W9-DIZ-412

LAW AND JUSTICE IN COMMUNITY

Law and Justice in Community

GARRETT BARDEN AND TIM MURPHY

OXFORD
UNIVERSITY PRESS

OXFORD
UNIVERSITY PRESS

Great Clarendon Street, Oxford OX2 6DP

Oxford University Press is a department of the University of Oxford.
It furthers the University's objective of excellence in research, scholarship,
and education by publishing worldwide in

Oxford New York

Auckland Cape Town Dar es Salaam Hong Kong Karachi
Kuala Lumpur Madrid Melbourne Mexico City Nairobi
New Delhi Shanghai Taipei Toronto

With offices in

Argentina Austria Brazil Chile Czech Republic France Greece
Guatemala Hungary Italy Japan Poland Portugal Singapore
South Korea Switzerland Thailand Turkey Ukraine Vietnam

Oxford is a registered trade mark of Oxford University Press
in the UK and in certain other countries

Published in the United States
by Oxford University Press Inc., New York

British Library Cataloguing in Publication Data

Data available

Library of Congress Cataloging-in-Publication Data
Barden, Garrett.
  Law and justice in community / Garrett Barden and Tim Murphy.
    p. cm.
Includes index.
  ISBN 978–0–19–959268–5
  1. Sociological jurisprudence. 2. Law—Philosophy. 3. Social structure.
  4. Community life. I. Murphy, Tim. II. Title.
  K370.B367 2010
  340'.115—dc22   2010023728

Typeset by Newgen Imaging Systems (P) Ltd., Chennai, India
Printed in Great Britain
on acid-free paper by
CPI Antony Rowe
Chippenham, Wiltshire

ISBN 978–0–19–959268–5 (Hardback)

1 3 5 7 9 10 8 6 4 2

This book is dedicated to the memory of Neil MacCormick

Acknowledgements

This book had its obscure – at the time unsuspected – origin in Cork in 1992. We both then worked at University College Cork, Garrett Barden in the Department of Philosophy and Tim Murphy in the Department of Law. In that year we began to work together in a very loose way; it was then that our discussions about the nature of law and justice began. They continued after Garrett Barden's retirement in 1999 and Tim Murphy's move to the University of Akureyri in 2005, where Garrett Barden was a regular visitor, and where, in February 2006, we decided to write a book of jurisprudence together.

We thank those friends and colleagues, too many to name – in China, the Czech Republic, France, Germany, Iceland, India, Ireland, Italy, Switzerland, the United Kingdom and the United States – whose help and support was generously given and gratefully received. Reluctantly we must limit our explicit acknowledgements to some who have been important intellectual influences on our work: Michel Bastit, Philippe Braud, N Ranganatha Desika, Gerald Goldberg, Patrick Hannon, Martin Hazell, François Monconduit, Vincent O'Connell, David O Mahony, Colm O'Sullivan, Peter Schäublin, Gerard Staunton, Michel Villey and, finally, Mikael Karlsson, without whose invitations to teach at Akureyri the book would not have been written.

On specific matters we gratefully acknowledge the advice of Páll Björnsson, Rachael Johnstone, Sigurður Líndal and Francesco Milazzo. We also gratefully acknowledge the insightful and stimulating comments and suggestions by the OUP readers who anonymously reviewed the book.

At Oxford University Press the kindness and professional acumen of Alex Flach, Natasha Knight, Ela Kotkowska, Deborah Harris and Gary Hill have been a constant support which has been much appreciated.

Garrett Barden gratefully acknowledges the award of a Fellowship in the Institute of Advanced Studies in the Humanities at the University of Edinburgh in 1991, where in good conversation seeds were sown. Of Beatrice, his partner, to say that *sine qua non* must, although inadequate, suffice.

Tim Murphy gratefully acknowledges the sabbatical leave granted to him by the University of Akureyri to undertake research for this book in 2008. He expresses also his gratitude to the library staff at the University of Akureyri, and to Nisthula in Pune.

Finally, we come to acknowledge our greatest debt, which is to the late Neil MacCormick, to whom the book is dedicated. Neil is the only person, apart from the anonymous reviewers, who read and commented on an entire draft manuscript of the book. Our debt to him is indeed great: we have been much influenced by his institutional theory of law, set out so eloquently in the quartet of OUP books that he successfully completed before his death in 2009. He brought our work to the attention of OUP and recommended it to the Delegates. In different ways he was a friend to us both. We remember him and thank him.

Garrett Barden and Tim Murphy
Tallow and Akureyri
Þjóðhátíðardagurinn (17 June), 2010

Contents

'It would be strange to make the happy man solitary. For none would choose to be solitary in order to have all good things; for man is social, and born apt to live with others.'

– Aristotle, *Nicomachean Ethics*

'By law is the land built; by lawlessness destroyed.'

– *Njál's Saga*

'The virtue of justice is the constant and enduring will to render to each what is due.'

– *The Institutes of Justinian*

Preface

The explicit idea that human society is the product of a contract between formerly separate individuals is easily enough rejected but the *image* is thoroughly extirpated only with considerable difficulty and often remains as an unacknowledged but operative presupposition. In contrast, evolutionary theory encourages us to imagine the social or political animals that we are as emergent in a web of inter-relationships such that the question as to how humans invented society – a question that led Kant to replace the idea of an actual historical contract by an *'idea of reason'* – no longer arises. Humans in no sense invented society or the social order within which they emerged but, from within the social forms in which at any time they already found themselves, they discovered new forms, sometimes discarding older forms, sometimes developing new ones as circumstances evoked new questions to which new answers were given.

There is present in every type and at every stage of every human society a differentiation of function to ensure the consistent availability of those things without which no society can survive; the production of food and shelter and the procreation and education of children are obvious examples. Somewhat less immediately obvious are the mutual rights or entitlements that must be honoured to prevent social collapse. Many writers – including for example the jurists who compiled the *Corpus Iuris Civilis*, as well as St Thomas Aquinas, Thomas Hobbes, and Adam Smith – have understood these mutual rights or entitlements as 'justice'. In this book we adopt that understanding of such rights and entitlements and emphasize throughout that they are *essential* to the maintenance and survival of civil society.

The function of customs and laws is to sustain the social or communal order. As peoples are faced with new problems, as new ways of living are discovered, some rights proper to an earlier order are discarded and replaced by others that sustain the new emergent order; thus the set of entitlements that sustain a society of hunters and gatherers will not be the same as the set that sustains a modern industrial society. The sets of entitlements, although not identical, will nonetheless intersect and within the lens of the intersecting circles will be entitlements common to every society. Of these Gaius in his *Institutes* wrote that what natural reason established among all mankind is kept equally among all peoples. It is called in English the 'law of nations' or the 'right of nations' because all peoples in their practices acknowledge and respect it. Throughout this work we suggest that there exist such sets of entitlements in as much as all peoples must live together in similar fundamental ways if the society in which they live is to survive. So, to introduce what is a recurrent example, all peoples must distinguish between physical possession of a thing and the right or entitlement to that thing. The thing that is physically possessed is corporeal and, as Gaius wrote, can be touched; the entitlement or right is incorporeal and cannot be.

We must make clear from the outset that when we claim that a right – such as the ownership of a thing – exists, we mean that it is recognized in the society. In an imaginary society in which possession but not in any sense ownership existed the right would not exist. Some members of that society might well discover the usefulness of introducing the right – that is, of introducing the practice, for the practice cannot exist without the right nor the right without the practice – and argue in favour of its introduction but until it is introduced the right does not yet exist. Similarly, a right to fair and unbiased adjudication that takes equal account of each litigant is a right that actually exists only when it is recognized and established. Where it is not established, its establishment might be advocated or claimed, and we argue in favour of the claim on the grounds that fair and unbiased adjudication is intrinsic or natural to adjudication. We argue, indeed, that biased adjudication is wrongly called adjudication because it lacks the impartiality intrinsic to that activity; in the same way a 'promise' that carries with it no demand that it be honoured is wrongly called a promise because it lacks a characteristic intrinsic to promising. If in an imaginary society people make 'promises' and no one understands that promising carries with it a demand that it be honoured, then no right accrues to the person to whom the 'promise' is made.

A 'promise' that imposes no obligation is bogus; so, too, is a 'right' that is not acknowledged, and so confers no actual entitlement. There is much debate as to whether or not human rights exist and much confusion. Again, we distinguish between what exists and what ought to exist but does not. Let X be a 'human right'. If X exists, there is a jurisdiction in which X is an acknowledged right; if there is no jurisdiction in which X is an acknowledged right, then X does not exist as a right, however much it exists as an idea or a claim. In as much as a right is acknowledged and called a 'human right' in, for example, an international agreement such as the Universal Declaration of Human Rights, that right exists in as much as it has purchase in the signatory jurisdictions. But there remain jurisdictions in which some of the rights agreed in the Declaration are not rights.

Human societies are networks of entitlements or rights. Societies do not first come into being and only then suggest, agree, and establish the set of rights within which the members of the society are to live. Humans from the beginning live in a network of entitlements; from an evolutionary perspective we may think of this network as the human version of the ordered pattern of the life of the animals from which humans evolved. Human society differs from animal society in that humans are not in the same way locked into the patterns but can and do reflect upon them and, in the light of discoveries and the questions thrown up by those discoveries, change and develop the patterns of their lives and discover new mutual entitlements – rights and duties – that allow them to live peaceably together in the new conditions. Throughout the many and profound changes that have come about in human societies since their original emergence, some very fundamental patterns survive. Humans, for example, communicate with one another – if they did not they would not survive as a species – and there are features spontaneously, intrinsically, naturally present in human communication upon which communication depends. Such features are the 'natural laws' of communication. One such feature is that most speakers most of the time tell what they hold to be true; if no one at any time could rely on their interlocutors to tell what they held to be true, communication would collapse. That is a 'natural law' or 'natural characteristic' of communication. Hence the injunction that for the most part and most of the time one ought to tell the truth. Hence also the idea that for the most part and most of the time one can expect to be told what the speaker holds to be the truth, and thence the idea that one has the right to be told it. But because both withholding information and lying are possible, it is likewise possible that in a particular society or part of society, the right to be told what the speaker holds to be true may not in all circumstances exist. There are situations in which a person or set of persons has the right to be told what the speaker holds to be true; for example, students normally have that right, which is intrinsic to teaching and learning, relative to their teacher, and a class in which that right does not exist is fraudulent; but fraud is possible and may on occasion be institutionally established so that teachers, for whatever reason, teach as true what they hold to be false; and when such institutionalization of fraud exists, the right ought to, but does not, exist.

Humans can be stupid, vain, covetous, malicious, envious, prone to anger, greedy, selfish, dishonest, and unjust as well as intelligent, fallible, generous, loving, caring, kind, temperate, empathetic, honourable, and just, and so it is a fundamental error to think of human judgments and human decisions as inevitably true and good. To seek certain or absolute truth and goodness in law or legal judgments or decisions is misguided. It may be that the search for this chimera was encouraged by the idea that natural science was both certain and true, a distorted image of science that itself came from the Greek ideal of science as the certain knowledge of the necessary. Now that natural science is correctly recognized to be the best available opinion, and truth the asymptote, the nostalgic quest for infallibility may be abandoned and positivism and relativism more easily let go. For at the heart of both positivism and relativism is the quest for infallibility; if we cannot be sure of reaching the true and the good, we can define the true and the good, right and wrong, as simply what has been decided. But no one, we argue, consistently holds, or can hold, this position.

This work is a study in jurisprudence that considers the proper function of law to be the promotion of a context in which, without impeding one another, we can lead our lives together in peace and justice. How does law carry out its function? Our book may be read as a sustained commentary on that assertion and that question.

Finally, a note on sources: This book draws on sources from different histori-cal periods and in different languages. The majority of these sources have been interpreted and translated in many different ways by various authors. Here we are eclectic. In some cases we use 'standard' translations; in other cases we translate passages ourselves; in yet others we draw on various interpretations and transla-tions in order to convey what we consider to be the primary meaning of the text in question. Obviously, there can be no substitute for the original, and the reader is well advised, if possible, to consult the original in cases where he is in doubt or where he senses ambiguity. Throughout this book, unless the context dictates otherwise, we use masculine pronouns as gender-neutral references.

1

Introduction: The Grey Goose

This book proposes a general account of law in community. By 'community' we mean human communal living of any kind and throughout this book we use the terms 'human community' and 'human society' interchangeably. We begin with reference to a particular community, namely, the group of people who first settled Iceland; and we discuss the 'Grey Goose Laws', a reference to the Icelandic text, *Grágás*, which was the first book containing written laws in Iceland.[1]

The settlement of Iceland is generally said to have began in the second half of the ninth century AD, when Norse settlers migrated across the North Atlantic from Scandinavia.[2] The year 874 is typically referred to as the first year of settlement and the Icelandic 'Age of Settlement' (Icelandic: *Landnámsöld*) is considered to have lasted from 874 to 930. By 930, most of the island had been claimed and the Icelandic parliament, *Althingi*, which today is widely acknowledged as the oldest parliament in the world, was founded. Prior to the establishment of the Grey Goose Laws – that is, prior to the publication of the book, *Grágás* – all the Icelandic laws were recited annually by the 'Law Speaker' (*lögsögumaður*) at the *Althingi*. In 1117 *Althingi* decided that all the laws should be written down and they were published subsequently as *Grágás*.[3] These laws remained in force

---

[1] *Grágás* is more properly translated as 'Greylag Goose'; it is sometimes referred to in its shortened form, 'Greylag', although the name 'Greylag' appears to date from the early 1700s only. In modern Icelandic, while the law book is referred to as *Grágás*, the bird is referred to as *grágæs*.

[2] Several sources claim that the Norse settlers encountered Irish monks, the *Papar*, when they first arrived in Iceland. Reference to these sources is made in the opening lines of *Independent People* [*Sjálfstætt Fólk*], the 1934 novel by the Icelandic writer, Halldór Laxness: 'In early times, say the Icelandic chronicles, men from the Western Islands came to live in this country, and when they departed, left behind them crosses, bells, and other objects used in the practice of sorcery. From Latin sources may be learned the names of those who sailed here from the Western Islands during the early days of the Papacy. Their leader was Kolumkilli the Irish...'. For a formal account of the various stages in the settlement of Iceland, see G Karlsson, *Iceland's 1100 Years: The History of a Marginal Society* (London: Hurst & Co, 2001), 9–15. Karlsson remarks that while some settlers were Celtic in origin, 'the Icelandic language shows clearly that the culture was predominantly of Norse origin' (14).

[3] Although *Grágás* constituted a codification it was not a unified corpus of law in that the name applies to some 130 codices and fragments of different dates compiled in the *Grágás* manuscripts. Gunnar Karlsson notes that at the same time as the codification in manuscript form 'a radical revision of the law took place', and that *Grágás* 'is now preserved in two manuscripts, which are both more than a century younger than the first codification. Their texts are only partly identical and

until the early 1270s, at which time the 'Ironside Laws' – based on Norwegian laws – were adopted.

Why the book was called *Grágás* is a matter of dispute amongst Icelandic historians,[4] but in the present context a far more pertinent question is what we can learn about the nature of law from a book like *Grágás*. The Icelandic case is an example only; as stated above, we wish to present a general account of law. But *Grágás*, as we shall now see, is a very good example. Before its publication there was no written law – that is, no statute; no code; no written judgment – setting out any law in Iceland. Yet there was 'law'; the recitations of the 'Law Speaker' were the basis of what we would now call a legal system. What was the source of the pre-*Grágás* laws? Where did the original legal system come from? What effect did the publication of *Grágás* have on the legal system? It is commonly thought that the first sets of written laws in any community express the customary law of the community. *Grágás*, after all, was clearly a *collection* of laws rather than a book that in any sense created or 'invented' laws. While we agree with this view of written law, we suggest that in one important sense it simply defers the issue. Important questions remain: What is the source of the customary laws? Where do they come from? What exactly, in the Icelandic example, was the 'Law Speaker' reciting?

There appear to be two possibilities. The first possibility is that, following the settlement of Iceland, there developed a need for a legal system and that this need was, probably gradually rather than suddenly, recognized and acknowledged by the settlers. As this need intensified it became inevitable that a system of legal regulation was not only required but would have to be introduced if civility of any kind was to be established. Ultimately, on this view, the settlers agreed to organize such a system – they somehow agreed upon various rules or customary laws. The *Althingi* or parliament pre-dated *Grágás* and so the idea of a gathering of representatives of the community to decide on various regulatory norms seems, on the face of it, reasonable. Such a gathering could have agreed that stealing and murder, for example, were to be forbidden; things that were borrowed were to be returned to the owner; promises of certain kinds were to give rise to enforceable obligations; and so on. Thus, this theory holds, was established the first set of customary laws in Iceland. These then provided the content of the Law Speaker's recitations at *Althingi*. In due course there was perceived a need to set these laws

---

may both have changed considerably after the first codification. The result is that the extant text of the law bears only slight marks of its oral ancestry...'. *Iceland's 1100 Years*, 21–2.

⁴ The book seems to have first been called *Grágás* in a document of the bishopric of Skálholt in 1548. The origin of the name is uncertain but it may refer to one of the following: that the laws were written with a Greylag goose quill; that the book containing the laws was bound in Greylag goose skin; or because of the age of the laws – it was then believed that geese lived longer than other birds. For discussion of this question, see Ó Lárusson, *Grágás: Lög og saga* (Reykjavík: Hlaðbúð, 1958), 119–34, esp 123–124, and P Briem, 'Um Grágás' (1885) *Tímarit Hins íslenzka bókmenntafélags*, 133, esp 176 et seq.

down in writing. After *Grágás*, one might say, the rest is recorded Icelandic legal history.

We argue in this book that the theory outlined above, this first possibility as to the origins of Icelandic customary law – and by implication the source of the tradition of written laws in any jurisdiction – is utterly mistaken and misleading. We suggest that this is *not* how the Icelandic legal system originated; nor is it how any legal system comes about; and nor does it tell us anything of value about the nature of law.

So how did *Grágás* come about? We propose that the first Icelandic settlers developed further whatever customs and laws they were familiar with and fashioned a kind of 'living law' in the new, settled context in which they found themselves.[5] The term 'law' is usually taken to refer to forms of what is typically called 'state law' or 'positive law' and including constitutional law (whether written or unwritten) and enacted legislation (for example, law contained in a common law statute or civil law code); law arising from or associated with the courts (common law, case law, or, sometimes, 'judge-made law'); and, from many perspectives, elements of international law.[6] But when we speak of 'living law' this is not the sense of 'law' that we have in mind. Rather, by 'law' in the sense of 'living law' we mean those judgments and choices that in recurrent kinds of circumstances are generally accepted and approved in a particular community. By saying that the Icelandic settlers developed a living law we mean that people in the settler community were brought up to do a whole host of things in particular ways, including, for example, the customs, practices, well-known and accepted procedures, and mutual expectations that establish the jural relationships particular to that community. This living law did not come into existence by any process of formal consideration, debate, or decree; it was not for the most part explicitly formulated in language; no individual or institution could change it; and when it changed it was usually a slow, incremental process of change. The living law is the *communal moral law*, or, even more simply, the *communal law* – and

---

[5] We initially took the term 'living law' from an account of lectures by FSC Northrop (1893–1992) in which Northrop discussed the distinction between the positive law and the living law. B Magee, *Confessions of a Philosopher* (London: Phoenix, 1997), 166–7. The theorist with whom the term is most associated is Eugen Ehrlich (1862–1922) but we do not endorse Ehrlich's complex and sometimes self-contradictory theory in its entirety. While we are in broad agreement with Ehrlich's central thesis – famously stated in the Foreword to his book, *Fundamental Principles of the Sociology of Law* (New Brunswick, NJ: Transaction Publishers, 2002) – that 'the centre of gravity of legal development lies not in legislation, nor in juristic science, nor in judicial decision, but in society itself' (xv), our conception of the living law bears only some resemblances to his. In particular we reject the sense in Ehrlich that there existed a pre-social condition prior to the emergence of the living law. We discuss some aspects of Ehrlich's book – which was published originally as *Grundlegung der Soziologie des Rechts* (Munich and Leipzig: Duncker and Humblot, 1913) and first translated into English by Walter L Moll in 1936 (Cambridge, Mass: Harvard University Press) – in ch 3.4 below.

[6] Many of the terms used here – eg 'positive law', 'judge-made law' – are slippery in the sense that they are used by different authors to mean different things. We clarify our use of these terms in ch 2.2 below.

throughout this book we shall use these three terms interchangeably. The living law is the set of communally accepted norms that express how, in certain types of situation, members of the community are obliged to act. Indeed, in many cases, we simply use the term 'custom' to refer to the living or communal law.

The living law of a community is originally unwritten and represents what is generally accepted as what constitutes the community as a community and what can, in some of its aspects, distinguish it from other communities. It constitutes the commonly accepted moral rules of the community, some of which, but rarely if ever all of which, may be written down.[7] In any community some norms will be taken to be of greater importance than others; some will be of such significance that failure to act in accord with them will occasion significant disapprobation; others will meet with only mild disapproval or disdain.[8]

The living law, in other words, is a moral tradition: it is the set of those ways of acting that, in a particular community, are admired and thought appropriate to common types of situations. The nature of morality is a constant theme of this book. 'What am I to do?' is *the* moral or ethical question because it is the question of deliberation and choice, the question that defines the moral or ethical domain. How we, as individuals, are to act in any given situation or circumstance is what ethics is fundamentally about. Counterintuitive though it may be, it is irrelevant whether what is at issue is a trivial or a serious matter: if it requires deliberation and choice then it is in the ethical or moral domain.[9]

What is admired and thought appropriate in the ethical domain is a value, and often those traditional values considered to be of paramount significance are expressed in laws that were, in archaic societies, frequently thought of as given by

---

[7] Indeed, whether or not it would be possible to list all the accepted moral rules of a community is moot. To refer to a comparison that we invoke throughout this book, we learn our morals as we learn our language, that is, without knowing or obeying formulated rules. The important thing about the commonly accepted ideas of what constitutes good behaviour is not that the ideas are written down but that they, or the practices that they describe, are known. In his recent book *Reality Hunger: A Manifesto* (New York: Alfred Knopf, 2010), David Shields makes this point in connection with the history of writing when he notes that the earliest manuscript of the Old Testament dates to 150 BC and that parts of the Bible incorporate 'real things' into the text; Shields remarks: 'The laws that have come to make up Mosaic Law, for instance, were undoubtedly real laws before they became canonized' (8). See also G Barden, *After Principles* (Notre Dame, Ind: University of Notre Dame Press, 1990), 30–111.

[8] The signal importance of the place of approbation and disapproval – respect, praise, scorn, derision, and so on – in social life is a constant theme in Adam Smith's *The Theory of Moral Sentiments* (1759; 6th edn extensively revised by the author in 1790). 'Human virtue is superior to pain, to poverty, to danger and to death; nor does it even require its utmost efforts to despise them. But to have its misery exposed to insult and derision, to be led in triumph, to be set up for the hand of scorn to point at, is a situation in which its constancy is much more apt to fail. Compared with the contempt of mankind, all other external evils are easily supported.' *The Theory of Moral Sentiments* (DD Raphael and AL Macfie eds) (Oxford: Clarendon Press, 1976) [I.iii.2.12], 61; this idea is repeated throughout [II.iii.3.1–3.8], 61–6 and [II.i.1.1–II.i.5.11], 67–78. Unless otherwise stated, when quoting from Adam Smith's writings we use *The Glasgow Edition of the Works and Correspondence of Adam Smith* (Oxford University Press) edited by RH Campbell, AS Skinner (general editors) and WB Todd (textual editor). [9] G Barden, *After Principles*, ch 2.

the gods or as of unknown and mysterious origin.[10] Our view is that the source of the communal moral law is the evolving practices of those who live together; the practices that become, for a variety of sometimes antagonistic reasons, not only communally accepted but also required in order that communal life may continue. We suggest that the living law, or the communal moral law, gives rise to the sense of justice in a community. By 'justice' we have in mind the Roman law definition of justice in Justinian's *Institutes*. In Latin the sentence reads: *Iustitia est constans et perpetua voluntas ius suum cuique tribuens.*[11] And in English: The virtue of justice is the constant and enduring will to render to each what is due. The communal or living law, in other words, establishes *entitlements*; the network of entitlements evolves as a consequence of people living together and dealing with the jural demands that ordinary living imposes upon them. Some of these entitlements are formalized as 'state' or 'positive' law when the communal sense of justice provides the basis for formulated law (constitutions, statutes, codes, etc) and contribute to the development of the framework within which law is judicially interpreted. Just as *natural* laws and the living law express an understanding of how the community lives and ought to live, so formulated *conventional* rules and judicial decisions express an understanding of how the community ought to, and for the most part actually does, operate, how it ought to live and for the most part actually lives. Formulated or written laws, whether natural or conventional, are not to be understood as 'new' laws that are, after political debate, imposed on

[10] The conviction that what is naturally just derives from a lawgiver above the community or state is by no means uncommon or historically unimportant in jurisprudential reflection. The basic image in the *Torah* is of laws given by God, the divine, and so unquestionable, lawgiver. The *Code of Hammurabi* (c 1780 BC) is not directly of divine origin but of Hammurabi himself it is written in the Prologue: 'Anu and Bel called by name me, Hammurabi, the exalted prince who feared God, to bring about the rule of righteousness in the land...'; and in the Epilogue: 'The great gods have called me, I am the salvation-bearing shepherd...' (trans LW King (1910); ed R Hooker (1996)) <http://www.wsu.edu/~dee/MESO/CODE.HTM>. In ancient Greece, the idea of the gods as the source of fundamental laws is found as is the related idea that these fundamental laws are of mysterious and unknown origin: 'They are not of today and yesterday; They live forever; none knows when they first were' (Sophocles, *Antigone*, 496–501); this translation is from *The Theban Plays* (EF Watling trans, Harmondsworth: Penguin, 1947). The conviction that what is naturally just derives from a lawgiver above the community is discussed more fully in G Barden, 'Of the Naturally and the Conventionally Just' in T Murphy (ed), *Western Jurisprudence* (Dublin: Thomson Round Hall, 2004), 17, 31–41.

[11] Justinian, *Institutes*, I.I.1. Modern reflection on law in the European and later Western tradition has its sources in Mesopotamian, Hebrew, Greek, Roman, and Christian traditions. Hebrew and Greek reflections were influenced by the cultures that surrounded them, so, for example, the *Decalogue* shows the influence of the *Code of Hammurabi*. The Roman tradition in Cicero, Gaius, Ulpian, Paul, and others flows in its early period from the Greek tradition, but develops the critically important idea of *ius* (or *jus*), for which there is no unambiguous translation into modern English, and which was only inchoately present in either Greek or Judaic thought. (A distinction between *ius* and *lex* is found in the main source of Roman law, Justinian's *Corpus Juris Civilis*. As we shall see, it is often impossible to express this distinction in modern English, for which reason, in some English translations, both terms become 'law' in passages where *ius* and *lex* appear in the original.) The Christian tradition flows from the confluence of the Judaic, Greek, and Roman, and includes the influence of medieval Islam, which itself shows the influence of its Judaic and Greek ancestors.

a *tabula rasa* of any kind. It is also crucially important to note, as we shall reiterate throughout this book, that whatever is discovered and formulated as law or developed through judicial interpretation will not be infallible: what is discovered will often be the subject of intense debate and disagreement. Law emerges, and cannot but emerge, within the developing communal moral context.

A distinction between 'law' and 'justice' is often found but it is not always the same distinction and different usages have led to considerable ambiguity in the study of jurisprudence. A very common way of understanding the distinction between 'law' and 'justice' imagines the latter as an ideal that the former should strive to emulate. 'Law', on this view, is a reference to forms of 'state law' or 'positive law' and it is supposed that it should be 'just' in the sense that it should accord with some vision of substantive justice, usually more or less formulated as a set of principles or axioms. These understandings of 'law' and 'justice' still dominate some modern jurisprudence; the common and underlying tendency of that modern juridical scholarship is to suggest that justice can be known as a set of unassailable principles that can be formulated and particular conclusions of justice deduced therefrom.

In our account of law, however, something very different is understood by the distinction between 'law' and 'justice'. By 'law', as we have said, we mean primarily the living law or communal moral law, those judgments and choices that in recurrent kinds of circumstances are generally accepted and approved in a particular community; by 'justice' we mean the willingness to give to each their due. This different – and, we suggest, better – understanding originates in Aristotle. Aristotle distinguished between, on the one hand, 'law' (*nómos, lex, loi, ley, gesetz*) and, on the other hand, 'the just' (*tò díkaion, jus, droit, derecho, recht*).[12] In the fifth book of his *Nicomachean Ethics*, Aristotle analyses justice and what is just and there makes it clear that the object of his enquiry is a 'justice which is a part of virtue', which he calls 'particular justice'.[13] The virtue of justice is one virtue among many (and therefore not the whole of virtue); 'particular justice' has to do with *rendering to each one what is due*.

When Aristotle analyses the moral life *as a whole* he discusses the distinct virtues that, in addition to particular justice, make it up. Aristotle uses the term 'law' to cover the moral life as a whole and therefore *all* the virtues – justice, courage, temperance, liberality, good temper, friendliness, and so on. In other words, when he uses the term 'law' he is referring to the living law:

...for practically the majority of the acts commanded by the law are those which are prescribed from the point of view of virtue as a whole; for the law bids us practise every virtue and forbids us to practise any vice.[14]

---

[12] See M Villey, *Leçons d'histoire de la philosophie du droit* (Paris: Dalloz, 1962), esp Part II, ch VII; *Seize essais de philosophie du droit* (Paris: Dalloz, 1969); and 'Torah et *tò díkaion*' in *La Formation de la pensée juridique moderne* (Paris: Montchrestien, 1968).
[13] Aristotle, *Nicomachean Ethics*, V.1130b.6.   [14] Ibid, V.1130b.23–5.

Since particular justice (ie the rendering to each what is due) is part of the moral life, that is, part of virtue and of law, the questions of justice and law are related but are not the same.[15]

The important point is that in much subsequent reflection on morality in the West, the 'law' covered the entire moral life, the entire living law or communal moral law or sense of justice of the community, and 'the just' was the rendering of what is due. This distinction is present in Roman law, from which later European and Western jurisprudence developed. Indeed the Roman invention of law may be understood as a method of dealing with questions of justice.[16]

St Thomas Aquinas was deeply versed in Roman law and he, following Aristotle, generally uses the term 'law' rather than 'justice' to cover the whole of the moral life. In other words, they both understood the living law or communal moral law to be the commonly accepted moral rules of the community rather than simply a set of rules or laws posited by a ruler. Again, this is also our basic understanding of law, and our basic understanding of justice is the Roman definition, that is, the rendering to each one what is due.

Let us clarify further our disagreement with the view that the law is invariably and exclusively state or positive law, that is, the set of positive rules or laws enacted and interpreted by those within a jurisdiction authorized to do so (or, in the case of international law, by relevant bodies authorized by the international community). From Plato and Aristotle, *nómos* – which is often translated by 'law', although the word can also mean 'usage' or 'custom' – carries with it some idea of command. The idea that law is necessarily command has endured and remains extremely powerful. That the *Torah* is the command of Yahweh (YHVH) is apparent particularly in *Exodus*, *Leviticus*, and *Deuteronomy*.[17] Although, as we

---

[15] However, as Aristotle also makes plain, the word 'justice', and associated words, were often used by his predecessors, by his contemporaries and sometimes by himself, as a synonym of 'virtue' and thus covering the whole moral life. *Nicomachean Ethics*, V.1 and V.1129a.1–1131a.7. Aristotle accepts the fluidity of usage, and used in that way to be 'just' is to be 'moral' (or 'good' or 'virtuous'). In early Greece, in the Jewish biblical and in the early Christian tradition, little if anything turns on a distinction between 'moral' or ('good' or 'virtuous') and 'just'. In *Genesis*, for example, Abraham intercedes with Yahweh who intends to destroy the city of Sodom by fire: 'Abraham remained standing before Yahweh. Approaching him he said, "Will you destroy the just man with the sinner?"' *Genesis* 18: 22–3. In St Matthew's Gospel the Father 'maketh his sun to rise on the evil and on the good and sendeth rain on the just and the unjust', *Matthew* 5: 45. (Unless otherwise stated, we cite from the Authorized King James Version of the Bible.)

[16] The Romans 'invented' law to the extent that they developed the first legal system in the West, where legal system is understood 'in the sense of a consciously articulated and systematized structure of legal institutions clearly differentiated from other social institutions and cultivated by a corps of persons specially trained for that task', HJ Berman, *Law and Revolution: The Formation of the Western Legal Tradition* (Cambridge, Mass: Harvard University Press, 1983), 76. For a succinct account of the Roman invention of law understood as a method of dealing with questions of justice, see M Villey, *Le droit et les droits de l'homme* (Paris: Presses Universitaires de France, 1983), 33–5.

[17] The *Torah* presents its many laws as Yahweh's edicts, ordinances, or statutes and this image has been extremely powerful in the Western tradition; our argument is that these commands represent laws that emerged in the practice of the community over time. The *Torah* is differently present in the three Near Eastern religions of the Book. In Judaism, it is a central text in the Hebrew Bible

have just mentioned, St Thomas *usually* uses the term 'law' rather than 'justice' to cover the whole of the moral life, in his set of questions on law in the first part of the second part of the *Summa Theologiae* he has dominantly positive law in mind, and gives as one of the essential elements in law that it states what is to be done, what people are bound to do, and is established either by the entire community or by whoever represents the community.[18] In a similar vein, Thomas Hobbes in *Leviathan* defines law thus:

> And first it is manifest, that Law in generall, is not Counsell, but Command; nor a Command of any man to any man; but only of him, whose Command is addressed to one formerly obliged to obey him. And as for Civill Law, it addeth only the name of the person Commanding, which is *Persona Civitatis*, the Person of the Commonwealth.[19]

Modern colloquial English, by whom and by whatsoever influenced, uses the term 'law' in a way close to how it is defined by Hobbes. Because the term 'law' is nowadays almost exclusively used to refer to state law or international convention, it is unusual to think of a rule within a community as a law quite independent of its being or not being state law or international convention. But when used to refer to communally accepted rules, law is the expression of a way of acting approved and expected within a given community.[20]

In our account of law and justice, people live together within a body of laws that evolve in response to new and unfamiliar situations and disputes. They

---

or TaNaKh; in Christianity its legal rhetoric and the Ten Commandments have greatly influenced jurisprudential discussion; in Islam it is an earlier revelation of which the Koran is the fulfilment: 'Yet before it [the Koran] the Book of Moses was revealed: a guide and a blessing. This book confirms it.' *The Koran*, 'The Sand Dunes', 46:10 (trans NJ Dawood, London: Penguin, 1999), 354. See also 'Hūd', 11:15, 157. (We refer in this book to the common English names for the books of the *Torah*; their names in Hebrew are *Bereshit* (Genesis), *Shemot* (Exodus), *Wayiqra'* (Leviticus), *Bemidbar* (Numbers), and *Devarim* (Deuteronomy).)

[18] It is in this set of questions (which is often referred to as the 'Treatise on Law') that St Thomas writes of 'natural law' and students of jurisprudence will come upon many references to this discussion; more rarely will they come upon references to his discussion of the 'naturally just'. In T Murphy (ed), *Western Jurisprudence* (Dublin: Thomson Round Hall, 2004), natural law in St Thomas's thought is the focus of T Murphy, 'St Thomas Aquinas and the Natural Law Tradition', 94, whereas his ideas concerning natural justice are discussed in G Barden, 'Of the Naturally and the Conventionally Just', 17. St Thomas's *Summa Theologiae* is divided into four parts: Part I deals with God and creation; Part I–II deals with human action and the virtues in general; Part II–II considers such actions and virtues in particular detail; and Part III deals with Christ. St Thomas's discussion of 'natural law' is to be found in the *first* part of the second part (I–II); his discussion of the 'naturally just' is found in the *second* part of the second part (II–II). The *Summa Theologiae* is cited by Part (I, I–II, II–II, III), Question (q 58), and Article (art 3).

[19] T Hobbes, *Leviathan*, 312 [137]. In the notes page references in *Leviathan* are to the Penguin edition edited by CB Macpherson (London: Penguin, 1968); the numbers in square brackets refer to the original pagination and are given in Macpherson's edition.

[20] In a modern state, many, but not all, enacted laws take up traditional laws and customs including those that have been discovered in the course of litigation. However, legislation that addresses the relation of people or institutions to the state is later than, and dependent upon, the emergence of particular types of state. Legislation, therefore, is not exclusively a selection of provisions from a pre-existing customary, living law of a particular community.

express the approved and expected ways of acting. As long as they remain effective they are the norms according to which most members of the community for the most part act, are in various ways required to act, and in various ways corrected if they act otherwise. We include the phrase 'as long as they remain effective' to indicate that a rule or law which no longer guides action is no longer a norm, and that the normative status of a rule or law that has become an uncertain guide has changed. A set of laws guides and sustains a social order. Some laws are discovered to be common to all social orders; some are peculiar to particular societies. As Gaius wrote, and as is incorporated in Justinian's *Institutes*:

Civil law [*ius civile*] is distinguished from the law of nations [*ius gentium*] in that every people that is ordered by laws [*leges*] and customs uses in part its own law [*ius*] and in part the law [*ius*] that is common to all men...[21]

Leslie Green has remarked in an essay on general jurisprudence that, 'Whatever else it does, a general theory of law has at its core an account of the nature of law'.[22] While we agree that such an account is required we suggest that it would be more accurate to say that at the core of a general theory of law should be an account of the nature of human community and how it is constituted and sustained. A central theme in this book is that humans have always lived together: civil society is conceived as a social *order* and not in any sense as a social contract-based *organization*.[23] Within the social order, the function of law – of the jural order – is to promote the common good, that is, to contribute to the maintenance of a social order within which people can pursue their lives in peace. We shall argue also that the living or communal moral law tends to cultivate a moral context spontaneously within which others' interests are to be considered, and we shall emphasize throughout the idea that this moral context is itself an expression of what is naturally just. What is 'natural' in human life and society is what is *intrinsic* to common human practices, whether at the individual or social level. On this view, to refer first to the ethical domain, to act reasonably and responsibly is the demand intrinsic to our moral experience as humans. We must and we

---

[21] Justinian, *Institutes*, I.II.1. Cf Gaius, *Institutes*, i.1: 'All peoples who are governed by laws [*legibus*] and customs [*moribus*] use law [*ius*] which is partly theirs alone and partly shared by all mankind.' *The Institutes of Gaius* (trans and ed WM Gordon and OF Robinson) (London: Duckworth, 1988), 18. We refer to this translation throughout the book. Gaius's *Institutes*, which date from the second century AD, presents Roman private law according to what came to be called the 'institutional scheme', in which all law concerns persons, things, and actions. It was an important source when the *Institutes* and *Digest* of Justinian were prepared in the sixth century AD. See our discussion of the *Corpus Iuris Civilis* at the beginning of ch 3 below. To avoid any possible confusion we indicate in the footnotes throughout the book to which *Institutes* we are referring.

[22] L Green, 'General Jurisprudence: A 25th Anniversary Essay' (2005) 25 *Oxford Journal of Legal Studies* 565, 567.

[23] The distinction between an order and an organization is a recurrent theme in the writings of FA Hayek. See, for instance, his *Law, Legislation and Liberty*, esp *Vol 1: Rules and Order* (Chicago: University of Chicago Press, 1973). See also *Vol 2: The Mirage of Social Justice* (Chicago: University of Chicago Press, 1976) and *Vol 3: The Political Order of a Free People* (Chicago: University of Chicago Press, 1979).

do, constantly and always, ask the moral question: how are we to act? Once we have discovered how to act then there is an intrinsic demand to act accordingly. This is the natural law in that it is natural to us. It is, in other words, the kind of beings that we are. The rule against stealing, on the other hand, is thought to be an understanding and a formulation of a social norm forbidding an act that is naturally or intrinsically unjust, and that no human decision can make just.[24] By examining and investigating the nature of the situation – rather than 'human nature' – we can discover what is naturally or intrinsically just or unjust. This is what St Thomas means when he writes that the just is 'in the thing', that is, it is discovered by an examination of the situation or case.[25]

This theme is strongly present in the work of the twentieth-century French jurisprudent, Michel Villey (1914–88). Villey observed that what characterizes all modern legal thinking is the tendency to regard law (*le droit*) as a coherent and rationalistic system of rules; with regard to interpreting and applying the law, modern juridical thinking is based on the idea that the legal outcome is derived deductively from the rule, and law (*le droit*) is thus 'the paradise of logic conceived as the art of deduction'.[26] His notion of law (*ius, le droit*) is quite different: the law (*ius, le droit*) is identified with the set of established entitlements and the concrete solution that will be found in each case. In this way the court of law is also a court of justice. The law (*ius, le droit*) is not exclusively the valid sources of law (*leges*, pre-existing laws or rules) but also the effort, in the light of previous discoveries, to discover what in the particular circumstances is just, what, in other words, is due to whom. There are, of course, rules, but these rules

are not the law [*le droit*], applicable as such to new cases, because to respond precisely to the conditions of each case, each solution must adapt itself to the 'nature of the matter at hand', to the nature of *each* case.[27]

Laws are essentially expressions of what is held to be just; sometimes of what is naturally, and sometimes of what is conventionally, just. When these laws come to be the subject of interpretation, when cases emerge within the framework of

[24] St Thomas Aquinas, *Summa Theologiae*, II–II, q 57, art 2.
[25] Ibid, II–II, q 58, art 10. The phrase 'in the thing' is a literal translation of *in re; res* and *in re* may also be translated as 'the case' and 'in the case'.
[26] See M Villey, 'Questions of Legal Logic in the History of the Philosophy of Law' in V Gessner, A Hoeland, and C Varga (eds), *European Legal Cultures* (Aldershot: Dartmouth, 1996), 113 (emphasis in original). This is a translation of part of 'Questions de logique juridique dans l'histoire de la philosophie du droit' (1967) 37 *Logique et Analyse*, 3–22. Because Villey insists on the critical importance of distinguishing 'droit' [*ius*] from 'loi' [*lex*], the difficulties encountered by translators of Roman Law are also met by those attempting to translate Villey's writings into English, as is evident both from a comparison between the original title of this article and its English translation, and from our translation of the quotation from Villey's *Seize essais* below (at n 28). See also C Perelman, 'Le raisonnement juridique' in his *Droit, morale et philosophie* (Paris: Librairie Génerale de Droit et de Jurisprudence, 1976), 93–100.
[27] M Villey, 'Questions of Legal Logic in the History of the Philosophy of Law', 114 (emphasis in original).

reference of the laws, the jurist must take note of existing laws, but the adjudicative process does not end there:

The jurist does, of course, take account of the existing laws [*lois existantes*]; but what is just [the just solution (*le droit*)] is not confined within them; the just solution [*le droit*] remains on each occasion and in each case an unknown to be discovered and not a solution that derives entirely from rules given in advance.[28]

The answer to the question of what is due to whom – the law in any given instance – is *discovered* in the course of the judicial proceedings, which are in effect a 'discussion' or 'controversy'. As Villey has suggested, in order for the judge's task in each particular case to be carried out, 'there is a method – supple, prudent, approximative – inherited from the ancients: the method of *discussion*'.[29] Moreover, the traditional understanding of the judicial 'discussion' or 'controversy'

had no other ambition than to arrive at the broadest possible agreement among the opinions: it aimed to convince, if not the losing litigant, at least the greatest possible number of the trial participants, of the wise men present in the audience and of the third parties who would agree the following day to help carry out the sentence. Yet this rational agreement was the sign of an approach to the truth.[30]

Justice must be discovered through the discursive judicial process. It represents the law because both law and justice demand a discovery based on the nature of each particular case with which it is confronted: a decision is required and the decision will relate to the particular facts of the case as well as to the pre-existing legal rules. The decision will not necessarily be correct, but will be, as Villey says, 'an approach to the truth'.

One final set of remarks before we turn to outline the structure of the book: We consider this book to be a work of jurisprudence in the sense that jurisprudence is the philosophical pursuit of wisdom about law, legal systems, and justice.[31] Although the question of whether 'jurisprudence', 'legal theory', and 'legal philosophy' should be considered as in some sense distinct has provoked much debate,[32] there is no agreed demarcation and we tend to the view that they constitute one more or less coherent body of knowledge.[33] This book proposes

---

[28] M Villey, *Seize essais*, 222.

[29] M Villey, *Critique de la pensée juridique moderne* (Paris: Dalloz, 1976), 136 (emphasis in original).

[30] M Villey, 'Questions of Legal Logic in the History of the Philosophy of Law', 115.

[31] See T Murphy, 'Introduction: The Nature and Scope of Jurisprudence' in T Murphy (ed), *Western Jurisprudence* (Dublin, Thomson Round Hall, 2004), 1.

[32] See, for example, J W Harris, *Legal Philosophies* (London: Butterworths, 2nd edn, 1997), 5; M Van Hoeke, 'Jurisprudence' in CB Gray (ed), *The Philosophy of Law: An Encyclopedia (Vol 1)* (New York: Garland, 1999), 459–61; and J Penner, D Schiff, and R Nobles, 'Approaches to Jurisprudence, Legal Theory, and the Philosophy of Law' in *Jurisprudence and Legal Theory: Commentary and Materials* (London: Butterworths, 2002), 3–5.

[33] If there is a case for any demarcation in the subject it is perhaps strongest in relation to the distinction between historical and contemporary jurisprudence. John Kelly, for example, while acknowledging the 'astonishing flowering' of Anglo-American jurisprudence during the latter part

a contemporary philosophy of law that draws on classical and medieval sources more heavily than most other such contemporary philosophies and indeed more than contemporary jurisprudential scholarship generally. But in no sense are we attempting to present anything like a history of legal theory: our focus throughout is on proposing a general theory of law. The reader may notice what may appear to be a tendency on our part to eschew some of the terms of reference of contemporary orthodox jurisprudential scholarship. To the extent that we do so is simply a consequence of the incorporation, into our general theory, of certain classical and medieval ideas and perspectives that are in our view wrongly neglected in current juridical thought. That said, we have taken care to address each of what are commonly regarded as the most significant themes in jurisprudence.

Moreover, in line with much modern jurisprudence, the historical and contemporary sources that we draw on are by no means exclusively 'legal' or 'jurisprudential'. Theorizing about law often involves substantial engagement with other disciplines: Julius Stone famously described jurisprudence as the lawyer's 'extraversion';[34] another writer has suggested that jurisprudence could be defined as 'critical external reflection on law', where 'external' means not from the internal point of view of the doctrinal analysis of a legal system.[35] The account proposed in this book is grounded in, for instance, anthropological, economic, philosophical, and theological thought as well as in legal or juridical reflection.

We do wish to acknowledge expressly, however, that there is one province of knowledge with which we do not engage in any depth. Throughout the book we refer to several examples of socio-legal differences between jurisdictions, and also to changes within jurisdictions over time. Consider, for example, the moral context in which the general injunction against murder is a fundamental feature. It is patently obvious that if one wants to change the mind of someone whose moral context includes the conviction that access to euthanasia or assisted suicide is right, one cannot do so simply by appealing to the shared conviction that murder is wrong. The change of mind demands a contextual shift. Over time and within jurisdictions change of mind has come about, and it is the province of the history and sociology of law to discern the often small and gradual, sometimes sudden, shifts within a context that lead from an earlier to a later position. A social change in attitude to, and consequent legalization of euthanasia or assisted suicide, may

---

of the twentieth century, considered that growth as 'so luxuriant that ... it seems to blot out everything else'; perhaps, he suggested, 'there is too much sailing under the flag "jurisprudence" and it might more rationally be divided into two teaching subjects: (a) history of legal theory; (b) modern philosophy of law'. Note by Tony Honoré in JM Kelly, *A Short History of Western Legal Theory* (Oxford: Clarendon Press, 1992), xvi. The quotation is from the last letter Kelly wrote to Honoré before his death in 1991.

[34] J Stone, *Legal System and Lawyers' Reasoning* (Sydney: Maitland, 1968), 16. This characterization of jurisprudence may mislead slightly in that it suggests perhaps that jurisprudence is the preserve of lawyers only, which is certainly not the case.

[35] M Van Hoecke, 'Jurisprudence' in CB Gray (ed), *The Philosophy of Law: An Encyclopedia (Vol 1)*, 459.

be associated with a decline in adherence to a religious community in which it was forbidden rather than simply with an increase in a demand for the rights of the terminally ill. In our view it is the province of the history and sociology of law and of political science – rather than of jurisprudence – to compare these differences, to discover intelligible relationships between legal and extra-legal attitudes, and to discern what in a particular jurisdiction took place.

It is time now to turn to the structural framework within which we set out our jurisprudence. An account of the nature of human community and how it is constituted and sustained is provided in Chapter 2, which begins by addressing the question of how human community or civil society arose. We suggest that humans originally live together in community and that civil society is, therefore, a spontaneous order constituted by the natural sociability of humans. In short, humans live together because they cannot do otherwise. In this chapter we discuss also the spontaneous jural order: what we refer to as the living law or the communal moral law. Some customs and practices are so fundamental that, were people not to act for the most part in accord with them, any social order would collapse. These customs and practices involve entitlements that are just in a *natural* sense: that what is borrowed is to be returned, for example, or that promises ought to be kept. Other more detailed laws – positive laws or state laws – are needed and are *conventional* to the extent that they select and enjoin one of several possible, disputable or, rarely enough, equally good ways of acting rather than others that might just as well have been chosen. In this chapter we emphasize also the similarity between the practice of language and the social and jural domains and we argue that the function of all law in the social order is the sustaining of a peaceful social and jural order.

Chapter 3 discusses the Roman definition of justice as the constant and enduring will to render to each what is due and we consider the general question of the context in which the question of what is just arises. The practice of the virtue of justice demands that one knows what is due, and so the question of justice is always of this form: What belongs to whom? *Entitlement* is the key issue here because, we argue, *ownership is a bundle of entitlements*. We argue that there is no human society without ownership; or, to put it another way, that there is no human society in which entitlement is absent. Different types of society have existed and continue to exist but we suggest that within each there is some concept of ownership and entitlement. Effectively, for a person to own something requires that both that person and others accept both the practice of ownership that prevails in the society, and the fact that the person owns this particular thing: for ownership, and indeed any entitlement or right, actually to exist it must be communally accepted. In this chapter we address also the issue of how one can discover what is just. If one is to be just and render to another that which is due, one must know what is due and to attempt to discover this involves various types of questions. Justice has to do with clearly expressing – and, in unforeseen circumstances, developing, and, in disputes, determining – the set of entitlements.

Laws, including positive or state laws, indicate what is just in *types* of circumstances; courts, in the light of the contextual background to an extent established and clarified by constitutions and in legislation, state what is just in *particular* circumstances. Finally, we discuss the living law and its relation to justice and to the communal moral order, and also the way in which the living law tends to cultivate a moral context in which to consider others' interests and not merely one's own is approved.

Chapter 4 introduces the distinction between natural justice and conventional justice. The common jurisprudential understanding of the term 'natural justice' is the justice inherent in a court's procedures but, within our account of the just, this understanding is only part of what is naturally just. We consider procedural justice in our discussion of adjudication in Chapter 6 but in this chapter we focus on the distinction between the naturally and the conventionally just. We begin with a discussion of nature and what is natural and then, in distinguishing between the naturally just and the conventionally just, we further distinguish justice into three types – distributive justice, rectificatory (or corrective or commutative) justice, and reciprocal justice. In this chapter we consider the cases of distributive and rectificatory justice. A distributively just allocation is achieved when shares in what is commonly owned are justly allocated; a correctively just allocation is achieved when what, rightly or wrongly, is held by a non-owner is returned to its owner. We argue that in each case there is a contrast, and possible conflict, between the naturally and the conventionally just but that this is never a contrast or conflict between a higher and an inferior command. What by any single person or community is considered to be naturally just can, of course, be formulated in a rule or law but this rule or law derives from an understanding of the social situation and is an expression of that understanding. In distributive and rectificatory justice, what is naturally just can be discovered by an intelligent enquiry into the nature of the particular situation in light of the general practice or context within which the situation arises.

Reciprocal justice, the justice at work in exchange or trading, is examined in Chapter 5. In a single exchange between two people, the relative value of what is exchanged is settled by agreement between the trading partners. The relative exchange values of the goods exchanged, their price, is that set by mutual agreement in that particular exchange, and the reciprocally just price is the agreed exchange value of what is exchanged. The trading or market order is simply the order of indefinitely many exchanges among indefinitely many people; it has a function, which is to allow participants to pursue their trading goals, but has itself no goal. In this chapter we consider the trading order as a model before examining the complementary roles of nature and convention in exchange. We discuss the elements of exchange in some detail and then the manner in which trading reallocates goods between participants. As we shall see, no particular later allocation can be expected, and any later allocation will not be just otherwise than being that brought about by the many reciprocally just transactions that took place between the earlier and the later time. In the concluding sections, we examine the *lex mercatoria*, we distinguish the entitlements intrinsic to a trading order from those extrinsic to it, and we discuss the roles of morality and self-interest in the trading order. Throughout the chapter we acknowledge that trading will, almost inevitably, have consequences that within the restricted context of the trading order itself are simply consequences, but within the encompassing social and political order may be, and often are, grave social problems.

Chapter 6 deals with adjudication and interpretation. Adjudication is the effort to resolve a dispute by determining, amid the clamour of rival claims, what is just. We argue that the movement towards the resolution and settlement of any dispute involves three things. First, the hearing of evidence; secondly, reflection on the evidence partly in the light of the prevailing laws and precedents, partly in the light of what are thought to be the prevailing local conventions, partly in the light of what is thought common to all mankind, and partly in the light of what appears to be the nature of the case; and thirdly, coming to a conclusion or verdict that, within the limits of human fallibility, states what is just. Because the just is to be discovered in an adjudicative or judicial procedure rather than in some aleatoric fashion such as drawing lots or tossing a coin, the nature of the procedure will also be examined: we examine the roles of evidence and impartiality. Because the just is to be discovered in the light of laws, precedent, and custom, that is, within the prevailing jural context, the interpretation of laws, particularly written laws, is an essential feature of adjudication, and so it too is examined.

The relationship between law and morality is discussed in Chapter 7. The term 'law' is usually taken to refer to what is variously called positive or state law, mainly in the form of legislation. 'Morality', on the other hand, is usually taken to refer to a pre-existing moral law or moral code containing an indefinitely large number of precepts only some of which are explicitly formulated, or, and perhaps more often, to a sub-set of the moral code containing only private as distinct from public precepts. We neither understand nor use the terms in this way, and we discuss the inter-relation between three, rather than between two, elements: namely, morality, law, and legislation. In our understanding and usage of these terms, 'morality' refers to that part of human living governed by deliberation and choice; 'law' refers primarily to the communal moral law, that is, those judgments and choices that in recurrent kinds of circumstances are generally accepted and approved in a particular community; and 'legislation' refers to decisions of the legislator, whether the legislator be a single individual or a legislative assembly. We argue that legislative acts are intrinsically and inevitably moral and therefore that a distinction between moral and non-moral legislative proposals is incoherent. We discuss aspects of the inter-relation between morality, law, and legislation throughout the remaining chapters also; here we make some initial remarks on the nature of obligation and on the proper range or scope of legislation.

Chapter 8 develops an understanding of natural law as referring primarily to the moral experience of being human. By 'moral experience of being human' we mean that, as humans, we must, constantly and always, ask the moral or ethical question: What am I to do? We must, constantly and always, ask this question because as humans we are constantly engaged in thought and action (or, as the case may be, inaction), and this is the moral or ethical question because it is the question of deliberation and choice, the question that defines the moral or ethical domain. The first principle or precept of morality, we shall argue, is the basic feature of natural law in humans: namely, that we, who are naturally social animals, are responsible for how we live and what we do. This first principle is the natural law in that it is natural to us. It indicates the kind of beings that we are. The account proposed in this chapter, in other words, is grounded in an analysis of human decision that finds that it is possible to discover, albeit fallibly, what is right. We suggest, but do not insist, that our theory of natural law is similar to that of St Thomas Aquinas, notwithstanding the fact that there are other, quite different interpretations of his natural law theory.

Chapter 9 proposes an account of rights as jural relations. The distinction between classical and modern theories of rights is that classical theory emphasizes the jural relation between people within society while modern theory emphasizes subjective rights, that is, the idea of the rights-bearing individual. We advance a version of classical theory. We argue that rights, whether they are classed as 'natural', 'individual', 'subjective', 'fundamental', or 'human', are a function of justice understood as the giving to each what is due. To put this another way, we consider rights to be entitlements that are discoverable objects of justice; what is discovered to be due to a party in instances of disagreement is established as a right. Rights – like claims – are three place relations and are necessarily social: A is entitled to X from B, or A claims X from B. This chapter also makes some observations on how the historical development of modern rights discourse has eclipsed the more insightful understanding of classical theory.

Chapter 10 addresses the theme of law and force or coercion. A person is *directly* forced to act (or to refrain from acting) when to refrain from acting (or to act) is made physically impossible for him; and a person is *indirectly* forced to act (or to refrain from acting) when the unavoidable or anticipated consequences of refraining from acting (or acting) are judged by him to outweigh the anticipated benefits of acting (or refraining from acting). In this chapter we are concerned only with force, direct or indirect, exerted by another's action. We first examine the force of law in the specialized sense of legislation – ie enacted or positive law – then consider custom and, following that, threat. Although it is not uncommon for jurisprudential writers to conflate the issue of law's force with that of law's authority or legitimacy, we do not do this because we concentrate on the fact that force can and does exist without authority or legitimacy. Because we prescind in this chapter from any questions of authority or legitimacy, we effectively subsume law, custom, and threat under command that is effective precisely because the person or persons commanding can exert force. We discuss different possible reasons for obedience and distinguish between autonomy and heteronomy, and we consider also the criterion of effectiveness as a measure for the severity of a threat. Finally, we consider another criterion – that of taking into account the interest of the person or persons subjected to a threat of force or coercion.

Chapter 11 discusses the authority of law in the realm of adjudication and in this discussion we prescind from force. It is commonly, although not always, the case that legal measures are combined with the power or force to ensure implementation but the source of the authority of custom, legislation, or judicial decision is not merely the force available to community, ruler, or judge, unless 'authority' is no more than a deliberately misleading name for a force the real character of which it is intended to conceal. We distinguish two modalities of authority. First, a ruler is said to be in a position of authority over his subject in that the ruler is entitled to command his subject who, reciprocally, is obliged to obey. Secondly, a person is said to be an authority in as much as he is expert in a domain and worthy of belief, although not infallible. This chapter addresses the relationship between these two different modalities of authority in the legal domain. It includes also an examination of the question of the legitimacy of law. In discussing legitimacy we switch focus from adjudication to legislation, but we hold that our conclusions concerning both authority and legitimacy are equally valid in the legislative and adjudicative domains respectively.

In proposing this account of the nature of law and justice we share the lofty goal of virtually all philosophers of law when they set out a general theory. Neil MacCormick described that goal when he said that his institutional theory of law 'aims to develop a better understanding of law than other current legal theories offer'.[36] We emphasize that our account is founded on a particular conception of praxis. We make much use throughout the book of actual and hypothetical examples in different historical contexts. In this regard the reader will notice the strong influence on us of the Roman lawyers as well as of the Aristotelian-Thomist tradition generally. In three places we invoke what could be called 'case studies': we make some remarks on the meaning of 'refugee' in international law as part of the analysis of adjudication and interpretation in Chapter 6; in Chapter 10 we draw on an ancient Irish tale of a king's judgment on damage caused by trespassing sheep; and in Chapter 11 we discuss the entitlement to reside in a state in the context of a real situation in which a deportation order was carried out before the case could come before a court. The use of examples serves not only the purpose of explicating the argument of the book but also indicates that central to the argument is that various practices are critical to the survival of society; that the 'natural laws' of such practices express their intrinsic character or nature; and that what is intrinsic or natural

---

[36] N MacCormick, *Institutions of Law* (Oxford: Oxford University Press, 2007), 1.

to them is not known in some peculiar or mysterious way: *investigating the situation discovers it.* So our examples are at once investigations and exemplars of the epistemological *method* proposed in this book. We argue that this is the method of law and justice and also the appropriate and dominant method of sound jurisprudential reflection. The final chapter of the book, Chapter 12, provides both a brief overview of the various strands of the argument and some concluding remarks.

2

The Origins of Civil Society and the Function of Law

2.1 Introduction

How did it come about that humans live together in community? How, in other words, did human society arise? Did one group of humans in some fashion 'invent' the idea of society and subsequently try to persuade others of its usefulness? Is society, to put this another way, an organization? Or is society a spontaneous order, that is, a spontaneous ordering of the natural sociability of humans? Some have feared that if human society is not an invention it must be 'irrational' and, fearing this irrationality, and being unable 'to conceive of an effective coordination of human activities without . . . deliberate organization by a commanding intelligence',[1] have attempted to understand society as an organization established by the agreement of pre-social individuals. This old idea, often called 'social contract theory', has dominated the modern imagination, in one version or another, since Thomas Hobbes's *Leviathan*.[2] In the English-speaking world at least, the best-known and most influential recent work in this approach is John Rawls's *A Theory of Justice*.[3] Precisely because there are several versions of social contract theory it is better to think of it as an approach rather than as a theory.

Immanuel Kant considered it impossible for the original, 'natural' condition to have been a fact and, persuaded of the need for the notion to make sense of society, referred to it as 'merely an *idea* of reason',[4] and with this, it is reasonable to suppose, many social contract theorists agree. Yet the domination of the modern *imagination* by the contract approach has had profound consequences for modern social and political theory generally. It has led to an emphasis on the idea of human society as an organization, and this has led in turn to a focus on how society should be organized and what means should be used to organize it.

[1] FA Hayek, *The Constitution of Liberty* (Chicago: University of Chicago Press, 1960), 159.
[2] For earlier versions of this story of origins, see R Tuck, *Natural Rights Theories* (Cambridge: Cambridge University Press, 1976).
[3] J Rawls, *A Theory of Justice* (Cambridge, Mass: Harvard University Press, 1971).
[4] I Kant, 'Of the Relationship of Theory to Practice in Political Right' in *Kant's Political Writings*, HS Reiss (ed), HB Nisbet (trans) (Cambridge: Cambridge University Press, 1991), 79 (emphasis in original).

The account of human society that we propose in this book is in contrast to the social contract approach. Indeed, we suggest that the idea that contract is in any way whatsoever the origin of human society is in fact inaccurate and misleading, and that its residual image must be extirpated.[5] Humans originally live together in community; civil society is a spontaneous order, a product of the natural sociability of humans; in short, humans live together because they cannot do otherwise.

In this chapter we first discuss the idea of civil society as a spontaneous order that gives rise to a 'living law', which state or positive law expresses in part and develops; we then discuss the function of law in such an order; and, finally, we draw these two discussions together with reference to Hobbes's *De Cive* (1642) and *Leviathan* (1652).

2.2 Civil Society as a Spontaneous Order

Neither Aristotle nor St Thomas say explicitly that humans have always lived in community: but this, for the very cogent reason that they think they cannot live otherwise, is taken for granted, and is, so to speak, the model or context of their discussions. In the *Nicomachean Ethics* Aristotle asks if the happy man can be happy alone, or if he needs friends, and he responds – in a passage that is one of the epigraphs to this book – that the latter is the case:

It would be strange to make the happy man solitary. For none would choose to be solitary in order to have all good things; for man is social, and born apt to live with others....[6]

St Thomas's commentary on this passage reads:

And [Aristotle] says that it would be strange, that the happy man should be solitary. For this is contrary to every choice of everyone. For none would choose to live always by himself, that is, alone, even if consequently he would have all other goods; for man is

---

[5] See Hume's twelfth essay, 'Of the Original Contract' in *The Essays of David Hume* [1741–43] (London: Grant Richards, 1903): 'Were you to preach in most parts of the world, that political connections are founded altogether on voluntary consent or a mutual promise, the magistrate would soon imprison you as seditious for loosening the ties of obedience; if your friends did not before shut you up as delirious, for advancing such absurdities. It is strange that an act of the mind, which every individual is supposed to have formed, and after he came to the use of reason too, otherwise it could have no authority; that this act, I say, should be so much unknown to all of them, that over the face of the whole earth, there scarcely remain any traces or memory of it.' See also Adam Smith's discussion of sentiment at the origin of human sociability and at the foundation of the distinction between good and evil in *The Theory of Moral Sentiments* (VII.iii.2), 452–73.

[6] Aristotle, *Nicomachean Ethics*, IX.1169b.18. See also Aristotle, *Politics*, I.1253a.2. The translation from the *Ethics* given here is from the Latin used by St Thomas in his commentary. The page numbers (*viz* IX.1169b.18) are common to all modern editions whether in the original Greek or in translation. Elsewhere in this book we have usually used David Ross's translation in *The Works of Aristotle* (Oxford: Clarendon Press, 1928).

naturally a political animal and born apt to live with others. Because the happy man has those things that are naturally good for humans, consequently he should have [friends] with whom to live.... [7]

That man is a social animal is asserted frequently by St Thomas in the *Summa Contra Gentiles*, in the *Summa Theologiae*, and in his commentaries on Aristotle's *Nicomachean Ethics* and *Politics*. In the *Summa Contra Gentiles*, to give another example, when he discusses how man, by the law of God, is ordered relative to his neighbour, St Thomas observes that it is 'natural to man that he be a social animal: as is shown by the fact that a man by himself cannot procure all that is needed for human life'. [8]

Both Aristotle and St Thomas rely on what they take to be a universal fact: no one chooses the solitary life. Humans inevitably live in community, and cannot live wholly solitary lives. Even if a choice were possible, humans would not choose otherwise, because outside community they would not be happy. [9] But only in a community in which peace prevails can happiness be achieved; and it is this order that is the object of choice.

That humans live communally is given; the order of concord or peace is chosen on a continuous or constant basis. Since they who are to choose civil society already live within it, civil society is not chosen by a founding contract between those living outside it. It is an order into which humans are born, as they have always been born, without any original choice;[10] that is maintained by those

---

[7] St Thomas Aquinas, *Commentary on Aristotle's Nicomachean Ethics*, IX.X.1891. St Thomas here writes that man is a 'political animal' rather than a 'social animal' because he is here commenting on the Latin translation of Aristotle where the relevant passage reads: '... *politicum enim homo, et convivere aptus natus'. In Decem Libros Ethicorum Aristotelis ad Nicomachum Expositio* (Turin: Marietti, 1934), 603.

[8] *Summa Contra Gentiles*, III.129. The context of St Thomas's discussion is an account, running from ch 111 to ch 163, of how humans are governed by God. In this set of chapters in the *Summa Contra Gentiles* the phrase 'social animal' appears for the first time in ch 117.

[9] The eremitic life and the anchoritic life would of course have been very familiar to St Thomas, and the reader may think of these styles of life, or of modern hermits or isolationists, and consider that they render Aristotle and St Thomas incorrect in this regard. Man is not, it might be said, necessarily a 'social' or 'political' animal because there are those who choose to withdraw completely from human society. But Aristotle says 'none would choose to be solitary in order to have all good things' and St Thomas's version is that 'none would choose to live always by himself, that is, alone, even if consequently he would have all other goods'. In both accounts there is the implicit idea that the 'goods' of life are to be found by living in community, that is, that human fulfilment is for the most part found in social life. The hermit, the anchorite, the isolationist – these are exceptional cases that to an extent prove but fail to refute the rule. Neither Aristotle nor St Thomas condemn these lifestyles but both writers take as given that such cases go against the social or political nature of humans; the consequence of this is that these lifestyles do not afford the possibility of enjoying the full range of the 'goods' of life. The 'eremitic option' may be thought of as a 'good' of social life only if one is careful to remember that only someone brought up in community can *choose* solitary life; the wolf-child, if such there is, does not live a human life.

[10] GK Chesterton put it well in his essay, 'The Flag of the World': 'A man belongs to this world before he begins to ask if it is nice to belong to it', *Essays and Poems* (W Sheed (ed), Harmondsworth: Penguin, 1958), 54. The essay was published originally in Chesterton's *Orthodoxy* (London: The Bodley Head, 1908).

within it acting well; and that is undermined by those within it acting badly. When a person, for example, tempted to steal, chooses not to steal, he chooses to maintain the peaceful order; when, tempted to steal, he chooses to steal, he chooses to undermine the peaceful order. The honest man chooses not to steal because he accepts that what he is tempted to steal belongs to another and he respects the owner's interest; when honest men and women live together their honest choices contribute to bringing about and sustaining the peaceful order, which is thus chosen, as it were, obliquely.

On this view, when humans live together they are brought up to do a whole host of things in particular ways. These 'ways of doing things' include, for example, customs, practices, well-known and accepted procedures and mutual expectations that establish the jural relationships particular to any community. These are ways of doing things that are 'extra-legal' in the sense only that they do not originate in state or positive law, that is, in constitutions, statutes, codes, or case law. They *are* 'legal', however, in that they constitute the living law of a community, which does not come into existence by any process of public and explicit formal consideration or debate. The communal living law – or the communal moral law – is not for the most part explicitly formulated in language; no individual or institution can change it; and when it changes it tends to be a relatively slow process of change. As humans interact with one another and deal with one another in different ways, as their mode of livelihood changes, the character of their societies changes; new practices arise to replace older ones, new questions come up, new solutions are offered, accepted more or less happily by some, acquiesced in by others, transmitted from generation to generation, questioned, retained, or eventually rejected. Human society is a dialectical order and the ever-evolving communal moral law is the jural order of society; it is constituted by those judgments and choices that in recurrent types of circumstances are generally accepted and approved of in a particular society.[11]

This recurrence of accepted and approved judgments and choices in particular types of circumstances is part of the process that leads to the formalization – usually in the form of inscription or writing – of law. So, as we said above, the first Icelandic laws were recited annually by the 'Law Speaker' (*lögsögumaður*) at the *Althingi* or parliament until in 1117 *Althingi* decided that all those laws should be written down and they were published subsequently as *Grágás*.

---

[11] Like language, synchronically the communal moral law, whether more or less comprehensively formally expressed in maxims and rules is what, at any given time, is generally accepted in the community as 'a prescription of what ought to be done and proscription of what ought not to be done', *Digest*, 1.3.2. Still, at any given time, there may be, and commonly is, major or minor disagreement. Such disagreement is one of the sources of change so that, diachronically, the moral law of a particular people, at a later time, will not be identical with what it formerly was. The moral law of different communities will be 'in part their own special law [its *ius civile*] and in part a law common to all men [the *ius gentium*]', *Digest*, 1.1.9. Both parts will be known but, only very rarely, will they be known *as* parts analytically distinguished in that way. The law will be known as a whole, and the relevant distinction will be between more and less important rules.

Obviously the Law Speaker did not recite the entire living law, the entire communal moral law, but only those laws that were considered to be the most important norms and rules of the community. Similarly the legal measures provided for in *Grágás* – including its provisions regarding legislative powers; truce and peace speeches; bethrotal; homicide; land claims; and so on – were those that referred to situations where formalization was considered necessary. Other aspects of the living law – norms of everyday social behaviour, for example – were not included.

In Chapter 1 we distinguished our sense of 'law' – as in the 'living law' – from the more common understanding of the term, that is, as state or positive law and including constitutional law (whether written or unwritten) and enacted legislation (for example, law contained in a common law statute or civil code); law arising from or associated with the courts (common law, case law, or, sometimes, 'judge-made law'); and, in many perspectives, elements of international law. In this book we tend to use the terms 'state law' or 'positive law' for this type of law.[12] It includes the *formulation* or *expression* of parts of the living law in constitutions, legislation, case law, and so on. The formulation, the written law, expresses an understanding of some (but not all) social practices and deals with some of the problems that have arisen in relation to these practices and that are likely to arise in the future. Rarely, however, as Hayek observed, does the jurist 'achieve more than an adequate and partial expression of what is well known in practice' because 'the rules that govern action will often be much more general and abstract than anything language can yet express'.[13] The jurist's task is 'one of discovering something which exists, not as one creating something new, even though the result of such efforts may be the creation of something that has not existed before'.[14] But state law, as we noted in Chapter

---

[12] We avoid identifying state law with what is sometimes called 'conventional law' because in one sense of that slippery term, the entire law – including the living law and state law – is 'conventional' in that it is agreed, for as Julian, quoted in the *Digest*, writing of custom, says '… given that statutes themselves are binding upon us for no other reason than that they have been accepted by the judgement of the populace, certainly it is fitting that what the populace has approved without any writing shall be binding upon everyone. What does it matter whether the populace declares its will by voting or by the very substance of its actions?', *Digest*, 1.3.32. The communal moral law of a community is the law because it is agreed to be the law; when it is no longer accepted it is no longer the communal moral law. The same applies to state or positive law. In that sense of the term, all law is conventional.

[13] FA Hayek, *Law, Legislation and Liberty – Vol I: Rules and Order* (Chicago: University of Chicago Press, 1973), 77.

[14] Ibid, 78. 'This remains true even where … those called upon to decide are driven to formulate rules on which nobody has acted before. They are concerned not only with a body of rules but also with an order of the actions resulting from the observance of these rules, which men find in an ongoing process and the preservation of which may require particular rules. The preservation of the existing order of action towards which all recognized rules are directed may well be seen to require some other rule for the decision of disputes for which the recognized rules supply no answer. In this sense a rule not yet existing in any sense may appear to be "implicit" in the body of existing rules, not in the sense that it is logically derivable from them, but in the sense that if the other rules are to achieve their aim, an additional rule is required.'

1, also includes the legislation that concerns the relation of people or institutions to particular types of state. State law, therefore, is not *exclusively* a selection of provisions expressing parts of a pre-existing customary, living law of a particular community.

We use the term 'positive law' to refer to those laws that have been legitimately posited,[15] and we use it interchangeably with 'state law'. In the account of law and justice proposed in this book, both judge-made law and international law are part of what we refer to as state or positive law. State or positive law includes the law that emerges from litigation on written rules and matters outside the scope of such rules. We shall elaborate in Chapter 6 on how judges, when adjudicating disputes and interpreting written law, cannot on some occasions avoid 'filling in the gaps' in the written law and to that extent 'making' law. We consider public international law on the one hand, and metropolitan or municipal law (that is, law confined to state entities) on the other hand, to be similar enterprises. They obviously refer to different domains, and they obviously differ crucially in terms of their authority and force, but ultimately they are both expressions of what has been discovered – although fallibly – to be either naturally or conventionally just. Much public international law is in many respects closer than metropolitan or municipal to the idea of the living law because of the significance of customary norms in inter-state relations, and this in turn draws attention to the relationship between custom and written law.

Although the significant role of custom as an *original* basis for the content of positive law is widely acknowledged, it is commonplace to hear suggestions that custom plays only a very small part in modern law. In the common law system, for example, in which custom is defined as 'such usage as has obtained the force of law',[16] it is often thought that the decisions of judges, in recognizing some customs as positive law because of their reasonableness and practicality, somehow transform these customs into something quite distinct, to the extent that they cease to be customs altogether. It is crucial to remember that such customs *remain* customs *in addition* to becoming part of the positive law. It is a grave mistake to consider positive law as completely separate from the generally accepted customs and moral norms of a community – that is, from the living law – because the latter generate the former on an ongoing, dialectical basis. Jean Porter has suggested that because written laws serve to formulate and correct custom, they will normally supersede and override customary law; yet, because they find their

---

[15] To use the term in that way is to prescind from the content of what is posited but does not require one to hold that only what is posited is law. For example, a presupposition that there is a natural law against stealing does not preclude an injunction against stealing being posited; it does not preclude the assertion that the natural law against stealing may not in a particular community be a positive law; and, finally, it does not preclude the assertion that a pre-existing customary law against stealing may become a positive law. A positive law, then, is simply a law that is posited in an established way; content is irrelevant. The radical positivist account of law, with which we disagree, adds that only laws posited in that particular way are laws, and that the law is just if properly posited, thus rendering 'just' redundant.   [16] *Tanistry Case* (1608) Dav Ir 28.

context and point within a broader framework of customary law, the customs of a people will provide the necessary context for their interpretation. What is more, Porter observes,

...written law will have no purchase on a community, unless it reflects the practices of that community in some way; even a law that sets out to correct custom will necessarily reflect other aspects of the customary practices of a community, or it will lack purchase in the community for which it is intended. Far from being a minor adjunct to the law properly so called, custom is seen from this perspective as the one essential component of any legal system, sufficient to sustain a rule of law under some circumstances, and one essential component of the rule of law under any and every circumstance.[17]

We are fully aware that the role of custom – or, as we have put it above, customs, practices, well-known and accepted procedures and mutual expectations – in our account of law is controversial. In many influential modern accounts – from which they differ – Amanda Perreau-Saussine and James Bernard Murphy have observed that

...reliance on customary practices is a mark of inadequacy: acceptance of customs should be minimal and provisional since an unreflective attachment to customary ways of thinking is inimical both to practical thought and to political harmony. Modern societies and their legal systems depend not on enslavement to customary habits and laws but on reasoned principles and doctrines; customary laws grow up only where legislators have done a particularly poor job, leaving a need for elaborate statutory construction and legislative gap-filling. The more coherent and consistent a legal system is, the less the need for such customary rules and practices....[18]

The views referred to by Perreau-Saussine and Murphy in this passage are intimately connected with the modern accounts that insist on contract-based explanations of the origins of human society. The modern tendency is to insist on the displacement of whatever order has evolved by an imposed organizational template or framework. However, in arguing that there is never a total 'displacement' of any natural order, we are expressing an ancient but also a topical jurisprudential view. For example, in Neil MacCormick's 2007 book, *Institutions of Law*, law is defined as 'institutional normative order'.[19] MacCormick refers to the practice of queuing

---

[17] J Porter, 'Custom, Ordinance and Natural Right in Gratian's *Decretum*' in A Perreau-Saussine and JB Murphy (eds), *The Nature of Customary Law: Legal, Historical and Philosophical Perspectives* (Cambridge: Cambridge University Press, 2007), 79, 100. We noted in ch 1 above that we initially took the term 'living law' from an account of lectures by FSC Northrop in which he discussed the distinction between the positive law and the living law. Northrop emphasized, as Porter does, that written law will have no purchase on a community unless it reflects the practices of that community in some way. B Magee, *Confessions of a Philosopher* (London: Phoenix, 1997), 166–7. See also FA Hayek, *The Constitution of Liberty* (Chicago: University of Chicago Press, 1960), esp ch 10, and G Barden and T Murphy, 'Society as a Source of Law' (2006) 95 *Studies* 407.

[18] A Perreau-Saussine and JB Murphy, 'The Character of Customary Law: An Introduction' in A Perreau-Saussine and JB Murphy (eds), *The Nature of Customary Law*, 1.

[19] 'Legal order is an instance of normative order. It obtains when life in a given society proceeds in an orderly way with reasonable security of mutual expectations among people, on the ground of reasonable conformity by most people to applicable norms of conduct.' N MacCormick, *Rhetoric*

to illustrate normative order, the kind of orderliness that we sometimes discern in human behaviour when people ('norm-users') follow common norms of conduct. Those in some kind of authority ('norm-givers') regulate and institutionalize this order via rules. The constitutional structure of the modern state and the international legal order are especially complex examples of institutionalization in this sense. MacCormick acknowledges that the institutionalization of rules and their application gives rise to disagreements concerning interpretation and scepticism concerning the extent to which the official rules truly account for conduct in real life, but he highlights the civility that permits the functioning of law, politics, and the economy and observes that this civility 'depends, it seems, on some measure of respect for the rule of law internally to states and among them'.[20] This respect is an element of custom, and indeed all formal normative order 'rests on a foundation of custom, that is, on informal normative order'.[21]

Ultimately, as will be reiterated throughout this book, we concur with Perreau-Saussine and Murphy's view that customary rules and practices underpin every legal system:

Customary rules of interpretation play a part in any legal system, however codified: no written law can give exhaustive directions on its own interpretation, so customary rules and practices inevitably guide judicial interpretation. And those customary rules and practices themselves in turn will be subject to change and development through interpretation. Ancient and modern, international, civilian and common law; every interpretation and application of a written law relies on a complicated set of shared customs. And, once given, each interpretation and application of a written law itself extends that same set of customs.[22]

Our account develops this perspective further by integrating it with our ideas concerning natural and conventional justice, adjudication, interpretation, morality, legislation, force, authority, and legitimacy – and we would add that underlying all of these enterprises is an ambiguity that recognizes the fallibility of all that has been established, and so continuously questions all that is given or decided. But our immediate concern is with the role of custom in our understanding of

---

and the Rule of Law (Oxford: Oxford University Press, 2005), 2. A norm of conduct expresses a value and enjoins that the value be realized in the appropriate circumstances. Thus, 'it is an offence to use mobile phones while driving' forbids the use of mobile phones in the described circumstances and expresses the value that it is bad to use, and good not to use, mobile phones while driving.

[20] N MacCormick, *Institutions of Law: An Essay in Legal Theory* (Oxford: Oxford University Press, 2007), 73. Here MacCormick seems to differ from our view that positive law also includes legislation that concerns the relation of people or institutions to particular types of state, and that legislation, therefore, is not exclusively a selection of provisions expressing parts of a pre-existing customary, living law of a particular community (see n 20 in ch 1 above), but we interpret MacCormick as holding that such 'new' or 'original' positive laws attain their authority as elements of formal normative order by virtue, in part at least, of that order's more general foundation in custom. [21] Ibid, 162.

[22] A Perreau-Saussine and JB Murphy, 'The Character of Customary Law: An Introduction' in A Perreau-Saussine and JB Murphy (eds), *The Nature of Customary Law*, 1, 9.

the *function* of law. When we refer to the function of law we are referring to *all* law, whether part of the customary living law only, or the part of that law that is expressed in positive law, or part of the positive law that concerns the relation of people or institutions to particular types of state.

Before considering law's function, we turn to what we hold to be the key element of the living or communal moral law, namely the tendency of this law to cultivate a moral context within which others' interests are to be considered and the related idea that this moral context is itself an expression of what is naturally just. The moral context within which others' interests are to be considered is to be found, more or less clearly and formally expressed, in many societes. In the Judeo-Christian tradition, the 'golden rule' is clearly formulated in *Leviticus*: 19: 18 as 'Love thy neighbour as thyself.' This becomes central in Christianity, and thence in the Western tradition, from the New Testament where Christ calls it the second of the two commandments upon which 'hang all the Law and the Prophets'.[23] St Paul's earlier formulation is especially interesting. He makes clear, as the Gospels do not, *why* the command to love one's neighbour fulfils the law:

… for he that loveth another hath fulfilled the law. For this, Thou shalt not commit adultery, Thou shalt not steal, Thou shalt not bear false witness, Thou shalt not covet and if there be any other commandment, it is briefly comprehended in this saying, namely, Thou shalt love thy neighbour as thyself. Love worketh no ill to his neighbour: *therefore* love is the fulfilling of the law.[24]

Equally significant in the Western tradition are the Greek and Roman streams with their enduring effort to formulate a clear idea of justice that has at its heart the notion that no one person's interest is exclusive; justice is essentially a communal virtue, 'to render to each what is due'. Cicero, in *On Duties*, expressed it well:

Of justice, the first office is that no man should harm another unless he has been provoked by injustice… We are not born for ourselves alone, to use Plato's splendid words, but our country claims one part of our birth, and our friends another. Moreover, as the

[23] *Matthew* 22: 34–40 in which passage Christ, in answer to a lawyer's question as to which commandment is the greatest, says that the first and greatest commandment is to 'love the Lord thy God with all thy heart and with all thy soul, and with all thy mind. And the second is like unto it, Thou shalt love thy neighbour as thyself'. The story with small variations is told in Mark's Gospel (12: 28–34) and in Luke's Gospel (10: 25–8). Hillel, the Jewish contemporary of Jesus summed up the Torah with the admonition: 'What is hateful to you do not do to your fellow', GW Plaut (ed), *The Torah: A Modern Commentary* (New York: Union of Hebrew Congregations, 1981), 892.

[24] *Epistle to the Romans* 13: 8–10 (emphasis added). See also *Epistle to the Galatians* 5: 14; the *Epistle of James* 2: 8; and the *1st Epistle of John* 3: 23–4. Erich Fromm describes this kind of love as 'brotherly love' and considers it the 'most fundamental kind of love'; by it Fromm means 'love for all human beings; it is characterized by its very lack of exclusiveness… Brotherly love is based on the experience that we are all one. The differences in talents, intelligence, knowledge are negligible in comparison with the identity of the human core common to all men', *The Art of Loving* [1956] (New York: Perennial Classics, 2000), 43–4.

Stoics believe, everything produced on earth is for the sake of men, and men are born for the sake of men, so that they may be able to assist one another . . . Of injustice there are two types: men may inflict injury; or else, when it is being inflicted on others, they may fail to deflect it even though they could.[25]

The association between doing harm to another and justice is taken up again in the second of the three precepts of justice in Justinian's *Digest*: 'The basic principles of right are to live honourably, not to harm any other person, to render to each his own.'[26]

St Thomas takes up the Jewish, Greek, Roman, and Christian streams in his reflections on law and justice and thinks of a natural law against injuring another as a more basic principle from which flows the injunction against murder.[27] So, too, does Hobbes, who in both *Leviathan* and *De Cive* relates the natural laws that, he thinks, must be followed if a society is to be maintained in peace, to the divine law: 'This is that law of the Gospell: *Whatsoever you require others should do to you, that do ye to them*. And that law of all men, *Quod tibi fieri non vis, alteri non feceris*.'[28]

We argue in favour of the judgment that humans in their decisions and actions should take account of others. We think of it as a reasonable conclusion to the question as to how we should live. Is the opposite conclusion – 'Humans in their decisions and actions should take no account of others' – equally reasonable? We suggest that it is not. The principle that one should act taking others into account becomes more or less well communally accepted; it acts as a presupposition of positive law although it is not posited in legislation. One whose effective

---

[25] Cicero, *On Duties* (M Griffin and M Atkins eds; M Atkins trans) (Cambridge: Cambridge University Press, 1991), [I.22], 9–10. The reference to Plato is to his ninth letter, 358a.

[26] *Digest*, I.I.10; *Institutes*, I.I.3.

[27] *Summa Theologiae*, I–II, q 95, art 2: 'Some [precepts] are derived from the common principles of natural law by way of conclusion: as "do not murder" may be derived as a kind of conclusion from "do not harm anyone".'

[28] *Leviathan*, 190 [64]. The Latin in this quotation translates as: 'What you do not wish to be done to you, do not to another'. See also *De Cive*, ch 4, where, referring to Matthew's Gospel (7: 12), Hobbes writes: 'Lastly, the rule by which I said any man might know, whether what he was doing were contrary to the law or not, to wit, what thou wouldst not be done to, do not that to another; is almost in the self-same words delivered by our Saviour: Therefore all things whatsoever ye would that men should do unto you, do you even so to them', *De Cive* [1642], edited with an introduction by Bernard Gert: *Man and Citizen (De Homine and De Cive)* (Indianopolis, Ind: Hackett, 1991), 162. We use the Gert edition throughout this book. Hobbes makes the same point in his earlier *The Elements of Law* (see Hobbes, *Human Nature and De Corpore Politico* (JCA Gaskin ed, Oxford: Oxford University Press, 1994), 96, 101; *The Elements of Law* is in two parts – *Part I: Human Nature* and *Part II: De Corpore Politico*). The verse from Matthew concludes with the phrase, not quoted by Hobbes: 'for this is the law and the prophets'. A version nearer to Hobbes's version is found in *Tobit* at 4: 16: 'See that thou never do to another what thou wouldst hate to have done to thee by another'. Because *Tobit* is within the Greek Bible or Septuagint and remained within the canon accepted by the Roman Catholic Church, but not within the Hebrew Bible which was accepted as canonical in the Church of England, it is uncertain whether or not Hobbes here referred knowingly to this passage. Hobbes's biblical quotations are from the Authorized King James Version; we have taken the text from *Tobit* from the near contemporary translation of the Old Testament first published by the English College at Douay in 1600.

and affective orientation is always to ignore others' interests in favour of his own advantage will find valuable what one whose effective and affective orientation is to take account of others' interests will find valueless. The choice is between taking account of others' interests and allowing one's own absolute primacy; between supporting society and subverting it. Thus, we argue, the choice between these orientations is the fundamental moral choice.[29]

2.3 The Function of Law and the Jural Order

The model we propose is of an original unchosen but given social order, the further development or decline of which depends upon the choices of those who live within it. The maintenance of the good or peaceful social order is the *common good*. This order emerges between people who act well together, and, by definition, it is not an organization; it is not in any sense the result of legislative command or set of commands. In this model, it is the function of law to contribute to the maintenance of this social order, that is, the common good. This contribution is made in the form of both the 'living law' of the community – customs, practices, well-known and accepted procedures and mutual expectations – *and* the positive law – the formulation of part of the living law in constitutions, legislation, and so on; the 'original' forms of written law that pertain to particular types of state; and the case law emergent from litigation. Ideally, 'law' of any kind looks to what St Thomas calls the order of communal happiness.[30]

The common good is sometimes imagined as an aim or goal common to everyone, but on reflection this is evidently not the case. No social outcome – that is, no particular configuration of the social order – is an aim or goal common to all. Neither does the common good refer to anything like the good of the majority or the good of any portion of the populace, whether calculated along utilitarian or other lines. The common good is a constant goal but it is in no sense a social outcome that is aimed for. It is better thought of as a framework since it allows people to pursue their individual and collective goals in community: the common good is peaceful and civil society in which humans can, for the most part, live their lives in cooperative harmony. Patrick Riordan distinguishes between two assumptions: first, the interest common to players on the same team in a competitive game, which is to win; and secondly, the common good of all the competitors that the game be played fairly.[31] Obviously, the desire to win may easily,

---

[29] See G Barden, *Essays on a Philosophical Interpretation of Justice: The Virtue of Justice* (Lampeter: Mellen Press, 1999), ch 9 and G Barden, *After Principles* (Notre Dame, Ind: University of Notre Dame Press, 1990), chs 7–9. See also the chapter on the human good in Bernard Lonergan's *Method in Theology* (London: Darton, Longman and Todd, 1972).

[30] *Summa Theologiae*, I–II, q 90, art 2.

[31] P Riordan, *A Politics of the Common Good* (Dublin: Institute of Public Administration, 1996), 18–19.

and often does, undermine a player's commitment to the common good understood in the second, broader sense. This second sense – the sense that refers to all
participants collectively – is the sense of the common good as we understand it.
Thomas Hobbes, whose theory of civil society includes an understanding of law's
function that is, perhaps surprisingly, similar to that of St Thomas,[32] had one
overarching question: what is needed if 'men in multitudes' are to live together
without a state of constant war 'where every man is an Enemy to every man'?[33]
Hobbes suggested that humans were motivated to seek peaceful social order by
the 'Feare of Death; Desire of such things as are necessary to commodious living; and a Hope by their means to obtain them'.[34] The desire for what allows
a good life and the hope of being able to live it are the desire and hope for the
common good.

   We shall say more on Hobbes in the final part of this chapter but now we must
focus on the fact that the law of a community is expressed in *jural* terms. The
jural order that fulfils the function of maintaining the peaceful order is a network
or bundle of entitlements in society *only parts of which* positive law – of whatever
type – expresses. Some of the entitlements in the network, on the other hand,
are entitlements *only* because they are established as such in the expression that
is positive law. Justice, as we shall see in detail in later chapters, is the rendering
to each what is their due. A person's *ius* or 'right' is the object of justice, that to
which he is entitled. It is essentially something within a community of people
related to one another in a network of *iura* ('rights' or 'entitlements'). This jural
community is chosen in a way that is similar to the way in which the social order
more generally is chosen. In jural terms it is chosen to the extent that each member of the community chooses to act so as to respect others' rights, or fails so to
choose. Were everyone in the jural community at every opportunity to choose
not to respect others' rights, the community would be destroyed. Just as the social
order does not emerge from an original pre-social situation or condition, the jural
community does not emerge from a pre-jural situation or condition. That the
community into which they are born is a jural community is something that children must learn. The continued existence of a viable jural community depends
on its members understanding in their daily practice what a jural community is,
knowing, again in practice and not theoretically, that their community is a jural
community, and, for the most part, choosing to act rightly in accordance with
that knowledge.[35]

---

   [32] G Barden and T Murphy, 'Law's Function in *Leviathan* and *De Cive* – A Re-appraisal of the
Jurisprudence of Thomas Hobbes' (2007) 29 *Dublin University Law Journal* 231.
   [33] T Hobbes, *Leviathan*, 186 [62].   [34] Ibid, 188 [63].
   [35] Humans in their ordinary lives together establish jural relationships between themselves and
live within a web of such relationships. This means that human juridical reality is not adequately
described in terms of what the Scandinavian realist, Karl Olivecrona (1897–1980), called 'material
space-time reality'. When Peter hands a book to Paul, we do not know what has happened until we
know what *jural* relationships have been established between them. Has Peter given Paul a gift; has
he sold him the book; has he lent it to him? Olivecrona's analysis overlooks the ambiguity of human

The first known *theory* of this practice is found in the work of the Roman jurists, who recognized that every society was governed partly by laws which were peculiarly its own – the *ius civile* of a particular society – and partly by laws which were common to all mankind.[36] These latter laws they termed the *ius gentium* or the law of nations:

What natural reason establishes among all men and is followed equally by all people is called the law of nations (*ius gentium*) for all nations use it...[I]t is common to all humankind for nations have established laws (*iura*) for themselves as occasion and the necessities of human life required.[37]

There is no suggestion that the *ius gentium* was the law that applied to Romans in their dealings with others, and that the *ius civile* was the law that governed dealings between Romans. Nor is there any suggestion that the *ius gentium* pre-exists the social group's existence and that the group's own legislative enactments – the *ius civile* – must conform to it, in the sense of conforming to a 'higher law', in order to be valid. The phrase 'higher law' is misleading because it gives the impression that the *ius gentium*, already fully formed, is in some sense imposed from above. It is not: its provisions are discovered to be common to different societies but, before they are *discovered* to be common, they are *in fact* common, and are similar responses to similar exigencies.

The *ius gentium* is another way of conceptualizing that *part* of the living law that is common to all human communities. The living law of a community is in part the *ius gentium* common to all humans and in part the customs, practices, well-known and accepted procedures, and mutual expectations that establish the jural relationships particular to that community. The *ius gentium* is not *invented* as a common law; rather it is, as we say, *in fact* common and only later *discovered* to be common. It is common because humans are spontaneously intersubjective, reasonable, and social beings whose lives together are in very basic and important ways similar in different societies; the Roman idea is that the *ius gentium* is a response to the very basic exigencies of human life that, as a matter of fact, are common to humankind. Some laws are fundamental in that they are essential to communal life: were people not to act for the most part in accord with them, the jural order and, by extension, the social order would not survive. No human society can survive in which random and indiscriminate killing is approved or practised; and no human society can survive if whatever is in any way owned may be taken against the owner's will by another at that

---

action abstracted from its jural context. See G Barden, *Essays on a Philosophical Interpretation of Justice*, esp chs 4 and 8; N MacCormick, *Institutions of Law*, esp chs 1, 2, and 8; and M La Torre, 'Institutionalist Philosophy of Law' in CB Gray (ed), *The Philosophy of Law: An Encyclopedia (Vol I)* (New York: Garland, 1999), 420–3.

[36] Justinian, *Institutes*, I.II.1: 'The people of Rome are governed partly by their own laws, and partly by the laws that are common to all mankind.' This is a direct quotation from Gaius's *Institutes* (i.I).   [37] Justinian, *Institutes*, I.II.1 and 2.

other's whim.[38] Other more detailed customs and laws are needed and are conventional to the extent that they select and enjoin one way of acting rather than another; so, for example, the detailed rules governing murder and larceny differ from jurisdiction to jurisdiction. This is the *ius civile*, but its detailed rules of murder and larceny cannot coherently undermine the fundamental laws that express an understanding of what is communal living.

We remarked above that children must learn that the community into which they are born is a jural community, and we observed that this community did not emerge from a pre-jural condition. In a similar way, the *ius gentium* – and the entire living law of a community – is learned and developed to some extent as language is, and emphatically not by following a set of rules. As the late French linguist, Jean Gagnepain, observed, we learn our morality as we learn our language.[39] The most important thing about language – and about the commonly accepted ideas of what constitutes good behaviour – is not that the rules or ideas be written down but that they are known.

The set of rules associated with an activity either establishes the activity or describes it. Sometimes people first agree upon the rules of a proposed activity such as a game, and, in that sense, invent the activity. Only when the activity is invented do they begin to engage in it. For example, a game of chess or cricket cannot be played if the rules are not known and assented to in advance. On the other hand, sometimes people engage in an activity and only later formulate its rules explicitly. Language is the obvious and difficult example of an activity that may be described in a set of rules but that exists as an activity before the rules are theoretically discovered. No speakers know the entire set of rules of their own language but every language, including its so-called irregular formations, is rule governed or regular. So we speak our language correctly without knowing formulated grammatical rules.[40] The rules formulate how we speak but when we speak we only in a very queer sense 'obey the rules'. Similarly, when a person acts well he is rarely 'obeying a rule'.[41] Children learn language by listening and

---

[38] Some may consider this claim regarding ownership to be controversial but it is absolutely central to our account of justice and is discussed in detail in ch 3 below. Suffice to say at this juncture that by ownership we mean an entitlement or set of entitlements.

[39] On this idea, see J Gagnepain, *Du vouloir dire* (Paris: Pergamon, 1982). Think of speaking your own language correctly; contrast this with writing in a language other than your own that you know reasonably well. It is true that children are also instructed how to speak, but more by example than by rule. Obviously, a child does not learn his mother tongue by first learning, and then applying, its rules.

[40] There are no non-grammatical languages; but there have been, and still are, languages the grammar of which has not been analysed and for which, therefore, there are as yet in a sense no rules to follow, and few, if any, speakers know all the rules of their mother tongue. By no means are all the rules of, for example, the Australian Aboriginal language, Ngatatjara, known; and, indeed, it is extremely doubtful, as Randolph Quirk's analysis of modern English shows, that all the rules according to which English is spoken are known; in neither case do native speakers have the least difficulty using their respective languages. R Quirk, *A Concise Grammar of Contemporary English* (New York: Harcourt Brace Jovanovich, 1973).

[41] L Wittgenstein, *Philosophical Investigations* (Oxford: Blackwell, 2001), 68 et seq.

understanding and, to some extent, by being corrected when they make mistakes. But those who correct them often do not know the explicit rules in the light of which they correct the children's usage; they know that 'this is what is said' and 'this is not what is said' in whatever version of the language they use. When mutual intelligibility disappears the speakers no longer form a single linguistic community.[42]

Language is in some respects natural, in some respects conventional. It is natural to humans in that humans communicate linguistically, but 'conventional' in the sense that languages differ, and none is more naturally related to what is meant than is another.[43] Language is conventional in at least two other senses. Speakers of the same language agree in practice to use words in the same way but, despite the best efforts of academies, the agreement is rarely successfully dictated in an obligatory rule; the agreement comes about as speakers communicate with one another. And linguistic communication is conventional in yet another sense, so obvious, that it is sometimes overlooked. When two people speak to each other, they agree to do so. They do not usually first make an agreement to speak – which it would be difficult to do without speaking – and only then speak about some other topic. Their agreement emerges in their mutual communication.

Language reveals a great deal about the character of communal discovery, yet it remains insufficiently understood; but it is what the Roman jurists had in mind when they wrote of the *ius gentium* being the response of a people to the changing demands of communal life. The sense of justice of a given community or society is a sense that evolves as a consequence of people living together and dealing with the continual jural demands that ordinary living imposes upon them.[44]

---

[42] Correct usage is to an extent a social and political thing but there is a purely linguistic limit in that within a single linguistic community there must be mutual intelligibility between speakers.

[43] Onomatopoeic words do have this quality but these do not detract significantly from the general conventionality of language.

[44] G Barden, 'Discovering a Constitution' in T Murphy and P Twomey (eds), *Ireland's Evolving Constitution 1937–1997: Collected Essays* (Oxford: Hart, 1998), 5–6. In the field of contemporary constitutional theory, Martin Loughlin has contrasted the 'essentially modern understanding' of a constitution as a formal framework of fundamental law that establishes and regulates the activity of governing a state with the views of the French thinker, Joseph de Maistre, who argued that 'the constitution of a nation is never the product of deliberation' and that so-called constitutional reform never establishes anything new but only declares existing rights, and hence that a country's constitution cannot be known from its written laws 'because these laws are made at different periods only to lay down forgotten or contested rights, and because there is always a host of things which are not written'. J de Maistre, 'Study on Sovereignty' [1794–95] in J Lively (ed), *The Works of Joseph de Maistre* (New York: Macmillan, 1965), 93, 103, 103–4, cited by M Loughlin, 'Constitutional Theory: A 25th Anniversary Essay' (2005) *Oxford Journal of Legal Studies* 183, 184. As Loughlin remarks (184), the contrast reveals that a constitution 'can be viewed not only as a text, but also as an expression of a political way of being. And in this latter sense, constitutions can no more be made than language is made, since constitutions evolve from the way of life of certain groups that come to conceive of themselves as "a people" or "nation"' (184).

This sense of justice, expressed originally in the living law, is the background context or tradition against which dialectic or debate on positive law takes place. It provides not only the basis of formulated law, that is, of constitutions and legislation, but also the framework within which law is judicially interpreted. Society is lived; the formulated rules express an understanding of social life, of how society actually operates. As we have said, however, whatever is discovered as law in the given social context – whether through formulation or interpretation – will not be infallible: what is discovered will often be the subject of intense debate and disagreement.

Given our understanding of law as not being confined to statute, code, or convention and the manner in which they are interpreted and applied, but rather as the set of understandings or norms covering the whole moral life, a question arises: could a human community or society exist and survive *without* positive law? We answer yes unequivocally, albeit probably a small community only. In its social aspect, the living law has no limits in terms of what it relates or refers to: it can be exhaustive. But such a community – sustained solely by the living law or the communal moral law, and having no positive law – would have to be what is sometimes called 'close-knit' and one where the degree and force of approval and disapproval – approbation and disapprobation, scorn and derision, and so on – would have to be significant indeed.

And what of dissonance, it may be objected? It is all very well to envisage a situation in which the positive law expresses a conceptualization of justice, at least partially, but what of the case where laws are posited in a community solely – or almost solely – for the advantage of some privileged, powerful elite? Such cases – where positive law deviates deliberately and markedly from the living law – are common, and not only historically so. Our view is that such regimes or such communities tend – not necessarily rapidly but inexorably – towards self-destruction and collapse and that in many, if not most, such cases, this self-destruction and collapse is signalled by civil strife or even civil war. As we shall elaborate further in our discussion of Thomas Hobbes below, the function of law and the jural order is ultimately to express, defend, and preserve the order in which humans can live together in peace. If the jural order fails in that task then the common good is compromised and the community endangered.

The jural order or community that we describe is founded on a particular idea of justice. This idea of justice – the rendering to each what is due – is central to this book, and in Chapter 3 we examine its meaning and argue that a concept of ownership or entitlement is essential to it. In Chapter 4 we contrast natural and conventional justice and examine also distributive and rectificatory justice; reciprocal justice is discussed in Chapter 5 as part of our account of the trading order. Before turning to consider justice, however, it is worth pausing to reflect further on the place of law in our theory of human community. We shall do so by examining briefly Hobbes's account of law's function.

2.4 Law's Function in *De Cive* and *Leviathan*

Our account of how human community is constituted differs radically from social contract approaches. We hold that human community or civil society is chosen, although not from within a Hobbesian natural condition imagined as an original state. St Thomas writes that it is reasonable to choose civil communal life because it is proper that 'there should be between men, lest they mutually impede one another, an order of concord, which is peace'.[45] Read through a Hobbesian lens, the condition in which they 'mutually impede one another' is the natural condition, and the 'order of concord, which is peace' is civil society.

Despite the differences in approach, however, there is striking similarity between Hobbes's theory of civil society and ours as to what the function of law is: both theories regard the fundamental function of law as the achievement and maintenance of peaceful and civil human society. In the thirteenth chapter of *Leviathan* Hobbes describes the natural condition of mankind. It may be disputed as to whether Hobbes thought that humans were ever in such a condition, or whether he simply used the description as an imaginary picture of a condition – what we should now call a model – to be contrasted with an image of civil society. We incline to the second interpretation, but it is of no consequence for this discussion:[46] what is important is the contrast between civil society and the natural condition. As well as making that contrast, Hobbes makes another; that between a society at peace, and one in the grip of civil war:

… it may be perceived what manner of life there would be, where there were no common Power to feare; by the manner of life, which men that have formerly lived under a peaceful government, use to degenerate into in a civill Warre.[47]

Another, similar contrast might be between life under a peaceful government and the manner of life into which people tend to degenerate in the aftermath of natural or humanly provoked disaster with the emergence of widespread looting and loss of mutual respect.

Hobbes's use of the word 'degenerate' in the passage quoted above is significant. For him, the natural condition is worse, and is, by those living within it, experienced as worse, than civil society. He takes it for granted that his readers will share this evaluation of the contrasted conditions. Hobbes does not so much argue that it is better, as show or remind us that it is. That is how he expects the

---

[45] *Summa Contra Gentiles*, III.128.4.
[46] Hobbes discusses the matter briefly in *Leviathan*, 187 [63], and in the first chapter of *De Cive*. In *Leviathan* he writes: 'It may peradventure be thought, there was never such a time, nor condition of warre as this; and I believe it was never generally so, over all the world…', and, in the following paragraph there is, 'But though there had never been any time wherein particular men were in a condition of warre one against another…'. In the earlier *De Cive* he does not clearly acknowledge the possibility that the state of nature never actually existed.   [47] *Leviathan*, 187 [63].

reader to respond to the contrast. In the first chapter of Hobbes's *De Cive* there is support for the view that civil society is preferable to the natural state:

> ...the natural state of men, before they entered into society was a mere war, and that not simply, but a war of all men against all men.... But it is easily judged how disagreeable a thing it is to the preservation of all mankind, or of each single man, a perpetual war is... [That state is] deprived of all that pleasure and beauty of life, which peace and society are wont to bring with them. Whosoever, therefore, holds that it had been best to have continued in that state in which all things were lawful to all men, he contradicts himself. For every man by natural necessity desires that which is good for him; nor is there any that esteems a war of all against all, which necessarily adheres to such a state, to be good for him....[48]

It is perfectly clear that Hobbes takes it to be an empirical fact, and takes it for a premise in his discussion, that no one 'esteems a war of all against all...to be good for him'. The argument is this: Everyone desires his own good; No one finds the natural state good; Therefore, no one desires the natural state. To hold that it had been best to continue in the natural state contradicts not another proposition but an unavoidable desire; to choose the natural state over against civil society is to choose against one's unavoidable desire. A reader who genuinely took the natural state to be better than, or as good as, civil society would find Hobbes' discussion deeply puzzling.

In what is undoubtedly the best-known quotation from Hobbes, the natural condition is described in *Leviathan* as one in which 'the life of man [is] solitary, poore, nasty, brutish, and short'.[49] The adjective 'solitary' does not describe a condition in which humans live isolated from one another, as if, for example, each one had to fend for himself, alone on his own island, unimpeded by others. The natural condition is nothing of the kind. Even if it is described as non-social, it is not a condition in which humans live alone. They live in proximity to one another, yet not in harmony, in a state of continual war. For Hobbes, humans are naturally and inevitably social beings; but their society is neither naturally nor inevitably civil; that is, it is neither necessarily nor inevitably peaceful.[50]

The natural condition is the war 'of every man against every man'.[51] Men find this hateful, and incline to its opposite, peace. We referred near the outset of the previous section of this chapter to what Hobbes considered to be the motivations underlying this inclination:

> The Passions that encline men to Peace, are Feare of Death; Desire of such things as are necessary to commodious living; and a hope by their means to obtain them.[52]

---

[48] *De Cive*, 118.   [49] *Leviathan*, 186 [62].

[50] In ch 1 of *De Cive* Hobbes argues against the idea that man is a political animal born fit for society – because children must learn to become social – but takes it for granted that humans live in inevitable proximity and association with one another. It is worth remembering that, eg infant chimpanzees also must learn to become social.   [51] *Leviathan*, 185 [62]; *De Cive*, 118.

[52] *Leviathan*, 188 [63].

Of these three passions that incline to peace, one is negative, the fear of death; and two are positive, the desire for what allows a good life, and the hope of being able to live it. It is possible to hate a condition, to desire to escape from it, and to seek another condition without having a very clear idea or image of that other condition. Hobbes, however, does have a clear idea of the desirable condition, and expects his readers to share it. The desirable condition is civil society in which humans, for the most part, live in cooperative harmony and 'under a peacefull government'.[53] For Hobbes, such a situation is the product of social contract borne out of the desire to escape the natural condition.

He calls this the condition of peace, and expects his readers to know, from their own experience, what it is, and to desire it. Why do they desire it? Because, outside it, they live in fear of death in a condition in which 'there can be no security to any man . . . of living out the time, which Nature ordinarily alloweth men to live'.[54] The fourteenth and fifteenth chapters in *Leviathan* and the second and third chapters in *De Cive* set out the 'laws of nature' that indicate the means to achieve peace and the conservation of civil society. These laws are fundamental in as much as they are laws

which, being taken away, the Common-wealth faileth, and is utterly destroyed; as a building whose Foundation is utterly destroyed. And therefore a Fundamentall law is that . . . without which the Common-wealth cannot stand . . . .[55]

What, then, is the *function* of law in Hobbes's scheme? Hobbes is perfectly clear that the appropriate means to achieve and maintain civil society – the fundamental laws of nature or 'theorems of reason' – have a function, and are good or bad to the extent that they fulfil or fail to fulfil their function. Let us consider some of these fundamental laws or 'theorems'. The first law of nature is

to seek peace, where there is any hopes of attaining it, and where there is none, to enquire out for auxiliaries of war, is the dictate of right reason, that is, the law of nature.[56]

---

[53] Ibid, 187 [63].

[54] Ibid, 190 [64]. As is well known, since Hobbes wrote in time of civil war, the immediate purpose of his theoretical account of human civil society was to inculcate a desire for, and to assist in the bringing about of, civil security in the England of his time. Anything that tended to undermine the security of the sovereign was to him anathema. His 'plausible model of absolute government' (JM Kelly, *A Short History of Western Legal Theory* (Oxford: Clarendon, 1992), 214) is thus said to be one in which 'the authority of law rested solely on the fact that it was promulgated by the authorized ruler' (M Loughlin, *Public Law and Political Theory* (Oxford: Clarendon, 1992), 80). In fact, there is an unresolved tension in Hobbes between, on the one hand, his view that law expressed the will of the sovereign – who, for Hobbes, necessarily sought his own good, as he understood it to be – and, on the other hand, Hobbes's acknowledgement that this might or might not coincide with the good of civil society. On this tension, see G Barden and T Murphy, 'Law's Function in *Leviathan* and *De Cive* – A Re-appraisal of the Jurisprudence of Thomas Hobbes' (2007) 29 *Dublin University Law Journal* 231.

[55] *Leviathan*, 334 [150]. This recalls Njál's dictum in the Icelandic saga that we have used as one of the epigraphs to this book: *Með lögum skall land byggja og ólögum eyða* ('By law is the land built; by lawlessness [unlaw] destroyed'). *Njál's Saga*, ch 70.   [56] *De Cive*, 119.

The function of this law is to contribute to the maintenance of a social order within which people can pursue their lives in peace.

Hobbes's second law of nature in *Leviathan* addresses the issue as to how civil society is to be established. His answer is that it can be established only among those who agree to it, that is, who agree to act in a way that both establishes and maintains it. The second law is:

That a man be willing, when others are so too, as farr forth, as for Peace, and for the defence of himself he shall think necessary, to lay down [his] right to all things....[57]

'Right' in the Hobbesian natural condition is simply the freedom to do whatever one wills and is in one's power but such a benefit must be relinquished in a jural community in which each respects others' rights. If, for example, the continuance of civil society depends on its members respecting each other's property, it is perfectly clear that such respect must be mutual. If Peter respects Paul's property but Paul does not respect Peter's, then Peter and Paul live together in a state of conflict or, in Hobbesian terms, 'war'. The same is true at an even more fundamental level. If Peter thinks of possession not merely as a physical fact but also as a juridical fact, he thinks of both his own and Paul's possessions as severally *owned*, and not merely *possessed*. If, on the other hand, Paul has no concept of a juridical fact, and no concept of ownership, he cannot but think of what Peter possesses as merely physically possessed.

Hobbes thus argued that the establishment of civil society depends on the mutual surrender of original 'rights', the function of the second law. He held that such mutual surrender depends on mutual agreement or contract, and would be unreasonable in the absence of any guarantee that such contracts would be honoured.[58] This is the function of the third law:

That men performe their covenants made: without which covenants are in vain and but Empty words; and the Right of all men to all things remaining, wee are still in the condition of Warre.[59]

For Hobbes, the principles of law and the more particular or less fundamental laws of civil society – the detailed principles and provisions of the criminal law, for example, or of the law of contract – must be in keeping with the fundamental

---

[57] *Leviathan*, 190 [65]. The equivalent in *De Cive* is 'that the right of all men to all things ought not to be retained; but that some certain rights ought to be transferred or relinquished', which, were it not done, 'war would follow. He therefore acts against the reason of peace, that is against the law of nature, whosoever he be, that doth not part with his right to all things', *De Cive*, 123–4, where it is derived from the first and fundamental law but is not numbered.

[58] Within Hobbes's model the natural condition is given and to establish civil society is in some sense chosen. On one, as we think superficial, reading of Hobbes, civil society is chosen once and for all. Hobbes at times seems to suggest a foundational contract; but it may be more fruitful to emphasize – as we have done – his insistence on the centrality of agreement for the ongoing survival of civil society; for society is constantly open to collapse and so must be constantly chosen. This reading is nearer to St Thomas, for whom the achievement of the peaceful order is a constant choice.   [59] *Leviathan*, 201–2 [71].

laws of nature that he sets out in *De Cive* and *Leviathan*. This concordance must exist because the fundamental laws share the same basic function of sustaining civil society; any deviation from them would undermine that function. We shall observe this further as we proceed with our argument and refer to other of Hobbes's fundamental laws.[60] (In *De Cive* Hobbes lists 20 fundamental laws; in *Leviathan* 19 are listed. The laws are substantially the same in both works but are numbered differently.)

In sum, then, we suggest that communal living is natural to humans and that within the community the living law and the positive or state law share the function of sustaining a peaceful order. Any jural order requires a common core of some fundamental human customs and practices. That is the *ius gentium* of Roman law. Generally speaking, other more detailed customs and laws select and enjoin one way of acting rather than another when there are several, often disputed, possibilities. These conventions include detailed rules of law – the rules of the *ius civile* – and differ from jurisdiction to jurisdiction. But the detailed rules cannot coherently undermine or conflict with the fundamental customs and practices, which express an understanding of common and necessary social practices without which any society would disintegrate.

---

[60] See chs 6.3.2 (on impartiality) and 11.3 (on authoritative adjudication).

3

Justice, Ownership, and Law

3.1 Introduction

The opening sentence of the first book of Justinian's *Institutes* offers a definition of 'justice' and 'the just' that has survived, through the centuries and through many vicissitudes, in Western jurisprudence.[1] Because of its significance for our account of law and justice in community, we have quoted this definition twice already in this book: as one of the epigraphs and in Chapter 1. The reader will recall that in Latin the sentence reads: *Iustitia est constans et perpetua voluntas ius suum cuique tribuens.*[2] And in English: The virtue of justice is the constant and enduring will to render to each what is due.

The virtue or practice of justice is the practice of being just when the occasion arises, and 'being just' is 'rendering to each what is due'. The English phrase 'what is due' translates *ius suum*. A person's *ius* – which may also be rendered as *jus* – is what that person is entitled to.[3]

---

[1] In AD 528, the Roman Emperor Justinian (AD 482–565) instructed the jurist Tribonian to make a new code of laws which was to be a compilation or digest of earlier writings including the opinions of the great Roman jurists, Gaius (fl AD 130–180), and Papinianus, Paul, and Ulpian (all three fl about AD 200–220). Tribonian and 16 colleagues selected what they considered most valuable in the writings of their predecessors, and in AD 533 the *Digest* was approved. As well as the immense *Digest*, a shorter and more elementary work, the *Institutes*, based upon the *Digest* and compiled by Tribonian, Theophilus, and Berythus, was likewise approved. So too were the *Codex* and the *Novellae*. Collectively the four books make up what is known as the *Corpus Iuris Civilis*.

[2] Justinian, *Institutes*, I.I.1. The definition is attributed in the *Digest* (1.1.10 Prologue) to Ulpian (d 228 AD) but the idea appears at least as early as Cicero's *On Duties*, I.15, where it is said to be the second of the four parts of the honourable: '[The honourable] is involved either with the perception of truth and with ingenuity; or with preserving fellowship among men, with assigning to each his own, and with faithfulness to agreements one has made; or with the greatness and strength of a lofty and unconquered spirit; or with order and limit in everything that is said and done (modesty and restraint are included here)' (M Griffin and M Atkins eds; M Atkins trans) (Cambridge: Cambridge University Press, 1991), 7.

[3] In this book we tend to use *ius* rather than *jus*. The Latin word *ius* in *ius suum* refers linguistically to *iustitia* more clearly than 'what is due' refers to 'justice'. Another translation, then, is: *The virtue of justice is the constant and enduring will to render to each that to which he is entitled.* Yet another:... *to render to each what belongs to him.* As many translators despairingly remark, there is no easy translation of *ius* into English. 'Right' will sometimes serve reasonably well ('Justice is a steady and enduring will to render unto everyone his right'); but the couple 'Right–Law' does not sit easily as do the couples *Diritto–Lei, Derecho–Ley, Droit–Loi, Recht–Gesetz, Rettur–Lög*, etc. A right is nowadays usually thought to refer to a freedom to do or forbear. In Roman law, however,

The virtue of justice is the settled determination to render to each what is due. The practice of the virtue of justice demands that one knows what is due, and so the question of justice is always of this form: What belongs to whom?[4] This question is not yet a moral question. Only when one has discovered what is just, does the personal, practical, or properly moral question arise, namely, will I on this occasion, in these circumstances, be just? By a 'moral question' is meant a question as to what one will do. Moral questions, as we reiterate throughout this book, arise within the domain of deliberation and choice; morality is *not* a subcategory of choice. But the question as to what is just, in and of itself, is not yet a moral question. 'Who owns this house?', 'What is due to those involved when someone

and in our account of law and justice, a right (*ius* or *jus*) is an entitlement. One may, for example, have a *ius* to allow one's neighbour's drain to pass through one's yard. A right, in other words, may be a benefit *or* a burden, in which latter case it is traditionally called a 'servitude'. See Gaius, *Institutes*, ii.14. For our treatment of rights, see ch 9 below. In very many places in English translations of the *Institutes*, the term 'law' – the common English translation – is a translation of *ius* not *lex*. What in English is almost always referred to as 'the law of nations' is in Latin not *lex gentium* but *ius gentium*; and in Justinian what has come into English as 'natural *law*' is almost invariably '*ius* naturale'. A rare exception in the *Institutes* is in the definition of theft at IV.I.1 where it is said that theft is recognized as forbidden by the natural law (*lege naturali prohibitum est*).

[4] It is sometimes said that it is in the nature of arbitration, for example, to try and obtain peace rather than secure justice. '[In Far Eastern legal systems, at any rate until recently,] law is a secondary and subordinate means of achieving social order, and it is used only as a last resort. The harmony of society is seen as reflecting the general harmony of the world as evidenced in nature and the cosmos. The arid logic and external compulsion inherent in law make it a very rudimentary means of achieving order, though no doubt it is suitable for uncivilized peoples. Among civilized peoples, principles of behaviour should be obeyed voluntarily, and then they will prove effective in the community life of family, clan, and village; they come not from the law, but from the mass of unwritten rules of behaviour harmoniously integrated by tradition. These rules are not directed to procuring that everyone obtains his due, but to preserving social harmony. In consequence it is no solution to a dispute to have a winner and a loser; instead the claimant must take great care to let his opponent "save face". Thus in the Far East law does not lead to a judicial decision in favour of one party, but to a peaceable settlement or amicable composition. There is much of the wisdom of the Orient here, and there are some echoes of it in the West. Thus a bad settlement, we say, is better than a good lawsuit, and a legal adviser may pride himself on never having had to go to court. Despite this, there is still this critical difference in style, that in the West man naturally fights for his rights and seeks a clear decision, treating a compromise as a thing perhaps to be settled for, and in the East the face-saving compromise is the ideal and a firm decision only a necessary evil', K Zweigert and H Kötz, *An Introduction to Comparative Law* (Oxford: Clarendon Press, 3rd edn, 1998), 70–1. While we acknowledge that the living law of different communities may place differing degrees of emphases on the value of social harmony, we suggest that there is a danger in exaggerating this point. If two parties are at odds they might agree to abide by a judgment but hardly if they considered that the adjudicator had no interest at all in what is just. It may sometimes be better to accept a solution that one finds unjust for the sake of peace but one would find it hard to accept that one ought to do that all the time and on every issue. Not only is imposed peace without justice likely to bring about a sense of instability, in general; it also seems unlikely that peace could be reached unless the solution seemed to both disputants to be sufficiently just. It is also important to reiterate in this context Michel Villey's suggestion, noted in ch 1 above, that the traditional understanding of the judicial 'discussion' or 'controversy' that sought the just outcome 'had no other ambition than to arrive at the broadest possible agreement among the opinions: it aimed to convince, if not the losing litigant, at least the greatest possible number of the trial participants, of the wise men present in the audience and of the third parties who would agree the following day to help carry out the sentence', M Villey, 'Questions of Legal Logic', 115.

buys land in good faith from someone that he believes to be the owner but who in fact is not?' are not yet moral questions.[5] 'Now that I have discovered who owns this house, what am I going to do about it?', 'Now that I have determined what is due in case of the mistakenly bought land, what am I going to do about it?' – these are moral questions. Essential aspects of the virtue of justice are within the moral domain precisely because the question – 'Will I on this occasion do what is just?' – is a question about what one will do. The two questions – 'who owns this house?' and 'what is due to those involved when someone buys land in good faith from someone that he believes to be the owner but who in fact is not?' – may seem at first sight to be structurally different; in fact, they are not. 'Who owns this house?' translates into 'Who is entitled to possess this house?', and 'What is due…' translates into 'To what are those involved entitled when someone who buys land in good faith…?' 'Entitlement' is the key term. Ownership is a bundle of entitlements, and our claim that there is no human society without ownership translates into the claim that there is no human society in which entitlement is absent.

Ownership, entitlement, and justice are, therefore, inextricably linked. 'Who owns this thing?' and 'Who is entitled to possess this thing?' are two versions of the same question, namely, the question of justice. To own something is to be entitled to possess it under certain conditions. What one is entitled to possess may be a material or non-jural thing – a house, a horse, etc – or a jural thing – a debt, recognition as being the author of a work, punishment for a crime of which one has been found guilty, recompense for work done, etc. But, as Gaius makes clear, whether or not the thing owned is material, the crucial issue is that 'the actual right of inheritance is incorporeal, as is the actual right to the use and fruits of a thing, and the right inherent in an obligation'.[6] Land is material or corporeal; the ownership of land is jural or incorporeal. The *conditions* under which a thing – whether material or jural – can be possessed may vary considerably. For example, owning a house in entailment differs from owning it outright; an owner is entitled to alienate what is owned outright; an owner whose property is entailed is not so entitled. Again, where a state is entitled to compulsorily purchase what is privately owned, ownership is different from ownership in a state where no such entitlement exists. Similarly, the ownership of a debt may or may not be subject to

<hr />

[5] The second of these two questions is a familiar legal issue that is addressed in Justinian's *Institutes* at II.I.35. We refer to the issue here in order to clarify the structure of justice; we shall refer to it again in the discussion of rectificatory justice in ch 4.5 below. The answer to 'who owns this house?' and like questions does not always evoke the further question as to what one is to do, since the questioner may seek no more than an understanding of what the situation is. The court of law, on the other hand, is concerned to discover and establish entitlements within a disputatious or interpretive context in which the entitlement that the court does establish will be enforced.

[6] Gaius, *Institutes*, ii.14. As we noted in the Preface, the distinction between corporeal, in themselves non-jural, things, and incorporeal or jural things is made by Gaius (in his *Institutes*, ii.12, 13, and 14). In the sentence we quote here, what Gordon and Robinson translate by 'right' is '*ius*'. *The Institutes of Gaius* (trans and ed W M Gordon and OF Robinson) (London: Duckworth, 1988).

a statute of limitations, or the ownership of entitlement to recompense for work done may depend on the quality of the work.

In this chapter we examine various aspects of justice in some detail and begin with the general question of the context in which the question of what is just arises. We suggest that it can arise only in the context of ownership and entitlement. Where there is literally no ownership and no entitlement, then the question as to what is just simply does not and cannot arise. Different kinds of society have existed and continue to exist but within each there is some concept of ownership, certainly to the extent that 'ownership' is understood as entitlement of some kind. We only then address the issue of how one can discover what is just. If one is to be just and render to another that which is due, one must know what is due and to attempt to discover this involves various questions ranging from the very straightforward to the extremely difficult. Finally, we discuss the relationship between the living law and justice, and in particular how the living law tends to cultivate a moral context in which to consider others' interests and entitlements and not merely one's own is approved and valued.

3.2 Ownership and Entitlement

We may begin with a brief consideration of John Rawls's leading question in his *A Theory of Justice* (1971). Using the image of a social contract, but not to explain or explore the actual historical emergence of civil society, he presents an imaginary original condition as a model context in which to ask: 'What is the fair distribution of wealth among the members of a society?' In that imaginary initial state, the task is to discover a distribution scheme the outcome of which would be just. One is asked to choose a distribution scheme without knowing what one's own place will be in the resultant situation. The rational person, it is supposed, will choose what he thinks best for himself but, since he is choosing blind, he will include in his calculation the chance of his being very badly off were he to choose a very unequal distribution scheme. Rawls's suggestion is that the distribution and criterion of distribution that will be chosen by the rational person when faced with this choice will be what most would accept as just. *A Theory of Justice* argues in favour of the following two principles of justice:

First: each person is to have an equal right to the most extensive scheme of equal basic liberties compatible with a similar scheme of liberties for others. Second: social and economic inequalities are to be arranged so that they are both (a) reasonably expected to be to everyone's advantage, and (b) attached to positions and offices open to all.[7]

Rawls's principles of justice constitute an important contribution to the ongoing dialectical debate about what, in substantive or concrete terms, should be

---

[7] J Rawls, *A Theory of Justice* (Cambridge, Mass: Belknap Press, revised edn, 1999), 53.

considered as just.[8] Our account of law and justice, by contrast, does not include or sanction any substantive account of what constitutes 'justice' in society as a whole. This is one sense in which our theory differs not only from Rawls but also from many of the major schools of late twentieth-century jurisprudence. These schools of thought – for example, critical legal studies, law and economics, feminist jurisprudence, and critical race theory – are forms of normative, political jurisprudence to the extent that they all include strands that, like Rawls, ultimately propose visions of substantive justice to which they argue society and law should conform.[9] In contrast, the Roman idea that justice is the rendering to each what is due is an understanding of justice as involving a method of enquiry, which does not by itself indicate *what* is due to whom. Instead, what is due to whom must be discovered by *investigating* the particular case or dispute and more generally by considering types of cases.

Our primary concern here is with Rawls's approach rather than with his theory of justice. His approach is significant since it is an outstanding example of a very common way of conceptualizing the issue of justice. The wealth, including incomes, of an entire society is imagined as commonly owned until justly distributed, and the political question is how to distribute it. Rawls is not the only modern example of this approach to society either in theory or practice. It remains a very influential feature in the approach taken in modern liberal democracies, where it is generally agreed, or acquiesced in, that the state is both entitled and expected to redistribute wealth from tax revenue. It is also, in great measure, the approach taken in communist societies, where it is agreed, or acquiesced in, that the state, representing the people, owns everything and so becomes a vast organization that arranges for the creation and distribution of the wealth that is common to all.[10]

---

[8] David Hollenbach has described *A Theory of Justice* as 'the magna carta of that form of late twentieth-century liberal democracy that includes a commitment to the principles of the modern welfare state'. 'A Communitarian Reconstruction of Human Rights: Contributions from Catholic Tradition' in R Bruce Douglass and D Hollenbach (eds), *Catholicism and Liberalism* (Cambridge: Cambridge University Press, 1994), 127, 133.

[9] Marxist-influenced jurisprudence, for example, tends to endorse to some degree – either explicitly or implicitly – Marx's vision of justice under communism: 'from each according to his ability, to each according to his needs' (K Marx, 'Critique of the Gotha Programme' in D McLellan (ed), *Karl Marx: Selected Writings* (Oxford: Oxford University Press, 1977), 564, 569); while Posnerian 'law and economics' theories utilize measurements of justice such as Pareto and Kaldor-Hicks paradigms (see R Posner, *Economic Analysis of Law* (Boston: Little Brown, 4th edn, 1992), 13–14. See also, for another example, of this manner of conceptualizing justice as possessing substantive content, P Hillyard, 'Invoking Indignation: Reflections on Future Directions in Socio-legal Studies' (2002) 29 *Journal of Law and Society* 645, 655: '[W]e need the absolute value, a utopian concept of justice, in order to challenge [inequalities].'

[10] It is worth remembering that communist economies are, for that precise reason, deliberately not market orders but ideally and as far as practicable, centrally controlled organizations. Modern liberal democracies are not pure market orders either – state intervention in the form of taxation-redistribution and various forms of economic regulation constitute organizational elements imposed on the trading order – but such economies, in so far as the market is 'free', do resemble

In fact, the general question as to what is just arises, and can arise, only in the *context* of ownership and entitlement. Where there is literally no ownership and no entitlement, then the question as to what is just simply does not arise. If no one owns anything, then a question of the form, 'Whose is this?' is irrelevant and, if even the notion of ownership is absent, meaningless. In a society where, quite literally, no one in any way owns anything, including, for example, clothes or books or pens or bicycles or anything whatsoever, the question as to what is just simply cannot arise.[11] So we may ask: Is ownership just? Is it just that humans own things? The question seems at first sight clear but on reflection turns out to be very strange. If a just situation is one in which each quietly possesses what he owns, a situation in which no one owns anything cannot be just. The question of justice is irrelevant. Neither is such a situation unjust, for an unjust situation is one in which at least one person does not quietly possess what he owns, and where no one owns anything, no one lacks the possession of what he owns. If literally no one is entitled to anything, no one can be deprived of their entitlement and there is neither justice nor injustice; again, the issue of justice is an irrelevance.

We consider, however, that ownership of some kind is *necessary* for, and unavoidable in, communal human living. We take it that ownership has been and is present in all societies, that is, that humans have always owned – that is, have always been entitled to – things, although what they own and how they own them changes over time. There is no human community in which ownership does not exist, and no evidence that there ever has been. It is sometimes claimed that among such and such a people there is no 'private property' but this claim usually means that property is not owned in the way that it is owned in the writer's community. Land, for example, in a hunting and gathering community is not owned as it is in a community of nomadic pastoralists or in a settled agricultural community or in a community in which people make their living dominantly through exchanging one thing for another. But in each of these types of community, land or property *is* owned in the sense that there exist various types of entitlement to it. Even when a group tries to own literally everything communally, time and use are generally, perhaps necessarily, overlooked. Is the cup of coffee that a person has just poured for himself, in no sense whatsoever, his? Are the clothes that he is now wearing, in no sense whatsoever, his for the time being?[12]

We do not assume that, at any one moment, what is generally accepted as owned by whomsoever was originally justly acquired either by themselves or

market orders to a much greater extent. The justice proper to the market order is discussed in ch 5 below.

[11] For a discussion of an attempt to create such a society, see O Figes, *Natasha's Dance: A Cultural History of Russia* (London: Penguin, Allen Lane, 2002), 446.

[12] In the great communist upheaval of ownership in the twentieth century, the ownership of land and other sources of wealth shifted from private individuals or the *mir* to the state; nonetheless, questions of distributive justice arose under communism in the first instance because state or publicly owned positions had to be distributed to particular individuals who thus became entitled to hold them.

in cases of inheritance, by their ancestors from whom they have inherited it.[13] The assumption is simply that humans have always owned, or been entitled to, things.[14] Nomadic herders think of their regular routes as theirs. Street buskers in many modern societies often agree among themselves as to which of them owns a particular pitch at a particular time, but they know very well that they do not own their particular pitch as they own their musical instruments. Similarly, holiday-makers at a beach resort develop customs to book their patch for the day. Effectively, for a person to own something requires that both that person and others accept both the practice of ownership that prevails in the society, and the fact that the person owns this particular thing.

Ownership is a bundle of entitlements and what constitutes the bundle differs from society to society. Different kinds of society exist. Within each there is ownership but the precise character of ownership differs greatly from society to society. Where discrete plots of land are not individually owned, even the idea of this type of ownership is absent; for *ideas* of ownership arise as different *practices* emerge. In a hunting and gathering society, therefore, questions of justice arise that do not arise in an agricultural society and vice versa, and a hunting and gathering or nomadic pastoral society does not become a purely or dominantly agricultural society overnight. The development is slow, and as different practices of ownership emerge, ownership is understood differently and different questions as to what is just arise; for questions as to what is just arise in response to real situations that are seen as problems and have given rise to disputes. For example, in a society within which parcels of land are not individually owned, bought and sold, obviously no question would arise as to what is to be done if someone 'in good faith purchased land from another, whom he believed to the true owner, when in fact he was not'.[15] Equally obviously, this question is very likely to arise when land is individually owned, bought and sold.

Similarly, a land-locked community will not have to address questions or formulate rules concerning sea fishing, whereas the Icelandic law text, *Grágás*, 'contains more extensive regulation on whaling than on fishing or any other type

---

[13] For much of the medieval and modern history of Europe, it was generally accepted or acquiesced in that the ruler, when powerful enough to do so, was entitled to dispossess his opponents and grant the land to his supporters.

[14] How to account for the settling of ownership of what was formerly not owned is a disputed question. The Justinian solution is given in the *Institutes*, II.I.11 et seq: [12] 'Wild beasts, birds, fish, that is, all animals born on land, in the sea or sky, as soon as they are captured by anyone, by the law of nations, begin to be his; for what formerly belonged to none, natural reason gives to the first occupant.' It will seem reasonable to many that the first occupant of what belongs to none should become its owner but that he actually becomes the owner requires both an understanding of ownership and agreement, and so Grotius, in *De jure belli et pacis* (*On the Law of War and Peace*), I.2.II, stresses the social and conventional character of ownership when he writes that ownership is given 'by a kind of agreement, either express, as in division, or tacit, as in occupation'. That the very idea of ownership arose among people who formerly owned nothing is, to put it mildly, unlikely.   [15] Justinian, *Institutes*, II.I.35.

of hunting'.[16] The idea that the sea or rivers can be owned, or the way in which they can be owned, is explicitly excluded in Justinian's *Institutes*: 'By the law of nature these things are common to all: the air, running water, the sea and consequently the shores of the sea.'[17] In a fishing community whose livelihood is made upon the sea, it is likely to be equally obvious that the fishing grounds can be and often are owned and that the way in which they are owned must be settled. In many modern European states the fishing rights on some stretches of rivers, if not the rivers themselves, are privately owned. Most obviously, and historically disputatiously, sea areas are owned by states and, for example, in the European Union they are distributed between member states for fishing purposes.

Just as there are different types of ownership in different types of societies it is plain that ownership itself can take many different forms *within* a given society. Private ownership, like any other kind of ownership, is jural or institutional. Ownership is a jural relationship between people, not a physical description of an action or situation. In societies where land is individually owned, bought and sold, 'ownership-in-entail' is very different from 'outright ownership that allows alienation' – and these differ from ownership of a right of way through a property. If the property is a share, one may be entitled to dispose of it or not, however one sees fit, but alternatively one may be permitted to sell it only under particular conditions. The important point is that for ownership, and indeed any entitlement or right, actually to exist it must be communally accepted. What is in practice meant by ownership must be known, and from the acceptance of the practice there follows a rule, however expressed, that what one person owns, another is not entitled to take without permission. Who owns what must normally be known or discoverable, and their ownership of it generally respected. Children learn in practice what ownership means not usually by being first given a rule, but by discovering in their dealings with other children that they are not allowed to take home toys or clothes or other things that they would like to have, *because* they belong to another child, because 'That toy is John's'. Children thus gradually learn what ownership involves; they learn the practice and learn that it is approved and, on them, at least to some extent at first simply imposed.

As we remarked in Chapter 2, children learn these things in somewhat the same way as they learn their language; if their language is English they learn

---

[16] Gunnar Karlsson, *Iceland's 1100 Years: The History of a Marginal Society* (London: Hurst & Co, 2001), 48. Karlsson continues: 'In sagas, however, whales most often drift to the coast, where they are divided among the inhabitants of the neighbourhood. This may be due to the different nature of these sources. Whaling demanded extensive regulation because the hunter, or so it seems, killed the whale with some kind of harpoon, but did not catch it. While the whale drifted ashore, he could demand a part of its value if his harpoon was recognized in it. In sagas, on the other hand, the dividing of stranded whales is often the origin of disputes and killings'.

[17] Justinian, *Institutes*, II.I.1. The use of the common phrase 'By the law of nature' (*naturali jure*) here is interesting in that it seems to mean little more than 'it is obvious' as, indeed, it was to the jurists of Justinian's time. (We discuss various meanings of the word 'natural' in ch 4.2 below.) Because the shores are mentioned here, the sea shore is defined in II.I.3: 'The sea shore extends to the limit reached by the greatest winter flood.'

that statements are commonly transformed into questions by using the verb 'to do' as an auxiliary, eg 'I played with Peter yesterday' becomes 'Did I play with Peter yesterday?'; 'I went to Cork last week' becomes 'Did I go to Cork last week?' They learn this without formally studying English grammar. What they learn is how to make statements and how to ask questions, not the rules governing the relationship between statements and questions. Similarly, without any formal study or attempted justification of ownership, they learn that people own things and that stealing is disapproved of; which is why people are commonly nonplussed when asked why they should not steal. They learn to distinguish between owning something, and physically possessing it. They learn what ownership means by learning that it is not acceptable to take what another owns without the owner's consent. They learn in practice that not to steal is intrinsic to the practice of ownership; but the young child does not learn what ownership is by being told that 'not to steal is intrinsic to ownership and the survival of the community depends on most people most of the time respecting others' ownership of things'. So there emerges in the communal moral law – in the living law – an explicit rule against theft.[18] The rule states or implies that it is not good to take what belongs to another. Very obviously, it is a rule that can emerge only where there is ownership; if nothing belongs to anyone, nothing can be stolen. Only slightly less obvious is the fact that if anyone may take whatever he wants whenever he wants it, ownership would cease to exist – as happens during the widespread looting that often follows great natural disasters or political upheavals – and a society based upon it would collapse, that is, it would disintegrate to the extent that it would cease to be a civil society in which peaceful communal living is possible.

The idea that if theft were to become completely normal a society would collapse is not, of course, usually in the minds of those who accept that to steal is wrong. They accept that to steal is wrong because they have learnt that this is what is established and perhaps too – indeed usually too – because they accept this as right and proper: that what another owns he is entitled to keep and what they themselves own they are entitled to keep. Perhaps inchoately and as an unclarified presupposition they recognize that there is no reason why they alone should be entitled to keep what is theirs and no reason why others should respect their entitlement, while at the same time they themselves may simply ignore the entitlements of others. Such recognition highlights what we introduced in Chapter 2 as a key aspect of the living law or communal moral law, namely that

---

[18] A rule against theft ('Thou shalt not steal') is the eighth commandment of the *Decalogue* (*Exodus* 20:15; *Deuteronomy* 5:19) but more detailed rules concerning theft, with associated penalties or liabilities, are found in other places in the *Torah*, eg *Exodus* 22:1, 2, and 7. In the *Code of Hammurabi*, theft is not explicitly forbidden as it is in the *Decalogue* but punishments and liabilities associated with theft are given in, eg laws 20–24. Likewise, in the Roman *Twelve Tables* (c 450 BC), theft is not explicitly forbidden but punishments and liabilities for theft are found in Table VIII. Theft is treated by Gaius in his *Institutes* at iii.183–209; it is defined and explicitly forbidden in Justinian's *Institutes* at IV.I.1 and in the *Digest* at xlvii.2.1.3.

this law naturally tends to cultivate a moral context within which others' interests are to be considered and the related idea that this moral context is itself an expression of what is naturally just. As we said, the moral context within which others' interests are to be considered is to be found, more or less clearly and formally expressed, in every human society. We shall return to this issue in Chapter 3.4 but now we turn to the discovery of the just.

3.3 Discovering the Just

If one is to be just and render to another what is due, one must know what is due and to know this is not always easy. The effort to be just begins with a question that may be expressed in several ways, for example: 'Who is entitled to what?' 'Who owns what?' 'What belongs to whom?' 'What is due to whom?' If, say, a cat wanders into your house, seemingly with no intention of leaving, and you think that it belongs to someone, before you can give the cat to its owner you must discover who the owner is. Your question is: 'Who owns this cat?' If you ask the question, you are, in fact, making two very basic, banal, and everyday, presuppositions. You presuppose that the cat belongs to someone and that, in most cases, the owner is entitled to get the cat back.[19] If someone persuades you that the cat is feral and belongs to no one, then you accept that the question of ownership does not arise. The question, 'Who owns this cat?' turns out to be irrelevant if, in fact, the cat belongs to no one.

In the famous Scottish case of *Donoghue v Stevenson*,[20] Mrs Donoghue, whose friend had bought her ginger beer in a stone bottle and in which she found a decomposing snail, looked for redress from Mr Stevenson, the maker of the drink.[21] Mrs Donoghue had no contract with Mr Stevenson; she had not even bought the drink herself. The court ruled that Mrs Donoghue was entitled to redress and the case is authority within the common law tradition for the ousting of the privity of contract rule by the neighbour principle in cases of manufacturers' liability for defective products. The question before the court was: Who, in this instant case, is entitled to what? Another way of phrasing precisely the same question is this: What in this situation is just? In coming to its judgment that

---

[19] We say 'in most cases' because of the very old idea in Western thought of *epieikeia* or 'equity'. This arises when the proper, clear, and incontrovertible meaning of the text or rule as it applies to the envisaged situation gives rise to the conviction that it does not apply to the situation under consideration. We discuss *epieikeia* in the context of adjudication and interpretation in ch 6 below.

[20] *Donoghue v Stevenson* [1932] AC 562.

[21] During the case it was assumed that the bottle was opaque and so hid the presence of the snail (if it had been clear, it would not have been a latent defect but rather a patent defect as Mrs Donoghue could have seen through the glass). There is some speculation that it was not in fact stone but clear glass; that what Mrs Donoghue had was lemonade; and that the bottle was mistakenly taken to be stone because the Court was unaware that 'ginger' was a generic name in Scotland for lemonade, orangeade, ginger beer and so on, whereas in England this was not the case.

Mrs Donoghue was entitled to redress, the court did not follow an already set-tled rule or opinion. The court discerned a factual, non-jural association between the manufacturer of a drink and the end-user who drank it; on the basis of this association the court decided that the responsibility that already lay with the manufacturer to produce a safe product, and for which he was already liable to the person to whom he had sold the drink, should be extended to the end-user who, as in this case, had no contractual relation with the manufacturer. Mrs Donoghue's entitlement, which is jural, has its source in the prior factual and non-jural association but is distinct from it.

In the example of the cat, where the question as to who owns the cat does in fact arise – because the prior question as to whether or not the cat was owned has already been answered in the affirmative – it may well be that to discover the answer is not at all easy and may be in some cases in practice impossible. But although often difficult, or in practice impossible, to answer, it is in itself a sim-ple and straightforward question and it arises in particular circumstances about a particular cat; it cannot be asked or answered intelligently in the abstract. As we reiterate throughout this book, courts of law deal with particular questions; it is not normally their function to focus on abstractions except to the extent that they must consider the meaning of the laws that state what is just in *types* of circumstances. Courts, in the light of the contextual background to an extent established and clarified by constitutions and laws, are usually required to state what is just in *particular* circumstances.[22] So, for example, a traffic law may require drivers not to exceed 120 kilometres per hour on a motorway. Suppose that a driver, in this type of circumstance, and so not entitled to exceed 120 kilo-metres per hour, is brought before the court for having exceeded the limit. He pleads that he was driving a very sick person to hospital, that he was driving at two o'clock in the morning, and that the road was empty. The court is not asked to discover *exclusively* whether he acted in accord with the law; its ulti-mate question is 'to what, in the light of the law, is the driver on the one hand, and the state on the other hand, entitled in these particular circumstances?' Still, the court considers each particular case not only as particular but as to an extent typical and what is decided in a particular case can, and often will, act as a precedent for future like cases (as did *Donoghue v Stevenson*). The particular solution applies to similar cases on the spontaneous and unavoidable principle of intelligent enquiry that similar data are similarly understood. A different solution to an apparently similar case must appeal either to error in the previ-ous solution or to relevant differences between the two cases, ie the cases must be distinguished. The judge who discovers no relevant differences between the

---

[22] It is true that at the constitutional level courts and councils often appear to consider cases exclusively in the abstract, as when, for example, they judge the constitutionality of legislation dur-ing the ratification process, but in such cases courts are in fact ultimately assessing the entitlement of legislators to enact the law in question and are doing so in light of a particular constitutional order.

cases and who agrees with the previous solution *cannot* understand and honestly decide the cases differently.[23]

In discussing the meaning of 'justice', we are concerned not with particular questions but with the *form* or *structure* of such questions: 'Who owns what?' 'What belongs to whom?' 'What is due to whom and from whom?' This type of question, and this type of question only, addresses what is just in a particular case. The court of law is, in the end, trying to answer what may be called the 'justice question' in the context of a particular set of facts but, in order to reach the answer, prior questions of a different kind may have to be raised and answered. For example, in a criminal trial where Peter is accused of fraud, one of the prior questions is whether or not he is guilty of fraud but the final question is this: What is due to Peter if he has been found guilty of fraud? More generally, the final question in a criminal trial where an accused has been found guilty is always: What is due to this guilty person? This is the question to which the sentence passed is the answer. The first 'prior question' is always the question of jurisdiction and sometimes this is an extremely complex issue. In cases involving private international law, for example, that part of the private law of a particular country which deals with cases having a foreign element, there is always the preliminary question: has the national court that is seized of the case jurisdiction to hear and determine the case?[24] If jurisdiction is established the further question arises as to whether the

---

[23] For a discussion of this fundamental intelligent spontaneity, see B Lonergan, *Insight: a Study of Human Understanding* (London: Longmans, 1957), 37, 175, 288, 297. Different types of legal system have different formal perspectives on precedent but the rule that similars are to be similarly understood is the expression of an understanding of one of the spontaneities of intelligence. Not only do we not, but we *cannot*, understand differently data that seem to us relevantly similar. Thus, if having measured the movement of particle A down an inclined plane, one works out that the movement is a constant acceleration of the particle related to time and distance, then one *must* understand the relevantly similar movement of particle B down the same inclined plane in the same way if the measurements are similar. In the jurisprudence of adjudication the practical issue is not whether or not to understand similar situations similarly but to determine whether or not two situations are *relevantly* similar. Whether or not a difference is relevant is not always obvious and, indeed, may be the crux of an argument in litigation as it was when the question arose as to whether or not the judgment in *Donoghue v Stevenson* should apply in *Grant v Australian Knitting Mills Ltd* [1936] AC 36. (*Grant* concerned the purchaser of a pair of woollen long-johns which contained an excess of sulphite chemicals which should have been removed during the manufacturing process but which instead caused the purchaser to contract dermatitis. He sued the manufacturer successfully in negligence.) That the very obvious difference between a poor and a rich person should be considered to be irrelevant in litigation appeared very early in the Hebrew tradition in *Exodus* 23.3 and 6: '3.... you shall not be partial to the poor in a lawsuit. 6. You shall not pervert the justice due to your poor in a lawsuit.' And similarly in *Deuteronomy* 1:17: 'You must not be partial in judging: hear out the small and the great alike; you shall not be intimidated by anyone...'. Once the poor and the rich are considered to be similar within the context of litigation why one should not discriminate either in favour of or against the poor is spontaneously obvious, but it may take some time to recognize that rich and poor are relevantly similar; bias is not automatically always overcome, as at once appears if 'rich and poor' are replaced in this type of analysis by 'men and women' or 'white and black'.

[24] JHC Morris, *The Conflict of Laws* (ed D McClean and K Beevers, London: Sweet & Maxwell, 6th edn, 2005), ch 1, esp 5–6. The court approaches this question using legal categories such as are found in all fields of law (performance or breach of contract, succession to immovables, formal

court will apply its national law or the law of another country. Typically, only when these questions have been decided in this order may the court begin to address the justice question, that is, the question of what is due to whom. Thus, answering prior questions is essential to the methodology of deciding what is due to whom – but it is the justice question that aims to establish the entitlements arising from the jural relationship under examination.

3.4 Justice and the Living Law

In Chapter 2 we discussed the idea of civil society as a spontaneous order that gives rise to a living law, of which state law is but a later and partial expression. Human communities are in part jural orders defined by well-known and accepted customs and laws that indicate how it is acceptable to act in types of situation. These well-known and accepted customs and laws are the living law of that community. The living law, following Gaius's division, is in part the *ius gentium* and in part its *ius civile*: each society has, and must have if it is to survive, a core of customs and laws that are common to all societies, as well as a set of customs and laws that are peculiar to itself. The *ius gentium* is another way of conceptualizing that *part* of the living law that is common to all human communities. The living law of a community is in part the *ius gentium* common to all humans and in part the customs, practices, well-known and accepted procedures, and mutual expectations that establish the jural relationships particular to that community. If a living law rule is written or posited it is then a part of both the living law and the state law or *ius civile* of the community. That Gaius's analysis fits, so to speak, with the idea of the living law does not mean that the analysis itself is known to those living under it, any more than it would have been known or surmised by most of his non-jurist contemporaries.

What Justinian says of the *ius gentium* or the law of nations, that 'nations have established certain laws, as occasion and the necessities of human life required',[25] may be said of the living law in general. The living law is the set of customs and explicit rules that usage has approved and confirmed. How precisely they arose is obscure but it is commonly found that the provisions considered to be most significant are enshrined in a story that tells of their unquestionable and often divine source, as in the *Code of Hammurabi*, in the *Torah*, and as referred to in Sophocles' *Antigone*, where Antigone opposes the divine ordinances to Creon's command.[26]

---

validity of marriage, and capacity to marry, etc) but the distinctiveness of the private international law approach is its necessary use of 'localizing' elements or 'connecting factors'. These elements connect the facts of the case to jurisdictions. They include factors such as place of performance of contract, situation of property, place of celebration of marriage, nationality and domicile, JHC Morris, *The Conflict of Laws*, 8–9.

[25] Justinian, *Institutes*, I.II.2.

[26] 'I did not believe/Your proclamation had such power to enable/One who will someday die to override/God's ordinances, unwritten and secure./They are not of today and yesterday;/They live

There tends to be in any living law a division between those laws and customs that are changeable and those that are not. Still, whatever its source and whatever of any account of its authority, the living law is and remains the living law of a people because it is known, accepted, and in sufficiently large measure, followed. The living law is law 'sanctioned by the consent of those who adopt it'.[27]

As human societies changed and as reflection on law developed there came about a shift from law and custom to legislation, and in much jurisprudential discussion the implicit, and often the explicit, image of law became legislation, enactment, code, or statute.[28] The law becomes what the legislator enacts. Custom is thought to be 'like law', that is, it is treated as if it were legislation. Positive law is 'posited' by the legislator. Henceforth, it is so often taken for granted that it is hardly noticed that the analysis of law is dominantly an analysis of legislation. Perhaps almost inevitably, certainly understandably, later thinking on natural law, which was not thought of as posited by a human legislator, looked for a legislator, and stories of the mysterious and divine origin of fundamental laws – in Christian Europe the Hebrew story of Moses on Sinai – provided the answer. In Justinian's *Institutes* it is said that: 'The laws of nature, which all peoples observe, being established by a divine providence, remain fixed and immutable.'[29] When legislation begins to dominate, law is increasingly thought of as the commands of sovereign to subject; nonetheless, more or less strongly felt in the community, two things remain. First, the idea that there are basic or fundamental laws that legislation ought not override, and, secondly, even if much less clearly than the first, the idea that legislation does and often must add to the underlying living law. Legislation may only with great care override the living law because the latter, by definition, embodies communal jural attitudes. Yet the living law is not necessarily right and not necessarily universally shared. No human institution is

---

forever; none knows when they first were', Sophocles, *Antigone*, 496–501. This translation is from *Antigone* in *The Theban Plays* (EF Watling trans, Harmondsworth: Penguin, 1947).

[27] Justinian, *Institutes* I.II.9 and *Digest* I.3.35.

[28] As early as Plato's *Politicus* (*The Statesman*), law is thought of as discovered and handed down by a lawgiver. But the idea that the written rule expresses what is already accepted to be right remains in Justinian's *Digest* at, for example, 50.17.1, where the third century AD jurist, Paul, is quoted: 'A rule is something which briefly describes how a thing is. The right is not derived from a rule, but a rule from the right.' Peter Stein has observed that 'in origin *lex* was declaratory of *ius*' (P Stein, *Regulae Iuris* (Edinburgh: Edinburgh University Press, 1966), 20) and this is quoted and discussed by Hayek in *Law, Legislation and Liberty – Vol I: Rules and Order* (Chicago: University of Chicago Press, 1973), ch 4.

[29] Justinian, *Institutes*, I.III.11. The 'laws of nature' are here equivalent to Gaius's 'laws of nations'. References to the providential origin of law (*ius*) are rare in the *Digest* and *Institutes*. At *Digest* I.3.2 Marcian is quoted: 'For Demosthenes the orator also defines it thus: "Law is that which all men ought to obey for many reasons, and chiefly because all law is a discovery and a gift of God…"'. Evidently, in Demosthenes 'a gift of God' is pre-Christian; 'divine providence' in the passage from Justinian's *Institutes*, where a pre-Christian or early source is not directly quoted, is less evidently so. The question of the divine source of law, prompted by reflection of the *Torah*, became increasingly and controversially prominent in both theological and philosophical enquiry in Christian Europe.

utterly without bias and the living law is not an exception. It is not an unbiased, unchangeable, infallible supervening law but it does express what is, or has been, generally accepted to be good.

It is one of our constant themes that the proper function of law – both the living law and legislation – is to sustain a peaceful order. We acknowledge, of course, that it never perfectly fulfils that function. The law states what in different situations is just, and set out in this chapter is a theory of justice based on the idea that ownership is a bundle of entitlements, and that justice has to do with clearly expressing for the normal case – in unforeseen circumstances developing, and in disputes determining – the set of entitlements. Hence, the fundamental and recurrent question: who in these circumstances is entitled to what? In Chapters 4 and 5 we examine the distinction between natural and conventional justice, and the classification of justice into three types: distributive, rectificatory, and reciprocal. In the present chapter we discuss the living law and its relation to justice, the communal moral order, and the way in which the living law tends to cultivate a moral context in which to consider others' interests and not merely one's own is approved. This 'cultivation', however, is subject to the ordinary range of corrupting human influences.

A society is a set of relations between people. It is a solution to the problem of living together in a particular environment and is known and handed on in customs and laws. Known and approved laws and customs, the living communal law, express the character of the extant solution.[30] One who fails to act in accord with the solution is subject to some kind of sanction such as disapproval, ostracism, or other punishment. When disputes arise there is commonly an arbiter to whose judgment the disputants are required, under pain of sanction, to submit.[31]

---

[30] On the idea that species are solutions to a problem of living in a given environment, see B Lonergan, *Insight: a Study of Human Understanding* (London: Longmans, 1957), 265. The human environment includes the natural environment and human institutions. Different ways of living, that is, different social orders, resemble animal species and are more or less adequate solutions to the problem of living in a given environment. New problems call for new solutions and so, for example, the present great climatic shift in the natural environment, related to a greater or lesser extent to human action, is a new problem in living that demands a new solution.

[31] The methods may be very different and the limits set more or less great, but for a society to survive, a method of setting some limits to internal disputes is necessary. In his discussion of the political system among the Nuer, EE Evans-Pritchard wrote that 'In a strict sense Nuer have no law. There are conventional compensations for damage...but there is no authority with power to adjudicate on such matters or to enforce a verdict', *The Nuer* (Oxford: Oxford University Press, 1940), 162. But later in the same section he records that he had been told, but had not personally observed, that 'a way of settling disputes is to use a leopard-skin chief as mediator' (163). What is perfectly clear, however, is that the Nuer have well-known rules stating what behaviour is acceptable and what is not. Theft is wrong but only within one's own group: 'I have never heard of a Nuer stealing a cow from a fellow tribesman merely because he wanted one. He has, on the other hand, no hesitation in stealing cows from persons belonging to neighbouring tribes and will even go with friends to another tribe in order to steal from them. This theft (*kwal*) is in not considered in any way wrong' (165). The question is not whether or not theft is wrong but what is considered to be theft; in the same way, murder is universally forbidden but there are great differences between peoples as to what killing is considered to be murder. When Evans-Pritchard writes that the Nuer 'have no

The living law is, therefore, a communal *moral* law. As we said in Chapter 1, morality is about human choice, and choices are made in situations. An explicit moral tradition, the living or communal law, is the set of customs and rules that state the kind of choices that are in that tradition thought good, and indicate the generally approved ways of acting in recurrent types of situations. Because humans live, and cannot but live, in societies (however different those societies may be), moral traditions will emerge which members of a community will know both in practice and in the living or customary law in which they are expressed. Children learn it as they are taught how to behave properly and, in their turn, pass it on to their children. It becomes part of them in many, but not all, respects, as their language becomes part of them.

Moral traditions will *change* when sufficiently many of those living within them change their minds about how it is good to act. Since it is unlikely that minds will always change in unison, moral traditions at any one time will often be controversial. Changes are more or less great, more or less significant, and more or less controversial. When a community moves from being a pastoral nomadic society to being a settled agricultural society in which different families own different parcels of land, new questions arise and new solutions are established. When trade emerges and people live increasingly by trade, besides the rules intrinsic to that practice and without which it would not exist, more detailed solutions to more detailed problems are discovered;[32] so, for example, an acceptable solution must be found when the question arises as to who is liable if, through no fault or negligence on anyone's part, fruit dispatched in good condition rots before it is delivered to the buyer. People pass one another in streets, live and eat together, buy goods in the same shops and, that these things may be done in peace, rules of politeness emerge and evolve. Questions arise and solutions are discovered. If the solutions are generally found to be acceptable, they become common practice and part of the living communal law, much as new turns of phrase emerge, catch on, and, perhaps only for a time, become common currency in everyday speech. People could not live with one another in peace were it not generally known and generally accepted how in the recurrent circumstances of everyday life it was thought good to act. How it is thought

---

law' he means that there is nothing that he recognizes as legal procedure or legal institutions (168) as there were among the Azande. Cf EE Evans-Pritchard, *The Azande* (Oxford: Oxford University Press, 1971), 166–93. Among the Nuer, Evans-Pritchard found that 'if they [disputes] are not settled by the mediation of kinsmen, they are likely to lead to violence' (*The Neur*, 170). As Hobbes, in *Leviathan*, 215 [78], had predicted: '... unless the parties to the question, covenant mutually to stand to the sentence of another, they are as farre from Peace as ever.' Among the Azande, in contrast, 'Control of the poison oracle in all legal cases gave the princes enormous power. No death or adultery could be legally avenged without a verdict from their oracles, so that the court was the sole source of law. Although the procedure was a mystical one it was carried out in the king's name and he was vested with legal authority as completely as if a more commonsense system of justice had obtained', EE Evans-Pritchard, *Witchcraft, Oracles and Magic among the Azande* (Oxford: Oxford University Press, 1937), 293.

[32] See ch 5 below for a discussion of justice and the trading order.

good to act is expressed in a common, even if intrinsically controversial, moral tradition expressed in practices, customs, rules, and in the communal common sense.[33]

The living law may be either general or specific. It is general when it applies to all or most members of society. At least some of the rules of politeness that emerge in communal living and which, of course, are different in different communities, tend to apply generally and are not confined to any particular social group. For example, it is usually nowadays deemed unacceptable to push or shove other people out of one's way while walking down a street or browsing in a shop, no matter who you or the other people are. There may be exceptions, of course, such as when one is chasing a thief on the street or on the morning of a high-profile shop sale. Such exceptions, like the general communal rule itself, will be known to, and more or less accepted by, different members of different communities. Another general element of the living law – one that is found universally and not confined to a particular people – is the communal value, *pacta sunt servanda*. That promises are to be kept is an operative presupposition of the practice prior to any theoretical reflection on the practice and to any attempt to justify the presupposition.[34] One who 'promises' with no intention of keeping his promise has not promised but has only pretended to do so. One who – as might a young child – promises verbally, thinks that he has genuinely promised but does not know that he has thereby obligated himself to another, has simply failed to understand promising, and has failed to promise. The expectation and custom that promises be kept applies not to any one group of people but rather applies generally, and as in the case of politeness the rule regarding promises is subject to exceptions, as when fraud or misrepresentation or the like is present. The notable difference between the basic rule regarding politeness and that regarding promises is that the latter finds more direct and explicit expression than the former. The edifice of contract law is built on the premise that promises should be honoured whereas politeness exists primarily as a social expectation. There are of course criminal laws that protect individuals from assault and battery and the like, but while such laws facilitate ongoing polite and mannerly behaviour, their primary purpose is to prevent actions of this type.

The rules that make up the living law may be more specific in their application, confined to a particular group of people within the broader community. An example is found in the practice of seafarers' acceptance of a demand to help others in distress. A sailor competing in an Atlantic race hears that a rival some

---

[33] On common sense, see B Lonergan, *Insight: a Study of Human Understanding* (London: Longmans, 1957), chs VI and VII. See also N MacCormick, *Institutions of Law* (Oxford: Oxford University Press, 2007), 16, and recall Gagnepain's insight that we learn our morals as we learn our language: *Du vouloir dire* (Paris: Pergamon, 1982).

[34] An operative presupposition is a principle intrinsic to an act in the absence of which the act fails to be what it seems to be. Examples include: that we cannot knowingly affirm a contradiction (both P and not-P); that affirmations intend truth (either P or not-P); and that genuine questions arise upon ignorance and intend answers.

way behind him has capsized. The question as to what he should do in these new circumstances may throw up two contrasting possible courses of action: either to sacrifice his position in the race, and attempt to rescue the sailor who may otherwise be lost, or to carry on. These incompatible courses of action embody incompatible values. There are, obviously, other possible circumstances in which no question of sacrificing his position in the race would arise. In other words, considered only in the context of a race, the value of winning is an unquestioned good. But human action occurs in concrete circumstances and the new circumstances bring to bear another, and, in the circumstances, incompatible value, that evokes in the sailor hearing of his capsized rival the question as to which value he will choose. The circumstances are not only the fact that a boat has capsized, that another sailor is in grave danger, and that he is in a position to make a realistic attempt to save him. They include the fact that he knows of the situation, knows that he can make the attempt if he so chooses, and that the question arises, not in the abstract but in him, as to what in these circumstances he should do. So are introduced what may be called the moral, as distinct from the physical, facts; for the question as to what he should do is in the moral domain. It is possible to imagine someone to whom the question simply did not occur; to whom knowledge of the new circumstances is of no more moral consequence than is learning from the radio that an event in which he has no interest has been postponed owing to rain. In such an imaginary person no conflict of values occurs; he does not ask what he should do in these new circumstances, because they are to him utterly morally irrelevant. It is also possible to imagine one in whom the question arises, to whom the contrasting values occur, and who chooses to carry on. It is, finally, possible to imagine one in whom the question arises, and who chooses to abandon his chances in the race in favour of what seems to him the greater of the two incompatible values.

There is another hugely significant feature of the moral context. Sailors in contact with one another form a community within which certain values are accepted; anyone who takes up sailing learns – gradually and perhaps very slowly – that some ways of acting in certain circumstances are generally accepted and approved. These ways of acting have become accepted values within the community. The newcomer may or may not make these values his own; but he will learn what they are, and will learn how he is likely be treated if he ignores them. These accepted values are part of the communal law of the sailing community. Victor Mallet writes:

[I]t is completely routine for sailors to sacrifice their chances of winning a race, and even put themselves in danger, in order to save others... Probably the most extraordinary sea rescue of recent times is the saving of Ralph Dinelli by Pete Goss in the 1996–97 Vendée Globe round-the-world race. Goss turned back on Christmas Day 1996 to beat into a Southern Ocean Storm and saved Dinelli from certain death – a feat that earned him the Légion d'Honneur and a firm friendship with Dinelli...And yet Goss did not really have a choice. Most sailors assume that there is an unbreakable rule that obliges them to

go to the rescue of someone in trouble, and even if there is no law to that effect the tradition is deeply entrenched in sailing culture. Not every rescue attempt will succeed, but if
you hear a cry for help from those in peril on the sea there is no question but that you are
obliged to try.[35]

As we repeatedly insist throughout this book, within particular communities
there emerges a set of communally accepted ways of acting, that is, communally
accepted values, within recurrent and foreseeable circumstances. The living law
of a community is made up of such values. This does not ensure that everyone
within the community will act in these ways, and in the light of these values,
on each relevant occasion. But if fewer and fewer people within the community
were to take any account of the values, this would indicate that the communal
values were changing. Any reader of Mallet's article will understand perfectly
what he means when he writes 'Goss did not really have a choice'. But, to speak
more strictly, Goss did of course have a choice – as humans always do when
deliberating on the fundamental moral question, that is, what to do at a given
moment in given circumstances. He had to choose to act, or to fail to act, in
accord with the communal value. The choice that almost certainly he did not
have was to avoid the question as to what he should do when he learned of
Dinelli's situation. That the question was unavoidable is in part because the
value that in the circumstances gave rise to it was a communal value shared
by Goss and in part because, for the most part, humans, prior to accepting
the value at the level of deliberation and choice, find themselves spontaneously
related to one another in a manner that evokes the value. Spontaneously, and
prior to choice, another person is not present (in moral terms) as a neutral fact
but as a demand.[36] Once the question had arisen, that two possible courses
of action occurred to him was, equally probably, not a matter of choice; for,
whether we accept them or not, communal values are usually known to us and
they influence the way in which situations appear to us. The values that each one
accepts are an habitual element of himself. His circumstances include the tradition in which he lives, and in so far as he accepts the tradition, it, too, becomes
an habitual element of himself.

The value at work in the account of Goss's rescue of Dinelli is the saving
of another. That Goss had that value is certainly in part accounted for by

---

[35] V Mallet, 'Lost or hurt at sea? Phew!', *Financial Times*, London, 1 July/2 July 2006, W11.

[36] That the other person is present as demand is a constant and explicit theme in the writings of
Martin Buber and Emmanuel Lévinas but, not in the same words, is present, more or less centrally,
in the Western and other traditions. It is well to recall, for example, the Biblical golden rule and
that the second principle of justice in Justinian's *Institutes* (I.II.3) and *Digest* (1.1.10.1) is 'not to
harm any other person'. Lévinas spoke '... of responsibility as the essential, first and fundamental
structure of subjectivity. For I describe subjectivity in ethical terms. The ethical does not supplement a prior existential base; in the ethical understood as responsibility is found the kernel of
subjectivity. By responsibility I mean responsibility for the other person', *Éthique et infini: dialogues
avec Philippe Némo* (Paris: Fayard, 1982), 91. See also Martin Buber, *I and Thou* (trans RG Smith,
Edinburgh: T & T Clarke, 1987).

saying that it is a 'tradition deeply entrenched in sailing culture', but the tradition actually exists only in people, and it exists as actually operative in them,
increasingly as they go from childhood to maturity, by their choice. A tradition is expressed, in part, in language; but not only, or even primarily, in a set
of formulae. It is also handed down – often more powerfully – both through
example and in stories that express approval and disdain. The value that Goss
habitually accepted – that went to make up who he was – and upon which he
acted, comes across to those in the sailing community as (in Mallet's words) 'an
unbreakable rule that obliges [sailors] to go to the rescue of someone in trouble'.
The rule, more or less explicitly formulated (possibly less explicitly expressed
than the list of rules enjoining members how to behave at the yacht club), states
what is considered to be the good thing to do in certain circumstances; it is
a *specification* of the more general rule that enjoins one to love one's neighbour as oneself, that one should considers others' interests and not merely one's
own. This and other rules – some, as this one, of great importance, others more
casual and more changeable, what Hume calls 'a kind of lesser morality' and
Hobbes 'Small Morals'[37] – go towards making up the moral tradition of the
sailing community.

If what Mallet calls the deeply entrenched and unbreakable rule were to van-
ish from the sailing community, that community would be altered radically. But
where does 'the unbreakable rule...deeply entrenched in [the tradition]' come
from?[38] It is not legislated. Rather it emerges from the affective, intelligent, and
responsible practice of those who sail in proximity with one another in the peril
of the sea, and who, in practice and for the most part, deal each with another as he
would have the other deal with him: it is a practice consonant with the golden rule
that one should treat others as one would wish to be treated by them. The practice
exists before the rule is formulated. Sailors get into difficulty; other sailors choose
to try to rescue them; these attempts are admired within the sailing community;
failure to try is thought less well of. Sailors tell of courageous efforts both of those
that have succeeded, and of those that have not; they speak scornfully of those
who made no effort when an effort could have been made. To attempt to rescue those in danger is admired and becomes a communal value, and communal
values enjoin actions that are admired. In some such manner, the unbreakable
rule becomes entrenched in sailing culture, in the tradition. The contrary image
of people coming together to form a sailing community and, before actually taking to the sea, working out a complete set of values, and legislating a complete set
of laws is, to say the least, unrealistic.

---

[37] Hume, *An Enquiry concerning the Principles of Morals* [1751] (Oxford: Oxford University
Press, 1988) [IV.169], 209; Hobbes, *Leviathan*, 160 [47].
[38] This question recalls our questions at the outset of this book: 'What was the source of the
pre-*Grágás* laws? Where did the original system come from?...What is the source of the customary
laws? Where do they come from?'

In Chapter 1 we noted that the legal theorist with whom the term 'living law' is most associated is Eugen Ehrlich.[39] Ehrlich referred to the living law as 'the law which dominates life itself even though it has not been posited in legal propositions':[40] the law made and maintained by people in their 'associations' and in the broader community. His central thesis was that 'the centre of gravity of legal development lies not in legislation, nor in juristic science, nor in judicial decision, but in society itself'.[41] For Ehrlich society was 'the sum total of the [very heterogeneous] human associations that have mutual relations with one another',[42] and law's primary function is to create order in and between associations within society.[43] 'Just as we find everywhere the ordered community, wherever we follow its traces', Ehrlich wrote, 'so we also find the law everywhere, ordering and upholding every human association'.[44] The community of sailors and the communal rule that we have been discussing is, in Ehrlich's terms, an example of the living law of a particular 'human association' or 'social association'.

We are in agreement with these and many other aspects of Ehrlich's theory – for example, his evolutionary conception of society[45] – but the correctness of his primary insight – the existence of a 'social' or 'living' law of which formal, state law is but one expression – is not supported by a clear recognition that a core element of the living law is that specific mutual entitlements are discovered to be intrinsic to specific common human practices and these give rise to a sense of natural justice upon which conventional law, whether of the state or non-state variety, is founded.[46] For example, in *Fundamental Principles of the Sociology*

[39] While Ehrlich is the author most associated with the term, it is not surprising – given law's practical dimensions – that other authors have also referred to law as 'living'. Eligio Resta's book, *Diritto vivente* ['Living Law'] (Bari: Laterza, 2008), is a recent example. Resta's notion of the 'life of the law' includes consideration of the law as an evolving natural *corpus* and not as a static 'positive' body – in this sense it bears some general similarity to Ehrlich's idea and to our own. But Resta's paths of analysis seem to be otherwise very different. See the review by Carlo Cantaluppi in the online journal, *Nordicum-Mediterraneum* (2010, Vol 5, Nr 1): available at: <http://nome.unak.is/>.

[40] E Ehrlich, *Fundamental Principles of the Sociology of Law* [1913] (New Brunswick, NJ: Transaction Publishers, 2002), 493.   [41] Ibid, xv.

[42] Ibid, 26.

[43] Law, for Ehrlich, is an order of peace and not of war; debtors keep their promises to creditors, first of all, not because they are afraid of credit law or sanctions but because they are anxious to keep promises and desire to live peacefully in community: 'If one reads a contract of usufructuary lease… one marvels how it is possible for the lessee to move at all within this barbed-wire fence of paragraphs. Nevertheless the lessee gets on very well… One who is engaged in the practical affairs of life is anxious to deal peaceably with people', ibid, 497–8.   [44] Ibid, 25.

[45] Klaus Ziegert has observed that Ehrlich 'captured the essence of evolution theory as it relates to the human species' by considering society as 'a structural network of relations that individuals entertain together and with each other', 'World Society, Nation State and Living Law in the Twenty-first Century' in M Hertogh (ed), *Living Law: Reconsidering Eugen Ehrlich* (Oxford: Hart Publishing, 2009), 223, 226.

[46] As we have said, some customs and habits are so fundamental that, were people not to act for the most part in accord with them, any social order would collapse. These customs and habits involve entitlements that are just in a natural sense: that what is borrowed is to be returned, for example, or that promises ought to be kept, or that people ought not to be killed at a whim. Other

of Law we find the suggestion that each primitive association 'creates [its living law] quite independently' and thus the possibility of conceiving of the living law as in some sense posited from within a pre-lawful context, a view with which we disagree completely.[47] Humans evolve within a social order and live in a complex pattern of interrelations that they express linguistically in 'laws'; thus 'Thou shalt not kill' and 'Thou shalt not steal', or some linguistic equivalent of these, emerge within a society where indiscriminate killing and stealing is already thought to be wrong and disapproved.

The living law or communal moral law tends, generally speaking – yet not always avoiding bias – to cultivate a moral context within which others' interests are to be considered and this moral context is itself an expression of what is just. When others' interests are considered, and therefore not merely one's own, the tendency is to give to others what is due. The desire to live peaceably brings with it the requirement of neighbourliness: each person may realize, albeit to a greater or lesser degree, that in order for his interests to be considered by others, in order for him to get what is his due in the community, he must reciprocate by considering and respecting others' interests; in other words, as well as the spontaneous response that concentrates on what is due to oneself, there is an equally spontaneous if not always so dominant response of concern for what is due to others. The choice of that response – which by no means obliterates self-interest – over against selfishness is the virtue of justice: the settled determination (*constans et perpetua voluntas*) to render to each what is due.

As we saw in Chapter 2, the moral context within which others' interests are to be considered is to be found, more or less clearly and formally expressed, in every human society. We argue in favour of the judgment, which we take to be

more detailed customs and laws are needed and are conventional to the extent that they select and enjoin one way of acting rather than another, for example the specific rules governing the buying and selling of property or the formation of contracts.

[47] Marc Hertogh has noted that many of Ehrlich's arguments are subject to multiple interpretations ('From "Men of Files" to "Men of the Senses": A Brief Characterisation of Eugen Ehrlich's Sociology of Law' in M Hertogh (ed), *Living Law*, 1, 6–8); part of the reason for this is that *Fundamental Principles of the Sociology of Law*, as Roger Cotterrell observes, is repetitive, ambiguous, and sometimes seemingly self-contradictory – but it is, as Cotterrell also remarks, 'a virtuoso performance nonetheless' ('Ehrlich at the Edge of Empire: Centres and Peripheries in Legal Studies' in M Hertogh (ed), *Living Law*, 75, 78). Although it is not our intention to do so, there does exist the possibility of developing and constructively interpreting parts of *Fundamental Principles of the Sociology of Law* that suggest affinity with our account of law and justice. There is a recurring, almost teasing quality about Ehrlich in this regard, for he acknowledged that some universal norms have taken hold among 'the whole human race' and had become, in his terms, 'rules of conduct' for them; he attributed similarities in the the living law of associations, or orders in association of the same kind, 'to the similarity of the conditions of life'; and his account of adjudication included the judge's understanding of social utility, his innate sense of justice and the subject of the dispute ('the nature of the thing'). On this basis, Ehrlich's living law *could* be understood as those judgments and choices that in recurrent kinds of circumstances are generally accepted and approved in particular human 'associations' and in society at large; but it is notable that although Ehrlich was also a Professor of Roman Law *Fundamental Principles of the Sociology of Law* does not incorporate any understanding of the *ius gentium* along these lines.

prevalent, that we should take account of others. We think of it as a reasonable conclusion to the question as to how we should live. Is the opposite conclusion – that one should take no account of others – equally reasonable? We suggest both that it is not and that the conviction that it is not naturally evolves between humans living together. The principle that one should act taking others into account becomes communally accepted more or less explicitly; specific instances of the principle may be posited in state law – as in the case of the underlying principle of contract law, *pacta sunt servanda*, or the body of traffic laws that require drivers to drive carefully and not recklessly or dangerously.

If the demand to consider the interest of others completely, or nearly completely, disappears the society tends to decline towards the natural condition and what Hobbes described as 'the Warre of all against all'. This is what we see in the aftermath of great natural disasters or in last throes of the collapse of tyranny. Humans are social beings and cannot sustain their lives in the state of nature; they live and develop within a way of life in which each can pursue his goals in peace. As we have seen, that way of life is not produced by a single decision made once for all time, but is continuously chosen as individual decisions are taken with respect for others' interest and is continuously under threat as individual decisions take no account of others. It is not that individuals do not or should not pursue their own interests; it is that the context in which individual interests are pursued is one in which many interests are pursued. Communal life becomes impossible if this context is not sustained, and so it is that the communal law describes, approves, and requires behaviour that sustains that context and describes, disapproves, and forbids behaviour that tends to destroy it.

Consider another example of living law, the communal 'rule' stating or implying that it is not good to steal, to take what belongs to another. If a person finds that some of the money in his wallet has been stolen, the person's interest in having the money restored is not simply that he could be reasonably expected to want it; it is that he is entitled to it. Entitlement of this kind is present in all human communities. Had he been no more entitled to it than anyone else, there would be no issue, and to speak more accurately the money would have been not stolen but simply transferred from one person to another. As we noted earlier in this chapter, the important point is that for ownership actually to exist it must be communally accepted and we referred to the emergence in communal law of an explicit rule against theft. We pointed out that if anyone may take whatever he wants whenever he wants it, ownership would cease to exist and a society in which it is crucial – as all societies are – would collapse. People accept that to steal is wrong because they have first learnt that this is what is accepted, and have later come to accept that what another owns he is entitled to keep and what they themselves own they are entitled to keep.

Because moral traditions are necessary in human society, and because without them we could not live together, it is easy to be tempted to imagine such traditions as in all respects good or just, but this is not the case. The inevitable moral tension between taking only one's own and taking others' interest into account cannot but exist in human societies and therefore in its living law. The living law in a community is what is in that community taken to be just. A custom is no more than an accepted practice: to say that something is a custom is not to assign a moral value to it.

No moral tradition will be in all respects good; it will inevitably be corrupted by individual and group bias. Some powerful individuals or groups of individuals will, given time and opportunity, favour traditions that support and enhance their power over others.[48] So, throughout history, the powerful have required some form of tribute from those whom they have succeeded in subduing. Thus, the enlargement of the Roman Empire, upon which modern European and Western civilization so greatly depends, was not undertaken with that goal in view, but with the hope of increasing the wealth of Rome. Slavery, upon which, with conquest and pillage, the wealth of the early empires to a large extent depended, was for long an entrenched and insufficiently questioned tradition that denied freedom to some whose work sustained societies dedicated to the freedom of others. The exclusion of most people from any direct influence on the polity and the refusal of suffrage are traditions that in Europe have only recently been overcome. The ostracism of women who bore children out of wedlock and of their children, until recently common throughout much of Europe, and not entirely eliminated, is yet another horrible example of the refusal of the powerful – who in this case may well not have thought of themselves as powerful – to allow those of whom they disapproved to live a peaceful life. Examples of antagonism between groups are not hard to find, ranging from the antagonisms between recognizably different social or ethnic groups, through deliberate and systematic discrimination in political and social entitlements, to civil war, crimes against humanity, and genocide; for the immediate advantages of one group often demand the imposition of corresponding disadvantages upon another, and the survival of the powerful often demands that they discriminate in favour of those upon whom the continuance of their power relies, and against their opponents.

Even when antagonism between different social or ethnic groups is not great, its significance may well be. One of the features of what is described as 'globalization' is the increase in the rise of legally 'pluralist' communities throughout the world,[49] where for example religious or ethnic minority communities, with distinct sets of values and norms, exist within a larger community with values

---

[48] Theodore Beza remarked in 1574, '[S]ince the origin of the world, there has never been a king – even if you were to select the very best – who did not in some measure abuse his authority', *Concerning the Rights of Rulers Over Their Subjects and the Duty of Subjects Toward Their Rulers*, quoted in J Witte Jr, *The Reformation of Rights* (Cambridge: Cambridge University Press, 2007), 125.

[49] The term 'globalization' has been described by William Twining as meaning 'those processes which tend to create and consolidate a unified world economy, a single ecological system, and a complex network of communications that covers the whole globe, even if it does not penetrate to every part of it', *Globalisation and Legal Theory* (London: Butterworths, 2000), 4.

and norms that indicate and have shaped the dominant sense of justice of a given jurisdiction. One of the typical instances of this situation is the case of religious minorities in contemporary Europe and elsewhere. In our account of law and justice the issue arises as to how such situations are to be interpreted in terms of the living law. We have emphasized the link between the living law of a community and its sense of justice and how these in turn provide the basis for the community's conventions and state law. But what about a case where there are dual or multiple co-existing 'living laws'? For instance, the living law of the minority Muslim community in some western countries includes customs, practices, well-known and accepted procedures, and mutual expectations that establish jural relationships particular to that community *within* that community, but this living law seems in turn, on one view at least, to exist *within*, and be subservient to, the living law of the dominant Christian or secular community. We suggest that this is an instance of two living laws in conflict and that it is a case of the living laws being, as all living laws always are, in a state of flux. In most large modern jurisdictions there is not a uniform living law and flux is brought about often through conflict and resolution. Although it is not our task in this book to address the significant and often intractable difficulties that arise in multicultural jurisdictions owing to such flux,[50] they in no way detract from the value of living law as a conceptual tool with which to understand the nature of law and justice. We made the point earlier in this section that moral traditions will change when sufficiently many of those living within them change their minds about how it is good to act. Since it is unlikely that minds will always change in unison, moral traditions at any one time will *commonly* be controversial. New sets of customs, practices, well-known and accepted procedures, and mutual expectations that establish jural relationships different from those previously established present a perennial challenge, so to speak, to the existing sense of justice.

Yet the fact remains that in every community, some persons and some groups are more influential than others. Sometimes greater influence depends entirely on the person or group exerting it; sometimes on the person's or the group's social position. The solutions initiated by the more powerful may well suit their own desires rather than the desires of those on whom the solutions are imposed. The institutions of slavery, serfdom, indentured labour and the like are solutions of this kind, and show that the living communal law and the community that it both describes and regulates are not necessarily for the common good. Social position both evolves and is sustained by power, the emergence and increase of which is not legislated but emerges by imposition sufficiently successful to be exercised and accepted – or at least acquiesced in. The person or group imposes

---

[50] For discussion of some of the issues at stake in such situations, see, for example, T Hickey, 'Domination and the *Hijab* in Irish Schools' (2009) 31 *Dublin University Law Journal* 127 and E Daly, 'Restrictions on Religious Dress in French Republican Thought: Returning the Secularist Justification to a Rights-based Rationale' (2009) 31 *Dublin University Law Journal* 154.

its position when sufficiently powerful to do so. The commonplace that the duty of the prince is to care for the common good suggests the ideal that the state is always a benign institution dedicated to the wellbeing of its citizens. Between ideal and its realization there can be, and in a large number of modern states there is, a great gulf. That gulf may be smaller or greater but it cannot reasonably be expected to disappear since its original principle – selfishness and its resultant bias in individuals and in groups – is endemic and enduring.

The pure imposition of power of one over another is the refusal to take the other's interest into account. The interest of the powerful becomes the criterion. This is obvious in the case of slavery; less obvious in the case of chiefdoms, earldoms, kingdoms; perhaps less obvious still in the case of influential groups in a modern liberal democracy; but the tyrannies in the present and the last century are sufficient indication of the survival of this criterion in contemporary practice, as well as of its inevitable persistence. However, accompanying pure power there is commonly a justifying rhetoric that tries to hide the fact that the interest of the powerful is the actual criterion of judgment and decision, behind some supposed but illusory communally accepted criterion presented as the true source of action. The interest of the powerful is presented as the interest of those upon whom it bears, and so relies to an extent upon an argument that undermines it. Power tends to corrupt and attempts to legitimate its corruption which it cannot do otherwise than by jeopardizing its supposed legitimacy.[51] But however much communal moral traditions may be, have been, are, and will be, distorted to allow the more powerful to oppress the less powerful and however much they may allow or encourage antagonism between different communities, the proper function of the living law – of a communal moral tradition – is to allow a community to live in peace and harmony.

---

[51] G Barden, 'Rhetorics of Legitimacy' (1998) 2 *European Journal of Law, Philosophy and Computer Science* 47; see also our discussion of legitimacy in ch 11 below.

4

Natural Justice and Conventional Justice

4.1 Introduction

A common jurisprudential understanding of 'natural justice' – in English-language jurisprudence at least – is the justice inherent in a court's or tribunal's procedures. Within the account of the just put forward here this is only *part* of what is naturally just. We consider procedural justice when discussing adjudication in Chapter 6 – and show there how this type of justice is essential to adjudication properly so-called. In this chapter, however, we concentrate on the distinction between the naturally and the conventionally just.

We begin with a discussion of 'nature' and what is 'natural' and use those terms to refer to that which is intrinsic to a practice or circumstance. Using them in that way we distinguish between the naturally and the conventionally just. We distinguish three kinds of justice – distributive justice, rectificatory or correct-ive or commutative justice, and reciprocal justice – and in this chapter consider the first two.[1] A distributively just allocation is achieved when shares in what is common are justly allocated, as when, for example, shareholders in a com-pany are paid dividends according to the number of shares held. In rectifica-tory justice a just allocation is achieved when something, rightly or wrongly in the possession of one who does not own it, is returned to its owner, as when, for example, something stolen, taken in error or borrowed is returned, or when a debt is redeemed. Reciprocal justice – the justice in exchange or trading – is discussed in Chapter 5.

---

[1] The distinction stems from Aristotle although it is commonly thought that he distinguished, not three, but two types of justice – distributive justice and rectificatory justice – and, indeed, he does so explicitly at V.1131a.30 et seq, and in that place he considers transactions to be part of rectificatory justice; but later in the book, at V.1133b.30, he introduces reciprocal justice and there analyses transactions. There is some incoherence in the presentation probably owing to the fact that the *Nicomachean Ethics* is more a set of lecture notes than a fully worked out book. In his translation Tricot explicitly rejects the interpretation that there are three types of justice, *Éthique à Nicomaque* (Paris: Vrin, 1972) 231 (n 4). Whatever the better interpretation of Aristotle, we consider it more illuminating to distinguish justice into three types. The distinction should be thought of as a commonly convenient and clarifying division – as a rule of thumb – rather than as an exact theory.

4.2 On the Meaning of the Word 'Natural'

Generally – but particularly in jurisprudence – the term 'natural' is used in so many, sometimes incompatible, ways that it is at once difficult and imperative to clarify how we use it in this book.[2] In English-language jurisprudence 'natural justice' is, as was said above, usually equated with procedural justice,[3] but it is sometimes used as a synonym of 'natural law'. Natural law, which is a term often associated with the interface between law and ethics, is notoriously difficult to define. Paul Foriers and Chaïm Perelman refer to Erik Wolf's enumeration of multiple meanings of both 'nature' and 'law', which in turn yield multiple definitions of 'natural law'.[4] Given this ambiguity, one might be inclined to accept Hume's counsel of despair that, 'The word *natural* is commonly taken in so many senses and in so loose a signification, that it seems vain to dispute whether justice be natural or not.'[5]

That there is much in Hume's complaint is undeniable. Some of the uncertainty and confusion has come from different understandings of Roman Law throughout the ages. In English particularly there is, as is well known, no easy translation of the key term *ius*, with the result that it is difficult to distinguish between *ius naturale* and *lex naturalis* – and 'natural law' has been used for both.[6]

Gaius distinguishes 'the right of peoples', common to all peoples (*ius gentium*), from 'civil right', proper to a particular people (*ius civile*). Ulpian later introduced a threefold division by adding 'natural right' (*ius naturale*) which is

that which nature teaches to all animals. For this right does not belong exclusively to the human race, but belongs to all animals, whether of the air, the earth or the sea.[7]

In both the *Digest* and the *Institutes* all three terms are used but, except in the opposition between *ius naturale* and *ius gentium* with respect to slavery,[8] the

---

[2] In ch 3.2 above, we referred to the exclusion of the idea that the sea or rivers can be owned, or the way in which they can be owned, in Justinian's *Institutes*: 'By the law of nature these things are common to all: the air, running water, the sea and consequently the shores of the sea', II.I.1. There, as we said, the common phrase 'By the law of nature' (*naturali jure*) seems to mean little more than 'it is obvious' as, indeed, it was to the jurists of Justinian's time. But it is equally obvious that this is only one of many meanings that attach to 'natural'.

[3] See, for example, P Jackson, *Natural Justice* (London: Sweet & Maxwell, 1979); see also RA MacDonald, 'Natural Justice' in CB Gray (ed), *The Philosophy of Law: An Encyclopedia (Vol II)* (New York: Garland, 1999), 573–5.

[4] E Wolf, *Das Problem der Naturrechtslehre, Versuch einer Orientierung* (Karlsruhe: n.p.a., 1955), cited in P Foriers and C Perelman, 'Natural Law and Natural Rights' in PP Weiner (ed), *Dictionary of the History of Ideas* (New York: Charles Scribner's Sons, 1973), 13–14.

[5] Hume, *An Enquiry concerning the Principles of Morals* [1751] (Oxford: Oxford University Press, 1988) [Appendix 3: 258], 308.

[6] *Lex naturalis* occurs very infrequently and perhaps only once and in the ablative case in Justinian's *Institutes* (IV.I.1), where natural law is said to prohibit theft.

[7] Justinian, *Institutes*, I.II.Preamble; *Digest*, I.I.1.3. In the *Digest* wild animals are specified.

[8] *Institutes*, I.II.2 and *Digest*, i.4.5; *Institutes*, I.III.2 and *Digest*, i.5.4.1.

distinction between these two almost disappears and they are sometimes explicitly said to be the same.[9]

The idea of a natural right or law common to humans and other animals, although not wholly absent, is not prominent in later jurisprudential thought. We recall it to make clear one important way in which we use the term. The passage from Ulpian quoted above continues: '[non-human animals are] to be reckoned to have practical knowledge of this', which may be interpreted to mean that they act in accord with it, in some respects as a falling body acts in accord with the laws of physics. In this sense, for example, there is a natural law of human sexuality and human digestion that is not an instruction that humans obey or ignore but simply the regularity discovered in human sexuality and digestive systems.

It is in this way that humans are naturally social beings. They are naturally social beings as are other social animals, for example horses, elephants, and buffalo (and unlike, for example, tigers and hedgehogs, which are solitary animals except for mating and the rearing of offspring). Humans are naturally social just as they are, for example, naturally bipedal, naturally linguistic, naturally in need of food and sleep, naturally inclined to mate, procreate, and bring up children. Sociability is not chosen by humans any more than it is chosen by horses, elephants, or buffalo.[10] When St Thomas argues in the *Summa Contra Gentiles* that some actions are 'naturally right', he uses the word 'natural' in this way:

It is natural to man that he be a social animal, as is shown by the fact that one man by himself cannot procure all that is needed for human life. Those things without which human society cannot be sustained are naturally appropriate to humans. Among such things are to preserve for each person what is due, and to refrain from injuring another. Therefore, some human acts are naturally right.[11]

This sense of the *ius naturale* – the sense of something acting in accord with its own nature – is our sense of the English-language term 'natural law', a theme we develop in Chapter 8.

We discussed the *ius gentium* in Chapter 2. According to Justinian's *Institutes*, 'Natural reason establishes [the *ius gentium*] among all humans'.[12] The provisions of the *ius gentium* or 'right (law) of peoples (nations)' are discovered to be

---

[9] *Institutes* II.I.11 and *Digest* xli.1.1.

[10] Humans neither decide nor are commanded to be social animals. They do not choose to be social. Nonetheless, as we saw in ch 2 above, humans do choose and their choices are made within society. These choices may sustain or undermine society.

[11] *Summa Contra Gentiles*, III.129.5. It is presupposed in this argument, which is strikingly and perhaps unexpectedly similar to Hobbes's, that to sustain human society is a value, and to contribute to its destruction a disvalue. However, before that value is intelligently, reasonably, and responsibly chosen, it is spontaneously lived. What St Thomas thinks of as natural spontaneities, Hobbes thinks of as 'The Passions that encline men to Peace ...', and, for both, what are naturally right are those actions 'which, being taken away, the Common-wealth faileth, and is utterly dissolved; as a building whose Foundation is destroyed', *Leviathan*, 188 [63] and 334 [150].

[12] Justinian, *Institutes*, I.II.1. See also *Digest*, 1.1.1–4 and Gaius, *Institutes*, i.1.

common in as much as human reasonable enquiry is found to have reached similar solutions to similar problems, 'for nations have established for themselves certain laws [*iura*] as occasion and the necessities of human life required', and 'From this law of nations almost all contracts were first introduced, as, for instance, buying and selling, letting and hiring, partnership, deposits, loans returnable in kind, and very many others.'[13]

Roman jurisprudence makes three claims, all of which are of great importance. The first is that the practices of the *ius gentium* are the fruit of human intelligence and inquiry. Secondly, these practices are found in all societies – they occurred in all the societies with which the Romans were familiar – and they are, in that sense, common to humans. Thirdly, they are activities with their own intrinsic regularities – thus, it is intrinsic to lending and borrowing that what is borrowed is to be returned; but it is also the case that the activities are carried out correctly only by choice – thus, a specific case of lending and borrowing occurs in the correct way only if the lender in fact lends to the borrower, or if the borrower in fact decides to return what he has borrowed.

Because the making of contracts, buying, and selling and so on do not occur among non-human animals, they are not part of the *ius naturale* as this is defined in the preamble to I.II of Justinian's *Institutes* ('that which nature teaches all animals') or, to put this another way, not part of the idea of natural law when this is understood as something or someone acting in accordance with its own nature. However, the *ius gentium* is the fruit of natural reason, and the fruit of natural reason is also referred to as *ius naturale*, because, as was said above, the *ius gentium* and the *ius naturale* are, for the most part in Justinian, thought to be the same.[14]

We interpret the Roman *ius naturale* and *ius gentium* – that is, both natural justice and the right or law of nations – as meaning that it is naturally right that contracts are to be honoured, that what is borrowed for use is to be returned, or that when something is borrowed for consumption, not the thing but an equivalent is to be returned. It is naturally right, not for some arcane and mysterious reason, but quite simply because that is how contract or lending and borrowing are correctly understood. The mutual entitlements in buying and selling differ from those in lending and borrowing because the practice of buying and selling differs from that of lending and borrowing, and *specific mutual entitlements are discovered to be intrinsic to specific practices*. To understand the mutual

---

[13] Justinian, *Institutes*, I.II.2 (both quotations).

[14] Ibid, II.I.11: 'Things become the property of individuals in various ways; of some things we acquire ownership by natural law, which, as we have observed, is termed the law of nations'; II.I.12: 'Wild beasts . . . as soon as they are captured by anyone become by the law of nations the property of the captor; for natural reason gives the first occupant that which had no previous owner'; and *ius naturale* and *ius gentium* are again said to be the same at II.I.41. There is one, although somewhat ambiguous, exception: slavery is said to be against the *ius naturale* but is recognized as commonly found, as it was at that time (I.II.2). See also Cicero, *On Duties*, III.21–32, esp 23.

entitlements involved in lending and borrowing is simply to understand the practice. It is possible to imagine a society in which lending and borrowing did not occur, but it is not possible to imagine a society in which lending and borrowing occurred but in which what was lent and borrowed, or its equivalent, was not to be returned. Again, it is possible, if difficult, to imagine a society in which no contracts were made. That contracts are in fact made is thought to be common to humans, and that contracts made are to be kept is thought to be intrinsic to the practice of promising. Similarly, that things are severally owned is thought to be common, and to respect ownership and not to steal is thought to be intrinsic to ownership.

We use the word 'natural' to refer to that which is intrinsic to a practice or circumstance. The natural refers primarily to what is often called 'the nature of the case', as is implied in Adam Smith's remark on the obligatory character of promise:

A promise is a declaration of your desire that the person for whom you promise should depend on you for the performance of it. Of consequence the promise produces an obligation, and the breach of it is an injury.[15]

In other words, it is in the nature of a promise that it produce an obligation or, changing the words only, that a promise naturally produces an obligation. A corollary of the claim that a promise produces an obligation is that the production of the obligation does not depend on the sovereign's command to keep promises.[16] It is an entirely different question within a particular jurisdiction which promises are justiciable.

If we ask 'what is the nature of society or community?' we are asking what is intrinsic to the practice of social or communal life. That to sustain society is a value and to contribute to its destruction a disvalue may be derived from the propositions that to sustain human life is valuable, and that human life cannot be sustained outside society, but eventually one must come to a proposition that cannot be demonstrated as there is no more basic proposition from which it can be logically derived. The proposition that to sustain human life is valuable is such an indemonstrable proposition. We should emphasize that we do not think of it as in any way present in our minds as a proposition to which we must give our assent. To remain alive is a natural spontaneity. In most circumstances, we spontaneously act in accord with it but, when we think about it, intelligently, reasonably,

---

[15] Adam Smith, *Lectures on Jurisprudence,* Report dated 1766 (ed RL Meek, DD Raphael and PG Stein), 472 (Glasgow edn). A promise is the declaration of a desire; the declaration reveals the desire. Likewise St Thomas in the *Summa Theologiae,* II–II.88.1: 'A man obliges himself to another by means of a promise... but a promise by one man to another cannot be made except in words or some external sign.' And, according to Hobbes, as we saw in ch 2, if the intrinsic obligation to fulfil contracts or covenants is absent, they 'are vain, and but empty words; and the Right of all men to all things remaining, wee are still in the condition of Warre' (*Leviathan,* 210 [71]).

[16] See our discussion of natural law in ch 8 below.

and responsibly, we choose it as a value that ought in most circumstances to prevail.[17]

We referred in Chapter 2 to the function of law in Hobbes's theory of civil society. Hobbes's understanding of what is 'natural' is, in many respects, close to ours. Consider, for example, Hobbes's first law of nature – 'to seek peace where there is any hopes of attaining it, and where there is none to enquire out for the auxiliaries of war is the dictate of right reason, that is, the law of nature'.[18] Note that 'the dictate of right reason' and 'the law of nature' are two expressions for the same object. The truth of a proposition such as Hobbes's first 'dictate' or 'law' cannot be demonstrated because there is no more basic proposition from which it can be derived. It is obvious to the intelligent person engaged in action. It describes their spontaneous practice. The principles of action are how intelligent humans consciously reflect or act when engaged in the business of trying to discover what is to be achieved and how it is to be achieved; they are the way in which we exist when engaged in action as distinct, for example, from the way in which we exist when engaged in theoretical enquiry or when sleeping. In the realm of action we cannot choose what seems to us to be bad; we can choose the bad only when it seems to us to be good – that is, we choose the bad under the guise or appearance of good: *sub ratione boni*.[19]

In this discussion we must make one final thing clear. The term 'natural law' is sometimes understood either as a more or less covert synonym for the 'divine law' believed by religious Jews, Christians, and Muslims to have been in some sense revealed to Moses or as a set of inbuilt infallible moral axioms from which appropriate moral rules may be deduced.[20] There is one passage in Justinian in

---

[17] That this value ought not in all circumstances to prevail is expressed in what have become almost proverbs, well known in the Western tradition, *dulce et decorum est pro patria mori* ('it is admirable and fitting to die for one's country') (Horace, *Odes*, iii.1.40); *greater love than this no man hath than to lay down his life for his friends* (St John's Gospel 15:13); etc. That one ought to choose to die rather than to live dishonourably is a value in many cultures, perhaps in all.

[18] *De Cive*, 1.15. See also 2.2: 'But the first and fundamental law of nature is *that peace is to be sought after, where it may be found; and where not, there to provide ourselves for helps of war*' (emphasis in original). There is no idea in St Thomas comparable to Hobbes's first law because for St Thomas, as we discussed in ch 2 above, the peaceful order that is the goal of the law is to be found within an already given order; and it is this peaceful order that is the subject of constant choice.

[19] See G Barden, *After Principles* (Notre Dame, Ind: University of Notre Dame, 1990), especially ch 5. In the Aristotelian-Thomist tradition, the first indemonstrable principle of practical reason is based on the fact that every agent acts on account of an end, and to be an end carries the meaning of 'to be good'; every action, in other words, looks to achieve a result that the agent intends and finds good. The claim that a person chooses what is in fact bad because it seems to him to be good (that is, chooses the bad under the guise or appearance of good, *sub ratione boni*) depends upon there being an objective distinction between good and bad. We shall refer to the idea of *sub ratione boni* again in our discussion of choice in the trading order (ch 5.8 below); we discuss objectivity in morality in ch 7.2 below.

[20] We say 'in some sense revealed' to make clear that we do not suppose the story of the revelation of the law to Moses on Mount Sinai in *Exodus* 19–34 to be necessarily taken literally by believers, or that the revelation of the law has always been understood in the same way throughout the centuries.

which natural laws are said to be 'ever fixed and immutable having been established by divine providence' and which might lead one to conclude that these laws
were thought to have been inserted in, or are accessible by, human minds as fully
formed axioms or fundamental statutes.[21] Whatever about the interpretation of
this passage and of its significance in the work as a whole, it is crucial to point out
that in this book the terms 'natural law' or 'natural justice' are *never* used in this
way. We shall elaborate on this in the discussion of natural law in Chapter 8.

4.3 Natural Justice and Conventional Justice

Aristotle's preliminary description of the distinction between the naturally just
and the conventionally just is as follows:

What is just in the city is in part natural and in part conventional or legal. What is
naturally just ... does not depend on people deciding this or that; what is conventional
is that which is originally indifferent but which, when it is established, is no longer
indifferent.[22]

It is imperative to recognize that the naturally just is not discovered by discovering higher rules or laws laid down by a sovereign. In Aristotle's account, what
is naturally just is not originally a matter of indifference that becomes just only
following custom, convention, agreement, or legal edict. Writing of judgment in
the realm of justice St Thomas gives, almost incidentally, an account of the distinction between the naturally and the conventionally just:

... judgement is nothing else but a kind of definition or determination of what is just.
And something is just in one of two ways: first, *from the nature of the case itself, which is*

---

[21] In Justinian's *Institutes*, I.II.11, *naturalia jura* (laws of nature or natural law rights) are
defined, as was the *ius gentium* in I.II.2. The natural laws are said in I.II.11 to have been established
'by a divine providence' (*divina quadam providentia*) and for that reason are ever fixed and immutable. This is the only place in Justinian's *Institutes* where divine providence is mentioned, and there
is no explicit theoretical account of how the *naturalia jura* are discovered by humans. (In one place
in the *Digest*, as we have said, Marcian quotes approvingly Demosthenes' definition of law: 'Law is
that which all men ought to obey for many reasons, and chiefly because all law is a discovery and
a gift from God and yet at the same time is a resolution of wise men ...' (*Digest* 1.3.2)). At II.I.40
concerning the transfer of property the naturally just solution is related to natural equity and at
II.I.12 concerning the capture of wild animals the solution according to the law of nations is said
to be in accord with natural reason. The *ius naturale* is present in non-human animals but not in
the same way in humans (I.II, Preamble). Cicero, in *On Duties*, distinguishes the manner in which
natural orientations are present in human and other animals on the basis of the presence or absence
of reason and speech (I.50). The gods are variously treated in Cicero; the closest he comes in *On
Duties* to an idea of the *naturalia iura* being of divine origin is in III.28: 'Those who destroy them
(kindness, liberality, goodness, and justice so tear apart the common fellowship of the human race)
must be judged irreverent even in respect of the immortal gods; for the fellowship that they over-
turn was established by the gods....' (M Griffin and M Atkins eds; M Atkins trans) (Cambridge:
Cambridge University Press, 1991), 110.

[22] Aristotle, *Nicomachean Ethics*, V.1134b.18–23.

called naturally just; secondly, from a kind of agreement among men, which is called positively (or conventionally) just.[23]

The phrase in italics – our added emphasis – is crucial. In Latin it reads: *ex ipsa natura rei, quod dicitur ius naturale*. Literally translated the first phrase reads: 'from the very nature of the thing'. The 'thing' is 'the case', 'the situation', or 'the dispute'. What is naturally just is discovered through an intelligent and reasonable examination of the actual situation, and so the discovery of the naturally just is a method and not a doctrine. It is a search for what is intrinsic to the situation or case.

A very simple example of what is *naturally* just is that if one finds a wallet in a classroom, the just situation is restored when it is returned to whoever owns it. One may or may not be anxious to return the wallet, one may make no effort to discover the owner and, if one does know whose wallet it is, one may or may not return it, but none of this takes away from the simple fact that the naturally just situation is restored when the wallet is returned. Why anyone would be interested in bringing about the naturally just situation is an entirely different question.[24]

A simple example of what is *conventionally* just is a rule that states that a library book must be returned before five o'clock on the day when, as established by a conventional rule, it is to be returned. That the borrowed book is to be returned is natural, that is, it is intrinsic to the practice of lending and borrowing; precisely when it is to be returned is a matter of conventional justice that will be decided differently by different libraries. 'Conventionally' means that which may be settled legally *or* by agreement.[25]

---

[23] *Summa Theologiae*, II–II, q 60, art 5 (emphasis added).

[24] We emphasize that it being just to act in a certain way may or may not be, for a particular person, a reason to act in that way. In trivial as well as in important matters, what is a reason for one person may not be a reason for another. G Barden, *Essays on a Philosophical Interpretation of Justice: The Virtue of Justice* (Lampeter: Mellen Press, 1999), ch 9.

[25] For Aristotle, 'political justice' is justice in society, that is, justice between those living a common life for the purpose of satisfying their needs (cf *Nicomachean Ethics*, V.1134a.25). His demarcation of 'political justice' in the *Nicomachean Ethics* (V.1134b.18–1135a.15) is variously translated: 'Political justice is of two kinds, one natural, the other conventional' (H Rackham trans (Heinemann, London, 1975), 295); 'Of political justice part is natural, part legal' (D Ross, in the 1954 Clarendon Press edn, 124); 'There are two sorts of political justice, one natural and the other legal' (*The Ethics of Aristotle* (JAK Thomson trans) (Harmondsworth: Penguin, 1981), 189); 'La justice politique elle-même est de deux espèces, l'une naturelle et l'autre légale' *Éthique à Nicomaque* (J Tricot trans) (Paris: Vrin, 1959), 251. In each translation there is 'natural' but also *either* 'legal' or 'conventional', both of which are correct and both of which may, although differently, mislead. The dominant modern meaning of 'legal' in this context is 'legislative'; while 'conventional' in one fairly common modern usage refers to a practice for which there is no particular reason or for which, if there ever was a reason, it is forgotten. In Aristotle's usage – despite the word 'indifferent' – the idea that what is 'just by convention' is 'just for no particular reason' is totally absent; the dominant sense is that in many cases what is just *must* be settled by agreement. The transacting parties themselves may do this, as when someone who borrows a book agrees to return it by an agreed date, or it may be done by or within the community generally, as when, for example, what precisely constitutes a binding contract is settled

There are two features worth remembering when contrasting natural and conventional solutions. First, if a naturally just solution is to be effective in a given society it must be discovered, agreed, and established in custom or legislation. So there is no reason to be surprised when a discovered and agreed naturally just solution is expressed as a rule. It is, of course, obvious that until the naturally just solution is known it cannot be expressed as a rule. Secondly, a conventional solution is normally neither random nor arbitrary but is, rather, an agreed solution to a question or difficulty to which no 'natural' solution can be discovered. Whether a library book may be borrowed for two or three or four weeks may be conventional but the time period is not arrived at arbitrarily. It is a reasonable solution; a loan period of five minutes or one decade would be manifestly unreasonable and therefore not reasonably a conventional solution. Whether inheritance of land is to be according to a rule of primogeniture or of gavelkind or according to some other rule may be conventional but, again, such rules are not arrived at arbitrarily or unreasonably.

We may investigate the conventional further by examining why there can be no question of associating it with either randomness or arbitrariness. In the *Nicomachean Ethics*, as we have seen, Aristotle says that the legal or conventional is 'that which is originally indifferent but which, once laid down, is no longer indifferent'; he continues by giving some examples of the originally indifferent: 'that a prisoner's ransom be one mina, or that a goat shall be sacrificed and not two sheep...'. How conventional or legal is to be understood in this text and in jurisprudence generally may seem at first glance to be obvious. If it is a matter of utter indifference whether A or B be chosen, then there seems little reason why the matter should not be settled by some method of random selection, as when before a chess game begins which player is to be White and which Black is usually settled in some such way. But that some way of deciding be agreed is not a matter of indifference.

If we think of Aristotle's two examples we find that arbitrary choice between possibilities fits neither one. To develop very briefly the first example, suppose that Paul has taken one of Peter's soldiers a prisoner of war, a matter that has traditionally been considered an element of the 'right of conquest' and not, therefore, thought of as a case of unjust kidnapping or stealing. For the matter to go any further Paul must in principle be willing to return the prisoner for a ransom, and Peter in principle be willing to pay. What is the price to be? Aristotle's argument is that before the matter is settled between them there is no price, that is, the eventual price may be this or that. What the price is to be is whatever the negotiators can agree upon. Again, the situation is one in which there is no naturally just solution; it is rather a situation in which the just solution is reached through negotiation and eventual agreement or convention. The agreed or conventional

and expressed in legislation, or as when what constitutes proper etiquette in relation to queuing is implicitly agreed upon.

price reached is one that, in the detailed circumstances, seems reasonable – that is, in this situation, the best that could be got – to both negotiators. And it may turn out that what is agreed on one occasion may become the ordinarily agreed price in similar situations.[26]

His second example, the choice of a suitable sacrifice, shows another aspect of the conventional. That a sacrifice is required is not in question; but what should it be? It is assumed that someone or some group is entitled to decide what the appropriate sacrifice ought to be, and to impose the solution. It is assumed that, prior to deciding the issue, those who are to decide already think of goats or sheep as suitable. The comparison must have been familiar to the contemporary readers, and even to the modern reader appears plausible. Had Aristotle compared a goat with a small stone or with 50,000 sheep, readers would have been nonplussed simply because it would have struck them as unreasonable. He has chosen a comparison that will leave many readers with the conviction that either one or the other solution would serve but that, for some reason to do with the character of the cult, it is appropriate to choose only one.[27] In his example, the goat is chosen and, because those who decided were entitled to decide, to sacrifice a goat is what is just, legally or conventionally.

Likewise, the case St Thomas discusses in his commentary is not one in which the problem is to decide between several possible and equally good solutions: 'That punishment is due to the thief is naturally just; but that this or that ought to be the punishment is positive law.'[28] St Thomas's argument is that what the legislature decides is the appropriate punishment in the general case, and what the judge decides is the appropriate punishment in a particular case of theft, ought to be a responsible decision emergent from a careful analysis of the facts, an intelligent grasp of their jural character, including reference to any relevant legislation, and responsible and unbiased judgment as to what is due.

Between the natural and the conventional there is this affinity: both are in principle intelligent, reasonable, and responsible solutions to a problem. The natural solution is discovered when what is intrinsic to the situation is understood; the conventional solution is discovered at the point where the nature of the case leaves more than one possible, disputable and, in some cases, equally good solution, but where the different envisaged solutions either cannot be implemented together or where it seems more reasonable to implement only one. For example, it is obvious that, in determining which side of the road vehicles should drive on, both equally good solutions cannot be implemented together just as it is obvious that a custodial and non-custodial sentence cannot be implemented at the same time.

---

[26] The exchange of a prisoner for a ransom is a case of reciprocal justice. For an account of this type of justice, see ch 5 below.

[27] That bulls, cows, goats, and sheep were thought to be acceptable sacrificial offerings to the gods was well known. Examples from early Israelite society of more detailed laws concerning precisely what ought to be offered in different circumstances are given in *Leviticus* 4, 5, and 6.

[28] St Thomas Aquinas, *In Decem Libros Ethicorum Aristotelis ad Nicomachum Expositio* (Turin: Marietti, 1934), VI. XII.1023.

When the naturally just has been discovered one can still choose whether or not to do what is just. Once a particular solution becomes the agreed convention – whether it is merely agreed socially or, alternatively, enshrined in the positive law – it states what is just, but, as with the naturally just, one can choose whether or not to act in accord with it. About the conventionally just a question of authority arises, for its authority is *extrinsic* to it, whereas the authority of the naturally just is *intrinsic*. So, a promise intrinsically obliges, whereas the convention or agreement that the bank robber seeks to establish – that the teller hand over money – does not intrinsically oblige or, to adapt Hart's useful verbal distinction, does not obligate.[29] The natural solution obliges because it discovers what is intrinsically just – for example, that contracts be honoured – the conventional or positive solution obliges because, and only when, it is imposed. The conventionally just – again, whether it is agreed merely socially or, alternatively, enshrined in the positive law – is in principle a reasonable and agreed solution to a problem. The caveat 'in principle' is required because what a lawgiver powerful enough to impose does in fact positively impose may in practice be neither reasonable nor freely accepted, but only reluctantly acquiesced in.[30]

In addition to the distinction between the naturally and the conventionally just, we distinguish three types of justice: distributive, rectificatory, and reciprocal justice. In each type there is a contrast, and possible conflict, between the naturally and the conventionally just, but in each case this is never a contrast or conflict between a higher and an inferior command. What by any single person or community is considered to be naturally just can, of course, be formulated as a command, for example in a rule or law, but this rule or law derives from an understanding of what is intrinsic to the situation and is an expression of that understanding. In this chapter we consider distributive and rectificatory justice and we shall distinguish between the naturally and the conventionally just in each case. When a court is called upon to adjudicate on what is due to whom, it always does so in the context of either distributive or rectificatory justice, but never in reciprocal justice, which is confined to exchanges that make up the trading order. Commercial disputes fall for consideration by courts as matters of rectificatory or distributive justice even if it is sometimes debatable which of these is at issue. What is always crucial is the underlying question: what is due to whom?

4.4 Distributive Justice

The just situation is achieved when each has what is due. When that situation is achieved the situation is for the moment just and stable. For a variety of reasons,

---

[29] See HLA Hart, *The Concept of Law* (ed P Bulloch and J Raz) (Oxford: Clarendon Press, 2nd edn with Postscript, 1994), 82–91.

[30] Obligation is discussed further in ch 7, the force of law in ch 10, and authority and legitimacy in ch 12 below.

including the fact that human living is constantly changing, a just and stable situation may never be reached. The virtue of justice is the enduring determination to give to each what is due which supposes that at any particular time what is due has yet to be given; in other words, the stable just situation is what is to be achieved; and, indeed, if one considers all humans at any moment there is never such a stable situation. In the remaining sections of this chapter and in Chapter 5 the three types of justice are discussed separately: distributive justice in the present section; rectificatory justice in the next section; and reciprocal justice in Chapter 5.

Distributive justice arises when shares in what is commonly owned are to be distributed among those who share the ownership of it.[31] Commonplace instances of distributive justice are easy to find. In a raffle or lottery the ticket holders are joint owners of the exercise that will distribute the prizes among them according to some agreed method of random selection. Somewhat similarly, shareholders in a firm own shares in the firm, and receive an annual dividend according to a criterion – in this case, according to the number of shares held. What they are jointly entitled to is that the criterion be used. In an examination, marks are awarded to candidates relative to the quality of their papers. Each candidate is entitled not only to the mark due but also to the examination being fairly and competently administered: each candidate's entitlement is not simply that his own marks but also that others' marks be fair. In cases of separation or divorce, what the couple jointly own is to be divided between them according to some more or less explicit criterion or set of criteria that may be agreed between them or determined by the court in the light of their joint assets and commitments, and of the jurisprudential context. Similarly, the allocation of public offices among eligible candidates is a prime instance of distributive justice.

No question of distributive justice properly arises unless what is to be distributed is jointly owned by those between whom it is to be distributed.[32] It is, of course, perfectly possible to imagine a case where nothing whatsoever is jointly owned or shared between two or more people; and in such a case, obviously, no dispute about the just distribution of what is jointly owned or shared can arise. Whether or not there ever has been a human society in which nothing whatsoever was jointly owned or shared is an historical question,[33] but were such

[31] As we saw in ch 3.2, this justice is the theme of Rawls's *A Theory of Justice*. Rawls imagines a situation in which the idea of ownership is accepted but in which no one yet owns anything, and he addresses the question of what the most just distribution of wealth and income would be.

[32] All questions arise upon presuppositions. Thus, the question, 'How shall we share this among us?' arises upon the presupposition, however it is arrived at, that 'this' belongs jointly to us. On questions and presuppositions, see RG Collingwood, *An Essay on Metaphysics* (Oxford: Clarendon Press, 1940). Cf T Murphy and R Weber, 'Confucianizing Socrates and Socratizing Confucius – On Comparing *Analects* 13:18 and the *Euthyphro*' (2010) 60 *Philosophy East and West* 187.

[33] In the great communist upheaval of ownership in the twentieth century, the ownership of land and other sources of wealth shifted from private individuals or the *mir* to the state. Nonetheless, as we have noted (in ch 3.2 above), there were questions of distributive justice under communism; such questions arose in the first instance because state or publicly owned positions had to be distributed.

a society to exist no questions of distributive justice could arise within it. For the most part, however, no less than ownership by individuals, common or joint or shared ownership does exist, although what precisely is commonly or jointly owned or shared, and how it is owned differs from society to society and, within the one society, from time to time.[34]

Distributive justice is not benevolence, and does not supplant benevolence, as a simple example illustrates. If a group of children is given a bar of chocolate, the children in the group commonly own the chocolate, and each is entitled to a share when it is distributed among them. If they consider themselves as equals for this purpose – they will not, and cannot be, equals for all purposes – they will conclude that each should receive an equal share. This is an example of distributive justice, and each member of the group has a right or entitlement to his share. But if one of a group of children has a bar of chocolate that properly belongs to him, he may or may not decide to share it with the others. If he decides to share it with them, this is an example of benevolence because none of the others has a right or entitlement to a share.

Questions and disputes in the realm of distributive justice most often arise within the generally accepted prevailing context, although the prevailing context itself may at times become a matter of dispute. Whatever the context, distribution is necessarily according to a more or less explicit set of criteria. Two questions, therefore, arise in every discussion or dispute about distributive justice. First, was the distribution made according to the relevant set of criteria? Secondly, is the set of criteria just? Suppose that several people apply for one position. Clearly, since there is only one position available they do not jointly own the position. What they jointly own is the method according to which the position is awarded. Distributive justice requires that each be treated *equally according to the criteria in place.* The distributively just allocation is reached when each has what is due according to the criteria. Another example is when shareholders in a firm receive dividends according to the number of shares held. Someone who is not a shareholder and who applied or sued for the payment of a dividend would be unsuccessful but nonetheless treated equally according to the criterion in place. Similarly, a shareholder who applied or sued for a greater dividend than corresponded to the number of his shares would not succeed but would nonetheless be treated equally; for distributive justice, as we have said, operates necessarily according to a set of criteria. Disputes about equality, then, are either about the interpretation and application of the criteria or about their justice.

Is the set of criteria just? That the shareholders in a firm receive dividends according to the number of shares held is the prevailing criterion. Is it just? The question is not whether or not there should be firms, whether or not there

---

[34] Forms of common or joint or shared ownership are in this sense no different from ownership *simpliciter.* See the discussion of different types of ownership in different types of society in ch 3.2 above.

should be shareholders or whether or not there should be dividends. The question is simply this: in the context of there being firms with shareholders who receive dividends is it just that each shareholder should receive a dividend related to the number of shares held by that shareholder? There is certainly an element of convention or agreement. If someone buys shares in a firm he knows that it has been decided to sell part of the firm in this way, that one who buys shares becomes a shareholder and is entitled to an annual dividend related to the number of shares bought. This is what is offered for sale, and what he has agreed to buy.[35] Is the agreement that dividends be paid according to the number of shares held just? If it is just, is it just only because that criterion has been agreed or is it because it is consonant with an understanding of the nature of the situation? When, say, a firm in its entirety is divided into 1,000 shares that are then offered separately for sale, each share is one thousandth part of the firm. When the shares have been sold each shareholder has the number of shares that he has bought. It may be that not every shareholder will pay the same price per share; indeed, it may happen that a single buyer will buy shares at different prices. Nonetheless, what each one buys is a share in the firm, and the dividend is not paid according to the price paid for a particular share, but according to an agreed proportion of the firm's annual profit, if any. Each share will attract the same dividend because there is no relevant difference between one share and another, and, therefore, no reason to associate different dividends with different shares. The shares are relevantly equal and the shareholders relevantly comparable on the basis of the number of shares held. Consequently, the criterion that a dividend payment be related to the number of shares held is, in the nature of the case, just.[36]

It is commonly the case that shareholders will have bought shares at different prices. It is also often true that a single shareholder will have bought some of his shares at one price, and some at another. Why is this difference considered to be irrelevant to the payment of dividends per share? A very pedestrian example will illustrate why this should be so and, at the same time, reveal a presupposition in the example. Suppose that each of 10 people buy from the confectioner the entitlement to a number of slices of a cake that is to be divided into 30 equal parts. When the slices are distributed each will receive the number of slices to which he is entitled. But it may happen that before the distribution takes place, an eleventh person offers one of the original ten more money for some or all of his entitlement than

---

[35] The dividend is related to the number of shares bought and not to the amount of money that the shareholder has invested in the firm, which, had he bought his shares from an existing shareholder and not as a new issue, is nil. (If Peter buys shares from Paul, he pays Paul and not the firm. In a new issue the firm itself sells the shares and the money goes to the firm.)

[36] Neither in the original flotation or a new issue nor in the resale of shares is the price set a matter of distributive justice. It is, rather, as we discuss in the next chapter, a matter of reciprocal justice and, as such, paradigmatically conventional or by agreement. Again, distributive justice concerns only what is in some sense commonly owned.

he had paid.[37] If the offer is accepted, the eleventh person will pay more for each slice than had the original buyers, but that is considered to be irrelevant because he is given precisely what he has bought, namely, the entitlement to a defined number of slices (shares in the cake). The presupposition at work here is that each of the original 10 buyers is entitled to sell the slices that he has bought. This is not always the case with something that has been bought and is jointly owned, as when two people buy and jointly own a house it may well not be open to either one to sell his interest in the joint property without the consent of the other.

Another example of distributive justice will bring to light further conventional elements. In modern democracies members of parliament are elected but precisely how they are to be elected is not identical as between different states but is rather settled conventionally and posited by law. In some democracies, for example, candidates are elected in a 'first past the post' system, that is, there is in each constituency one seat, each elector has one vote, there is a single round, and the candidate who receives most votes is elected; in others there is some form of proportional representation based on an open or closed party-list system; in yet others the proportional representational system in place is linked with single transferable voting; and so on. Whatever the electoral system chosen, distributive justice demands that each candidate be treated equally according to the criteria in place.

Who is to be an elector? Again this is a matter of agreement and again agreement is not merely arbitrary. The history of the development of the several answers to this question is undoubtedly subtle and it would be naïve to suppose that bias and prejudice has played no part. To be an elector is to have some influence, however small, on political power in the polity but certainly to have more influence than one who is not an elector. Hence, established electors may be tempted to resist the enlargement of the franchise that would see their influence diluted, and may also be tempted to resist the franchise being given to those whom they expect to oppose their interests. It might seem that all those who are affected by the decisions of parliament ought to be electors but this, on reflection, is absurd. Nobody suggests that infants are to be enfranchised, and yet they are, often greatly, affected by political decisions. So is introduced the idea that electors ought to be capable of responsible choice. Once that idea gains currency, a decision to exclude some person or type of person who is capable of responsible choice becomes dubious. Nor does its dubious character seem to be merely conventional; once again it seems to be related to the nature of the situation. On the criterion of capacity for responsible choice, that infants ought to be excluded is obvious, but the age at which young people ought to be enfranchised is necessarily to an extent conventional. It is worth remembering that one of the reasons put forward in Europe to

---

[37] It is equally possible for one of the original ten to offer to buy shares in the cake from another member of the original group, in which case he may well pay more (or less) for these shares than he paid for those he already holds.

defend the exclusion of women from the electorate was that women were either incapable or relevantly less capable of responsibility than were men. What is true of the exclusion of women is true of the exclusion of many other types of people. Bias typically and commonly seeks rationalization.

Other questions arise that have to do not with a potential elector's capacity for responsible choice but with his association with the state in which the election is to take place. No one, for example, suggests that tourists who happen to be visiting when a parliamentary election is taking place should be enfranchised. The question as to whether non-citizen residents should be electors is more controversial. Ought a non-citizen resident who has been in the state for 10 years be enfranchised and one who has been there for only one year excluded? Are non-resident citizens to be disenfranchised? If yes, after how long a period of non-residence?

Distributive justice is always according to a criterion. Everyone is to be treated equally according to the criterion and the criterion itself ought to be the fruit of intelligent, reasonable, and responsible enquiry, judgment, and decision. Thus, underlying the choice of criterion is the inescapable demand to be intelligent, reasonable, and responsible. Because everyone is to be treated equally according to the criterion, we add that equality is, as it were, the default position or base line from which to depart requires a reason. A criterion that distinguishes one person from another requires a reason; so the electoral criterion distinguishes infants from responsible adults, the justifying reason being that capacity or lack of capacity for responsible choice enables or disables a person from carrying out the task. But it is obvious that this criterion does not distinguish residents from citizens or non-citizen residents from non-resident citizens. To make that distinction some other criterion is needed and that criterion in turn demands justification.

In sum, then, distributive justice is the distribution according to some criterion of what is commonly owned among those who own it.

4.5 Rectificatory Justice

Rectificatory justice – also known as corrective or commutative justice – comes into play when one person has, *rightly or wrongly*, what *belongs* to another. Again, examples of this type of justice are ready to hand and commonplace. Suppose that Peter goes to a restaurant and, after his dinner, leaves, taking with him by mistake, the umbrella that belongs to Paul. Peter now possesses what belongs to Paul. He does not yet know this, having taken the umbrella in error. Paul may not yet have discovered his loss. No one, perhaps, yet knows what is, in fact, the case. It begins to rain and Peter puts up what he thinks is his umbrella only to discover that it is not. He now knows that he has in his possession an umbrella that, justly, belongs to another. He knows, too, that the just situation will be restored if he brings the umbrella back to the restaurant, discovers who owns it, restores it to its owner, and collects his own umbrella. The unjust situation would then be rectified. It is important to notice that a situation may be unjust although no one has knowingly or willingly acted unjustly. In other words, an unjust situation may be brought about by accident or mistake.

Suppose, now, a situation similar in some respects. After his dinner, Peter goes to the umbrella stand, sees another's umbrella that he prefers to his own, takes it and leaves. Once again, he possesses what belongs to another. The difference is that he knows this and, having no interest in justice, has no intention of rectifying the unjust situation. Whether or not the situation can be rectified and, if it can, how it is to be rectified, are important questions but they are different questions from the question of justice. The answer to the question of justice – 'what is due to whom?' – is, again, that the owner of the umbrella is entitled to the return of his umbrella.

In both cases, Peter has, wrongly, what belongs to another; unknowingly and indeliberately in the first case; knowingly and deliberately in the second. In both cases, the situation is unjust. The possibility of an unjust situation, and so a need for rectificatory justice, rests on things being owned. Peter can neither take in error nor steal Paul's umbrella unless Paul owns the umbrella. If, quite literally, nothing in any way whatsoever belongs to anyone then to steal is impossible, and no question of what is just or unjust can arise. A rule against stealing would be irrelevant and literally unintelligible where there was no ownership, where there was no idea of ownership, and where nothing in any sense belonged to anyone at any time. Stealing is traditionally thought to be naturally unjust. This must mean that where there is ownership, stealing is unjust, and that, in turn, must mean that the ideas of ownership and of stealing fit together. Just as one cannot understand stealing without understanding ownership, so the understanding of ownership includes an understanding that stealing is unjust, that is, it includes an understanding of the fact that stealing brings about an unjust situation. Someone convinced that it was in no sense unjust that Peter took Paul's umbrella simply does not understand what is meant when the umbrella is said to belong to Paul.[38]

A comparison of two situations can show the distinction between the conventional and the natural in the context of rectificatory justice and indeed more generally. Suppose that Peter and Paul live in a community in which there is a legitimately formulated rule, command, or law against stealing. If Peter steals Paul's umbrella he has broken the rule. Suppose that they live in a community in which there is a legitimately formulated rule requiring that they make their tax return annually. If Peter fails to make his return he has broken the rule. The question about the natural and the conventional is whether the two situations are

---

[38] Again, it is important to distinguish between, on the one hand, the fact that stealing brings about an unjust situation and, on the other hand, the moral demand and the decision not to steal. A person may well recognize that his action will bring about an unjust situation without agreeing that he ought not, or will not, bring it about.

similar in that both may be adequately described by saying that in each case Peter broke a rule.

In fact, the first situation is natural, and the second conventional. The rule governing the making of tax returns is conventional: 'it is originally indifferent but when it has been laid down it is not indifferent' that tax returns be made annually.[39] The rule against stealing, on the other hand, is thought to be an understanding of, and a formulation forbidding, an act that is naturally or intrinsically unjust and that no human decision can make just.[40] An understanding, not of human nature but of the nature of the situation, discovers what is naturally or intrinsically just or unjust. This is what St Thomas means when he writes that the just is 'in the thing', that is, it is discovered by an examination of the situation or case.[41] It is worth looking at two types of situation in some detail: first, stealing; and secondly, lending and borrowing.

In a society where people own things, is it entirely a matter of command and convention that stealing is unjust or is stealing unjust because stealing is incompatible with owning? The question needs some commentary. First, it must be stressed again that the question of stealing arises only in a society in which things are owned. Secondly, to own something means more than merely to possess it. For Robinson Crusoe, living alone on a desert island, 'to possess' and 'to own' are synonymous or nearly so.[42] Were a man to spend his entire life alone – something in reality impossible – he would have no occasion to distinguish between ownership and possession. The very idea of ownership would not occur to him for ownership is essentially a social thing and as we have seen there is, in every human society, a recognized idea of ownership and, generally, a fairly good and fairly detailed idea as to who owns what. Thirdly, if each person quietly and agreeably possesses what he owns, neither more nor less, then the situation is just. Fourthly, what constitutes stealing is determined by what constitutes ownership and it is utterly crucial to remember that ownership is a bundle of entitlements, and that what constitutes the bundle differs from society to society.[43] We may now recall the question: In a society where people own things is it entirely a matter of command and convention that stealing is unjust or is stealing unjust because stealing

---

[39] Aristotle, *Nicomachean Ethics*, V.1134b.19. See ch 4.3 above.

[40] St Thomas Aquinas, *Summa Theologiae*, II–II, q 57, art 2.

[41] Ibid, II-II, q 58, art 10. See M Villey, 'La nature des choses' in *Seize essais*, 38–59. The phrase 'in the thing' is a literal translation of *in re*; *res* and *in re* may also be translated as 'the case' and 'in the case'. See ch 1 above.

[42] We say that for Crusoe 'to own' and 'to possess' were nearly identical. The caveat 'nearly' is needed because Crusoe was not in fact the only human ever to have existed. He lived isolated on the island but, having been brought to adulthood in society, knew that he owned what he possessed, and were he to come into contact with others, which in the story occurred, possession would be at once dominantly experienced as ownership.

[43] There are societies where no particular parcel of land is 'owned', as ownership is now generally understood, by a particular person; but there are none in which the land on which a people lives is *in no sense* 'owned', in no sense 'theirs'. There is always, in other words, ownership of land in that entitlements are associated with land.

is incompatible with owning? Or, to put it another way: Is a rule against steal-ing – for example, 'Thou shalt not steal' – simply *added on* to ownership, or is it intrinsic to it?

The argument for the assertion that to steal is intrinsically unjust is, in essence, very simple.

If Peter now possesses what he owns, there is a just situation.

If what he owns is taken from him against his will, he remains the owner of it but no longer possesses it, and there is an unjust situation.

An act that brings about an unjust situation is unjust.

Stealing brings about an unjust situation.

Therefore, stealing is unjust.

The argument for the assertion that to steal is not intrinsically unjust is likewise simple:

If Peter now possesses what he owns, there is simply a factual situation.

If what he owns is taken from him against his will he remains the owner of it, and there is simply a different factual situation.

An act that brings about simply a different factual situation is intrinsically indifferent.

Stealing brings about simply a different factual situation.

Therefore, stealing is intrinsically indifferent.

The difference between the arguments is clear. The first premise in the first argu-ment expresses an understanding and acceptance of ownership, and of the dif-ference between it and possession. In the first premise of the second argument, there is no more than a verbal difference between possession and ownership. In both arguments it is presumed that if Peter now possesses X, there is a factual situation that is correctly described in the proposition: 'Peter now possesses X'. In the first argument, a jural universe is presupposed which allows a distinction between the non-jural fact, 'Peter now possesses X', and the jural fact, 'Peter owns X'. Ownership is a jural fact; in Neil MacCormick's terms, an institutional fact; in Gaius's terms, an incorporeal thing, a thing that cannot be touched, a right.[44]

We suggest – in line with the first argument – that it is intrinsic to the idea of ownership that the situation is just when the owner of something possesses what he owns, and unjust when he does not. We suggest also that what is meant by 'naturally just' and 'naturally unjust' is 'intrinsic to the situation'. In most cases, in principle, it is just that the owner quietly possesses what he owns; in most cases

---

[44] N MacCormick, *Institutions of Law* (Oxford: Oxford University Press, 2007), 11–14, 163–4, 243, 289–93, and 304. Gaius, *Institutes*, ii.14. What one owns may be material – a house, an umbrella, a cricket bat – but that one owns it is non-material; to claim that one owns X is to assert a right; to own something is to possess it *right*fully – to possess not only the material object but also the title to it. See the discussion of rights as jural relations in ch 9.2 below.

to deprive him of this quiet possession is to produce an unjust situation; and in most cases, to deprive him of this quiet possession is to steal.[45]

In the examples we have discussed thus far we have considered situations in which one person has wrongly in his possession what belongs to another person. It may happen, of course, that one person has in his possession – but *rightly* – what belongs to another person, as in lending and borrowing. Suppose that Peter borrows a book from Paul. Peter now has the book in his possession and intends to read it before returning it. Paul has agreed to this arrangement. He is still the owner of the book. As long as Peter has the book he has, as a matter of fact, something that belongs to another. There is no injustice here but the situation is temporary – it can be described as provisional, unstable, or anticipatory – for, eventually, the book is to be restored to Paul. Aristotle thinks of a case of this kind – its technical name being 'a loan for use' – as one involving voluntary rectificatory justice and it is important to note that there is no injustice, which arises *only* if the borrower refuses to return what has been borrowed.[46] The practice of lending and borrowing, where it exists, exists within a context of ownership but when something is borrowed for use, the borrower not the lender – the original owner – temporarily possesses what is borrowed.

Is the understanding of the practice of lending and borrowing an understanding of what is naturally or of what is only conventionally just? The practice itself is conventional in two distinct ways. First, and indisputably, a single case of lending and borrowing is conventional in that it is a convention or contract between lender and borrower. Secondly, that the practice of lending and borrowing exists in a particular society at a particular time is conventional in that it is quite possible to imagine a human society in which the practice simply does not occur. Whether such a society exists or has ever existed is an empirical question in historical social anthropology. But it is worth reflecting on the fact that the practice emerges just as soon as two people decide to engage in it, and becomes commonplace as others take it up; it requires no central power or state to establish it.

Is there a justice intrinsic to – that is, inherent in, essential to, or natural to – the practice of lending and borrowing? We answer unequivocally that there is. The practice of lending and borrowing has a nature where the term 'nature' is used as it is in such questions as 'What is the nature of a free fall?' or 'What is the nature of tidal movement?' The idea that there is a justice intrinsic to the

---

[45] The argument that to steal is intrinsically unjust may be very simple but, as happens in human living, there are difficult cases. The recurrent classical and medieval example of a difficult or special case is that of the enraged owner of a sword who demands that his sword be returned to him by its borrower in order that he might do ill with it, or that of the enemy who demands the return of his weapon in order that he may continue to wage war against the city. As we have already noted (in ch 3.3 above, when we discussed the issue of discovering the just), the traditional name for the effort to discover what is just when the particular case does not fit easily into the mould of what is just for the most part is *epieikeia* in Greek, *aequitas* in Latin, and, from Latin, in English, 'equity'. We discuss this in the context of adjudication and interpretation in ch 6.5 below.

[46] Aristotle, *Nicomachean Ethics*, V.1131b.25.

practice of lending and borrowing rests on the idea that the practice cannot properly be understood without understanding the relations of justice established between borrower and lender, that is, without understanding that lending and borrowing is intrinsically – inherently, essentially, naturally – a coherent set of such relations.

What, then, *is* the practice of lending and borrowing? It involves two persons – one or both of whom may be legal persons, for example, a library – one of whom lends the thing borrowed by the other. The thing lent passes from the present possession of the owner-lender to the present possession of the borrower. What distinguishes this practice from gift-giving or stealing, both of which involve the passing of possession from one person to another, is precisely the jural relations that are established in the transfer, and that both lender and borrower understand and accept. What distinguishes lending and borrowing from gift-giving is that the thing – *or an agreed equivalent* – is to be returned to the owner-lender. This jural relation, established in the act of lending and borrowing, is not a rule added to the practice but what is naturally just in, or intrinsic to, the practice. It is discovered explicitly, as we always make discoveries, by examining carefully and trying to understand the practice but it is implicitly understood or presupposed by those engaged in the practice. Were a borrower not to understand that what he had borrowed was to be returned, he would not, as far as he knew, have borrowed it but perhaps would have thought that he had been given a present. The jural world is understood not seen.

The phrase 'or an agreed equivalent' had to be included when we referred to the returning of something by a borrower to a lender because there are, in fact, two types of thing that can be lent. First, there is the loan of something that is used without being consumed in the use of it, and so the identical thing rather than its equivalent can be returned; for example, if one borrows a book or a car or, to take the common Roman example, a horse, one is expected to return the same book, car, or horse. This is a 'loan for use', of the kind we have been discussing. Secondly, there is the loan of something that the borrower wants not only to use but to consume. So, if one borrows milk or coffee or the like one expects that these will be consumed and cannot be returned. This is a 'loan for consumption'.

Who now owns the milk if Paul borrows a bottle of milk from Peter? Does Peter still own the bottle of milk that Paul has borrowed from him? Let us suppose, as would normally be the case, that Paul intends to consume the milk. The answer in Roman jurisprudence is that Paul becomes the owner of the milk. In general, in a loan for consumption, what is lent becomes the property of the borrower:

An obligation is contracted in the actual transaction, as for example, in a loan for consumption. This always consists of things which may be weighed, numbered or measured, as wine, oil, corn, brass, silver or gold. In giving these things by number or measure, we so give them that they become the property of those who receive them. And identical things are not returned, but only others of the same nature and quality.[47]

Normally, when Peter lends Paul a bottle of milk, he no longer owns what he has lent. What does he now own? And Paul, while he does own the bottle of milk, is not simply in the position he would be had he bought it, or had he been given a present of it. What else, in addition to the milk, does he now own? He owns a debt. In fact, *both* Peter and Paul own a debt; one as creditor, one as debtor. This is what in the situation is naturally just. Again, it is in the nature of a debt that it be paid, that is, it is naturally just that Paul extinguish his debt to Peter. But *when* precisely is it naturally just to extinguish the debt? It would be absurd if two minutes after Paul had borrowed the milk, Peter called at his home to demand that the debt be now repaid. Equally, it would be absurd were Paul to suppose that he could repay the debt in 20 years' time. A common expectation develops in a community – normally, if one borrows a bottle of milk the expectation in most places is that the debt be repaid within a few days, or within an agreed time. This is the element of the conventionally, yet not arbitrarily or capriciously, just.

In the loan for use the identical thing borrowed is to be returned to the lender. If Paul borrows a book from Peter, it is naturally just that he return the identical book. It is naturally just because that is what is meant in the practice of a loan for use. When is the book to be returned? This may be explicitly agreed, as when books are lent and borrowed from a library, or it may be generally understood. Peter will normally lend the book so that Paul may read it, and so the anticipated length of time that it takes to read the book is included in the transaction. Another good and clear example of this is when, at a lecture, one student lends a pen to another student who is without one. The assumption, usually mutually understood, is that the borrower wants to use the pen during the lecture only, and not for the entire day, week, year, or duration of the whole course. In a 'loan for use' the lender remains the owner of the thing lent. The borrower owns, for a time, the use of the thing borrowed and the obligation to return it in good order:

A person to whom a thing ... is lent that he may make use of it ... [differs greatly from] the person who has received a loan for consumption; for the thing is not given to him that it may become his property, and he therefore is bound to restore the identical thing he received ... and he is indeed bound to employ the utmost diligence in keeping and preserving it; nor will it suffice that he should take the same care of it, which he was accustomed to take of his own property, if it appears that a more careful person might have preserved it in safety.[48]

---

[47] Justinian, *Institutes*, III.XIV.Preamble. What we have translated as 'An obligation is contracted in the actual transaction' is *Re contrahitur obligatio*: the idea is that in a *mandatum* or loan for consumption the obligation is contracted when the thing is handed over.

[48] Ibid, III.XIV.2.

The first part of this quotation describes the 'loan for use'. It does not establish the practice for the first time but rather formulates in writing a practice that is already common. Precisely how, when, and where the practice arose cannot now be discovered for lack of evidence. But why it arose can be known, because why it arose is why it survived: the practice of lending and borrowing for use was discovered to be useful in the course of human living where, quite commonly, not everyone at every moment has everything he needs. A person borrows a pen because he now needs, but has not now got, a pen.

But the quotation does more than simply describe a loan for use. In a loan for use the borrower does not own the thing borrowed – as he does in a loan for consumption – and, precisely because he does not, a question as to how to treat what he has borrowed arises, and is dealt with in the latter part of the passage quoted. It can happen that the thing borrowed gets accidentally destroyed, for example, in a fire, for which the borrower may be in no way responsible and, again in the nature of the case, the question as to what is then due between owner-lender and borrower arises. It can happen that the thing borrowed deteriorates while it is in the possession of the borrower and, again naturally, the question arises as to what is now due. The Roman jurisprudents suggest that, following an examination of the kind of practice that lending and borrowing is, the borrower is bound to take good care of what is borrowed, precisely because, in a loan for use, he does not own it. The Roman answer remains in the French *Code Civil*.[49] In most jurisdictions, one who rents accommodation is bound to return it in good order except for normal 'wear and tear'; typically it is required by law that this be a part of tenancy agreements. This answer reflects the expectation of lenders and borrowers for normally no one would lend his car to someone who, he confidently expected, would drive it so badly that the likelihood of its being returned in good order was minimal.

The purpose of this examination of the practice of lending and borrowing is to show that what is naturally just is what is intrinsic to a practice and not some supervening law imposed upon it. The formulation, the written law, expresses the understanding of the practice, and deals with some of the problems that have arisen and are likely to arise in the future. For it happens that what is borrowed is destroyed or broken or badly treated, and further questions as to what is due arise. Some of these questions will reveal what is naturally just and some what is 'originally indifferent' and to be solved by the establishment of some convention or agreement. What is crucial is that what is naturally just is not discovered by consulting some higher law nor by consulting human nature but by examining and trying to understand the jural nature of the 'thing', the case.

---

[49] *Code Civil*, III.X.I.II.1880: 'L'emprunteur est tenu de veiller, en bon père de famille, à la garde et à la conservation de la chose prêtée.' ('The borrower is bound to watch over, like a good father of the family, the security and preservation of the thing lent.')

We may now return to the familiar legal question, referred to at the outset of Chapter 3, as to who owns what in a case where someone buys, or otherwise obtains, and has worked, land from another whom he believes to be the owner but who in fact turns out not to be. Justinian's *Institutes* give an answer to the question and to some issues to which the situation gives rise. Who owns the land? Who owns the produce of the work put in by the person who has worked the land in good faith? It is worth quoting and commenting upon the suggested answer to show more clearly that the naturally just here has nothing to do with appeal to some higher law but is discovered through a jurisprudential enquiry into the situation:

> If anyone has in good faith purchased land from another, whom he believed to be the true owner, when in fact he was not, or has in good faith acquired it from such a person by gift or by any other good title, natural reason demands that the fruits that he has gathered shall be his in return for his care and culture. And, therefore, if the true owner afterwards appears and claims his land, he can have no action for fruits which the possessor has consumed. But the same allowance is not made to him who has knowingly been in possession of another's land; and, therefore, he is compelled to restore, together with the lands, all the fruits although they may have been consumed.[50]

First, it is obvious that the question arises only within a society in which land is privately owned, bought, sold, given as a gift or the like. Secondly, private ownership of land, like any other kind of ownership, is jural or institutional. Ownership is a jural relationship between people, not a physical description of an action or situation; hence, in the quotation above, the distinctions between ownership, possession, and usufruct are distinguished.[51] Thirdly, the specific question to which this is an answer is not in fact whether or not the land should be restored to its owner. That is here taken as settled. The specific question is: who owns the produce of the land? The possessor, who possesses the land in good faith, who thinks that he owns it but in fact does not, has worked and cultivated the land; the produce or fruits of the land are the fruits of his work. Who owns these? Is it the owner or the possessor in good faith? The suggestion here is that the possessor in good faith who has worked the land is entitled to the fruits that he has gathered. A moment's reflection will provoke further questions. What, for instance, is just if the possessor in good faith has ploughed but not yet sown when the true

---

[50] Justinian, *Institutes*, II.I.35. It is worth noting that the clause 'natural reason demands' translates '*naturali ratione placuit*' which is precisely the locution used when it is laid down in I.II.6 that 'That also which has been decided Emperor has the force of law' (*quod principi placuit*). Both may be translated by 'what is resolved or agreed on', 'what is decided by', or 'what is demanded by'. Although the conjunction of the Emperor's will and the force of law is often associated with the Roman jurist, Ulpian (fl AD 211–222), and with positivism, there is no suggestion in Roman law that a purely arbitrary or tyrannical decision is as good as any other.

[51] In Latin 'ownership' is *dominium*; the 'owner' is the *dominus* or 'lord' – from which we get 'landlord'; 'possession' is *possessio*; the English word 'usufruct', no longer in common use, is from the Latin meaning 'use of the fruits or produce'; the one who is entitled to usufruct is the 'usufructuary' – again no longer in common use but which in some ways resembles the modern 'tenant'.

owner claims the land? What if the crops are ripening but not yet harvested? Again these are questions as to what is just, as to who is entitled to what. They are questions that arise from the nature of the case. Some solutions will discern what is naturally, and some what is conventionally, just.

The text states that this is what 'natural reason demands'. Natural reason is not an appeal to some higher law or to some hidden axiom; it is simply that it seemed to the Roman jurists from an examination of the situation that the possessor in good faith owns those fruits that are the result of his care and culture. But why should this be? The argument seems to be that an owner who works his land is naturally entitled to its fruits; that someone who rents the land that he works is entitled to its fruits once he has paid the rent due to the owner; and that in this context the possessor in good faith is sufficiently like an owner or like one who has genuinely rented land to be entitled to the fruits of his labour. The opinion – fallible and tentative – arises from a careful consideration of the case. The possessor in bad faith who has knowingly been in possession of another's land is not entitled to the fruits of his labour because he is insufficiently like an owner or usufructuary. To say that this solution is 'natural' simply means that it appears to the reasonable and responsible enquirer to be rooted in the nature of the case. But there will also be situations where what is just does not appear from an examination of the case and must be settled by decision or convention. As we have been said, the *method* of investigation and discovery is always intelligent enquiry into the situation, not recourse to some higher law. Finally, no solution – whether natural or conventional – that is not known and accepted can have purchase in the community.

The theory of the naturally and conventionally just worked out here is not a doctrine but a method, an approach to the discovery of what is just. We may now turn to the third type of justice, namely, reciprocal justice, which is the justice involved in the individual exchanges of one thing for another that make up the trading order.

5

Justice and the Trading Order

5.1 Introduction

Reciprocal justice – justice in exchange – is the justice proper to the trading order in which people make their livelihoods in a market society. In this chapter we concentrate on the analysis of that justice but also refer to the relationship between the reciprocal justice proper to trading and justice in the political and social orders. Our task in this chapter is the modest one of showing, first, what reciprocal justice is; secondly, that it is the justice intrinsic to trade; thirdly, that it cannot bring about any particular desired distribution of wealth; and fourthly, that it cannot resolve all socio-political problems.

A trading or market order is constituted by an indefinitely large number of exchanges between an indefinitely large number of people each of whom may, in theory at least, trade indefinitely many times with any other. Ownership is prior to trade: trading orders emerge within a surrounding socio-political context in which people own things that they are prepared to trade for things others own and are prepared to trade. The function of a trading order is to facilitate the reassignment of ownership, and requires that traders own, and are recognized, at least between the trading partners, to own, what they propose to trade.[1] Justice – the giving to each what is due – within the trading order is not, and cannot be, concerned with the overall outcome at any given time of the assignment of participants' resources. Justice within the trading order is reciprocal and concerned only with the justice involved in the individual transactions that constitute the order.

We begin the chapter with some preliminary remarks that are intended to provide background for our analysis of reciprocal justice by placing the trading order in its social context. We suggest that *in the trading order free exchanges are reciprocally just*. Reciprocal justice, by definition, exists *only* in the context of exchange and the trading order (which is the set of exchanges). It is, however, crucial to recognize that a trading order governed solely by reciprocal justice does not exist.

---

[1] Readers may detect a difficulty in the suggestion that traders must own what they propose to trade. Is it not possible for two thieves to trade between themselves what each acknowledges the other does not own? We shall discuss this issue, which we describe as 'pseudo-ownership', in ch 5.4 below.

No trading order exists in a vacuum: trading orders exist as one order – along with, for example, jural, linguistic, and many other orders – within the broader, all-encompassing social order. Within the larger social and political order, trading will, almost inevitably, have consequences that within the restricted context of the trading order itself are simply consequences, but within the all-encompassing social and political order may be, and often are, grave social problems.

Reciprocal justice is the justice involved in free exchange and we examine the complementary roles of nature and convention in this type of justice. Trading is conventional in that there cannot be a genuine trade except by mutual agreement, contract, or convention between the trading partners. Where either partner is compelled, there may be the appearance of trade but, in reality, there is not. When two partners trade with each other they establish themselves in a jural relationship; this is not added on to the trading but is intrinsic to it. Trading is a jural fact arising out of the establishment of a jural relationship. Not only is reciprocal justice conventional in that what is reciprocally just is determined in the transaction by agreement or convention between the trading partners, but it is also natural to exchange in that it is not added on to an exchange; in other words, the exchange would not take place without the partners being satisfied: the exchange is reciprocally just when and because it is mutually agreed. Paradoxically, what is natural to exchange is that the justice intrinsic or natural to it is conventional: a mutually satisfactory agreement constitutes the reciprocally just. But there are non-conventional elements natural or intrinsic to exchange, namely, first, that the person who proposes to trade a thing must both own and be entitled to alienate it, for what is traded is not only the thing but title to the thing, and, secondly, that what is proposed for trade is not fraudulently presented, as might be, for example, counterfeit money.

The elements of exchange are then examined and this involves a more precise analysis of the elements of both natural and conventional justice in the single transaction. A great deal of debate about exchanges in the trading order focuses on issues of coercion, rationality, and freedom. We emphasize that coercion in exchange is brought about by the use or threat of direct or indirect force. Where such coercion exists there is no free exchange and so no reciprocal justice. It is sometimes said that humans do not always act rationally when they trade. We contend, however, that when someone chooses freely to trade X for Y he chooses rationally *at the time of choosing* and that, therefore, reciprocal justice does exist in the exchange. Similarly, to choose to engage in trade is to choose freely to exchange, to work within the province of reciprocal justice.

We continue our analysis by showing how the trading or market order is simply the order of indefinitely many exchanges among indefinitely many people; it has a function, which is to allow participants to pursue their trading goals, but has itself no goal. Trading reallocates goods between participants, and their allocation at one time will not be their allocation at a later time. No particular later allocation can be expected, and any later allocation will not be just otherwise than being that brought about by the many reciprocally just transactions that took place between the earlier and the later time. The common good of the trading order is not a particular outcome but the reciprocally just working of the order, the function of which is to allow the fulfilment of many purposes. The most immediate social function of a trading order is to allow trading partners to gain what each wants by exchanging for it what each values less highly and so to make their living by trading.

Our discussion then moves to an account of the *lex mercatoria* or 'law merchant'. Although a trading order emerges within a surrounding context, the temptation to imagine that context to be necessarily an already established jurisdiction, community, society, nation, town, or village must be resisted. The trading order is essentially trans-jurisdictional and is simply the set of exchanges between those who trade. The *lex mercatoria* or 'law merchant' is the set of customary norms governing the trans-jurisdictional trading order. The relation between reciprocal justice and entitlements in the trading order is then discussed. Within the surrounding context of ownership there are entitlements that have nothing, or need have nothing, to do with trading; there are entitlements intrinsically associated with trade, namely, rules according to which the order works; and within particular jurisdictions there are particular entitlements, restrictions, or impositions extrinsic to the trading order. In the closing section we examine the roles of morality and self-interest in the trading order.

5.2 The Model of the Trading Order

Trading is extremely widespread – Adam Smith remarks that it is 'common to all men' and, perhaps, 'the consequence of a certain propensity in human nature'[2] – but its practice and consequences nonetheless remain highly contentious. Much modern jurisprudential debate refers – whether explicitly or implicitly – to the 'politics' of law and this debate usually relates to economic perspectives underlying the various jurisprudential schools of thought. The most obvious instance of this relates to the opposition between law and economics theory on the one hand,[3] and critical legal studies on the other hand,[4] which was typically characterized

---

[2] A Smith, *An Inquiry into the Nature and Causes of the Wealth of Nations* [1776] (Glasgow edn), (I.ii.1) 25. In fact, as anthropological research has shown, exchange of some kind – not by any means always market or commercial exchange – is commonly of great significance in human societies.

[3] The economic analysis of law from the perspective of 'Chicago school' economics is associated with figures such as Ronald Coase, Gary Becker, Frank Easterbrook, and Richard Posner. A Haugh, 'Law and Economics' in T Murphy (ed), *Western Jurisprudence*, 324.

[4] The writings of the critical legal studies movement (CLS) – which have their roots in Marxist thought and American sociological and realist jurisprudence – have been characterized as embracing four themes: a radical indeterminacy thesis; a concern for the mystification function of law; a concern for the role of ideology in law; and the radical transformative possibilities of law. G Quinn,

as the expression in jurisprudence of a 'left-right' political divide. According to John Kelly's 1992 account of legal theory, for example, the law and economics movement could be regarded, 'in crude terms, as the right wing of American Jurisprudence, critical legal studies [CLS] being its left'.[5] We reject the terms 'left' and 'right' as a means of understanding political ideology – in our view this terminology is unhelpful and misleading[6] – yet we acknowledge that accounts of law and justice are often examined partly with reference to underlying economic perspectives. When John Kelly placed the Chicago-school law and economics at the 'right' end of the spectrum and CLS at the 'left' he had primarily in mind the attitudes in these camps towards what is often referred to as 'capitalist' or 'free market' relations of production. We wish to emphasize that the account of the trading order in this chapter is neither an account nor advocacy of any particular set of economic arrangements; rather it is an account or *model* of a trading order considered largely in abstraction from rules that, from the limited perspective of the model, are imposed from various sources, but which are necessarily imposed in practice.[7]

'Critical Legal Studies' in T Murphy (ed), *Western Jurisprudence*, 308. Above all, CLS writers stridently rejected the existence of a viable distinction between legal reasoning and political debate: adjudication was ineradicably indeterminate and political when it claimed to be determinate and judicial. It is now generally agreed that, unlike law and economics theory, which continues to exert a strong influence in jurisprudence, CLS scholarship had declined and faded out by the end of the 1990s, although its influence is still felt in other jurisprudential movements, MDA Freeman, *Lloyd's Introduction to Jurisprudence* (London: Sweet & Maxwell, 8th edn, 2008), 1224.

[5] JM Kelly, *A Short History of Western Legal Theory*, 436. Of course a great deal has happened – in jurisprudence and in the terms of broader political developments – since 1992, most notably, in the terms of Kelly's dichotomy at least, a marked decline in both the fortunes of what is sometimes called 'actually existing socialism' and the influence of CLS scholarship, but such developments are not our concern in this book. In this chapter we refer generically to what Kelly would today term 'left-wing' jurisprudence – that is, contemporary CLS-style thinking, Marxist jurisprudence, and jurisprudence influenced by Marxist thought – as 'critical jurisprudence' or 'critical legal thought'.

[6] 'Politics' in its broad and proper sense refers to the general questions of how people do and should live together in community. A very large range of subjects is addressed by general political questions – the proper regulation of banking, the scope of government power, the role of religion in public life, the rights of prisoners, the degree of liability attached to various forms of negligence, the best method of constitutional interpretation, the nature and meaning of discrimination, the legitimate scope of the criminal law, and so indefinitely on. These are only some examples of political matters and it is immediately obvious that the range is such that many outlooks and combinations of outlooks – and not just a 'left'/'right' dichotomy – are possible. Ronald Dworkin put this well when he wrote: 'There seems no natural reason why people who favor more celebration of the Christian religion in their community's public life should also favor lower taxes for the very rich, for example, or why they should be less sensitive to violations of the human rights of accused terrorists, or why they should be more likely to resist regulations that might slow environmental pollution', *Is Democracy Possible Here?* (Princeton, NJ: Princeton University Press, 2006), 3.

[7] Jurists often engage in political argument. Advocates, whose task it is to argue in favour of one rather than another decision, engage in jural-political argument. When the decision of a lower court is challenged in a higher court, the advocates engage in jural-political argument, and the court's decision, which establishes entitlements, is inevitably political. The contents of legislation and the decisions of the courts on any matter are jural-political decisions in that they prescribe or proscribe individual or social activity in the context of communal life. To write in support or in opposition to such measures is to engage in jural-political argument. Clearly, to engage in

In this chapter we suggest that *in the model of the trading order free exchanges are reciprocally just*. Our main focus is on justice rather than on trade. In earlier chapters we have made the Roman definition of justice central to our jurisprudence; we have distinguished between natural and conventional justice, and have examined that distinction in the context of the tripartite classification of justice into distributive, rectificatory, and reciprocal. It is, as we have said, easy to overlook the fact that reciprocal justice exists *only* in the context of exchange and the trading order (which is the set of exchanges).

It is crucial to recognize that a trading order governed *solely* by reciprocal justice does not exist. No trading order exists in a vacuum: trading orders exist as one order – along with, for example, jural, linguistic, and many other orders – within the broader, all-encompassing *social* order. Reciprocal justice is within the order as it exists; it is the justice intrinsic to trading but it does not determine the social parameters of the order.[8] Frank H Knight remarked in 1948 that no reputable economist ever believed in literal economic *laissez-faire*; 'certainly', he observed, 'neither Smith and Ricardo, nor Cobden and Bright would have restricted the state entirely to the negative functions of policing individual liberty and defense against outside attack'.[9] State legislation can and does contribute, often greatly, to the production of the social, human world, as we have said. We agree with – but it is not our task to argue for – Hayek's observation that it is 'unquestionable that in an advanced society government ought to use its power of raising funds by taxation to provide a number of services which for a variety of reasons cannot be provided, or cannot be provided adequately, by the market'.[10] There will be

jural-political argument is at once valuable and essential to human living but in this book we do not engage in that type of argument. Our concern in this chapter is with the model of the trading order and in particular with the nature and place of reciprocal justice in that order.

[8] The reader will recall the discussion in ch 2 above where we argued that human community is a spontaneous ordering of the natural sociability of humans. Both the social order and the trading order exist in association with the state organization and both are subject to various organizational influences, which, in the case of the trading order take the form primarily of the state interventionism to which we refer at various points in this chapter.

[9] FH Knight in his *Risk, Uncertainty and Profit* [1921] (New York: Augustus M Kelley, 1964), in the 'Preface for the Reprint of 1948', xlix. Knight does argue that individualism must be 'the political philosophy of intelligent and morally serious men', and his articulation of the moral choice that he had in mind is worth quoting: 'The choice lies between allowing people to fix the general form and terms of association by mutual consent, and having all conduct ordered by some authority, ultimately one based on a claim to a prescriptive right to power. Both reasoning and historical experience seem to show that in spite of the crudities of free society, and the undoubted fact that a majority may be a tyrant of the worst sort, authoritarian control is worse. It is both expedient and fundamentally right for the normal human adult to be responsible for himself, "to make his own mistakes", and to carry his share of responsibility for the community. Accordingly it seems demonstrable that both representative political institutions and free exchange and free enterprise are essential to the general framework of a truly moral social order', ibid.

[10] FA Hayek, *Law, Legislation and Liberty – Vol 3* (Chicago: Universiy of Chicago Press, 1979), ch 14. Hayek in *The Road to Serfdom*, first published in 1944, wrote: 'To create conditions in which competition will be made as effective as possible, to supplement it where it cannot be made effective, to provide the services which, in the words of Adam Smith, "though they may be in the highest degree advantageous to a great society, are, however, of such a nature, that the profit could never

extrinsic constraints many of which will be legislated. The jural-political question is what should be the *nature and extent* of that contribution.[11]

The nature and precise extent of state intervention in modern polities is something about which people (including the co-authors of this book) can – and do – legitimately disagree. Modern governments provide – through tax revenue or other compulsory contribution such as a television licence – an enormous range of services. The question arises as to which ought to be and which ought not to be so provided; people disagree and argue quite sensibly about these matters because there are serious arguments on both sides; and of course such disputes cannot be intelligently carried on if the inevitable scarcity of resources, either in supply or demand, is overlooked. Taxation raises crucial moral questions. The most obvious of these concerns the very notion of taxation but objections to state imposition of taxation of any kind lead to questions as to whether and how the state could provide any of the basic infrastructure and services that states, to differing degrees, always do provide. Manifestly, such questions are not soluble within the trading order itself, and one can sustain the claim that all relevant socio-political questions are solved within that order only by assuming that any questions not solved in that way are irrelevant. There are, finally, theorists who oppose the very existence of the state. These are all undoubtedly questions of great importance but they are more political than jurisprudential, and we do not deal with them.

Within particular jurisdictions there are particular entitlements, restrictions, or impositions *extrinsic* to the model of the trading order. These are in part customary and in part imposed by legislation, and differ from one jurisdiction to another. State intervention in the trading order is ubiquitous and includes, for instance, fiat currency, control of the money supply, and the granting of licences or monopolies that allow some but not others to trade in certain goods or services. There are also restrictions upon *what* may legally be traded, some of which may have become part of the living law as, for example, trading in people (people trafficking) that is now, but was not always, universally forbidden. Other restrictions may be the product of legislation and may differ from place to place. Trade in cannabis is forbidden in some jurisdictions but not in others. The sale of alcohol or tobacco to minors is often forbidden although the age that defines a minor differs. The buying or selling of labour below a minimum wage is forbidden in some jurisdictions but not in others. Various taxes surrounding the sale and purchase

repay the expense to any individual or small number of individuals", these tasks provide indeed a wide and unquestioned field for state activity. In no system that could be rationally defended would the state just do nothing. An effective competitive system needs an intelligently designed and continuously adjusted legal framework as any other. Even the most essential prerequisite of its proper functioning, the prevention of fraud and deception (including exploitation of ignorance) provides a great and by no means yet fully accomplished object of legislative activity' (London: Routledge, 2001), 40–1.

[11] D O Mahony, 'The Market: A Social Order' (2007) 59–60 *Milltown Studies* 45.

of goods and services such as VAT, stamp duty on the purchase of houses and other immovable property, capital gains tax, and income tax are commonplace examples of impositions that exist in many jurisdictions but differ in extent from jurisdiction to jurisdiction as well as, at different times, within the same jurisdiction, as when the rate of income tax or VAT is changed. We are not concerned here with the many important and various effects of such particular entitlements, restrictions, or impositions on the trading order, noting only that there are such effects, and that it is impossible accurately and in detail to gauge in advance what their effects will be.

The question of state control of the economic order is admittedly very divisive. Those who consider that the containing context should be one in which the purpose of legislation is the achievement of greater equality of wealth are likely to think of an economy as a set of activities to be centrally organized. Those who consider that the containing context is one in which the purpose of legislation is the maintenance of an order in which many can pursue their various goals in harmony are more likely to think of the economy as an order that cannot be centrally organized. The trading order may not be the only possible economic system within which very many people unknown to one another can live together, but if the economic order that has evolved is a trading order, then in order to discover what legislation is necessary and appropriate, one must first discover how the order works. Whether or not the trading order is an organization that can be centrally managed is not an ideological question but a difficult question of fact, but the effort to answer it may be vitiated by ideological bias. It is the case that the two strands of jurisprudence associated with critical theory on the one hand and 'law and economics' on the other do have markedly different views regarding the trading order. The underlying and pervasive presupposition in much critical legal scholarship is that the human world, socially, economically, and politically can, and should, be the product of centralized decision. So the purpose of egalitarian politics is to devise legislation that will produce a human world organized in such a way as to distribute resources in some sense equally.

From the fact that we hold that the trading order cannot be centrally managed, and that, consequently, it is unreasonable to try so to manage it, it does not follow that it deals, or can in principle deal, with all social problems or that no problems that it fails to resolve are to be brushed aside as of little or no importance. In any commercial or trading society there will be some – incontrovertible cases include children below a certain age, the chronically infirm, those who through no fault of their own are unemployed, and the victims of great and sudden natural disasters – who, for whatever reason, cannot, or cannot yet, sustain their lives by trading and, if they are to survive at all, or survive in a humanly dignified manner, must survive in some other way.[12] Few if any consider their survival

---

[12] There is no economic order, and there can be none, where children are left to fend entirely for themselves. In this the trading order is not exceptional. At what age children are expected to sustain, or to contribute to sustaining, themselves differs from society to society, economy to

or their dignity to be of no importance, but how they are to survive and who is responsible for their survival are questions that, since by definition they cannot survive by participating in the trading order, are not answered by suggesting that they must survive by participating in it. What is clear, therefore, is that their survival is not a matter of reciprocal justice.

The trading order does not, then, eliminate all socio-political problems, and precisely because it does not, reciprocal justice, which is confined to, and justly orders, free exchange, is irrelevant to their solution. No chosen distributively just allocation of the combined wealth of the members of a particular community or jurisdiction can be achieved unless that combined wealth is commonly owned and to be distributed by some institution authorized to distribute it according to some criterion that will bring about the desired distribution. The trading order brings about a constantly changing allocation of resources but it neither intends nor can bring about any such particular distributively just allocation. Participants in the order intend to achieve their goals; the order intends nothing.

5.3 Natural Justice and Conventional Justice in Exchange

In a trade or exchange there are at least two partners, Peter and Paul, and two goods to be exchanged, X and Y, the one belonging to Peter, the other to Paul. Peter offers X to Paul on condition that Paul gives him Y in return. The exchange succeeds only if Paul is willing to accept X in return for Y. Peter will not offer X in return for Y, unless, for whatever reason, he wants Y more than he wants X; and Paul will not give Y in order to get X, unless, for whatever reason, he wants X more than he wants Y. The *structural* analysis of a trade between two partners requires no further account of the partners' reasons than that there is reciprocal demand for the offered goods. Why Peter wants Paul's goods more than he wants his own is irrelevant for the analysis.[13] In trading, *both* partners profit. Children swapping marbles know this in practice just as well as do the owners of companies who sell their companies. No one freely swaps his marbles, no one freely sells his shares, if he wants to keep them more than to swap or sell them. That is

---

economy, and time to time. For humans to survive over generations there must be an arrangement to care for children. To care for their rearing is a moral demand and is usually the responsibility of parents who find the resources to do so in their participation in the prevailing economic order. When the prevailing economic order is the trading order, one or both parents or sometimes other kindred, find the resources to do so by trading their resources.

[13] There are, of course, other analyses within which Peter's reason for his preference might be of great significance. For example, his preference will be influenced by demands put upon him by his present situation, his desires, his interests, his wealth, his standard of education, his level of knowledge of other available possibilities, and so on, but in an analysis of a single transaction none of these is relevant; what is relevant is solely that he engaged in the transaction.

what 'economic rationality' means and that is the only coherent way of using this commonly misunderstood, commonly misused, and largely redundant term.

Without this mutual or reciprocal demand there will be no exchange. Demand, as Aristotle wrote, is the yardstick of exchange:

All goods must be measured by some one yardstick or measure. And this yardstick is, in reality, demand, which is the universal bond (for if men were in need of nothing, or if there were no proportion between their needs, there would either be no exchange whatsoever or the exchanges would be other than they are); but money has become, by convention, a sort of representative of demand.[14]

Demand is common to all trading orders, and if such an order is to function over time and many exchanges, most exchanges must be mutually, that is, reciprocally satisfactory when the exchange occurs. Both Aristotle and St Thomas knew that many exchanges went on between many people (which is what a trading or market order is) but they had no theory of this order. There is a very elliptical remark on money in Aristotle that does in principle lead into questions about the trading or market order as distinct from the analysis of a single transaction;[15] but in fact it did not, and the Aristotelian analysis and St Thomas's commentary are almost wholly confined to the investigation of the single transaction. Both are clear that the outcome of each transaction is agreed. But since neither asks about the outcome of the entire set of indefinitely many exchanges between indefinitely many trading partners, neither remarks that the outcome of the entire set is not, and cannot be, envisaged or agreed.

Each exchange shifts the ownership of goods from one partner to another, and in a commercial society there is an immense multitude of exchanges hourly, daily, monthly, yearly, and so on over time. The pattern of ownership in any society at the beginning of any chosen period will differ from that at the end of that period. In the trading system the pattern will change by means of the many exchanges between the trading partners but what the pattern will be at the end of the

---

[14] Aristotle, *Nicomachean Ethics*, V.1133a.25–30.

[15] Aristotle is sometimes credited with the 'just wage' idea that if it takes x hours to make a pair of shoes and 100x hours to make a house, then the 'natural' exchange rate between shoes and houses is 100 pairs of shoes = 1 house. See the note by D Ross (ed and trans) on V.1133a.6 (Oxford: Clarendon Press, 1928). That this is in fact Aristotle's position is plausible but his repeated reference to demand, as in the passage quoted, throws some doubt upon this interpretation. It seems likely that Aristotle's position is insufficiently worked out. St Thomas in his commentary on the fifth book of the *Nicomachean Ethics* seems clear that price is set by mutual demand: 'what in reality measures all things (relative to one another in exchange) is demand', Lectio IX. Whatever the case, the search for a 'natural' or 'just' exchange rate apart from a rate set by mutual demand persisted for centuries and, to an extent, persists. In the model of a trading order, an exchange rate set otherwise than by mutual demand and agreement does not exist. In existing political-economic orders exchange rates may on occasion be set otherwise, as in minimum wage legislation. Similarly, interventions like privileged monopolies may serve to limit supply in various ways and thereby effect demand and consequently price. The nature and scope of such interventions – rather than simply questions as to the nature of the trading order – is the subject of most political debate and disagreement.

selected period *cannot* be predicted from the pattern at the outset. But although
the trading order has no aims, it does perform certain social functions, its most
immediate function being to allow trading partners to gain what each wants by
exchanging for it what each values less highly.[16]

In the trading system, each participant owns whatever he offers in exchange.
When he exchanges a good or service for something else, he now owns what he
has accepted in exchange. The exchange is just – that is, each person has what is
due to him – if it has been free and not vitiated by fraud, undue influence, culp-
able and, in some cases, simple mistake, misrepresentation or the like, in which
case a court may be involved in the resolution of a dispute. But there can be no
guarantee that a participant has made what he will later think of as a wise choice.
This is crucial to a correct understanding of justice in exchange. At the time of the
exchange, both partners are satisfied with the exchange; *otherwise they would not
exchange.* But it is perfectly possible that either or both will later regret it. Peter,
having come in to some money, may decide to open a clothes shop. He does so
because he hopes to trade sufficiently well to cover his costs, including his living
costs, and, usually, even to make a profit. He rents premises and buys clothes that
he thinks will sell in sufficiently great numbers at a satisfactory price. If his shop
succeeds, he will be retrospectively pleased with the original exchange. If his shop
fails, he will consider, again retrospectively, that he chose unwisely. At the end of
his first year it is unlikely, although possible, that his situation will be precisely as
it was at the outset; he is more likely to be richer or poorer than he was. Not only
may he compare his position at the end with his position at the outset, he may
compare himself with Paul who, we may imagine, began the year with the same
amount of money as Peter and, like him, also opened a clothes shop. Suppose that
Peter failed and Paul succeeded. Where both at the outset were equally well off,
at the end of the year one was better off than the other. That this will sometimes
be the outcome is inevitable in a trading order. It has nothing whatsoever to do
with reciprocal justice for reciprocal justice has nothing whatsoever to do with
outcomes other than bringing about the outcome of *each* exchange.

In this convention – trade or exchange through mutual demand – is there
room for what is naturally just? We suggest that there are elements of both natural
and conventional justice in the single transaction. At first sight it may appear that
such transactions are purely conventional. Suppose Paul to be a cabinet-maker
who shows Peter a dining table that he describes as a dining table in walnut.

---

[16] 'In an occasional act of barter in which men who ordinarily do not resort to trading with
other people exchange goods ordinarily not negotiated, the ratio of exchange is determined only
within broad margins. Catallactics, the theory of exchange ratios and prices, cannot determine
at what point within these margins the concrete ratio will be established. *All that it can assert with
regard to such exchanges is that they can be effected only if each party values what he receives more highly
than what he gives away*', L von Mises, *Human Action: A Treatise on Economics* [1949] (Auburn:
Ludwig von Mises Institute, 1998), 327 (emphasis added). The 'ratio of exchange' is the agreed relative value of the things exchanged and, when one of the things exchanged is money, is expressed in
the agreed price.

Peter looks at the table and buys it for €1,500. Paul has sold the table and Peter has bought it for €1,500.[17] Each has agreed to the exchange and together they have settled the price. In the transaction €1,500 is the agreed representative of their reciprocal demand. An agreed price establishes the relative values of the goods to be exchanged; within a trading or market order, price cannot be set in any other way. The conventional element is shown in that the relative values of the goods exchanged in a single transaction are set by agreement between the trading partners. The exchange is therefore reciprocally just and is arrived at conventionally or by agreement. But agreement on the relative values of the goods is intrinsic or natural to trading; this is the only way value can be established. What is natural to an exchange is not what precise value is to be put on the goods to be exchanged but the method in which the values are to be arrived at. In the example of the walnut table, the natural element is shown in that the transaction is just only if the money offered is not counterfeit, and the table offered as a walnut table is in fact a walnut table. This natural element is expressed in the ancient rule: 'You shall not cheat in measuring length, weight, or quantity. You shall have honest balances, honest weights, an honest ephah, and an honest hin.'[18] This is not a rule added on to trading but expresses a moral demand intrinsic or natural to it.

In summary, then, reciprocal justice is the mutual agreement between trading partners, and a transaction is reciprocally just if both trading partners freely agree to the exchange when the exchange takes place. The reciprocally just price is set by agreement or convention between the trading partners. It is, therefore, conventional. But it is natural – that is, intrinsic – to exchange that the price should be set in this way, for without agreement there would be no exchange.

Reciprocal justice is justice in exchange but things are not always exchanged at the same time. Peter orders a number of cylinders of gas from Paul on a given day; Paul delivers the gas the following day but Peter is not expected to pay for the gas until early in the following month. Time has entered into the arrangement; the completion of the contract is deferred and the situation is unstable: Peter possesses, rightly, what he has not paid for and so does not yet own. He possesses the gas and owns a debt. Paul no longer possesses what he has not yet been paid for; instead he owns the entitlement to be paid. When Peter pays for the gas his debt is expunged and Paul is given what he is entitled to. Thus, once time deferral enters into the reciprocally just contract, rectificatory justice comes in. It may happen that Peter reneges on his debt. Peter now possesses wrongly what he has not paid for and does not own. If Paul chooses to sue Peter, the court's question as to what is due is one involving rectificatory justice. That something is due to Paul follows from the intrinsic character of contract. What precisely is due is the question before the court. Natural reason demands that Paul, in the absence of other

---

[17] We use the common but theoretically misleading terms, 'buyer' and 'seller'. In reality, in an exchange each participant is both a buyer and a seller. If Peter gives Paul €3 in exchange for bread, Peter sells his money to Paul from whom he buys bread, and Paul sells his bread to Peter from whom he buys money. [18] *Leviticus* 19:35–6.

relevant circumstances, receive at least what Peter had agreed to pay but perhaps more than this. The task of the court once again is to discover in the instant case what is due.

It may happen that Peter cannot pay the entire debt. Between agreeing to buy the gas and the time when payment fell due his business may have failed. What now is Paul due? In case Paul is not Peter's sole creditor the question arises as to what is due to each creditor. An attempt may be made to resolve the problem in discussion between the creditors and Peter and they may negotiate a new distributively just solution. The creditors, for example, may consider themselves to be relevantly equal and agree to accept an equal proportion of what was originally owed. But the situation may be such that they do not consider themselves to be equal.[19] Andrew, knowing that the business was in danger of failing, may have lent Peter money in the hope of saving it, while the others may have traded in the normal way, and may not accept that Andrew's position is equal to theirs. They may consider that Andrew, having knowingly taken a risk, is not now entitled to an equal proportion in the overall settlement. If they fail to reach agreement and have recourse to the court, once again the question before the court is what in these circumstances is due to whom, in this case, how are the available funds or other property to be distributed among the creditors.

Whether the justice involved in such cases is distributive or rectificatory may be disputed. It seems to be distributive in as much as the court must discover what proportion of what is to be distributed is to be assigned to each litigant; it seems to be rectificatory in as much as what is at issue is a debt, and the repayment of a debt seems to be almost a paradigm of rectificatory justice. We do not consider the matter to be of great importance. What is always crucial is the underlying question: what is due to whom?

5.4 The Elements of Exchange

The trading order, like language, is an activity that people first engage in, and only later formulate its rules explicitly. What are the elements of the individual exchanges that make up the trading order? To trade is voluntarily to exchange one thing for another. Eight things are necessary to an exchange. The first four elements involve the parties to the exchange and what is exchanged: at least two people must make the exchange, and at least two things must be exchanged between them. The fifth and sixth elements are that each person must understand what is involved in exchange. If Peter wants to exchange his book for Paul's

---

[19] It may be possible, of course, to impose inequality and to make, for example, a particular person, or type of person, a preferred creditor such that what is due to him is to be paid in full before the other creditors are considered. In some jurisdictions, the state or banks are preferred creditors; it seems difficult to sustain the position that such preferential treatment, at least for what are privately owned companies such as banks, stands in need of no argument.

pen, before he can begin to look for Paul's agreement, he must explain to Paul, if Paul does not already know, what is involved in exchange. Exchange is mutual, and *must* be mutually understood. The seventh and eighth elements are the decisions that produce the mutual agreement to exchange one thing for another; for without agreement no exchange will take place. If any one of these eight elements is missing an exchange cannot take place. Of the eight elements, the first six are natural to exchange. The remaining two elements, the two decisions of which mutual agreement is the product, are both natural and conventional. As we have seen in the preceding section, they are natural in that without agreement there can be no exchange, and conventional in that actual exchange is an agreement or convention between people to trade one thing against another.

Peter and Paul agree to exchange X and Y. It is obvious that Peter will not agree to exchange X that he has for Y that Paul has, unless he wants to have Y more than he wants to keep X. Reciprocally, Paul will not agree to exchange Y for X unless he wants to have X more than he wants to keep Y. An agreed exchange is reciprocally just precisely because it is agreed. This is the basic model of a single exchange. Very obviously, Peter and Paul represent any two people whomsoever; X and Y represent any two things, whether goods or services, of any kind whatsoever. At this level of analysis, what is to be exchanged is of no significance. Children, heroin, sex, or internal organs are examples of tradable goods, precisely as are umbrellas, vegetables, work, or xylophones. Whether or not children ought to be tradable – we think not but we do not argue the matter – is disputable but that they *can* be, and in the case of illegal child-trafficking in fact are, is not disputable.

The case of child-trafficking draws attention to the requirement that trading partners in an individual exchange need to *own* what they trade may be satisfied by, so to speak, *pseudo-ownership*, as when, for instance, two thieves trade between themselves what each acknowledges the other has stolen and so does not own. Within the wider context in which they live and which they acknowledge in as much as they agree that they do not own what they propose to exchange, they exchange the goods but not the ownership of, or title to, the goods. Within the restricted context of their own trading, however, each acknowledges that the other owns the good that he proposes to trade in as much as each accepts that, within the restricted context, when the physical goods have changed hands their ownership has changed hands. This ownership within the restricted context is not recognized within the wider context and for clarity we call it 'pseudo-ownership'. What is crucial to the order is that those exchanging goods accept that each owns (or pseudo-owns) what he proposes to trade. What is needed for individual exchanges is neither legal nor moral ownership, but an acceptance by those involved that the exchange of goods will be by trade and not by force. What is traded is not the good or service only but also title to it. Trade between thieves is, within their restricted context, the same as that between those who genuinely own what they propose to trade, only that the title asserted by each thief is not recognized within the surrounding context. This is what the trad-itional saw means that there is honour among thieves. Trade within the context of 'pseudo-ownership' is, however, based upon pretence and necessarily parasitic on the trading order where what is traded is genuinely owned. The justice within it is inevitably flawed; it is 'pseudo-justice' as the transaction does not produce what is due, for what is due is what is required in rectificatory justice, namely, that the stolen goods be returned to their owners.

The example of trafficking in children is chosen deliberately in the expectation that every reader will accept that almost everything about the transaction is unjust. Peter possesses, unjustly, children whom he proposes to sell, and Paul has money that he proposes to give in exchange for Peter's goods.[20] We argue that reciprocal justice remains relevant despite this unjust context. The exchange *itself* is just if Peter freely accepts the mutually agreed amount of money from Paul in exchange for the mutually agreed number of children, and, reciprocally, Paul freely accepts the mutually agreed number of children in exchange for the mutually agreed sum of money. The difference between the transaction in this example and a slave mar-ket is only that in the jurisdiction in which the slave market took place the buyers and sellers were assumed to own and to be entitled to alienate their slaves.[21]

Consider a different example: the exchange of cannabis for money. In such a situation both seller and buyer own what each proposes to exchange. Peter wants to sell cannabis to Paul who wants to buy it. Peter owns the cannabis and Paul owns the money with which he wants to buy it. In many jurisdictions the sale of cannabis is illegal; in others it is not. Were an exchange agreed in a jurisdiction in which it is legal to sell cannabis, the transaction would be, by definition, legal; in jurisdictions in which it is illegal to sell cannabis, the transaction would be, again by definition, illegal. But the exchange in both instances is reciprocally just because the reciprocal justice involved has nothing to do with the surrounding jural context; it has to do only with the context of the exchange itself. Were that not so, the same transaction would be reciprocally just in one jural context and reciprocally unjust in another.

---

[20] That Paul may properly own the money with which he proposes to buy the children accounts for the restriction 'almost' in the previous sentence.

[21] Slavery is discussed in Justinian's *Institutes* in I.II.2 and I.III–VIII. Slavery is said to belong to the law of nations (*ius gentium*) in I.II.2, I.III.2, and I.VIII.1 and to be contrary to the law of nature (*ius naturale*) 'for by that law all men are originally born free' in I.II.2 and I.III.2: 'Slavery is an institution of the law of nations, by which one man is made the property of another, contrary to natural right [literally *contra naturam*, "against nature"].' Although masters were considered to own and to be entitled to sell their slaves, and at one time to be entitled to kill them, by a decree of the Emperor Antoninus Pius (AD 138–61) that entitlement was revoked and they were not permitted to treat them howsoever they wished (I.VIII.2). Some readers may incline to hold that people *cannot* be owned but this is untrue. What may be owned and how it may be owned is deter-mined conventionally or institutionally. Conventional or institutional determination may be, or be thought to be, unjust but this does not prevent it from being conventionally or institutionally determined; this tension is discussed in ch 7 below on morality, law, and legislation. In Justinian, only on the question of slavery is the *ius naturale* said to differ from the *ius gentium*.

In the surrounding context there may be, and often are, prohibitions against the trading of some goods or services. There may also be, and often are, laws forbidding some types of people from trading certain goods or services that may be legally traded between other types of people. So, for example, in many jurisdictions, alcohol may be legally traded, but only between people over a given age. There may be, and often are, prohibitions against the trading of some goods or services below a certain price. So, for example, a minimum wage per hour may be set prohibiting the sale or purchase of labour below that price. To trade in breach of such prohibitions is, by definition, illegal. Our contention, however, is that to trade illegally is not *ipso facto* to trade reciprocally unjustly. Justice in exchange, to put this point bluntly, is a matter that can be considered entirely separately from the issue of either state law or living law. *A particular exchange may be profoundly evil yet reciprocally just.*

As we have said, a transaction is reciprocally just if both trading partners freely agree to the exchange when the exchange takes place. Genuine mutual agreement is based on neither partner being misled by the other as to what the other is actually selling. Peter is willing, legally or illegally, to sell his kidney to Paul for, say, €400. Paul agrees, and the bargain is made. Paul gives Peter counterfeit money. The exchange which actually takes place is reciprocally unjust but not because what was agreed was otherwise illegal or unjust. It is reciprocally unjust because it is not the exchange that was agreed.

One of the partners in a proposed trade may be ignorant of the true character of what he has for sale. Peter, the proprietor of a bric-a-brac shop, is willing to sell a painting for €500. Paul, convinced that the painting is by Caravaggio, thinks that, were he to buy it for that amount, he could later sell it for a very much greater sum. Paul buys the painting from Peter for €500. Is the transaction reciprocally just? It may be allowed that Paul's action is neither generous nor particularly honourable, and that it has not the magnanimous character that goes beyond justice. But the question is not whether or not Paul's action is magnanimous. The question, raised as early as Cicero's *On Duties*, is whether or not it vitiates the transaction to the extent that justice is denied.[22]

Misrepresentation by either party of what he proposes to exchange is traditionally said to vitiate the transaction because the trading partners agree to exchange goods as they have been represented. When a good is merely presented for inspection by the seller, for example, a carpet, what the buyer agrees to buy is the carpet that he is free to examine. If he thinks, wrongly, that it is naturally, rather than chemically dyed, it is arguably his responsibility: *Caveat emptor.*[23]

---

[22] In *On Duties*, III.92, Cicero, in discussing his example of a seller offering what he thinks is brass but which the buyer knows to be in fact gold, concentrates on the distinction between the honourable, the expedient, and the legal. The theme runs throughout Book III. See also, *inter alia*, III.21 and 57.

[23] Consumer protection laws may be established requiring a carpet seller to state if a particular carpet is naturally or chemically dyed. Such a law forbids the sale of undifferentiated carpets and is

In the example of the painting, Peter does not misrepresent what he offers for sale, namely, a painting that a prospective buyer is free to examine.[24] What Paul buys is what is offered for sale. He misrepresents nothing. That he is convinced it is by Caravaggio, and so likely to fetch a much greater price when he tries to sell it, is not misrepresentation to the extent that it vitiates the justice in the exchange. Peter sells the painting as described, and Paul buys it as described; the description may well be incomplete but is not mistaken. The transaction is reciprocally just although hardly exceedingly honourable: *Caveat vendor.*

Cicero gives a powerful example of the competing attractions of honour and expediency:

> Suppose that a good man had brought a large quantity of corn from Alexandria to Rhodes at a time when corn was extremely expensive among the Rhodians because of shortage and famine. If he also knew that several more merchants had set sail for Alexandria, and had seen their boats *en route* laden with corn and heading for Rhodes, would he tell the Rhodians? Or would he keep silent and sell his own produce at as high a price as possible? We are imagining that he is a wise and good man; our question is about the deliberations and considerations of a man who would not conceal the fact from the Rhodians if he judged it dishonourable, but is uncertain as to whether it is dishonourable.[25]

Cicero refers to a discussion of this example between the Stoic philosopher, Diogenes of Babylon, and his pupil, Antipater. Diogenes held that the seller ought to declare any faults in his goods in so far as the metropolitan law demanded but about other facts surrounding the transaction may honourably remain silent if he is guilty of no explicit misrepresentation. Antipater, on the other hand, maintained that all pertinent facts should be disclosed. In this example, there are two related but not identical questions at issue: First, is to disclose the imminent arrival of other merchants the more honourable course? Secondly, does failure to disclose this information constitute fraud or misrepresentation to the extent of vitiating justice in the exchange? These questions, and the discussion between Diogenes and Antipater, raise a third question: What rule of justice is best established in

---

structurally identical with a law that forbids the sale of people or heroin or internal organs; it is, in other words, an extrinsic regulation imposed on trading within a particular jurisdiction. We discuss entitlements, restrictions or impositions extrinsic to the trading order in ch 5.7 below.

[24] Misrepresentation may be perfectly explicit or may be more or less veiled as when a dealer encourages the prospective buyer to think that a painting is an original without actually saying so. Someone may subtly insinuate that a particular company's results are likely to be worse than expected in order to encourage shareholders to sell at a price at which he may buy the shares in the hope that, when the rumour is shown to be unfounded, he may sell at a profit.

[25] Cicero, *On Duties*, III.50 (M Griffin and M Atkins eds; M Atkins trans) (Cambridge: Cambridge University Press, 1991), 118–19. In Cicero's opinion (III.57), 121: 'The fact is that merely holding one's peace about a thing does not constitute concealment, but concealment consists in trying for your own profit to keep others from finding out something that you know, when it is for their interest to know it' (Miller's translation from the Loeb edn (London, 2001 [1913]), 325–7). Cicero's position may seem at first convincing but ought a shopkeeper be required to tell a customer that what the customer intends to buy from him for €40 is available at another shop for €30?

that context within a society of traders? And this shows another and crucial conventional feature of the trading order, namely, that it is crucial that traders know what constitutes an enforceable contract. It is clear that different agreements or conventions are possible concerning the declaration or concealment of flaws in the goods offered for sale. Which known flaws or defects must be declared to an intending purchaser, and which may be left to the purchaser to discover, is conventionally set. The range of *caveat emptor* changes from jurisdiction to jurisdiction and from time to time as the history and content both of commercial custom and of consumer law illustrate. Cicero's concern with honourable conduct comes from an appreciation of the difference between sharp but not quite fraudulent practice and outright fraud. Fraud tends to destroy the order, sharp practice undermines the confidence on which it depends.

Another requirement of a reciprocally just exchange is the free agreement of each partner. A coerced exchange is not reciprocally just. An instructive example is compulsory purchase by the state. In many jurisdictions the state is legally entitled to purchase land on foot of a properly issued compulsory purchase order. The state is required to compensate the owner but the owner is not free to refuse the exchange. An exchange of this kind is not reciprocally just even if the compensation equals or exceeds the estimated 'market price' of the land.[26] For the same reason, namely, the absence of free agreement, someone invited to hand over his wallet in exchange for the withdrawal of further threats or actual harm is not involved in a reciprocally just transaction. The examples are, of course, very different. Most readers will readily assume that the robber is not entitled to force the exchange. Many, perhaps most, will readily assume that the state is in some circumstances entitled to purchase land compulsorily. But from the assumption that the state is so entitled, it does not follow that the exchange is reciprocally just.

These are examples of coerced exchange. Coercion in exchange is a particular type of coercion. It must be compulsory, that is, it must be brought about by the use or threat of force whether direct or indirect.[27] To say, therefore, that *need* in any sense – whether it be economic or psychological or social or whatever – gives rise to coercion and thus vitiates the justice of the exchange is in our view incorrect. Forms of need in exchange *are* relevant to analyses of trading within particular social orders at particular times and in particular circumstances, but *not* to an analysis of the trading order as such. We are concerned here with the *model* of a trading order but repeat, as we have explicitly acknowledged above, that within the encompassing social order there will remain social problems that in its actual working the trading order will not solve. We return to this question

---

[26] Strictly speaking, the market price is the price agreed by the transacting partners. In the compulsory purchase context and other contexts, the term is somewhat misleadingly – even, one might say, incorrectly – used to refer to an anticipated price based on recent previous sales of fairly similar goods.   [27] Direct force and indirect force are discussed in ch 10 below.

but now give a fuller account of the 'free' agreement intrinsic to reciprocally just transactions.

The initiator proposes to give what he has in exchange for what the prospective trading partner has. Suppose that a mistake has been made: Peter and Paul both have tickets for the same flight from Glasgow to Keflavík. The airline company guarantees to compensate whoever does not take the flight, but the problem remains: the flight is overbooked by one. Peter, having already checked in, has a seat, but his appointment in Iceland allows him to travel the next day. Knowing that Paul has no seat, and that his business is more urgent than his own, Peter offers to stand aside if Paul will pay him €300 in addition to whatever compensation he receives. Paul – who, for whatever reason, wants to fly now rather than tomorrow – considers the proposal. He weighs the loss of €300 against the gain of flying today. If he agrees to Peter's proposal, he may well later say that he had no choice, that he was forced to agree. Paul's description is readily understandable in everyday conversation, but is mistaken. He remained free to keep his €300. And yet the example illustrates the fact that free exchanges, although reciprocally just, are not necessarily in all respects desirable. Paul would have preferred his original arrangements to have gone smoothly; he did not choose to be in the situation in which Peter's offer held any attraction; but he is in that situation, and asks the question that must be asked when any exchange is proposed: 'Is what I shall get in return for what I must give a good way of using my resources in this situation?' The clause 'what I must give' is deliberate; every instance of free exchange includes the necessary element of loss on both sides; in order to gain what one wants one must lose what one has. Equally, every instance of free exchange includes the necessary element of gaining something that one prefers to the inevitable losses; but in a free exchange the loss is always less than the gain; were it not, the exchange would not be freely agreed to.

It is in principle obvious, but may be worth making clear, that a person may not be free to effect an exchange because he has not the resources necessary to persuade the other to give him what he wants. If Paul in the example lacks €300 and Peter is unwilling to forego his flight for less, then no exchange can take place. People are, by definition, unable to effect exchanges that demand resources that they have not got. A person cannot buy a house that costs more than he can afford; the person is not 'free' to buy the house. Here again, reciprocal justice is not involved because reciprocal justice comes into play only when an exchange takes place; reciprocal justice is justice *in* exchange.

It is not possible to provide a definition of 'free exchange' which when applied to a disputed case will automatically determine the character of the disputed contract, and so it falls to the court to examine the instant case, to determine the matter as best it can, and to decide what the litigants are entitled to. How 'free' is to be understood is not settled by recourse to a dictionary but within the background context of legislation and precedent, the practices of the trading community and indeed the practices of the wider community. It is 'naturally just' that the exchange is free but what precisely constitutes freedom must be agreed and, in case of dispute, adjudicated.

In the story of the two travellers faced with only one remaining seat, we deliberately invented a case where the need of one would appear to most readers as quite significantly greater than the need of the other – had their needs been in no way unequal there would have been no question of exchange. And yet we called the transaction 'free'. We supposed that Peter had been assigned the seat and that it would not be reassigned to Paul unless Peter gave it to him or exchanged it with him for an agreed amount. Peter was free to give his seat to Paul even if, by doing so, he would have incurred a cost, namely, the cost in inconvenience, time, and money attendant on changing his plans. For Peter to be unwilling simply to give away the seat is not unjust. Nor would it have been unjust had Peter been unwilling to sell it. The possibility of any transaction between them is based on Peter being in principle willing to sell, and Paul in principle being willing to buy, the seat. The only question is whether or not they can agree a price. In the story it was supposed that Paul was very anxious to have the seat, and Peter more or less indifferent about keeping it. Peter is in a position to drive a hard bargain. Suppose that he is prepared to drive as hard a bargain as he can, that is, to get as high a price as possible. When the negotiations begin Peter may be clear about how little he is prepared to accept; not less, say, than €200. Paul may be prepared to pay €400. Neither knows the other's limit.

Perhaps neither wants to be in the situation in which they find themselves but that is where they are. Here is where the term 'free' becomes multivalent. Is Peter free to accept less than he has decided? Is Paul free to pay above the limit he has decided upon? If we suppose that to postpone his departure would cost Peter €100 and disregard his cost in time and inconvenience, then clearly Peter is free to accept less than €200. Is he free to accept less than €100? By accepting €80 he in effect makes Paul a present of €20. What does it now mean to ask if he is free to do so? If he can afford to make Paul a present he is free to do so; if he cannot, he is not. Is Paul free to breach his limit of €400? Perhaps he can afford to do so, perhaps he cannot. If he cannot, he is not free to do so. If Peter cannot afford to take less than €100, and Paul cannot afford to offer more than €400, then their joint range of freedom in this sense of the term is between €100 and €400. They are free to exchange within that range but neither is coerced into making any exchange whatsoever and it is that absence of coercion that makes whatever exchange they may make free.

'Freedom', therefore, has at least three distinct senses: first, the range within which one has the required resources (a person who has not the resources to trade within the actually existing range is not free to trade); secondly, the absence of coercion by others in negotiation within that range;[28] and thirdly, in a trading

---

[28] In our model of the trading order, what is meant by 'free' is that participants are free and uncoerced by others to offer for exchange their available resources. For that reason, neither theft

order or market society, where most make their living by trading, most are not effectively free to make their living in any other way. So much is true of all economic arrangements; members of the society are free to make their living in the prevailing economy, and not effectively free to do so otherwise. Karl Marx influentially wrote that this was so in the trading order (what he called and subsequently has been called 'capitalism'):

> For the conversion of his money into capital, therefore, the owner of money must meet in the market with the free labourer, free in the double sense, that as a free man he can dispose of his labour-power as his own commodity, and that on the other hand he has no other commodity for sale, is short of [ie free of] everything necessary for the realisation of his labour power.[29]

The three senses of freedom are at work in that passage. First, there is at least the possibility that he can survive by trading within the actual range. Secondly, he is free to negotiate the trading of his labour. Whether or not he actually does so depends on his being hired. Thirdly, he is not effectively free to make his living in any other way. Consequent is that one who is not free – that is, is unable – to make his living otherwise than by trading his labour cannot survive within that order if he fails to trade at a price sufficient to sustain him, and, unless sustained by another, will soon die.

It is reasonable to suppose that to survive is for the labourer a fundamental good. Therefore, he must try to trade his labour. His need to be hired – even to be hired by this person now – may be overwhelming. He is open to exploitation in the modern and now perhaps more common sense of the word, 'to utilize for selfish purposes... take advantage of (esp. of a person) for one's own ends'.[30] Exploitation is possible when the power of one – person, group, or state – is significantly greater than the power of another. The powerful have the opportunity to oppress the less powerful, and because power that gives rein to selfishness tends to corrupt, they will sometimes do so. Slavery, the paradigm of selfishness, is the great and appalling historical example: the control of another entirely for the advantage of the owner. Selfishness can and does become in some the dominant criterion of action, leading to disregard for the other's interest. Opposed to it is the moral perspective in which others and their interests are taken into account. The fault-line between the opposing perspectives is *within* rather than *between* individuals, in individuals rather than in institutions – although institutions, such as slavery, may be no more than

---

nor taxation are within the trading order; whatever their other and important differences both are coerced reallocations of a person's resources. For example, the taxpayer gets many things, many of which he may be pleased to have and at least some of which he could otherwise get only with difficulty or not all, in exchange for his tax but the crucial difference remains: taxes are coerced, exchanges within the trading order are free.

[29] K Marx, *Capital – Part II: The Transformation of Money into Capital* (S Moore and E Aveling trans) (New York: The Modern Library, 1906) [ch VI], 187–8.

[30] *The Shorter Oxford Dictionary* (1938), Vol I, 707 and *The Concise Oxford Dictionary* (1991), 412.

expressions of pure selfishness and of 'the pride... [that makes man] love to domineer'.[31] From the perspective of pure selfishness, the employee is no more than an instrument – a factor of production differing little from a machine – whose interests may be ignored unless to take account of them is to the selfish advantage of the employer. That more or less unadulterated selfishness was the only engine of the labour market in which, as he saw it, the buyers had more or less absolute power over the sellers, is the presupposition of Marx's analysis of the buying and selling of labour power.[32] Only from the perspective of taking the employees' interests into account does the question as to the cost and conditions of employment arise apart from their advantages to the employer. In other words, only within that context and from that perspective do questions of justice arise that consider labour to be other than a factor of production like any other: 'what is due from employer to employee?'; 'what is due from employee to employer?' Selfishness is endemic and enduring in the trading order in practice but that is true of all human endeavour. Laws and customs can either mitigate or support it. Laws permitting, or at least not forbidding, employers to combine to force wages down and forbidding workers to combine to force them up evidently support the selfish interest of employers against workers. Laws permitting and forbidding the opposite evidently support the selfish interest of workers against employers.[33]

When a particular worker's need to be employed is significantly greater than the employer's need to employ that particular worker, the possibility of exploitation is greater than it otherwise would have been. The reverse is also true. Marx, however, basing his view on his understanding of surplus value, considered the employment of labour to be inherently corrupt, and consequently corrupting of any trading order that included the hiring of one person by another. This position is adopted by some thinkers in the tradition of critical jurisprudence. Although we fully acknowledge the very real possibility and, indeed, the existence, of exploitation, we do not share the view that employment of one person is inherently and unavoidably unjust.

Because in modern economies most make their living by trading, and most do so by trading their time and skill for a money income, the question as to whether or not the employment of one person by another is reciprocally just is not alone important but fundamental. Suppose

... the case of two men proposing to carry out a project together, with no other 'factors' involved. They would have a choice: either to negotiate agreement in advance of all details of what is to be done by each and sharing the result; or a much simpler arrangement would be for one of them to take charge and assure to the other a more or less definite

---

[31] Smith, *Wealth of Nations* [III.ii.10], 388.   [32] *Capital – Part II* [ch VI], 185–196.
[33] The relative positions of employers and workers, or the nature of each group's influence on law-making processes, while relevant to other types of analysis, has no bearing whatsoever on this analysis.

return, his own 'share' (positive or negative) to depend on the outcome... This hypothetical case exemplifies all the theoretical essentials of entrepreneurship and profit.[34]

'Capital' is often popularly but erroneously thought of exclusively as money. In fact, capital is the set of resources that are needed to establish and carry through an enterprise. In Knight's model the one taking charge provides one factor of production, the financial-capital, and the one assured of the more or less definite return – a money income – provides the labour-capital. For simplicity we suppose that the supplier of the financial-capital has no further input. In Knight's model, the labour-capital is assured of a return. The return on the financial-capital depends on the outcome. The labourer invests his labour in order to get a return that, had he not invested it, he would not have got. Evidently, the labourer would not have invested his labour – that is, his time and skill – had he not expected the return. Equally evidently, if irrespective of the outcome there was to be no return on the financial-capital, it would not have been invested in the first place. But the return on the financial-capital is the return over and above all the costs incurred including those of the labour-capital's assured return, that is, on the surplus-value produced through the joint operation of both forms of capital investment. What the prospective employee negotiates is, therefore, a more or less assured and more or less definite return on his investment of labour-capital. It is precisely for this reason that the eighteenth-century Irish economist, Richard Cantillon, considered the labourer to be the entrepreneur of his own labour.[35]

5.5 The Trading Order and the Allocation of Resources

Reciprocally just exchange is the agreed exchange of the ownership of the traded goods. Prior to the emergence of a trading order the potential trading partners already own different things, no matter how the particular allocation of resources originally came about. Once exchanges have been made the prior allocation is replaced by a new allocation within which in turn the next set of exchanges takes place. Considered synchronically, at any moment, each participant holds a set of potentially tradable resources; considered diachronically, the resources actually traded between participants, and the new resources that participants have produced, bring about a new set of potentially tradable resources.

It is possible to imagine a trading order within which each participant begins with a limited number of goods, and in which there is no further production of tradable goods. These goods will be traded between the participants until each one either has a number of goods none of which he wants to trade against any

[34] FH Knight in his *Risk, Uncertainty and Profit* [1921] (New York: Augustus M Kelley, 1964), 'Preface for the Reprint of 1957', lxi.

[35] R Cantillon, *Essay on the Nature of Commerce in General* (trans H Higgs, 1931) (New Brunswick, NJ: Transaction Publishers, 2001).

good held by any other participant, or has some goods that he would gladly trade but which no other participant wants. A trading order of this type then becomes extinct because the order is nothing other than the set of transactions, and disappears when, as in this case, there can be no further transactions. Conversely, the order will continue if and only if potential participants have goods that they are willing and able to trade. To be a potential participant in the order one must want what some other participant has and have what some other participant wants. Alone one can be a potential participant but alone one cannot be an actual participant. A shopkeeper may have a bottle of lemonade that a shopper would like to have but may want more money from him than he is willing to spend. Actual participation occurs only when the exchange is agreed between the two potential participants. There are two prerequisites for a trading order to continue indefinitely: first, that the participants own, and are entitled to trade, what they offer; and secondly, that the participants can indefinitely continue to produce what others want. When what someone offers is no longer wanted, he must produce something else that is wanted or fall out of the trading order. A participant will survive within the order only if he can get from others what he wants from them in exchange for the goods or services that he produces. A potential participant who already has everything that he wants will not produce goods or services for exchange and a potential participant who fails to offer what others want at a price they are willing to pay cannot get from them what he wants. Neither potential participant actually participates.

Money is a good that, in the normal course of events, and excluding rampant hyperinflation, every participant in the order is willing to accept in exchange for any other good. When money becomes commonplace, direct exchange or barter tends to diminish or die out. In an order that includes money, most participants will at any given moment have some money, and so be able to exchange their money for some other good. Over time, however, to continue to participate in the order, each participant must have some good that can be exchanged against money, for example, labour against a wage. So, for example, an electrician, a lawyer, or a professor has a skill the use of which he is willing to 'hire out' in exchange for money.[36] Besides labour and skill, participants may have other goods that

---

[36] It is more accurate to say that the labourer 'hires out' rather than 'sells' his labour. Karl Marx in *Capital* wrote: 'The second essential condition to the owner of money finding labour-power in the market as a commodity is this – that the labourer instead of being in a position to sell commodities in which his labour is incorporate, must be obliged to offer for sale as a commodity that very labour-power, which exists only in his living self', *Capital – Part II* [ch VI], 187. It is undeniably the case that labour-power, unlike the other means of production, exists in the labourer's 'living self', but where Marx thought of the labourer 'selling' his 'labour-power', we think of it as 'hiring out' because the labourer – of whatever type – retains the ownership of his skill and hires out the use of it; perhaps it may be said that he sells his time and the agreed way of using his skill during that time. To hire out one's skill to an extent resembles the renting out of one's land. As the one who hires out labour is paid by the one who hires it, so the one who rents out land is paid by the one who rents it. In similar vein, Adam Smith in the *Wealth of Nations* [I.viii.1, 2, and 6] ('Of the wages of labour') remarked that: 'The produce of labour constitutes the natural recom-

may be offered in exchange for money – for example, real property, or goods that they have produced using their skill. Money, skill, and other goods are similar in that they are tradable resources;[37] they differ in that money is immediately acceptable to every participant as an exchange-good, whereas only those who want the fruit of a particular skill or who want particular goods will accept skill and other goods as exchange-goods. At any one time, then, most participants have the three kinds of tradable resource: money, skill, and other goods. At no time will all participants have identical resources. After many exchanges, the same will be true, but each participant will then have different resources from those he had initially. (It is possible to *imagine* all to have identical resources but even then, trade would be possible as long as at least two participants were willing to exchange something that one had for something the other had, as could happen if X and Y both had apples and pears but X wanted only pears, and Y only apples. Absent reciprocal demand trade ceases, for reciprocal demand is the engine of exchange.)

The difference between the participants' resources at the earlier and later time is the result of the indefinitely many transactions. Each transaction changes the resources of those involved. But no single participant knows or can know what all the earlier resources were, or can choose what the later resources will be.[38] Thus, a trading order emerges upon an assignment of ownership – the participants' resources – and, as a result of the many transactions, results in a different assignment of resources that cannot as a whole be predicted or chosen. It is obvious that, with some presuppositions, limited prediction is possible since some future sets of holdings are necessary or probable consequences of prior choices. If, say, the price of oil rises relative to the prevailing prices of other goods and services, while the resources of other participants in the order who want oil remain the same, then necessarily the choices made in the use of their resources must change. How precisely they will change cannot be predicted

---

pense or wages of labour. In that original state of things, which precedes both the appropriation of land and the accumulation of stock, the whole produce of labour belongs to the labourer. He has neither landlord nor master to share with him...As soon as land becomes private property, the landlord demands a share of almost all the produce which the labourer can either raise or collect from it' (Glasgow edn, 82–3). Note that Adam Smith writes of 'the produce of labour' and, of course, the produce may be sold and thus permanent title to it (the produce) transferred rather than hired out. To sell one's skill and thus permanently transfer title to its use to another is to sell oneself into slavery.

[37] We concentrate here on immediately tradable resources rather than on the resources that enable participants in the trading order to produce immediately tradable resources, as when, for example, a participant has sufficient resources to allow him to plant seed potatoes and wait until the potatoes are grown and become immediately tradable.

[38] No single participant knows or can know what the earlier resources were simply because resources are too varied and there are too many people; even if one knows a person well one rarely has anything like an exact idea of what his resources are; and there is a very real sense in which at a particular time one does not know one's own; certainly no one can possibly know the present resources of everyone who participates in the trading order.

in detail but, all things being equal, it is not unreasonable to expect that the changes will not differ greatly from changes made in similar circumstances in the past.[39]

To say that the set of choices must change is to say that the set of exchanges must change. The very many consequences of changes in the set of exchanges cannot be predicted and, indeed, can be discovered retrospectively only with the utmost difficulty. As we have made clear, justice within the trading order is not, and cannot be, concerned with the overall assignment of participants' resources. It is concerned only with the justice involved in the individual transactions. If a 'just situation' is taken to be some ideal assignment of resources other than that brought about by indefinitely many reciprocally just transactions – as it is taken to be by, for example, liberals such as John Rawls, many socialists, many conservatives, and most fascists – then a 'just situation' cannot be brought about within the trading order. Such a 'just situation', in other words, could be brought about only by imposition of an assignment or allocation of resources by the state or another such centralized power.

But such an assignment or allocation could not be definitive or permanent were trading to continue. In 'Of Human Societies', which is the second chapter of his *Essay on the Nature of Commerce in General*, Richard Cantillon wrote – correctly, in our view – that *even if* everyone begins with an equal allotment of land they will shortly not be equal:

> Even if the Prince distribute the Land equally among all the Inhabitants it will ultimately be divided among a small number. One man will have several Children and cannot leave to each of them a portion of Land equal to his own; another will die without Children, and will leave his portion to some one who has Land already rather than to one who has none; a third will be lazy, prodigal, or sickly, and be obliged to sell to another who is frugal and industrious, who will continually add to his Estate by new purchases and will employ upon it the Labour of those who having no Land of their own are compelled to offer him their Labour in order to live.
>
> At the first settlement of Rome each Citizen had two Journaux of Land allotted to him. Yet there was soon after as great an inequality in the estates as that which we see today in all the countries of Europe.[40]

---

[39] The commonplace 'all things being equal' (*ceteris paribus*) includes the assumption, riskier in some circumstances than in others, that the future will be conformable to the past. See Hume's discussion of prediction in *An Enquiry Concerning Human Understanding*, IV.II and V.I. In a model, the proviso 'all things being equal' refers to the accepted defining elements in the surrounding context. To say that a shopper, *all things being equal*, will buy the cheaper of two identical goods, means that provided the shopper has no reason other than price – which in reality a shopper may well have – to distinguish between two identical goods, he will buy the cheaper of the two. The underlying presupposition is that a person will economize his scarce resources, that is, use as few of them as he can to gain what he wants.

[40] R Cantillon, *Essay on the Nature of Commerce in General* (trans H Higgs (1931)) (New Brunswick, NJ: Transaction Publishers, 2001), 6. Scholars now think that Cantillon's essay was originally written in French in 1730. It was published posthumously (Cantillon is thought to have been murdered in 1734 in London) in France in 1755.

In a dominantly agricultural society an equal allotment of resources in land is a possibility, albeit a very remote one, but for a trading order to exist there cannot be an equal allotment of resources, for exchange can come about only when potential partners have different things. Thus, the trading order is a continuous circulation of goods through many exchanges; the intended result of each exchange is the good of the partners in that exchange; and the intended result can be achieved only if the exchange is reciprocally just. The assignment of goods at any given moment between all the participants in the order is brought about in great measure by these exchanges but neither is, nor can be, envisaged or intended by anyone. (We say 'in great measure' because what a person produces for himself rather than for exchange is, of course, a greater or lesser part of his set of resources at any time.) The common good of the trading order is not a particular outcome but the reciprocally just working of the order, the function of which is to allow the fulfilment of many purposes.

5.6 The *Lex Mercatoria*

Although a trading order emerges within a surrounding context, the temptation to imagine that context to be necessarily an already established jurisdiction, community, society, nation, town, or village must be resisted. The order begins as soon as two people trade with each other; it enlarges as each one trades with a third and fourth, and exponentially increases as the third and fourth trade with a fifth and sixth and the original two trade with a seventh and eighth, and so on indefinitely. It is obviously and easily possible to imagine that each of the eight traders live in the same village but, unless there is a law forbidding trade with any outsider, it is equally possible, and more realistic, to imagine traders within the village trading with others outside it. What is true of a village is true of any jurisdiction whatsoever. Consequent is that the trading order is essentially trans-jurisdictional and is simply the set of exchanges between those people who trade.[41]

From this two things follow. First, in so far as discussions of the economy of a nation concentrate on citizens' participation in the trading order, and prescind from the non-trading elements in their production of goods for their own use that they do not propose to offer in exchange, and prescind also from their various choices as to how best to use their scarce resources (as when a family grows vegetables only for its own consumption or as when an individual devotes time which he could have devoted to making money to listening to music, cooking, or watching a film, etc), what is being discussed is not the national trading order but the precise manner in which citizens participate in the trading order which will almost certainly not be contained within the jurisdiction. In short, the trading

---

[41] See T Murphy, 'Globalization, Legal Pluralism, and the New Constitutionalism' (2007) 25 *Nordisk Tidsskrift for Menneskerettigheter* [*Nordic Journal of Human Rights*] 73.

order tends naturally to globalization. A locally restricted trading order does not indefinitely persist except by the unusual accident of being totally isolated from any other, or, within a particular jurisdiction, by the successful enforcement of a rule emanating from the state or another such centralized power forbidding all trade outside the jurisdiction.

Secondly, because traders live within different jurisdictions, and carry on their business in different jurisdictions, and because the conventional rules – for instance, the rules that determine what constitutes a contract – differ in different jurisdictions, there will emerge disputes that would be settled differently in different jurisdictions. To overcome this manifestly unsatisfactory situation, there tends to emerge a trans-national *lex mercatoria* or 'law merchant' by the conventions of which merchants among themselves agree to be bound. The emergence of the agreed conventions that constitute the *lex mercatoria* takes place within the trading order and not prior to it.

Harold Berman has characterized the medieval *lex mercatoria* as a coherent, European-wide body of general commercial law, driven by merchants, and more or less universally accepted and formalized into well-known and well-established customs during the period from 1050 to 1150.[42] Although it is generally accepted, Berman's account is not undisputed,[43] and some suggest that the law merchant evolved from *two* sources: legislation by public authorities and, only secondarily, from the practices of merchant communities. Emily Kadens, for example, suggests that the documents produced by merchants, such as contracts, bills of lading, and arbitration decisions, 'give little indication that medieval merchants thought of their practices as anything more than "the way we do things"'.[44] This characterization of the *lex mercatoria* as nothing more than 'the way [merchants] do things' is in our view critically significant. It is critically significant because it describes perfectly a central component of the account of law and justice that this book proposes and defends. As we have said, humans living together in civil society 'do' a whole host of 'things' in particular 'ways'. These ways include the customs, practices, well-known and accepted procedures, and mutual expectations that establish the jural relationships particular to communites. As customs, methods, and practices constitute the living law of a community, so in the trading order they constitute the *lex mercatoria*.

---

[42] 'It was then that the basic concepts and institutions of modern Western mercantile law – *lex mercatoria* ("the law merchant") – were formed, and, even more important, it was then that mercantile law in the West first came to be viewed as an integrated, developing system, a body of law', HJ Berman, *Law and Revolution: The Formation of the Western Legal Tradition* (Cambridge, Mass: Harvard University Press, 1983), 333.

[43] See, as examples of other perspectives, E Kadens, 'Order within Law, Variety within Custom: The Character of the Medieval Merchant Law' (2004) 5 *Chicago Journal of International Law* 39; C Wasserstein Fassberg, '*Lex Mercatoria* – Hoist with Its Own Petard?' (2004) 5 *Chicago Journal of International Law* 67; C Donahue Jr, 'Medieval and Early Modern *Lex Mercatoria*: An Attempt at the *probatio diabolica*' (2004) 5 *Chicago Journal of International Law* 21; and O Volckart and A Mangels, 'Are the Roots of the Modern *Lex Mercatoria* Really Medieval?' (1999) 65 *Southern Economic Journal* 427.   [44] E Kadens, 'Order within Law, Variety within Custom', 43.

The debates concerning the medieval *lex mercatoria* are of more than historical interest. It is generally thought that the *lex mercatoria* – whatever its precise nature – declined in significance with the growing status and power of urban and, later, national legal systems. However, with the advent of globalization in its contemporary form, and because, on the international level, there is no binding authority that protects merchants' property rights, guarantees their freedom of contract, and enforces legitimate claims, a modern or new *lex mercatoria* is said to have emerged. This modern version of the law merchant – which is also referred to as international, transnational, or supranational commercial law, international customs or usages, or the general principles of international commercial law – is considered to be 'a set of rules of conduct for border-crossing transactions developed autonomously by the international business community and applied by arbitrators in case of trade disputes'.[45]

The modern *lex mercatoria* relies heavily on the increasingly common modern practice of international commercial arbitration: it is said to be 'an autonomous non-state legal order with special rules and special adjudicating [and in particular arbitral] bodies'.[46] Arbitration is the hearing and determining of a dispute or the settling of differences between parties – using quasi-judicial methods – by a person or persons appointed by mutual consent or statutory provision. State law is becoming ever more irrelevant to the development of international commerce because of the hugely significant role of *lex mercatoria* in arbitration. The increasing role of arbitration in international commercial contracts and disputes is said to be a reflection of the international merchant community's inherent jurisdictional power, and an arbitrator applying the law merchant is considered to better effectuate the parties' intent than does a national court applying national positive law, including its private international law.[47]

Michael Medwig provides a compelling analysis of the historical and contemporary *lex mercatoria*.[48] The merchant judges, he suggests, like modern arbitrators, relied on their knowledge of commercial custom and on their familiarity with the evolving needs of commerce to resolve disputes. Medwig cites Hayek's views, to which we have already referred, that rarely does the jurist achieve more than an adequate and partial expression of what is well known in practice because of the general and abstract nature of the rules that govern

[45] O Volckart and A Mangels, 'Are the Roots of the Modern *Lex Mercatoria* Really Medieval?', 427.

[46] R Michaels, 'The Re-Statement of Non-State Law: The State, Choice of Law, and the Challenge from Global Legal Pluralism' (2005) 51 *Wayne Law Review* 1209, 1219.

[47] 'Notwithstanding the differences in the political, economic and legal systems of the world a new law merchant is rapidly developing in the world of international trade. It is time that recognition be given to the existence of an autonomous commercial law that has grown independent of the national systems of law', A Goldstajn, 'The New Law Merchant' (1961) *Journal of Business Law* 12, 12.

[48] MT Medwig, 'The New Law Merchant: Legal Rhetoric and Commercial Reality' (1993) 24 *Law and Policy in International Business* 589.

action, and that the jurist's task is one of discovering something which exists, not one of creating something new.

A great imaginative leap is needed in order to understand how the role of a merchant jurist differs from the role envisioned for judges under our present positivist conception of the judiciary. One must begin by observing that merchants are guided by rules that they know how to follow but are unable to state. The merchant jurist's function is to articulate these pre-existing rules that merchants observe in practice but might be unable to express. His task is to tell merchants what rule ought to have informed their expectations, not because anyone had told them that this was the rule, but because this was the established custom that they ought to have known. The merchant jurist's articulation of the custom as a verbal rule aims only at obtaining the merchant's consent about the custom's existence, and not at formulating a new rule.[49]

Ultimately, the body of *lex mercatoria* represents a prime instance of contemporary 'non-state' law, although it is not the only such more or less coherent body of law.[50] The significance of the *lex mercatoria* in our analysis of law and justice lies in its advanced state of development relative to most other forms of non-state law, and in its emphasis on the fact that trade is not confined within any one jurisdiction but tends naturally, as we said above, to globalization.

5.7 Entitlements and the Trading Order

Because what are traded are not simply goods and services but the ownership of these, and because the order emerges within the surrounding context of ownership, the given arrangement of resources within the surrounding context must be taken for granted. Thus, every participant in the order is presumed to own both what is to be traded, and whatever means he has of producing tradable goods and services. Within the surrounding context of ownership there are entitlements that have nothing, or need have nothing, to do with trading; there are entitlements intrinsically associated with trade; and within particular jurisdictions there are particular entitlements, restrictions, or impositions extrinsic to the trading order. These three types of entitlement will now be discussed in turn.

First, there are entitlements that have nothing, or need have nothing, to do with trading. These are the fundamental entitlements found in the jural order

---

[49] Ibid, 591.
[50] For instance, recent work by Marc Hertogh has compared the *lex mercatoria* with the emergence of a *lex sportiva internationalis* and non-state law associated with the internet. M Hertogh, 'What is Non-State Law? Mapping the Other Hemisphere of the Legal World' in J van Schooten and JM Verschuuren (eds), *International Governance and Law: State Regulation and Non-State Law* (Cheltenham/Northhampton: Edward Elgar Publishing, 2008), 11. On the *lex mercatoria* and the governance of the internet, see also D Nelken, 'Ehrlich's Legacies: Back to the Future in the Sociology of Law?' in M Hertogh (ed), *Living Law: Reconsidering Eugen Ehrlich* (Oxford: Hart Publishing, 2009), 237, 247–54.

that pre-exist any trading. We have referred to many of these entitlements in the preceding chapters. In a community of subsistence farmers, families own and work their holdings and livestock and little (although rarely nothing) is traded. In such a community ownership and its attendant entitlements, including those relating to lending and borrowing, and those prohibiting stealing, will all exist. In such a community justice will be concerned with, for example, the inevitable disputes about access to water from a river that no particular person or family owns, about damage caused to one holding by cattle breaking in from another, about alleged interference with boundaries, and so on. In such a community promises outside or prior to any trading will be given and either fulfilled or broken. As we have said, that promises are to be kept (*pacta sunt servanda*) is not a rule added to promising; rather it makes explicit, and to an extent commands, what is already intrinsic to the act. Disputes about entitlement may arise in case promises are broken, or in case there is disagreement as to whether or not a promise was made.

Secondly, there are entitlements intrinsically associated with trade. If Peter and Paul mutually agree to exchange work for money, Peter is entitled to the agreed sum of money, and Paul to the agreed work, where Paul is entitled to alienate his money, and Peter to alienate his work. As we have said also, promises exist outside or prior to any trading, but promises are also intrinsic to transactions. Transactions within a trading order are based on mutual contracts.[51] The fundamental rule of contract, namely, that contracts are to be kept simply states what a contract is; it is natural to a contract, which is a legally binding promise, that it be kept. A contract establishes a set of agreed entitlements between the contractors. Someone may verbally or in writing state that he will do something without having the least intention of doing it; he has not contracted but has pretended to contract. And yet he may have performed an action that will be judged by a court to have formed a contract and to have bound him to fulfil the terms of the contract. One who has given an undertaking that he has no intention of honouring cannot escape on the grounds that his undertaking was fraudulent. A contract *naturally* produces an obligation and breach of contract is an injury.

A contract naturally obliges the contractor but the determination of what exactly constitutes an actionable contract is *conventional* and so varies from jurisdiction to jurisdiction. If a company makes an offer to a shop for the sale of clothes but decides subsequently to withdraw the offer, is the company contractually bound if it is found that the shop posted a letter of acceptance before the decision to withdraw the offer was communicated? Courts deal with particular cases. Suppose that the shop has posted such a letter but the company, claiming it had no knowledge of the acceptance at the time of the offer's withdrawal, refuses to perform. The shop sues the company. Does a valid, actionable contract exist? The context – the element of natural justice – is not in question. The material

---

[51] See Adam Smith's discussion in the *Lectures of Jurisprudence*, Report dated 1766, 472–85 (Glasgow edn).

facts are not disputed. The primary question before the court is whether or not the material facts are to be understood as a contract between the company and the shop. If the court finds that there was a contract, the question of justice arises: what is now due to the shop from the company? If the court finds that there was not a contract, a different version of the question of justice arises: specifically, how are costs to be apportioned between the parties to the case? Whichever way the court decides the specific dispute, it cannot do so without establishing whether or not a contract existed in the particular circumstances; and (as we shall see in more detail when we consider adjudication and interpretation in Chapter 6) the court will necessarily consider the particular circumstances in the context of the type of situation in which the circumstances have arisen. In other words, in dealing with the particular case, the court cannot avoid determining the character of a type of situation even if that has not already been determined in legislation.

In the example of the company and the shop the issue is to what extent an offer in contract law is binding. The basic common law principle is that an offer may be freely withdrawn at any time until the offeree has accepted it. In the English common law this principle was mitigated by the 'postal rule', according to which it is not when the acceptance reaches the offeror that the contract is formed but at the earlier time when the offeree dispatches it, that is, puts it in a postbox or otherwise entrusts it to the Post Office.[52] It has been remarked that those unfamiliar with English common law may find it hard to reconcile this rule with the consensual nature of contract,[53] but it is explained by the common law doctrine of consideration, the doctrine whereby a promise, unless contained in a deed, generates a binding obligation only if the promisee has rendered or promised a counter-performance. This doctrine and the basic common law principle regarding offers reflect and inform conventions as to when a contract is formed. In French law, by contrast, the premature withdrawal of an offer leads to liability in damages, always in the case of offers with fixed periods, usually for offers without such periods attached. The convention is different again in German law, where every offer is irrevocable: a purported withdrawal has no legal effect whatever unless the offeror has excluded the binding effect of his proposal.[54]

These different jurisdictional regimes are, however, and indeed must be, similar in that the basic context is that described in the rule that contracts are to be kept. Trade can be carried on only when this basic context exists; and when it exists, trade can be carried on in any one of the different conventional contexts.

---

[52] *Adams v Lindsell* (1818) 1 B & Ald 681, 106 Eng Rep 250.

[53] 'Even in the Common Law all other declarations (offers, withdrawal of offers, the giving of notice, and so on) must reach the addressee before they are effective, yet a *contract* can come into existence without the offeror's knowledge. A valid contract arises even if the acceptance is lost in the post, though of course the offeree must be able to prove that he really did post his acceptance', K Zweigert and H Kötz, *An Introduction to Comparative Law* (Oxford: Oxford University Press, 3rd edn, 1998), 359 (emphasis in original).   [54] Ibid, 356–64.

Because trade can be carried on in different conventional contexts, it is easy to overlook the fact that conventional contexts must be established. A substantial proportion of trade in modern societies cannot be carried on if the status of offers is neither known nor agreed. Thus, although the particular character of the context within which trade is carried on is conventional, and so may differ from one jurisdiction to another, nonetheless it is essential to trade that *some* particular context be agreed between, and known to, traders.

In his *Promises, Morals, and Law*, PS Atiyah argues against the theory of contract that bases promissory obligation upon individual will or intention and in favour of the theory that reliance and benefit are the conditions for primary obligation.[55] But both the will theory and Atiyah's basic idea, that promises are binding if there is a pre-existing obligation in the form of a benefit received or detrimental reliance incurred, acknowledge that the basic context within which the matter arises is established by the principle that contracts are to be kept. Jack Balkin has interpreted Atiyah's analysis as a 'quite successful' deconstructive reading that does *not* show that a new ground of explanation will succeed where the old one has failed:

> Rather, he has demonstrated that the will theory and the benefit/reliance theory of promissory obligation exist in a relation of *différance*, that is, of mutual differentiation and dependence. This conclusion is unsatisfying to someone who seeks an ultimate ground for contractual obligation but [deconstructionism] suggests that this is the best that can be done.[56]

But an 'ultimate ground for contractual obligation' *does* exist. It is that a binding promise establishes a new jural relationship between the contracting parties; this is intrinsic to contracting and without this the words, actions, and intentions associated with the new jural relationship would be vacuous. The tag *pacta sunt servanda* is less a command than a statement of the nature of contract. We see precisely the same in less meta-theoretical debates such as discussion of the tension surrounding sources of contract law. Hugh Collins has suggested, for example, that the type of law that best contributes to the construction of markets and a vibrant economy would be one that 'avoids clear-cut entitlements based upon the contractual framework in favour of a more contextual examination of business expectations based upon the business relation and the business deal',[57] whereas a strong opposing view favours a greater formalism in the sense of increased focus on written contracts.[58] Neither opinion disputes the fundamental principle of *pacta sunt servanda*.

[55] PS Atiyah, *Promises, Morals, and Law* (Oxford: Oxford University Press, 1983), 66–7, 129, 193–4.

[56] JM Balkin, 'Deconstructive Practice and Legal Theory' (1987) 96 *Yale Law Journal* 743, 772.

[57] H Collins, *Regulating Contracts* (Oxford: Oxford University Press, 1999), 176.

[58] RA Hillman, 'The "New Conservatism" in Contract Law and the Process of Legal Change (1999) 40 *Boston College Law Review* 879; O Ben-Shahar, 'The Tentative Case Against Flexibility in Commercial Law' (1999) 66 *University of Chicago Law Review* 781.

Thirdly and finally, within particular jurisdictions there are particular entitlements, restrictions, or impositions *extrinsic* to the trading order. These are in large measure imposed by legislation, and in many cases differ from one jurisdiction to another. We have referred in our discussion – for example when we discussed how language is learned – to the way in which a set of rules may either establish or describe an activity; extrinsic constraints show how rules may *modify* the trading order. Banking law, for example, that allows fractional as against 100 per cent reserve, is an extrinsic rule with enormous consequences at least some of which can be foreseen. State intervention in the trading order is ubiquitous and we referred to several examples in the second section of this chapter. We are not primarily concerned here with the many important and various effects of such particular permissions, restrictions, or impositions on the trading order. We remark only that there are such effects, and that it is impossible accurately and in detail to gauge in advance what their effects will be. Inevitably there will be unintended results or effects, some of which will be foreseeable and some of which will not be. Still, they are statutorily established conventions and, as such, like any laws, are expected to produce a desired result. With respect to each proposed convention many questions arise: Is the intended result good? Is it reasonable to expect that the establishment of the convention will bring about the intended result? Is it reasonable to expect that the production of the intended result will not bring about other 'unintended' results? Is it reasonable to expect that the good brought about by the intended results will not be outweighed by the harm occasioned by the unintended results?[59] Although the notion of 'unintended result' is somewhat confused, it is possible to note that, to be reasonable, a law establishing an extrinsic constraint must, like any law, intend a result. To be a good law, the

---

[59] Wage agreements, with statutory effect, are nowadays often made between labour unions, employers' unions, and governments. These agreements have an intended result: to secure wages acceptable to both parties and thus to reduce the likelihood of strikes or other manifestations of industrial unrest. Suppose there emerges an agreement to a general wage increase of 2 per cent. Suppose that the agreement produces the intended result in that the wage increase is awarded and salaries are raised. A completely foreseeable and inevitable consequence is an increase in inequality between employees, that is, an increase in the absolute disparity in income between the less and better off employees. An employee who before the agreement earned €2,000 per month will, after the agreement, earn €2,040; one who formerly earned €1,000 will now earn €1,020. Although the relative or proportional difference has remained the same, the absolute or arithmetical difference has increased as the disparity between their monthly incomes has increased from €1,000 to €1,020. If the process is repeated in a later national agreement, the disparity will increase further, from €1,020 to €1,040.40. The disparity will continue inexorably to increase as the process is repeated. Is this foreseeable result actually foreseen and if foreseen intended? What unforeseen and perhaps unforeseeable consequences will result are by definition unknown. If the inevitable increase in absolute disparity in income is foreseen, it is unreasonable to ignore it. Even if originally unnoticed and unintended, once it has become known, it cannot be considered to be unintended in quite the same way as before. Is it a good, bad, or quite indifferent consequence? If it is thought good or quite indifferent, there is no further problem. If it is thought bad, then it would be unreasonable not to weigh the anticipated harm against the anticipated good. What is said here of this very simple case is obviously applicable to more difficult cases such as banking law about which there is considerable disagreement among contemporary political economists.

intended result must be good, and the established constraint or liberty must be judged to be a likely means of achieving the result.

5.8 Morality, Self-interest, and the Trading Order

Anyone who would trade proposes to exchange one thing for another. An actual trade occurs when there is mutual agreement between trading partners. Each partner decides to trade what he has for what the other has. In every transaction each partner makes a decision – a choice as to how to use his available resources at this time and in these circumstances – and, as we have said repeatedly, a decision or choice is a moral action. A transaction is vitiated if, for example, a participant misrepresents what he offers in exchange, as when a dealer offers as an original painting what he knows to be a forgery.[60] Ways to behave illegally, immorally, or dishonourably are many and devious and behaving in such ways is sometimes thought of as expressing the materialism associated with 'market values'. It is, of course, true that the trading order offers opportunities for enrichment through illegal, immoral, and dishonourable behaviour but this does not distinguish it from any other aspect of human living. Greed, dishonesty, immorality, and dishonour are not values intrinsically or uniquely associated with trading and to participate in the order does not require one to be greedy, dishonest, immoral, or dishonourable. In fact the contrary is closer to the truth, for the continued survival of the order depends on most people being honest, moral, and honourable most of the time.

The relatively common idea that the engine of the trading order is greed rather than mutual demand may have its source in a misreading of Adam Smith's contrast between self-interest and benevolence or beneficence.[61] There is a vague sense that to be self-interested is to be selfish; and to be selfish is, for the most part, thought ill of. But to equate self-interestedness with selfishness is a mistake,[62] as

---

[60] We discussed misrepresentation in ch 5.4 above. The offer may likewise be vitiated if, unknown to the dealer, the painting is a forgery; it is enough that, as part of the contract, he asserts, although in ignorance, what is not the case.

[61] 'It is not from the benevolence of the butcher, the brewer, or the baker, that we expect our dinner, but from their regard to their own interest. We address ourselves, not to their humanity, but to their self-love…', Smith, *The Wealth of Nations* (I.II.2), 26–7. In this passage 'their own interest' and 'their self-love' are wrongly understood if they are taken to mean 'selfishness' which is to pursue our own interests with no care for another's and 'how ruinous soever to him', Smith, *The Theory of Moral Sentiments* (III.3.3), 135. What is meant in the famous – even infamous – passage from *The Wealth of Nations* is that the butcher, brewer, and baker sell us beef, beer, or bread in order to make a living and, conversely, we buy them because we want to eat or drink. And that is obviously and uncontrovertibly true. That there is no conflict between *The Theory of Moral Sentiments* and *The Wealth of Nations* on the matter is well argued by Raphael and Macfie in their introduction to the former, pp 20–5.

[62] See Alasdair MacIntyre's brief discussion of self-interest in the Homeric poems in which he points out that 'there is not the same contrast between what is to one's own interest and what is to the interest of others as that which is conveyed by modern uses of "self-interest" and cognate terms',

a very ordinary example shows. Consider someone who buys a ticket from the airline company to fly from Akureyri to Reykjavík. He normally does so because he wants to get from one place to the other; normally he does not do so because he wants to keep the airline in business or those who work in the ticket office in a job. He is, in other words, self-interested. Perhaps he intends to go to Reykjavík for selfish reasons – he might want to engage in a fraud that demanded his presence there – or he might just as well want to go for reasons that many would think were benevolent – he might want to visit a friend who was dying. Whether his reason for going to Reykjavík is benevolent or selfish, his reason for buying the air ticket is self-interested. And this is all that self-interest is. Self-interest is intrinsic to trade: a person will not exchange X for Y unless, for whatever reason, he wants Y more than he wants X. Selfishness in trade is the desire to get what one wants with no care for one's trading partner's interest. Selfishness in trade is common, as the incidence of fraud and other forms of dishonesty show. A particular person's self-interest may be predominantly selfish – greed is neither unknown nor particularly uncommon – but the trading order intrinsically serves mutual self-interest rather than selfishness, and the inverse is also true: mutual self-interest and not selfishness is what serves and sustains the trading order. The person's self-interested buying of the air ticket contributes to keeping the airline in business and those who work in the ticket office in their jobs. Counterintuitive though it may seem, the trading order is a vast *cooperative* order within which people pursuing their own interests allow others to pursue theirs. The trading partners' interests are respected to the extent that one acts honestly and honourably, and ignored and undermined to the extent that one acts selfishly, greedily, dishonestly, or dishonourably; and selfishness, greed, dishonesty, and dishonour not only ignore others' immediate interests but also contribute to the collapse of the cooperative order.

Humans are social beings who sustain their lives by using their scarce resources, and how particular groups do so is their economy. It is cooperation in the use of scarce resources that is universal; the particular character and extent of cooperation differs in different economic systems. The trading order is a vast cooperative network within which there are two types of cooperation. First, there is cooperative exchange as when A gives X to B in exchange for Y. In that exchange X is a resource that A deploys in order to get Y, which he wants more than he wants X and B deploys his resource Y in order to get X which he wants more than he wants Y. Secondly, there is the pooling of resources as when A and B deploy their resources X + Y in order to get Z from C in exchange. A perfectly commonplace example of this is when two people agree to share a taxi fare when the cost of two separate journeys is greater than the cost of the joint journey. In the model of the trading order each adult participant (children, being unable at first to sustain

---

Whose Justice? Which Rationality? (London: Duckworth, 1988), 20. We consistently distinguish between 'self-interest' that takes others' interests into account and 'selfishness' which does not.

themselves, must be sustained by adults)[63] uses the available resources to sustain his life. In no modern state is living sustained purely by trade. States impose taxes of various kinds and use the resources gained to pay for an array of products that may be used by residents often at no additional direct cost, such as the government and civil service, army, police, judiciary, public health and education, roads, public lighting, and so on; the list differs from state to state and time to time so that what is now in a particular state taken for granted would have been formerly thought bizarre.[64]

In the cooperative trading order, every decision is a choice of one thing rather than another, and what is preferred and chosen seems to the person choosing, at the time, in the prevailing circumstances and for whatever reason, to be more advantageous – that is to say, better and more valuable to that person – than what is not chosen. In the Western philosophical tradition, this understanding has been expressed in, for example, Aristotle's remark at the beginning of the *Nicomachean Ethics*:

Every art and every inquiry, every action and choice, is thought to aim at some good; and for this reason the good has rightly been declared to be that at which all things aim.[65]

In his commentary, St Thomas clarifies the meaning of 'good' when he asserts that what is bad is not desired except *sub ratione boni*; that is, what is 'objectively' bad is chosen because the one who chooses it considers it to be good.[66]

---

[63] Necessarily children are at first sustained by the adults who are, and who have chosen to be, responsible for them and who are, consequently, responsible for the considerable costs involved in their upbringing to adulthood.

[64] Within the political world in which most readers live a great deal is provided by the state and paid for by taxes on income earned in the trading order and which residents are compelled to pay. What the state ought to provide and how much tax ought to be levied are perennially disputed questions. Within the *model* of the trading or market order, absolutely nothing is provided centrally by the state and no taxes are levied. The justice proper to the model trading order is reciprocal and bears on the many individual transactions that make it up. Within the trading order each participant agrees to exchange the resources that he has for resources that another has. The allocation of resources at any one time is the result of the exchanges that have taken place until that time. Often the resultant allocation leads to great disparities between participants – disparities that often occasion great resentment and a deep sense of unfairness. How to deal with such disparities is a real question – often called the question of distributive or social justice – but it is not one that arises within the trading order. That question simply does not arise within the trading order considered in abstraction from the surrounding social and political arrangements in which we live. That fact about the market or trading order has led some to repudiate it and to seek another economic order in which distributive or social justice that the trading order cannot bring about may be assured. We are not concerned with that argument although we do raise the issue of the relation between the trading order and the surrounding orders and state organization. Our question here is the elucidation of reciprocal justice, which is the justice in exchange.

[65] Aristotle, *Nicomachean Ethics*, I.1094a.1.

[66] St Thomas Aquinas, *Commentary on Aristotle's Nicomachean Ethics*, I.I.9–10. As we observed in ch 4.2 above, the claim that a person chooses what is in fact bad because it seems to him to be good (that is, chooses the bad under the guise or appearance of good, *sub ratione boni*) depends upon there being an objective distinction between good and bad. We discuss this distinction in our discussion of morality in ch 7.2 below.

And Hobbes: 'But whatsoever is the object of any mans Appetite or Desire; that is it, which he for his part calleth *Good*...'.[67] In economic writing this insight into the nature or character of choice is expressed in some version of the sentence that 'all people are rational maximizers of their own satisfactions'.[68] Economists have further illuminated the character of choice by insisting on the cost of choice and on the tendency to reduce it.[69] Thus, a person will in principle tend to try to achieve his chosen goal by using as few of his available resources as possible, although in practice he may overlook resources that are in fact available to him or squander resources by using more than he need. In other words, he will try to use his scarce resources to achieve what he thinks, at the time and however much he may retrospectively regret it, to be the best overall result possible. Precisely and only because resources are scarce, to choose is to economize.

Two things are worth keeping in mind when considering the intrinsically economic nature of choice. First, what a person, in the circumstances and at the moment of choice, will find good cannot be known in advance and different people will, often for easily understood reasons, choose differently. For example, a person thinking of taking out a mortgage may find that he can choose between a tracker (variable rate) and a fixed rate mortgage. The tracker mortgage may be financially more attractive but present a greater risk. Which to choose depends on the person's willingness to live with risk. But whatever the choice, it is rational.[70] Often, in common usage, to call a choice 'rational' is to deem it

---

[67] T Hobbes, *Leviathan*, 120 [24]. Here Hobbes does not define the good but describes how the word is commonly used. In *The Elements of Law* he defines the good as the object of reason rather than of passion (*Human Nature and De Corpore Politico* (JCA Gaskin ed, Oxford: Oxford University Press, 1994), 82). In our study of Hobbes ('Law's Function in *De Cive* and *Leviathan*: A Re-appraisal of the Jurisprudence of Thomas Hobbes' (2007) 29 *Dublin University Law Journal* 231), we suggest that his theory of the good is more nuanced than might appear from this passage taken in isolation and that for him the good is discovered by and related to reason rather than exclusively to immediate appetite.

[68] R Posner, *The Problems of Jurisprudence* (Cambridge, Mass: Harvard University Press, 1990), 353.

[69] Most obviously, the cost of a good is its price – when someone asks how much something cost what he wants to know is how much money it took to buy it – but there are, of course, other costs – opportunity costs – whether or not they are noticed. The time and energy expended is a cost: to save €5 a person might well choose to cross the road to another shop but might well think that to walk five miles to save that amount would be too costly. Inevitably, every choice is the rejection of incompatible possibilities or opportunities: one cannot, for example, choose to spend the same week's holiday abroad and at home.

[70] J Tricot in his translation of Aristotle's *Nicomachean Ethics* notes that choice is properly '*rational choice, deliberate and reflective*', *Éthique à Nicomaque* (Paris: Vrin, 1959), [1.1094a.1] 31 (note 4) (emphasis in original). St Thomas in his *Commentary* (I.1.3) is clear that by 'irrational' (or what he calls in this passage 'natural') actions he means those actions that occur in humans below the level of reason: 'I call *human operations* those actions that proceed from the will according to the order of reason. If there are operations found in humans that are not subject to reason and will, these are not called properly human but natural, as is plain of the operations of the vegetative soul. Which operations in no way concern moral philosophy' (emphasis in original). For that reason, with which we agree, Ludwig von Mises, in his *Human Action: A Treatise on Economics*, thought the epithet 'rational' to be redundant in the expression 'rational choice', [1949] (Auburn: Ludwig von Mises Institute, 1998).

wise, prudent, intelligent or the like as distinct from unwise or foolish. In some economic writing the reader gets the impression that by a rational choice is meant one that maximizes monetary gain. In contrast to these views, we use the adjective 'rational', in the traditional technical sense, to indicate that the action so qualified is deliberate and one for which the person is responsible. The rational action – choice – is properly contrasted with the irrational action which occurs below the level or reason and choice, for example, the spontaneous effort to regain one's balance when one stumbles, the dilation and contraction of one's pupils in response to light and dark, various habitual linguistic tics, and gestures such as the indeliberate stroking of one's beard and the like. Since every choice is rational, what a person will choose in the prevailing circumstances cannot be predicted simply by labelling the choice rational. What a person will find good is always influenced, and cannot but be influenced, by that person's temperament and habitual values, that is, by his moral context or, changing the words only, by what that person morally is.

Secondly, what a person chooses may in retrospect seem to have been a mistake, but choices are not made retrospectively. Even an impulsive choice from which reflection is nearly wholly absent is the choice of what seemed best at the time, however much in retrospect it may be regretted. Thus, to amend a formulation common in economic writing, people tend to maximize *what seems to them at the time* to be their utility. Or, changing the words only, people choose what seems to them, at the time and in the prevailing circumstances, to be both good and preferable to any other possibility that has occurred to them. Obviously, error is possible, and in practice frequent.[71]

Ultimately, when 'economics' is taken to refer to the analysis of choice and to the fact that choice is a decision as to how best to exploit one's scarce resources, all choices are 'economic'.[72] To say that choices are moral is to stress that they are deliberate decisions as to what is to be done when the proposed action can bring

---

[71] Analysis of the widespread banking collapse in 2008–9, in which charges of 'irrationality' are frequent, illustrates different usages of the term 'irrational'. First, the collapse came about owing to bankers' choices. Its causes were not 'irrational'. Secondly, no banker chose to do X in order to achieve Y because he was convinced that to do X would not achieve Y. No choice was 'irrational' in that sense. Thirdly, many choices were extremely foolish but were, obviously, not at the time known to be. They were at the time, and in retrospect known to be, 'irrational' in the popular and misleading use of the word. The terms 'foolish' and 'stupid' are more perspicuous. Indeed, we suggest that stupidity is frequent in *everyone's* life, and its effect in human life generally is both great and greatly underestimated.

[72] The study of an economy is, therefore, a study of human choices and their inter-relations. To discover what determines the employment of the available resources in the trading order is the leading question in Keynes's *The General Theory of Employment, Interest and Money* [1936] (London: Macmillan, 1973). 'The next step [in the effort to determine the employment of resources] is to recall that it is entrepreneurs who employ resources. Hence the method of addressing the question has to be rooted in the firm, the firm being the entrepreneurial entity or unit which consists of the entrepreneur and the resources employed... but in such a way that it can be extended to the economy as a whole in a coherent manner.' C Fanning and D O Mahony, *The General Theory of Profit Equilibrium: Keynes and the Entrepreneur Economy* (London: Macmillan, 1998), 184.

about change; to say that they are economic is to stress the fact that every choice is the use of one's resources to achieve one among many possibilities. Choices are, among other things, at once moral and economic. We therefore agree with Richard Posner when, later in the paragraph quoted above, he writes that his definition that all people are rational maximizers

> embraces the criminal deciding whether to commit another crime, the litigant deciding whether to settle a case, the legislator deciding whether to vote for or against a bill, the judge deciding how to cast a vote in a case, the party to a contract deciding whether to break it...

provided only that 'to be a rational maximizer' is understood to be strictly synonymous with 'to decide what seems best at the time'. 'To be rational maximizers', 'to choose what seems good and preferable to them at the time' is not what people choose to be; it is what they cannot but be, what they inescapably are.[73]

Both the criminal who decides to commit another crime, and the person who decides to break his contract, seek to maximize what seems to them to be their own satisfaction. What distinguishes the person who chooses to commit a crime from the person who chooses not to do so, or distinguishes the person who breaks his contract from the person who keeps his, is not that one 'maximizes his own satisfaction' whereas the other does not, it is simply that one chooses X whereas the other chooses Y. In that case, one person considers that X will 'maximize his satisfaction' whereas the other person considers that Y will do so. The criminal and the person who breaks his contract seek to achieve what is in fact bad but what seems to them to be good; again, they choose what is bad under the appearance of good (*sub ratione boni*).[74]

The litigant who considers whether or not to settle out of court – to give a different example – seeks also his own good. But, whether or not a particular litigant will consider it best to settle or to go before the court cannot be known in advance; to know that someone will choose what seems best is not yet to know what will seem best to him. And there is once more an ambiguity. The proper goal of the court is to discover what is just in the instant case, to discover, as we have repeatedly said, who is entitled to what. The proper or just and honourable goal of each litigant is to discover and agree upon what is just but, as is obvious, litigants submit to the court's enquiry and sentence precisely because they

---

[73] It is possible and sometimes valuable to construct a model in which what constitutes 'rational maximizing' is specified. For example, in the effort to understand the activity of sellers and buyers in a stock market, an intelligent first specification in the model is that each participant seeks to increase his financial gains and to minimize his financial losses. Thus, within the model, no participant will be expected to buy shares at €30 in the expectation of selling at €15 and, all things being equal, no one will sell at €30 who can afford to wait for an expected rise in the sale price of his shares.

[74] Non-fulfilment of contract for a sufficiently good reason is different but no less self-interested and is discussed in G Barden, *Essays on a Philosophical Interpretation of Justice: The Virtue of Justice* (Lampeter: Mellen Press, 1999), ch 6.

have failed to agree. Equally obvious is that a litigant may be blinded by bias in his own cause and seek not what is just but what, without regard to the other, is to his immediate selfish advantage. Because the litigants do not know how the court will assess their rival claims, they may think it wise to try to reach a mutually acceptable solution in discussion out of court. There are in fact several possible reasons why litigants would try to pre-empt the court's investigation. One is that the litigants, having discussed their differences, are quietly and agreeably convinced that they have themselves discovered what is just, and have agreed to implement their discovery. They have resolved their dispute in the way that both think that the court, were it to have judged correctly, would have resolved it. Another possible reason is that each litigant wants more than the other is initially prepared to give, and that they bargain with each other until each is uncertain as to whether the court would grant him more, or until at least one disputant thinks that any better arrangement likely in his estimation to be imposed by the court does not warrant any further expenditure of his scarce resources (time and loss of other opportunities, stress, money, and so on). We do not suppose that a mutually agreed or conventional solution and a just solution are in principle and in all cases identical. On the other hand, a disputant, more interested in the just solution, which he thinks the court better placed to discover, than in any out of court mutually agreed settlement, might insist upon a hearing.

That type of discussion is similar to, yet not identical with, an exchange within a market. The similarity is that in both the result is agreed. The differences are more significant. They are: first, that in a market either party may at any time withdraw before the contract is made, whereas in the out-of-court discussion each disputant is committed either to a mutual agreement or to a court imposed solution, and so cannot simply withdraw from the dispute, and secondly, that in a disputatious situation there is a just to be discovered even if the disputants may content themselves with an agreement that may or may not be just, whereas in an exchange there is no just solution other than the reciprocally just solution which is simply what is eventually agreed. A disputant may be willing to agree to an arrangement that he does not find just because he considers that the cost of pursuing the matter would be too great whereas in a free exchange what is agreed is by definition just.

The trading order is the dynamic interplay of a vast multitude of interconnecting choices and transactions that depend on one another in ways that can be known in theory; that can be to some extent anticipated in practice; that cannot be known in detail in prospect, and only with great difficulty in retrospect. Upon the success, decline, or failure of one set of transactions depends the success, decline, or failure of many others leading to the development or decline of the well-being – in as much as that depends, as to some extent it must, on the wealth – of those who live within the social order in which the trading order operates. Virtuous self-interested action in the mutual cooperation essential to the survival of the trading order follows the golden rule, 'Whatsoever you require that others should do to you, that do ye to them' or, negatively expressed, 'Do not that to another, which thou wouldest not have done to thyself'.[75] Virtuous self-interest – good will – is not enough; decisions and actions in the trading order must also be intelligent and reasonable. But even discounting human fallibility and human greed, risk remains. The trading order is a network of interdependent enterprises some of which will inevitably fail; upon their failure will follow the failure or decline of other enterprises, and the consequent failure of some people, for a shorter or longer time, to live by participating in the order. From the restricted perspective of the trading order that seems to be simply a fact; within the wider perspective of the social order it is a problem. But one that, as we have said, is not a matter of reciprocal justice, and that the trading order does not – and cannot – solve.

---

[75] These versions of the rule are from Hobbes's *Leviathan* (190 [65] and 214 [79]): the first he calls the 'Law of the Gospell' – from *Matthew* 7:12 – and the second the 'Law of all men' (the latter is, perhaps, as we suggested earlier, from *Tobit* 4.16).

6

Adjudication and Interpretation

6.1 Introduction

Adjudication is the effort to resolve a dispute by determining, amid the clamour of rival claims, what is just. The movement towards resolution and settlement of the dispute involves three things. First, the hearing of evidence; secondly, reflection on the evidence partly in the light of the prevailing legislation and precedents, partly in the light of what are thought to be the prevailing local conventions, partly in the light of what is thought common to all mankind, and partly in the light of what appears to be the nature, intrinsically, of the case; and thirdly, coming to a conclusion or verdict that, within the limits of human fallibility, states what is just. Interpretation is the elucidation or explanation of the meaning of a text, and in disputes that refer to or involve a written text or texts it is an essential part of the process of adjudication.

Historically, many different kinds of adjudication have been established. In archaic societies, for example, the king or prince was as much a judge as a ruler. In modern societies the courts fulfil the adjudicative function, and jurisprudents are, or are hoped to be, what the Romans called the 'priests of justice'.[1] Aristotle said much the same: 'when people dispute they take refuge in the judge; and to go to the judge is to go to justice; for the nature of the judge is to be a sort of living justice'.[2] Even when an oracle of some kind is preferred to reasonable enquiry, it is assumed to be impartial, and to be capable of discerning what is just.[3] In societies

---

[1] *Digest*, I.1.1. In the *Institutes* jurisprudence is said to be '...the science of the just and the unjust', I.I.1.

[2] *Nicomachean Ethics*, V.1132a.20.

[3] G Barden, *After Principles* (Notre Dame, Ind: University of Notre Dame, 1990), ch 5 (esp 90–8 and fnn 43, 44); EE Evans-Pritchard, *Witchcraft, Oracles and Magic among the Azande* (Oxford: Clarendon Press, 1976); and P Winch, *The Idea of a Social Science* (London: Routledge and Kegan Paul, 1970). The desire for impartiality and reliability, rather than simply irrational superstition, accounts for the very widespread and trans-cultural appeal to adjudicative methods beyond the human realm and free from the limitations, both intellectual and moral, of human enquiry. Adjudicative methods of this kind were found in Europe until comparatively recently. Frank acknowledgement of judicial fallibility is hard to live with; the certainty provided by an oracular judgment brings a tempting, even if in fact ungrounded, peace of mind. In some archaic societies, disputants bring their disagreements before non-human oracles for resolution; but here, too, these presuppositions are at work; for it is assumed that there is a just outcome, and that the oracle will discover it. Others may consider that to consult the oracle is no better than tossing a coin;

in which it is thought that what is just is to be intelligently, reasonably, and responsibly discovered, the ideal is that an impartial, intelligent, reasonable, and responsible person is chosen to arbitrate: 'The law is always an effort towards (the discernment of what is) the just in each case, and the judgement that does not rest upon the virtue of justice (including, in the first place, the cognitive part of the virtue) in the judge cannot succeed.'[4]

In this chapter we give an account of the adjudicative process and later an account, because of its role in adjudication, of the interpretive process. We argue that the adjudicative question – that is, the question before a court of law – is *always* of this form: 'In the case now being considered, what is due to whom?' In adjudication, it is sometimes possible, by an examination of the circumstances, to discover what is intrinsically and in that sense naturally just, and sometimes impossible to do so. When it is possible to do so, this is not done by appeal to a set of principles or axioms or to any higher law but through an examination and discussion of the case in the prevailing jural background. When it is impossible to discover a just intrinsic to a situation, what is just must be established by convention.

Our analysis of procedural justice begins with an examination of the natural rule of enquiry concerning evidence, that is, the rule that expresses what is intrinsic to the nature of enquiry and is not merely conventional: namely, that a conclusion is to be based on sufficient evidence. Turning then to impartiality we suggest that it too is not simply a matter of convention that, in a dispute between litigants, the court should hear both sides, or that an adjudicator between litigants should be disinterested, impartial, unbiased. These ideas – *audi alteram partem* and *nemo iudex in causa sua* – are intrinsic to the nature of adjudicative investigation.

We then discuss interpretation. An interpretation is a text that expresses the interpreter's understanding of another text. Understanding a text or an utterance is just a particular case of understanding where the object to be understood is a text or utterance and the goal is to grasp its meaning. Knowing is a movement from questioning data, through understanding and producing hypotheses, to the conviction that there is sufficient evidence reasonably to affirm one's hypotheses to be correct, probable, or mistaken. To know the meaning of a text is to understand it correctly; the claim to know a text's meaning is based on a reasonable judgment of the adequacy of an hypothesis. Reasonable judgment is not of course infallibility: there is the possibility that a critical feature of the text has been overlooked, for example, or that there are insufficient data to allow the investigator reasonably to prefer one possible meaning to another, yet a judgment

but this opinion is not shared by those who consult the oracle. And, indeed, it is possible to think of tossing a coin or drawing lots as a way to reach the just outcome or the right solution, as did Christ's Apostles when they chose between Matthias and Barnabas by lot, *The Acts of the Apostles* 1:26.

[4] M Villey, *Réflexions sur la philosophie et le droit* (Paris: Presses Universitaires de France, 1995), 305.

must be made. Finally in this chapter, to bring together the various aspects of our discussion, we discuss some parts of the definition of a 'refugee' under the 1951 United Nations Convention relating to the Status of Refugees.

6.2 The Adjudicative Process

The court is faced with a difficulty, a dispute, or a claim. The guiding question is of the form: What in this case belongs to whom? What in this case is due to whom? Who is entitled to what? Difficulties, disputes, and claims arise within particular societies, at particular times, and in particular circumstances. The court, in its effort to discover what is just, considers disputes in many different contexts simultaneously. Consideration must be given to the prevailing state laws and precedents, to the prevailing local conventions – that were described in the draft of the Dutch civil code as 'the common opinions about law held by the Dutch people', and that includes that part of the living law that is not the product of legislation[5] – to what is thought common to all mankind, and to what appears to be the nature of the case.

The Roman jurists adverted to the several strands of the jural background and context when they distinguished civil justice (*ius civile*) from the right or law of nations (*ius gentium*), and legislation from custom.

Civil justice [*ius civile*] and the justice of nations [*ius gentium*] are distinguished in this way: every people ruled by laws [*leges*] and customs uses partly its own law [*ius*] and partly laws [*ius*] common to all mankind. The laws [*ius*] that a people makes for itself belongs to that city and is called civil law [*ius*] as being proper to that city. That which is established by natural reason among all men is operative in all peoples and is called the law [*ius*] of nations since all peoples make use of it.[6]

The unwritten law [*ius*] is that which usage has established; for ancient customs, being sanctioned by those who adopt them, are like laws.[7]

The *ius gentium* is not a set of rules automatically known by everyone but is discovered as occasion and the necessities of human living require.[8] Intelligent questioning and understanding of situations discover it, and the question that gives rise to this investigation is always of the form: what, in this type of situation, belongs to whom? The rule of *natural* justice, which refers to types of situations,

---

[5] The place of unlegislated features of the jural context in adjudication is examined in JLM Elders, 'Equity in Dutch Law' in RA Newman (ed), *Equity in the World's Legal Systems* (Brussels: Bruylant, 1973), 354–65. The reference to the common opinions about law is at 363.

[6] Justinian, *Institutes*, I.II.1. We have put the word *ius* in parentheses to remind the reader that here, as in very many places in the *Institutes*, the term 'law' – the common English translation – does not translate *lex*. What in English is almost always referred to as 'the law of nations' is in Latin not *lex gentium* but *ius gentium*. As many translators despairingly remark and as we have said before, there is no easy translation.   [7] Ibid, I.II.9; *Digest*, I.3.32.

[8] Justinian, *Institutes*, I.II.2. See ch 2.3 above.

is the suggested answer to this question and is, therefore, always of the form: X in this type of circumstance belongs to Y. The *conventional* rule of justice has the same structure; the only difference being that the convention is a decision when the nature of the situation does not yield a unique solution. For example, the provisions of the 1951 United Nations Convention relating to the Status of Refugees, some of which we examine in greater detail later in this chapter are, as are those in other international conventions, and as the title itself implies, conventional. It is also the case, although perhaps not so immediately obvious, that the decision to accept refugees is conventional in that individual states agree or do not agree to be bound by the Convention. However, once the Convention is established within a jurisdiction it is then naturally just that an applicant is entitled to a just hearing and, if deemed to be eligible under the Convention's criteria, is entitled to residence, for these are particular cases of the intrinsic norms that adjudication is to be just and that contracts are to be honoured.

As we repeatedly emphasize, what is considered to be natural, universal, and intrinsic is not known in some peculiar or mysterious way: *investigating the situation discovers it*. Suppose that Peter wishes to sell a house that he claims belongs to him whereas Paul, on the contrary, claims that the house is his. It is not simply a matter of convention that Peter cannot sell what does not belong to him; the nature or meaning of ownership and sale includes the idea that one cannot sell what one does not own. A written rule, such as 'No one can sell what does not belong to him', simply formulates in writing an understanding of the nature of the situation, that is, the nature or meaning of ownership and sale. If Peter is to sell the house, his ownership of it must be established against Paul's claim. Why does the idea of ownership include the idea that one cannot sell what one does not own? The answer is clear: if Peter sells a thing to Paul, the ownership of the thing is transferred from Peter to Paul. But the ownership of the thing cannot be transferred from Peter if it is not vested in Peter in the first place.[9] Peter can, of course, physically transfer the thing to Paul without owning it but what is transferred in sale is not only the thing but the title to and ownership of the thing. It is naturally just – that is, it is intrinsic to the practice – that if one person transfers the ownership of a thing to another, the person purporting to transfer the ownership must be the owner. What is true of sale is true of gift-giving; for gift-giving is not simply the physical handing over of the gift to the recipient but the handing over of the ownership of what is given. In the Roman law formulation no distinction is made between the transfer (or handing over) of ownership by gift or by sale in as much as there is an assumption that what is owned may be alienated – that is, that the owner is entitled to transfer the ownership of what he owns to another.[10] In other words, ownership is thought generally

---

[9] See our discussion of this issue in the Roman law context in ch 4.5 above.

[10] 'Another way of acquiring things according to what is naturally just is by transfer; for nothing is more conformable to natural equity than that the will of an owner who wishes to transfer what is his to another should be ratified. And, therefore, a material thing of whatever kind can be transferred and, when so transferred by the owner, becomes the property of another', Justinian, *Institutes*, II.I.40.

to include that entitlement. That entitlement, however, is not necessarily part of *all* forms of ownership; the ownership of land held in entail, for example, cannot be transferred to whomsoever simply according to the will of the present owner.[11] Here, then, is a nice conjunction of what is naturally and what is conventionally just. That only the owner of the thing owned can transfer ownership of the thing to another is naturally just in that it is intrinsic to both gift-giving and selling. That a particular person owns a particular thing in such a way that he is entitled to transfer ownership only in a particular way is conventional.

The elements that form the background or context of adjudication are in part conventional and peculiar to the particular society and situation and in part natural in as much as they discern the nature of the case and, for that reason, are commonly found in human societies. To adjudicate, the adjudicator should have the subtle intellectual background that is the understanding of what is just both naturally and conventionally. One who totally lacked this background – as a small child might lack it – cannot distinguish between the physical handing over of a thing on the one hand and gift-giving or selling or lending on the other; and if he cannot make that basic distinction, much less can he distinguish more subtly between the latter three.

It is easy to know when a thing has been physically transferred from Peter to Paul (a material or non-jural fact); more difficult to discover when ownership of the thing has been transferred (a jural fact). To enable people to discover this, customs grow up in different societies and, for the most part, the transfer of ownership from seller to buyer is achieved without difficulty. Millions of such transfers occur daily between shopkeepers and customers. It is more difficult to determine when a contract has been formed in other contexts. What constitutes a legally binding unwritten agreement? What distinguishes it from a sale? In Roman law before Justinian, following Gaius, the agreement or contract of sale is reached when the negotiating parties agree upon a price and before the price is paid:

The contract of sale is formed as soon as the price is agreed upon, although it has not yet been paid, nor even a deposit [*arra*] given; for what is given as a deposit serves [only] as proof that the contract has been made.[12]

What is meant by 'natural equity' is not some mysterious or mystical knowledge, it simply means that most readers to whom the text was addressed, reading as they did in the jural context of their ordinary lives at the time, would find it reasonable to allow someone who owned his horse to sell it. In other words, the original readers would have read the text within a context in which the rule fitted with the prevailing idea of ownership. Readers from a context in which things were owned exclusively in entail would, obviously, not have found the rule in accord with 'natural equity'.

[11] The practical problem faced by the Bennet sisters in Jane Austen's *Pride and Prejudice* stems from the fact that their father owns his house and land in entail and so cannot transfer these to his daughters – a situation not serenely accepted by Mrs Bennet.

[12] Justinian, *Institutes*, III.XXIII.Preamble; the first two sentences of which repeat, in almost the same words, Gaius, *Institutes*, III.139. The Latin *arra* is rendered by Sandars as 'earnest' – *Institutes of Justinian* (trans TC Sandars, Westport, Conn: Greenwood, 1970), 362 – and by Gordon and Robinson as 'token of agreement'. See the note on 'token' in Gordon and Robinson's translation of Gaius, 554.

That sentence is clearly the proposed answer to the question: When is an unwritten contract of sale held to be formed? It is an answer that expresses an understanding of the practice. Before the price is agreed upon, it may well be that the buyer would like to buy what the seller would like to sell. The buyer is not willing to buy nor the seller to sell at any price whatsoever; what each is looking for is an agreed price and, once they reach a mutually agreeable price, there is usually nothing more to be done except to bring about what they have agreed. For this reason, it is considered to be of the nature of the contract of sale that it is completed when a mutually agreed price is reached.

In contrast is the set of conventional rules in Roman law governing a written, but not an unwritten, contract:

But, where there is a written contract, *we have enacted* that a sale is not to be considered completed unless an instrument of sale has been drawn up, being either written by the contracting parties, or at least signed by them, if written by others.[13]

The clause that we have emphasized – 'we have enacted' – indicates that this rule is a convention or public agreement. It is civil justice: how things are done in Rome. The convention is not an arbitrary, random imposition but an answer to a practical problem. Before the contracting parties begin to write the contract they will normally have verbally agreed the price. What then is the 'instrument of sale' or written contract? Is it simply no more than proof that a contract was made? Or is it to be taken both as a detailed description of what was contracted and as the act of contracting. In other words, is the contracting act the verbal agreement of price or the signing of the written text? A choice has to be made and under the Emperor Justinian it was enacted that, where a written contract existed, the signing of the text was the contracting act: henceforth, the Roman judges will understand contract in the light of this convention.

It can and does happen that one or other party reneges on the agreement, at which point the court may be asked to adjudicate. It may be that one of the parties to the alleged contract denies that there was a contract. The court's first question, then, is to discover whether or not there was a contract. Whether or not there was a contract is a question of jural fact, that is, of an action understood within a jural context; the same action performed between characters in a play mimes, but is not, a contract. If this question cannot be answered, that is, if the fact cannot be discovered, no further properly jural question arises. However, if the discovery of the existence of a deposit given and accepted is sufficient proof that there was a contract, the second question arises: What now is due to the parties? The answer, given in the same preamble, is:

If a deposit has been given, then, whether the contract was written or unwritten, the purchaser, if he refuses to fulfill it, loses what he has given as deposit, and the seller, if

---

[13] Justinian, *Institutes*, III.XXIII.Preamble (emphasis added).

he refuses, has to restore double; although no agreement on the subject was expressly made.

This answer rests upon the implicit assumption that in such a case something is required to restore a just situation beyond simply returning the deposit. That assumption rests on the prior conviction that the existence of the contract established a new jural relationship between the parties upon which each was entitled to rely. This implicit assumption expresses an understanding of the nature of the situation. Precisely what is to be done is conventional in that the purchaser loses the deposit or the seller should restore double. A rule establishing a different convention, for instance that the purchaser should lose double the deposit and the seller restore treble would also serve. Or, as does sometimes happen, the court may insist that the contract be honoured.[14]

   The task of the court is to determine who in this case is owed what by whom. The rule states, for the type of situation described, who owns what; but the rule is general and the case before the court is particular. In so far as the particular case is, in the court's judgment, an instance of the type of case envisaged in the rule, the rule is applied. In so far as the particular situation diverges from the general case, anticipated and envisaged in the rule, the task of the court is not to apply the rule but to determine, in the light of that and other rules, what is just. As we discuss later in this chapter in the context of interpretation, the effort to judge a case not perfectly covered by legislation, traditional rule or precedent is what Aristotle calls *epieikeia* or 'equity'. The difficulty surrounding the application of general rules to individual cases is not confined to rules expressing what is naturally just; it arises also in cases of the conventionally just. What this indicates is that what is just in any situation is not discovered and brought about simply by the application of a formulated rule; even in the ordinary circumstances where the rule does apply, it must be discovered that the situation under scrutiny is in fact one to which the rule applies. The discovery of what is just in a particular situation, in other words, requires an understanding of the particular situation, for which an understanding of the general case is illuminating.

   What is to be done if no deposit has been given? One party claims that a price was agreed; the other party claims that no price was agreed. Suppose that to this question there is as yet no established answer. A question before the court is, as before, whether or not there was a contract. The preamble states that in cases where a price was agreed there was a contract. Accordingly, in the absence of evidence of a deposit serving as proof of agreement, the court is faced with the prior question: Was there an agreed price? It will not always, and may only

---

[14] The court states not only what is just but works also within a context that requires that what is just be done. The court does not always decide that a contract be honoured, sometimes for no other reason than that it cannot be, as when someone who agrees to buy or sell something but goes bankrupt before the sale is complete and is unable to honour the agreement. But the court must decide something and what is decided must be done.

rarely, be possible to discover the answer. In the absence of the answer, what is just?

If, in a particular case, it is impossible to discover the answer, should the court decide the matter as if there had been no agreement and so no contract or as if there had been an agreement and so a contract? In reality, either there was or there was not. If there was, then, apparently, justice is not done if the court judges that there was not. If there was not, then, apparently, justice is not done if the court decides that there was. That a court or any human institution is not infallible must be constantly borne in mind. The deliberations of a court come to a conclusion, a sentence, or decision. The French term for a legal ruling *arrêt*, which literally means a 'stop', indicates that the jurisprudential conclusion differs from the demonstrative conclusion of a logical argument in which the conclusion follows inexorably from the given premises. The jurisprudential conclusion is fallible, revisable, or, to use an older and nearly defunct term, prudential.[15] The scientific conclusion – which also differs from the logical conclusion although it has been confused with it – is likewise fallible and revisable.[16] But it differs from the jurisprudential conclusion in that the jurisprudential conclusion is about particular cases and looks to a practical decision that must be made within a reasonable time. The court's decision states what, in the particular case, is due and it works within the accepted context that what is judged to be just must be realized within a reasonable time. Time presses upon practice as it does not upon theory. In principle, pure scientific enquiry is free of such limitation.

Our claim is the very traditional one that intrinsic to adjudication is the demand to try to discover what is just, which is why the virtue proper to the adjudicator is justice, that is, 'the constant and enduring will to render to each what is due'. But we do not claim that each judge in each case is unbiased; nor do we claim that each judge in each case is intent on discovering what is just. *Analytically*, the goal of the court's enquiry is the discernment of what in the instant case is just; *ideally*, each judge in each case should share this goal. Whether or not a particular judge in a particular case does in fact share the goal intrinsic to jural enquiry is a matter of contingent fact; and here, as in all human affairs, some corruption is inevitable. Bribery and other pressures from the powerful – whether their power be from wealth, or numbers, or force, or some of the innumerable forms of human prejudice – tend to distort judgment. The existence and corrupting influence of these have been long known. This influence cannot reasonably be expected to disappear since its original principle – selfishness and its resultant

---

[15] See Aristotle, *Nicomachean Ethics*, V.I.5 and P Aubenque, *La prudence chez Aristote* (Paris: Presses Universitaires de France, 1963). 'Prudence' nowadays has a somewhat negative ring to it; formerly it meant 'intelligent judgement in practical affairs' and was a compliment.

[16] The structure of the logical argument is: [1] If P, then Q; [2] And P; and [3] Therefore, Q. Here [3] follows logically and necessarily from [1] and [2] taken together. The structure of the scientific argument is: [4] If P, then Q; [5] And Q; and [6] Therefore (probably) P. Here [6] does not follow logically or necessarily from [4] and [5] taken together because Q could exist for some reason other than the existence of P.

bias in individuals and in groups – is endemic and enduring. We shall discuss bias in more detail when we discuss impartiality later in this chapter.

The process of adjudicative deliberation gives rise to questions that have to do with how the court is to proceed. The effort to answer these questions requires us to investigate the nature of judicial enquiry and to acknowledge that the natural justice intrinsic to the procedure includes, first, adequate evidence and, secondly, impartiality. We shall use the term 'procedural justice' to describe the justice inherent in a court's procedures, using it therefore to describe what, in English, is usually – but in our view somewhat confusingly – called 'natural justice'.

6.3 Procedural Justice: Evidence

Suppose that in business dealings between Peter and Paul there had been, in fact, an agreement and a properly binding oral contract. Peter claims that there was agreement. Paul claims that there was not. In fact, Paul is lying but this, by hypothesis, cannot be discovered in this case. If the court were to conclude that there had been an agreement, it would have concluded that Paul was lying and, for this conclusion, it has insufficient evidence. There might arise a general principle that a person is to be believed unless the contrary be shown. In the light of that principle, the court would decide that, in the absence of sufficient evidence of agreement, it must decide the case *as if* there had been no agreement and so no contract and so Peter's claim – since he cannot show the contrary to what Paul claims – is dismissed. Has a just solution been reached? In one sense, it has not. In reality there was an agreement and, had that been discovered, Peter's claim would have succeeded. In another sense, however, justice *has* been done. The court's decision to dismiss Peter's claim against Paul is made in a situation in which what had in fact happened cannot be discovered. The court's question is no longer what is to be decided if there had been an agreement but what is to be decided in the situation when what had actually happened cannot be discovered. Again, that a court or any human institution is not infallible must be borne constantly in mind.

At first sight, it might seem that to decide *as if* there had been no agreement is to decide that Peter had lied but, on reflection, this turns out not to be so. Peter is in fact not lying although this, by hypothesis, cannot be discovered. The court does not conclude that he was in fact lying. The conclusion is that Peter cannot produce sufficient evidence to show that what he says occurred did in fact occur and for that reason the court dismisses the case. Strictly, in this example, the court does not determine that there was no contract, but that there is insufficient evidence to conclude that there was.

The same structure is present in criminal cases. Mary accuses Peter of rape; again the first task of the court is to discover whether or not Peter raped Mary. Suppose that Peter had in fact raped Mary: Mary is telling the truth and Peter, who denies raping Mary, is lying but Mary is unable to establish this. In the absence of sufficient evidence the court will decide *as if* Paul had not raped Mary because, were it to decide on insufficient evidence that he had done so, it would, on insufficient evidence, decide that Peter was lying. Mary, on the other hand, is not convicted of lying but of failing to establish her version of the event. Mary's case fails. What is due to Mary and to Peter? That Mary's accusation against Peter be dismissed. Will justice have been done? In one sense, it will not, because Peter did in fact rape Mary, but in another sense it will, because the court concluded reasonably in the light of the evidence before it. And that is all we – or any court – can ever reasonably do.

In each of these examples, there was a fact. In the first example, there was a contract. In the second example, there had been a rape. The facts were in each case denied. In both examples, there was insufficient evidence to allow the court reliably to conclude that what was alleged to have happened had in fact happened. Being unable reasonably to conclude that a contract had been agreed or that there had been a rape, the court had no reasonable choice but to state this. In the first case, the court rejects Peter's action against Paul, and in so doing acts as if no contract had been agreed, and in the second example, the court rejects Mary's accusation that Peter raped her, and in so doing acts as if there had been no rape. The difference between the civil and the criminal example is that in the civil example the conclusion is that there is insufficient evidence to conclude that a contract had been agreed, whereas in the criminal example, in many jurisdictions, the court hands down a verdict of 'not guilty' which is often understood as an assertion that Peter did not rape Mary. In Scotland, the verdict of 'not proven' is allowed which is understood to assert not alone that Mary had insufficient evidence to prove her case but also that Paul had insufficient evidence to refute it. There is ambiguity in the verdict of 'not guilty': sometimes it is a conclusion based on the evidence that the accused did not do what he was accused of doing, and sometimes a conclusion based on the prosecution's failure to produce sufficient evidence to show that the accused did what he was accused of doing. The verdict 'not guilty' is ambiguous in a context in which 'not proven' does not exist because it does not distinguish between 'sufficient evidence to declare innocence' and 'insufficient evidence to declare guilt'.

The natural rule, that is, the rule that expresses what is intrinsic to enquiry, is that a conclusion is to be based on sufficient evidence and that in the absence of sufficient evidence no conclusion can be reached other than a declaration that the evidence is insufficient. This intrinsic characteristic is not confined to judicial enquiry but is found in everyday and in scientific enquiries. The enquirer begins with a question about something that he wants to understand but, as yet, does not. For example, 'As the radius of a circle increases from r = 1 to r = 2 to r = 3 and so on, how does the area increase?' The question looks for an answer. Once a suggested answer has occurred to the enquirer, a further question arises: Is there sufficient evidence for me to accept the suggested answer? In the absence of sufficient evidence the enquirer remains unconvinced and cannot reasonably accept the suggested answer. Consider this suggested answer: as the radius increases from r = n to r = n + 1, the area increases by $\pi\,(n + 1)^2 - \pi\,(n)^2$. No one can reasonably claim to know this in the absence of sufficient personally convincing evidence.[17] When one has insufficient evidence, one can neither reasonably assert nor reasonably deny but must remain unconvinced. This is not a rule imposed upon enquiry; it is a rule that expresses an understanding of what is intrinsic to enquiry. Obviously, no doubt in part because the conventional rules of evidence differ among jurisdictions, even in a single jurisdiction what is sufficient evidence for one person may not be for another.[18]

There is, however, a crucial difference between the geometrical example and a court case. In the absence of convincing evidence the scientific enquirer can neither accept nor reject the hypothesis. The enquirer ought to rest in the undecided position until evidence that he finds convincing one way or the other emerges. The deliberations of a court, on the other hand, *must* come to a conclusion, a sentence, or decision. In the court case, one cannot simply rest in the position that the evidence is insufficient to allow one to conclude either that there was or that there was not a contract or a rape. For the properly judicial question is yet to be asked: In the absence of sufficient evidence what is due? Unless the court answers that question it has failed to be a judicial – as distinct from being a merely factual – enquiry. For this reason, article 4 of the French *Code Civil* prompts the suggestion that a court that fails to decide is guilty of an injustice.[19] The idea that justice is denied if a decision is not reached is behind the related idea that one should not be tried more than once for the same crime.

The court of law is a court of justice. The court's question is: 'What is due to the protagonists?' In the absence of sufficient evidence no one is to be declared guilty. What is due to someone who has been accused but who cannot reasonably be declared guilty? Perhaps nothing other than the verdict 'Not guilty' or 'Not proven' and the freedom that follows, perhaps more than that. It is not possible to say in general.[20] But what is clear is that one who cannot reasonably be declared

---

[17] A reader might, of course, choose to *believe* the purveyor of this information but then the demand for sufficient evidence shifts to a demand for sufficient evidence for believing, not believing, or withholding belief from, the purveyor.

[18] On the general structure of enquiry, see B Lonergan, *Insight: a Study of Human Understanding* (London: Longmans, 1957). See also G Barden and P McShane, *Towards Self-Meaning* (Dublin: Gill and Macmillan, 1969), 34–41. In criminal cases where members of a jury are asked if there is sufficient evidence to judge the accused person guilty as charged, this formulation obscures the fact that each juror is really asked, and cannot but be asked, whether or not there is in his judgment sufficient evidence. In this way, each juror takes personal responsibility for his own judgment which is, therefore, inescapably subjective.

[19] 'Le juge qui refusera de juger, sous prétexte du silence, de l'obscurité ou de l'insuffisance de la loi, pourra être poursuivi comme coupable de déni de justice' (Loi 1803–03-05 promulguée le 15 mars 1803) ['The judge who refuses to judge, under pretext of the silence, obscurity or insufficiency of the law, may be charged with committing a denial of justice'].

[20] The judge in a criminal trial will sometimes dismisss the accused who has been declared not to be guilty with words indicating that they have been absolved of any wrongdoing. For instance,

guilty is not due that which is due only to one who is reasonably declared guilty. This is an intrinsic principle of intelligent and reasonable enquiry, not an extrinsic imposition.

When the facts are settled, the court asks what is due. In a criminal case, if Peter is judged guilty of a crime, the question as to what is now due to him arises. The answer to this question – the sentence – concludes the court's work. In some cases, of course, the question is not of guilt or innocence but of, say, the proper division of property following intestate death, separation, or divorce. Here again, the first question to be settled is what the relevant facts are. Here again, when the relevant facts are settled, the question as to what is due to each litigant or partner arises and the court's answer to this question concludes its work. In cases of intestate death, separation, or divorce, where a settlement is disputed, the court is concerned with distributive justice; it determines what is commonly owned and how this is to be shared. In cases of, for example, theft or embezzlement, the court is concerned with rectificatory justice for the theft or embezzlement has brought about an unjust situation and a just situation is to be restored.

In some cases of injury – for example, rape – it is difficult to discover how a just situation is to be restored. Perhaps it is because it is so difficult that it seems to many that the injury to the victim is forgotten and the question as to what is due to the victim simply ignored. The question as to what is due to the victim of rape is not that she not be raped. She cannot be unraped. She has been raped and, if sufficient evidence has been adduced to convict Peter, the question as to what is due to her arises in that horrible circumstance.[21] It is hardly plausible to suggest

in July 2009 a jury at Liverpool Crown Court cleared the Liverpool FC player Steven Gerrard of affray. The jury agreed with Mr Gerrard's assertion that he was acting in self-defence at the time of the incident in question. In concluding the hearing, Judge Henry Globe remarked, 'The verdict is a credible verdict on the full facts of this case, and you walk away from this court with your reputation intact.' In cases where such a public statement is made, although the statement itself is without legal significance, the judge decides that the accused person is entitled to be so described; that, in addition to the verdict, is his due or *ius*. It is perhaps worth remarking also that sometimes it is thought that a person's *ius* is something that, although impossible to implement, is nonetheless the deserved or appropriate entitlement. For instance, in June 2009 New York District Judge Denny Chin received more than 100 letters from victims of the disgraced US financier Bernard Madoff before Madoff, then 71, was sentenced, many urging the judge to impose the maximum sentence of 150 years in prison. This was the sentence that was handed down and against which Madoff decided not to appeal. Since an actual prison term of 150 years is impossible, for the judgment to make good sense it must in fact be understood to include both a possible term, which cannot be longer than life, and what may be called a rhetorical element signifying extreme jural disapproval.

[21] Richard Posner writes of what is due to the victim as, perhaps, 'a more or less emotionally satisfactory (legal) substitute for vengeance', 'Corrective Justice' in CB Gray (ed), *The Philosophy of Law: An Encyclopedia (Vol I)* (New York: Garland, 1999), 163. The popular demand 'to get one's own back' no doubt expresses a desire for vengeance but surely also for what is thought to be 'due'. Until recently, what is due to the victims of crime was to some extent – and to a greater or lesser extent in different types of situation – lost sight of. That situation is now changing somewhat. For examples of work on this subject, see B Williams, *Working With Victims of Crime: Policies, Politics and Practice* (London: Jessica Kingsley, 1998); B Williams, *Victims of Crime and Community Justice: Justice Rebalanced?* (London: Jessica Kingsley, 2005); and RC Davis, AJ Lurigio, and SA Herman (eds), *Victims of Crime* (Thousand Oaks, CA: Sage, 3rd edn, 2007).

that absolutely nothing is. Is Peter's punishment enough? Is Peter's punishment to be understood as what is due to Peter only or also as what is due also to Mary? It seems to be naturally just that both questions – 'What is due to Peter?' and 'What is due to Mary?' – be asked. More generally, it seems to be naturally, not simply conventionally, just that both questions – 'What is due to the criminal?' and 'What is due to the victim of the crime?' – be asked.[22] (In cases where the victim of a crime dies his *ius* may be judged to transfer to the victim's next of kin.) The victim of a crime has suffered an injustice; there seems to be no reason why that injustice ought not to be rectified.

6.4 Procedural Justice: Impartiality

In cases of uncertainty or dispute about what is just, there is no human society in which it has not been discovered that it is crucial to establish independent and, or so it is hoped, impartial and reliable adjudication. Richard Posner remarks that Aristotle's idea 'of judging a dispute without regard to the character, merit, or social status of the disputants... is a notable milestone on the road to the modern conception of the rule of law'.[23] Certainly, Aristotle's influence has been great but the idea appears much earlier; it can be found already in the *Torah*: 'You must not show partiality to the poor nor favour to the great; you must pass judgment on your neighbour according to justice.'[24] An early modern source is Thomas Hobbes's eleventh law of nature in *Leviathan*, the law of Equity, or the law of 'impartial', and in that sense 'equitable', judgment:[25]

Also, if *a man be trusted to judge between man and man*, it is a precept of the Law of Nature, *that he deal Equally between them*. For without that, the controversies of men cannot be determined but by Warre. He therefore that is partiall in judgment, doth what in him lies, to deterre men from the use of Judges and Arbitrators; and consequently, (against the fundamentall Lawe of Nature) is the cause of Warre. The observance of this

---

[22] What is due, as we argued in ch 4 above, is sometimes naturally due and sometimes conventionally due. If Peter has stolen €100,000 from Paul, it is 'naturally just' that Peter should restore the money to Paul. In other words, Paul is due from Peter the restoration of €100,000. Is Paul due any more than this? He has borne the loss of the use of his money for some time. Is he due some interest? In an economy in which money can be used in this way it would seem so. Precisely how much? Is he due something beyond this? The answers to these questions must be at least to some extent conventional.   [23] R Posner, 'Corrective Justice', 163.

[24] *Leviticus* 19:15. Much of *Leviticus* dates from the 7th century BC but parts of it – including the nineteenth chapter – are considered older. See also *Exodus* (10th century BC) 23:2–3; and *Deuteronomy* (7th century BC) 16:18–20. Another translation of *Leviticus* 19:15 is: 'You must not be guilty of unjust verdicts. You shall not respect the person of the poor, nor honour the person of the mighty; but in justice shall you judge your neighbour.'

[25] What Hobbes calls 'Equity' is neither a supplement to the Common Law; nor is it 'Equity' (*epieikeia* or *aequitas*) as used by Aristotle and St Thomas and which we discuss in the next section of this chapter.

law, from the equall distribution to each man, of that which in reason belongeth to him, is called EQUITY....[26]

As Hobbes explains, the reason for this law is that unless there is impartial arbitration litigants will be dissatisfied with the adjudicative practice, will be disinclined to use it, and will resort to war. Hobbes takes it as obvious that controversies will arise. Likewise he takes it as obvious and inevitable that partiality is intrinsically inappropriate to adjudication; which, when one considers the nature of partiality, is true.[27] With Hobbes, we hold that impartiality is not a moral feature added to the practice of adjudication; it is essential and intrinsic to it, such that without it what purports to be adjudication ceases to be. The partial or biased arbitrator is one whose own perceived good, in whatever form, is served by one rather than the other outcome, and who allows his bias to influence his enquiry. He will decide in favour of A rather than B irrespective of the actual situation whenever he can get away with doing so, in which case the hearing is a farce that serves only as an attempt to persuade onlookers of its appropriateness.[28]

We have observed that the elements that form the background or context of adjudication are in part conventional and peculiar to the particular society and situation and in part natural in as much as they discern the nature of the case and, for that reason, are commonly found in human societies. Ideally, the adjudicator should have the subtle intellectual background that is the understanding of what is just both naturally and conventionally. Is the establishment of impartial adjudication merely conventional or is it the establishment of what has been discovered to be the nature of the case? The only way in which one can discover whether or not impartiality is intrinsic to adjudication is by examining the practice of adjudication. If impartiality is intrinsic, then the rule 'Be impartial' is not simply a precept imposed on the practice; rather, it is also a methodological clarification of the practice. And the only way in which one can intelligently examine the practice of adjudication is by examining one's own spontaneous conscious practice while actually engaged in adjudicating.[29] Neither the precept 'Be impartial' nor the proposition that impartiality is intrinsic to adjudication is a logical conclusion from some undeniable, self-justifying axiom.[30] But it is important to

[26] *Leviathan*, 212 [77].

[27] Hobbes's argument is this: Controversies will arise; They will be solved peaceably or by force; It follows from the first fundamental law of nature that if a means of solving them peaceably is found, it is to be taken; Impartial arbitration is the appropriate means; To such arbitration litigants ought to submit 'for the reason which commands the end, commands also the means necessary to the end', *De Cive*, 145. That litigants ought to submit to such arbitration is the sixteenth law in *Leviathan*, the fifteenth in *De Cive*.

[28] See G Barden, 'Rhetorics of Legitimacy' (1998) 2 *European Journal of Law, Philosophy and Computer Science* 47.

[29] On methodological clarification and prescription, see B Lonergan, *Method in Theology* (London: Darton Longman and Todd, 1972), ch 1.

[30] That there are no first principles in the form of given, unquestionable axioms or propositions is the central theme of G Barden, *After Principles* (Notre Dame, Ind: University of Notre Dame, 1990). See esp ch 4, in which it is suggested that the common paradigm of human knowing

recognize that a willingness to be impartial does not follow logically or always in practice from the proposition that impartiality is intrinsic to adjudication.

The key elements of impartial adjudication are usually referred to as the rules or principles of natural justice (sometimes called 'constitutional justice'): that, in a dispute between litigants, the court should hear both sides (*audi alteram partem*) and that an adjudicator between litigants should be disinterested, impartial, unbiased (*nemo iudex in causa sua*). These may be wrongly understood to be conventional rules, that is, 'add-ons' to improve the quality of adjudication by emphasizing the significance and necessity of impartiality. But it is not simply a matter of conventional rule that, in a dispute between litigants, the court should hear both sides: *audi alteram partem* is in fact intrinsic to the nature of investigation. Proper or impartial adjudication requires that both sides be heard; otherwise, something other than adjudication is taking place. Similarly, that an adjudicator between litigants should be disinterested, impartial, unbiased – *nemo iudex in causa sua* – is not simply a matter of conventional rule: it, too, is intrinsic to the nature of investigation.

The ideal of unbiased judgment has been a jurisprudential ideal since time immemorial and lack of bias is in principle possible, but there is not the smallest reason to suppose that impartiality is discovered or implemented easily, nor that, once implemented in principle, it governs enquiry peacefully and without pressure. As we indicated previously, we do not claim that each judge in each case is unbiased; nor do we claim that each judge in each case is intent on discovering what is just. As we observed, bribery and other pressures from the powerful – whether their power be from wealth, or numbers, or force, or some of the innumerable forms of human prejudice – tend to distort judgment.[31] The corruption of power is great enough sometimes to prevent not alone the practice of impartiality but even the very idea of its value. Unless there are correct and incorrect answers to questions as to who is entitled to what in given circumstances, bias is

and valuing as logical system is mistaken. Logically to conclude that, for example, 'Impartiality is intrinsic to adjudication', one must hold prior proposition(s) from which this conclusion follows. In our view, it is not necessary to hold any prior propositions in order to understand that impartiality is indeed intrinsic to adjudication. See also PJ McGrath, *The Objectivity of Morals* (Durrus: Estragon, 2003).

[31] On individual, group, and general bias, see B Lonergan, *Insight: a Study of Human Understanding* (London: Longmans, 1957), ch VII, esp sections 6 and 7. If one is examining a particular adjudicative system, the question as to whether or not it is impartial is a question of social fact. Imagine a system in which impartial adjudication does not exist. If it is now asked whether or not the people living within that jurisdiction have the right to impartial adjudication, the answer clearly is that as a matter of social fact they have not. That is, impartial adjudication is not an entitlement within the system. Whether or not they ought to have that right, whether or not that entitlement ought to be within the system, is a good but different question. If it is intrinsic to adjudication that it should be impartial, then an established adjudicative practice that is not impartial is defective. If, on the other hand, there are simply two indifferently just general systems of adjudication – one impartial, the other biased – then an established adjudicative practice that is biased rather than impartial is not defective.

of no consequence, for bias is important only in that it distorts enquiry and tends to prevent the emergence of the true and the good.[32]

When a judge decides to cast his vote in a particular way – since he is, according to our definition of a decision maker,[33] a rational maximizer – he must be thought to have cast it because, for whatever reason, he thought that the best way to cast it. This may not, of course, be the just way. He may have decided as he did for any or many of several reasons. If one's concern is to discover why a particular judge in a particular case decided as he did, one is engaged in discovering the biography – which is only in part juridical – of the judge in question.

Consider a judge adjudicating on an application for refugee status. He may have been bribed or threatened; he may have wished to ingratiate himself with a more senior colleague through whose influence he hopes to gain preferment; he may have allowed his habitual dislike of people from the national or social or cultural group of which the appellant is a member to bias his judgment; he may quite simply have disliked the appellant and allowed his conviction that the appellant would not be a valuable addition to the community to sway his decision; or he may, on the contrary, have allowed his enthusiasm for immigration to have inclined him to grant the appeal. And so on indefinitely. If one's concern is to discover why a particular judge in a particular case decided as he did, one is engaged in biography, as we said above. If one's concern is to discover how within a jurisdiction judges have tended to decide cases, one is engaged in the social history of adjudication in that jurisdiction. One may go on to try to discover correlations between the observed tendencies and other features common to the corps of judges.[34] This is what, for example, the American legal realists and some of those within the critical legal studies tradition have attempted to do and we in no way reject this as a valueless exercise. The social history of adjudication is important and relevant to many different types of non-jurisprudential analyses. It may also have relevance – as some writers have claimed – to predicting how certain judges, or indeed most judges, will decide cases.[35] But however the individual judge decides or however several judges decide, each decision is a choice of what at the time and in the circumstances seemed good to those deciding.[36]

The ideal of a totally open judicial mind is one implied by formalist legal theory. Legal formalism seeks to explain or justify the existence of any given law by reference to authoritative and valid *sources* of law – for example, constitutions, legislation, precedents, etc. In these sources of law, the formalist theory goes, can be found the legal rules that provide a uniquely correct solution to any legal

---

[32] The reason behind the ancient prohibition on bribery is that a judge should not accept a bribe *because* a bribe blinds and leads to unjust decisions. See the discussion in ch 11.3 below.

[33] See our discussion in ch 5.8 above.

[34] JAG Griffith, *The Politics of the Judiciary* [1977] (London: Fontana, 5th edn, 1997).

[35] See P McCutcheon, 'American Legal Realism' in T Murphy (ed), *Western Jurisprudence* (Dublin: Thomson Round Hall, 2004), 212, 216–18. Cf D Kennedy, *A Critique of Adjudication* (Cambridge, Mass: Harvard University Press, 1997).

[36] P Devlin, *The Judge* (Oxford: Oxford University Press, 1979), esp 23–4.

problem. Formalism acknowledges that the rules cannot be applied automatically; they must be interpreted and applied in a reasoned way, but formalism claims that interpretation does not involve any individual judicial 'discretion' and so the very possibility of bias is excluded. In the formalist model of adjudication, judges exercise improper discretion if they reach conclusions about legal disputes by reasoning in ways *not* sanctioned or justified by 'legal reasons' (valid sources of law, valid interpretive principles, and valid principles of reasoning); formalism suggests that law is in fact rationally determinate; judging is 'mechanical'; and legal reasoning is autonomous, since legal reasons suffice to justify a unique outcome, and no recourse to non-legal reasons is permitted or required.[37]

That the ideal was not always realized was known and disapproved, but it was not until the work of the American legal realists that the empirical analysis of the presence and consequence of bias was undertaken. We do not deal with this empirical question but our methodological analysis acknowledges both the theoretical possibility and the practical inevitability of bias and of its distorting effect. We consider that the totally open or blank mind does not exist. The judge comes, and must come, to the particular case with a background from within which he tries to understand the case, and to determine who is entitled to what. That background may well include various kinds of often unnoticed bias that incline him to favour one person or group over another or one type of solution over another, but the intellectual and moral background of the judge is not essentially bias. Bias is the distortion of background. We do not think that a totally blank mind is an ideal to be sought. Bias is not overcome by increasing ignorance but rather by increasing and incessant self-criticism that seeks to articulate one's background in order to distinguish what in it is biased and to be eliminated from what is true and to be developed and refined.[38] Adjudication requires a conclusion or verdict that, within the limits of human fallibility, states what is just. We may now turn to the specific aspect of adjudication that involves the discovery and elucidation of the meaning of texts, namely, interpretation.

6.5 The Interpretative Process

An interpretation is a text that attempts to express the interpreter's understanding of another text. Natalie Stoljar observes that in very general terms an interpretation is 'an hypothesis, based on data generated by an object of interpretation,

---

[37] B Leiter, 'Positivism, Formalism, Realism' (1999) 99 *Columbia Law Review* 1138, 1145–6. See also G Barden and T Murphy, 'Society as a Source of Law' (2006) 95 *Studies* 407.

[38] For criticism of the blank mind, see B Lonergan, *Method in Theology* (London: Darton Longman and Todd, 1972), 157–8 and the quotation from Rudolph Bultmann in fn 3, 158. The classic jurisprudential argument against the blank judicial mind is J Frank, *Law and the Modern Mind* (New York: Brentano's, 1930).

about the meaning of the object of interpretation',[39] but it is critically important to distinguish between a *hypothesis* and the *expression of a hypothesis*. When
interpreting a text, the reader reads the text, considers the text in light of other
relevant data, invents a hypothesis as to what the text means, and then expresses
this hypothesis in another text. This latter text is the expression of the hypothesis,
or the interpretation.

But how precisely – before the development of an hypothesis and the expressing of it – does one move from reading the text to *understanding* it? There will be
levels of understanding. If a monoglot English-speaker reads a text in English
about something of which he has some understanding, his linguistic context enables him to go immediately to a level that he could not reach in, say, Icelandic,
although the Icelandic text might be about the same thing – for example, the
report of a football match. Roughly speaking, this is the first level of understanding, or not understanding, the words and sentences.

The next level is to understand, through one's understanding of words and
sentences, what the text *means*. The meaning of the text is not on the page; it is
in, or not yet in, the reader's mind. Necessarily, the reader's first hypothesis is that
the text means what he, the reader, would have meant had he written the text.
If, quite literally, and it must be understood quite literally, the reader has nothing but, say, a single sentence, he cannot, for want or sufficient data, go further.
Of course, it may be that the reader could have meant several different things by
the sentence. The text might have been: 'I played ball yesterday'. It might occur
to the reader that the author might have meant by that sentence either that he
played a ball game yesterday, or that he went along with someone's plan yesterday. Without further data – that is, another text or some information about the
context in which the text was written or spoken – he can go very little further;
perhaps he might incline to say, more tentatively, that the original author probably did not mean both. He would be able to give an interpretation like this:
'When John said that he played ball yesterday he could have meant that he played
a ball game or that he went along with someone's plan but it is unlikely that he
meant both.' Does the text mean both? It is clearer to say that the same text can
be used in different contexts and that in one context it is used to mean one thing,
and in the other context it is used to mean the other.

Suppose that the reader is unfamiliar with the usage of that sentence to mean
'going along with someone's plan' but that this was in fact what the author meant.
For that reader, the text can mean only that the speaker played a ball game.
Suppose that there are more sentences – that is, more relevant data – and that the
reader continues. He soon discovers that his hypothesis that the author meant he
had played a ball game does not make sense in the expanded context. Now he does
not know what the sentence means. Perhaps, reading further, he may hazard the

---

[39] N Stoljar, 'Interpretation, Indeterminacy and Authority: Some Recent Controversies in the
Philosophy of Law' (2003) 11 *Journal of Political Philosophy* 470, 470.

guess that it has something to do with agreeing with someone or something like that. He then reads the entire text again with this hypothesis in mind and if the text now begins to make sense to him, he will incline to accept his hypothesis.

What we have outlined here is in one sense a theory of reading and interpretation but it must be emphasized that the reader does these things *spontaneously*: we ask for more data – that is, more text, more sentences – if we suspect that we have not grasped what someone means. Can indeterminacy exist? The answer is unequivocally yes. A particular text – the single sentence in the example – may be indeterminate and there may be no way of determining its meaning if there are no further data. This theory – the idea of interpretation as the articulation of the spontaneously intelligent response to a text – thus imposes a constraint: a text's meaning should not be determined from insufficient data.

Traditionally in jurisprudence the issue of interpretation is conceived in terms of 'textual' and 'intentionalist' or 'purposive' theories of interpretation. In the former, the literal meaning of the words of the text generate constraints and standards whereas in the latter the constraints on interpretation are author-centred and the standard of authoritative legal interpretation is correspondence with the author's intentions. These theories underlie the basic approaches to statutory interpretation that have developed in the common law,[40] and they also underpin the main civil law techniques of statutory interpretation.[41] What these approaches do *not* do is take adequate account of the broader juridical

---

[40] The three traditional approaches to statutory interpretation that have developed in the common law are the 'literal rule', the 'golden rule', and the 'mischief rule'. The literal rule gives all the words in a statute their ordinary and natural meaning even if this leads to a 'manifest absurdity', per Lord Esher in *R v City of London Court Judge* (1892). The golden rule provides that if the literal rule gives an absurd result, which the legislature could not have intended, then the judge can substitute a reasonable meaning in the light of the statute as a whole. The golden rule was defined by Lord Wensleydale in *Grey v Pearson* (1857): 'The grammatical and ordinary sense of the word is to be adhered to, unless that would lead to some absurdity, or some repugnance or inconsistency with the rest of the instrument, in which case the grammatical and ordinary sense of the words may be modified so as to avoid that absurdity and inconsistency, but no further.' The mischief rule, which was laid down in *Heydon's Case* in the sixteenth century, provides that judges should consider, first, what the law was before the legislation was passed; secondly, what problem or 'mischief' the legislation was trying to remedy; and thirdly, what remedy the legislature was trying to provide. These three approaches are often broken down into a dichotomy between literal and purposive approaches, K Zweigert and H Kötz, *An Introduction to Comparative Law* (Oxford: Clarendon Press, 3rd edn, 1998), 265–7.
[41] In Germany, for example, the first two of these techniques include grammatical interpretation (*grammatische Auslegung*), which is the equivalent of the common law literal rule, and logical (*logische Auslegung*) and systematic (*systematische Auslegung*) interpretations, which are sometimes considered separately but together form a kind of contextual rule – not dissimilar to the golden rule – to interpret the provision in the context or light of the system of rules or the provision as a whole. The other two techniques can be understood roughly as versions of the mischief rule. They are the historical rule (*historische Auslegung*), which considers the state of affairs at the time the provision was drafted in order to determine what the draftsman or legislator wanted or was seeking to protect or correct, and the teleological rule (*teleogische Auslegung*), which aims to determine the meaning of the provision in the light of the purpose or aim of the provision or provisions, NG Foster and S Sule, *German Legal System and Laws* (Oxford: Oxford University Press, 3rd edn, 2002), 61–2.

effort, that is, the effort to discover what is due to the parties with the intention of rendering what is due.

In legal disputes, the task of the court is to discover and impose what in the instant case is just, or who, in the instant case, is entitled to what. The judge is not a computer; his task is to discover what is just, not simply automatically, unintelligently, and irresponsibly to apply statute and precedent. To judge well, the judge must discover the material or non-jural facts of the dispute. He must also discern the dispute's jural character in the light of legislation and precedents; for these in part describe, and institute, the jural world in which the dispute has arisen. But this jural world includes also the living law – the prevailing local customs and conventions and those that are common to all mankind – and what appears to be the nature, intrinsically, of the case. Moreover, to discover the just requires in the judge a moral context, described by Michel Villey as the virtue of justice, including the cognitive part of that virtue, and by Aristotle as a context demanding in the judge a mind totally possessed by justice. To be possessed by justice – to have, in other words, the required subtle intellectual background and the settled determination to render what is due – is the proper moral context of the judge whose task is to discover in the light of all the relevant factors – that is, all the relevant data – what in this particular situation is just.

In the *Rhetoric* and in the *Nicomachean Ethics*, Aristotle presumes that the law is understood and agreed to state what is just – that is, what is properly due to whom – in the envisaged situations. This presumption may jar with the contemporary reader. Since so much controversy surrounds the justness of so many laws, why presume that each law expresses justice, that is, that each law seeks to render properly what is due to whom? Since it is a presumption or presupposition for analytic purposes, it may be set aside, and of course Aristotle and St Thomas recognized that there could be unjust laws. But the emphasis here in Aristotle – and in St Thomas – is on the application of presumably just laws to *envisaged situations*. To understand a rule at all, one must understand it to refer to some identifiable type of situation; we always understand rules with reference to an envisaged situation.

The significant point for the present discussion is that laws may be just in the general case but inadequate in that they seem not to fit the instant case, and this may require 'going beyond the written law'.[42] There is a crucial difference between a law that is unjust and one that is just in the envisaged circumstances but that, were it to be applied in the instant case, would produce an unjust result. The traditional name for the effort to discover what is just when the particular case does not fit easily into the mould of what is just for the most part is *epieikeia*

---

[42] Aristotle, *Rhetoric* (London: Heinemann, 1968), I.1374a.23, 144 et seq; *Nicomachean Ethics*, V.1137a.35–1138a.3. In the *Rhetoric*, '...equity is justice that goes beyond the written law'; in the *Nicomachean Ethics*, equity is said to go beyond the law, and it is possible that Aristotle had written law dominantly in mind in this passage too. Plato, in *Politicus* (*The Statesman*), knows the problem but, for him, the human ruler must follow the rule.

in Greek, *aequitas* in Latin, and, from Latin, in English, 'equity'. The translation may mislead for, in the common law, this is no longer how the term is used.[43] Equity in the sense used here is a procedure or method not a doctrine or set of laws; the practice or procedure emerges spontaneously before there is any account of it.

Epieikeia has to do with those occasions when to apply the proper, clear, general, and uncontroverted meaning of the text to the instant case would be unjust. No question of going beyond the law arises unless in the course of the enquiry it appears to the judge that to apply it in the circumstances would be unjust. When the question of going beyond the law does arise the judge may 'reinterpret' the law; that is, he may, so to say, *adjust its scope*.[44] Whether or not the law applies without adjustment to the instant case cannot be known merely by an examination of the law itself, for the law states what is accepted to be just in the type of situation that it envisages, and to know whether or not the present situation is of that type requires an examination and understanding of the situation. The 'interpretation' of law includes a sustained effort to understand legislation and precedent, which understanding is part of the judge's moral context, but it includes also the effort to discover what is just in the instant case, and this effort neither is, nor can be, restricted to an understanding of a legal text.

We have argued that it is intrinsic to the idea of ownership that the situation is just when the owner of something quietly possesses what he owns and unjust when he does not. We argued also that what is meant by 'naturally just' and 'naturally unjust' is 'intrinsic to the situation'. In most cases, in principle, it is just that the owner quietly possesses what he owns and to deprive him of this quiet possession is to produce an unjust situation. In other words, to deprive him of this quiet possession is to steal. The argument that to steal is intrinsically unjust may be very simple but, as happens in human living, there are difficult cases. The recurrent classical and medieval example of a difficult or special case is that of the enraged owner of a sword who demands that his sword be returned to him by its borrower in order that he might do ill with it or the case of the enemy who demands the return of his weapon that he may continue to wage war against the city. St Thomas suggests that in such cases it is *not just* to return the weapon to the owner. In the *Summa Theologiae* St Thomas asks whether or not the practice of

---

[43] We have made clear already – but it is worth repeating – that *epieikeia* or *aequitas* or equity differs significantly from equity in the common law tradition, and also from Hobbes's eleventh law of nature, the law of Equity, or the law of 'impartial' – and in that sense 'equitable' – judgment. See ch 6.4 above.

[44] There tends to be in hermeneutic theory a verbal ambiguity. If an interpretation is a second text that expresses the interpreter's understanding of the original text for other readers, then it seems that a judge, in adjusting the rule's scope, is doing something different from simply applying clearly understood law. If both are to be called 'interpretation', at least they are different kinds of interpretation. There are in fact several distinct enquiries and, confusingly, 'the most striking feature of much contemporary discussion of hermeneutics is that it attempts to treat all these issues as if they were hermeneutical. They are not', B Lonergan, *Method in Theology* (London: Darton Longman and Todd, 1972), 155.

epieikeia is virtuous, that is, whether or not it is good to proceed in this manner.[45] His answer is that it is virtuous; it is worth quoting in full:

As has been said above [I-II, q 96, art 6], when we are dealing with laws, because human acts, about which laws are concerned, consist in particular and contingent events that may vary almost infinitely, it is not possible to frame laws that will in no instance fail to fit the case. Legislators concentrate on what happens for the most part, and make laws accordingly; in some instances to apply these laws runs against the character of justice, and counter to the common good that the laws intend. Thus, the law states that what is deposited is to be returned because for the most part this is just. However, it can sometimes happen that to do so would be harmful, as when someone maddened by anger hands over his sword and, while still enraged, demands it back; or if someone should look for the return of what he has deposited in order to damage the community. In these and similar cases it is bad to follow the established law; it is good in such cases, having put aside the verbal formula of the law, to follow what is just and for the common utility. This is the function of *epieikeia* – what we call *aequitas* (equity). Hence it is plain that *epieikeia* is a virtue.[46]

In general, the idea of ownership is incoherent and makes no sense if what is owned is not to be returned to its owner – hence, the idea of ownership is incoherent if it does not include the idea that to steal is unjust. And yet sometimes the situation is such that what is owned is not to be returned. So it would seem that the general formulation, which purports to express what is naturally just, is not always applicable. The argument here is that the formulation or law expresses what is just, that is, what is applicable in most cases but not in all. Where St Thomas writes 'for the most part', we might be inclined to write 'in principle' or 'all things being equal'.

A new question now arises: If the borrower refuses to return the sword because its owner is maddened with anger, is he breaking a rule of natural justice? Consider a more modern example: Peter and Paul go to the pub in Peter's car. During the course of the evening Peter drinks heavily and becomes incapable of driving safely. While he is buying another drink Paul takes the keys from Peter's overcoat pocket and refuses to give them back. The two examples are structurally identical. No one denies that the keys belong to Peter. No one denies that, in principle, in ordinary circumstances, the just situation would be restored were Paul to give the keys back to their owner. There may well be a formulated law stating that what belongs to someone is to be restored to him. In refusing to give back the keys in these circumstances, is Paul breaking the rule? Obviously he is. Is he going against what is naturally just? He is, if the formulation expresses what

---

[45] St Thomas Aquinas deals with the question of equity in his *Summa Theologiae* in the second part of the second part at Question 120 (II.II, q 120) and in his commentary on Aristotle: *In Decem Libros Ethicorum Aristotelis ad Nicomachum Expositio*, V.XVI. See G Barden, 'Aristotle's Notion of *Epieikeia*' in *Creativity and Method* (M Lamb ed, Milwaukee: Marquette University Press, 1981); H-G Gadamer, *Truth and Method* (London: Sheed and Ward, 1975), 284; and M Villey, *Seize essais*, ch 12*bis*.   [46] *Summa Theologiae*, II-II, q 120, art 1.

is naturally just in all circumstances. St Thomas's argument is that the formulation does not, and cannot, always express this. What is naturally just in these
circumstances is to be discovered in the circumstances but, of course, it cannot be
discovered, except by lucky accident, by someone who has no idea whatsoever of
what is in principle just.

The difficulty surrounding the application of general rules to individual cases
is not confined to rules expressing what is naturally just; it arises equally often
in cases of the conventionally just. What this indicates is that what is just in any
situation is not discovered and realized simply by the application of a formulated
rule; even in the ordinary circumstances where the rule does apply, it must be discovered that the situation under scrutiny is in fact one to which this rather than
another rule applies. After the theatre, the playgoer who has left his coat in the
cloakroom, hands in the ticket and asks for his coat. Both he and the attendant
understand the situation to be an instance of the ordinary, and in part conventional, case where what has been deposited is to be returned when the owner prof-
fers his ticket and asks for it. But were the attendant to suspect that the case was
in some relevant way out of the ordinary – for example, if a sniffer dog had shown
the coat to be suspicious – he would be culpably irresponsible not to ask himself
whether or not the general rule applied. Understanding the particular situation
discovers what is just in a particular situation; for which understanding, as we
have said, an understanding of the general case is illuminating.

How is the judge to know whether or not the instant case is an exception? The
text of the law does not, and cannot give a complete list of situations to which it
is applicable or inapplicable; did it do so, no question of going beyond it would
arise. And yet every reasonable person presumes that an injunction against sleeping in a railway station does not apply to babies. Why? It cannot be from a simple
reading of the law. The moral context of the judge will often be the key factor at
work here. The presumption flows from the judge's conviction that to apply to
babies a law against sleeping in a railway station would be unreasonable, absurd,
and unjust. And that conviction derives not from an understanding of the text
of the law, but from a moral context in which, to anyone within that moral context, any suggestion that as a universal rule babies are forbidden to sleep in railway stations appears to be ludicrous and unreasonable.[47] Because to apply the
law would be unreasonable, the law is then interpreted to have excluded babies
from its scope. The lawgiver is presumed to have excluded babies – although he
is not thought to have done so explicitly – because he is presumed to have legislated within the *same moral context* as that within which the judge now exam-
ines the case. The lawgiver is therefore presumed to be in agreement with the

---

[47] The possibility of a different moral context within which it would not be clearly unreasonable
must be roundly acknowledged. This *de facto* relativism exists; whether or not it can be in principle
overcome is another matter. If there are situations in which the command not to sleep would reasonably apply to babies (medical situations, for example), still that the baby is in a railway station
is not one of them.

adjustment.[48] Aristotle suggests that when the judge departs from the explicit law, he attempts 'to say what the legislator would have said had he been present'.[49] This seems to suggest that the task of the judge is to read the legislator's mind but there is commonly no, or very little, evidence for what an actual legislator would have said had he been actually dealing with the matter; rather, there is a presumption that the legislator would have judged wisely and, therefore, that the judge, if he judges wisely, will 'say what the legislator would have said'.

The effort to reach another's meaning through a spoken or written text pre-supposes that humans share the basic context, or mind, which is the ground of the possibility of understanding one another. The effort to understand another presumes and rests upon the basic intellectual context that is human intelligence, or mind, and which is the possibility of all contexts or, in Aristotle's words, 'the possibility of becoming and making all things'.[50] More concretely, the possibility of understanding another is the fact that what one person can understand so, in principle, can another. That is what we call 'basic context': the public character of understanding. If in principle one person cannot understand what another has understood and tried to express in a text, then understanding and expression are private and no one can correctly interpret another's text. Mind is given, but is used reasonably and responsibly, or not so used. Hence, there is the inevitable moral context of the investigator. As we have noted, bias towards one rather than another result is a real, even if not a constant, temptation, and reveals the signifi-cance of the investigator's moral context.

We understand before we speak. Unless we had come to understand others, we could not become speakers. When we learn to understand and to speak, we realize language in ourselves, and learn the specific linguistic context within which expressions make sense; that is, not only how to understand and speak grammatically but also the common sense, which includes the often internally controversial moral sense, of our linguistic community. Hence, most commu-nication between speakers and writers who share the same language is instantly understood. However, as cultures become more differentiated, within the same linguistic community different more specialized contexts develop (the jural and scientific contexts being but two examples), and to understand what is said or written within any one of these specialized contexts requires an understanding of that context. Furthermore, to understand new hypotheses within a context, read-ers must make the effort to understand what the original thinker understood, and has tried to express in a text which may have called for the development of the language, since the current state of the language may not easily have

---

[48] It might be objected here that an adjustment of scope stems from how anyone would under-stand the rule, and hence that the issue is linguistic, not moral. It is certainly linguistic; but to understand language as it is used is to understand the common sense, which includes the moral sense or context, of the community.

[49] Aristotle, *Nicomachean Ethics*, V.1137b.22; *Rhetoric*, I.11374b.

[50] Aristotle, *On the Soul*, III.V.

accommodated the new, and perhaps immensely difficult, insight. Still, because we share basic context, in principle another can understand what one person has understood. And because we share language, we can in principle learn any particular language; a meaning that can be expressed in one language can in principle be expressed in another;[51] and in principle what one person can mean can be understood by another. Yet what is in principle possible is not at every moment, and in every situation, proximately possible for, or easily achieved by, whomsoever. Each of us at any moment is limited; if that were not so, we should have no *need* to learn. Were we unable to go beyond our present limitations, we *could not* learn; we could not come to understand the utterances of those whose contexts differed from our own.

To know what is meant is correctly to understand what is meant. Knowing is a movement from questioning data, through understanding and producing hypotheses, to the grasp that there is sufficient evidence reasonably to affirm one's hypotheses to be correct, probable, possible, mistaken or for the moment to allow no conclusion. Reasonable judgment is not infallibility. The data for understanding what is meant are utterances, and if there is unclarity, misunderstanding or ambiguity, spontaneously we look for and, by asking questions, evoke further data, that is, more and different utterances. It can happen that there are insufficient data to allow the investigator reasonably to prefer one possible meaning over another. So, a fragment, or indeed a legislative provision, may be inadequate to allow one reasonably to settle its meaning. There is the effort to understand what the law means because disputes arise between people who share a common sense, and who live together in societies that are in part constituted by the prevailing laws and customs that to a great extent define the social world, and that enable us to live within a context of more or less well-known and accepted expectations.[52] So, in litigation over a particular contract it is important to know, to the greatest extent possible, what in the particular jurisdiction, in the particular community, is recognized as constituting a binding contract.

Where the application of the law would be patently unreasonable, the law is interpreted in a way that does go 'beyond' it: the law's scope, as we have said, is adjusted. When considering a legal text, two questions are quite distinct. The first is interpretive: what did X mean when he wrote Y about Z? The second question is, let us say, in quotation marks, 'theoretical': how is Z, the object that X wrote about, to be understood? The first is how to interpret the earlier author; the second is how to understand what the earlier author was writing about.

---

[51] The Sapir-Whorff hypothesis – that because language is the means by which culture is transmitted, the very basis of culture is language itself – is sometimes mistakenly understood as contradicting this assertion. What is of course true is that it is not always proximately possible to express in a language in its present state of development what is readily expressed in another; but its speakers can learn what is meant and develop their language to express it.

[52] This is what Neil MacCormick calls the institutional character of a normative order: *Institutions of Law* (Oxford: Oxford University Press, 2007).

A law or custom informs a person how to behave in the envisaged circumstances. Sometimes what is required is clear, but sometimes what is required must be discerned in the light of a law or custom that is less specific. Consider the issue of whether a speeding car was driven 'recklessly'. The word 'recklessly' is not difficult to understand but it is often extremely difficult to know how to use, and whether or not a particular act was reckless cannot be settled simply by consulting a dictionary. We tend to surround a term like 'recklessly' with precise and measurable descriptions, so that, for example, to drive a car on a given stretch of road at more than 80kph is forbidden as being reckless. But such specific limitations do not, and cannot, cover the entire range of reckless driving; the speed limit imposed in a town may be 50kph but it is often extremely reckless to drive at that speed. The specific limits assist the judge to come to judgment but they do not adequately define reckless. The judgment that a driver drove recklessly is based on an understanding of his actions. Obviously, we could not understand his driving as reckless if we did not understand the word 'reckless', but it is not enough to understand the word; we must understand *driving*. For that reason, and generalizing, it is usually necessary, but not enough, to know what the law means, what the words commonly mean, what the original legislator meant, and so on. When trying to decide whether or not the driver drove recklessly we are not trying to understand the verbal meaning of the law but, in the light of the law, the way in which the car was driven.

We have been discussing laws that are defective because they are inadequate, that is, because they seem not to fit the instant case. When a law is in that way inadequate, to discover what is just requires the judge 'to go beyond the written law', to judge equitably. In going beyond the written law does the judge make law? Legislators, to paraphrase St Thomas's discussion of *epieikeia* quoted above, concentrate on what happens for the most part and because events and situations are contingent and vary almost infinitely, it is not possible to frame laws that will in no case fail to fit the instant use. The legislative process properly so-called involves deliberation of policy as well as different stages of debate and discussion, in the public domain, regarding appropriate general legal measures. The court, on the other hand, must address the question: *in the case now being considered*, what is due to whom, and from whom is it due? In answering this question the court gives a judgment in the instant case that ought to be impartial, intelligent, reasoned, and fair but that on any specific occasion may be biased, unintelligent, unreasonable, and unfair. The court in handing down its judgment in the instant case does not make general law precisely as does the legislature but because similars are similarly understood and no particular case can be so peculiar that it in principle can in no way resemble any other case, the scope of the judgment cannot but go beyond the instant case to influence the course of future efforts to discern what is just. So while the court in these situations is not making law in the same way as the legislature is, it is nonetheless making law, as courts *must* on occasion do in fulfilling their task of determining what is due to whom in the particular case. It is justice that necessitates judicial 'law-making'.

But, of course, laws, as we discuss below in Chapter 8, may also be defective because they are unjust. In other words, the law may operate in some way against the goal of rendering to each what is due. Here the question is: how is a judge to deal with a law that he finds so unjust that he cannot in conscience apply it? He may try to 'interpret' it so that its injustice is either sufficiently diminished or removed. But what if he fails in the attempt? This is not a case of *epieikeia*; it is not a case of a just law failing to deal with the exceptional case. The legislature's intention is clear. The law unquestionably applies to the situation. To be possessed by justice is the proper moral context of the judge whose task is to discover in the light of all the relevant factors – that is, all the relevant data – what in this particular situation is just, and, by hypothesis, precisely because the relevant law is unjust to apply it would bring about an unjust result. The judge is not a computer but a moral agent whose task is to bring justice, not merely to apply the law. Accordingly, if he is convinced that a law is so unjust that it ought not be applied, then he ought not apply it and ought, if need be, resign his position.[53] The rule of justice here overcomes the rule of unjust law.[54]

In finding a law unjust a judge might, of course, be mistaken but fallibility is human, and laws do not come with the labels 'just' or 'unjust' conveniently attached. Laws may be just or unjust, as propositions may be true or false, but to discover whether or not they are is both the task and the responsibility of the enquirer. The judgment that a law is unjust (or just) is, as are all judgments, inescapably subjective but is not inevitably mistaken. Unless there can be no unjust laws, that is, unless all properly legislated laws are by definition just – so that the word 'just' is a synonym of 'properly legislated' – there will be unjust laws, and the judge who finds them unjust and in conscience inapplicable will be faced with a moral crux either to apply them against his conscience or to resign. Such cruces are not confined to adjudication.

6.6 Understanding and Interpreting a Definition of 'Refugee'

To bring together the various parts of the discussion of the interpretation and application we shall consider some aspects of the 1951 United Nations Convention relating to the Status of Refugees, hereinafter 'the Refugee Convention' or 'the Convention', in which what constitutes a refugee is defined.

---

[53] C Perelman, *Droit, morale et philosophie* (Paris: Librairie Générale de Droit et de Jurisprudence, 1976), 100: 'When clearly iniquitous legislation prevents him, for whatever reason, from carrying out his task in accord with his conscience, the judge is morally obliged to resign. He is not merely a calculating machine; and if by his participation he contributes to the functioning of an iniquitous order, he cannot hope to evade his personal responsibility.'

[54] The authority of law, upon which the rule of law is based, has two sources: the first, that it is law and not mere recommendation; the second, that it is just. The two modalities of authority are discussed in ch 11 below.

Suppose a person leaves his own state, arrives in another in which, being not otherwise entitled to residence, he claims refugee status based on the Refugee Convention in a jurisdiction where the Convention is binding law. The court's task is to decide whether or not the claimant is entitled to refugee status. There are already some presuppositions in operation that may easily pass unnoticed. That the claimant is not entitled to residence unless he is judged to be a refugee rests on the underlying presupposition that not everyone is entitled to residence everywhere. In other words, it is taken for granted that a state is entitled to enact laws granting or withholding entitlement to residence within it. That the prevailing residency legislation is in fact just is not inevitable, but when considering a claim for refugee status the court will normally presume that it is. Thus, the court, when undertaking its enquiry, accepts that the claimant is not entitled to refugee status unless he fulfils the criteria set out in the Convention. Accordingly, in order reasonably to determine whether or not the claimant is entitled to refugee status, the court must discover three things: first, what the facts are; secondly, what the criteria are; and thirdly, whether or not, in the light of the criteria, the facts show the claimant to be a refugee. These three elements are easily set out; that they are complicated appears on reflection and in practice.

When one thinks even for a moment, it becomes instantly clear, even without knowing the actual criteria, that there are indefinitely many facts about claimants that are almost certain to be irrelevant to the claim. It is irrelevant whether the claimant is a man rather than a woman; whether he has brown hair; whether he is highly educated; whether he speaks the language of the state where he seeks refugee status; and so on indefinitely. Such facts seem irrelevant because, within the surrounding jural common sense which is shared by the court, to include them would be simply bizarre and unjust; but it is worth noticing that 'to be highly educated' is often a criterion in a decision to allow immigration, thus showing that in the jural common sense – the living law, the communal sense of what is just – there is a clear and accepted distinction between a refugee and an immigrant. When we speak of 'the facts of a case', we have in mind those facts that are arguably relevant in the light of the established criteria.

The criteria relevant to a claim for refugee status are set out in Article 1(A)2 of the Convention and the Convention includes in its definition of 'refugee' any person who

owing to a well founded fear of being persecuted for reasons of race, religion, nationality, membership of a particular social group or political opinion, is outside the country of his nationality and is unable or, owing to such fear, is unwilling to avail himself of the protection of his country.[55]

---

[55] Article 1(A)2, Convention relating to the Status of Refugees, adopted 28 July 1951, 189 UNTS 137, entered into force 22 April 1954.

A claimant who would base his claim exclusively on his being a member of a particular social group must show five things: first, that he is a member of a particular social group; secondly, that he has a well-founded fear of being persecuted; thirdly, that the feared persecution is based on his being a member of that group; fourthly, that he is outside the country of his nationality; and, fifthly, that he is unable or unwilling, owing to his fear, to avail himself of the protection of the country of his nationality. *The criteria indicate what facts are relevant to the particular basis for the claim*; so, if the claim is based exclusively on being a member of a particular social group, then nationality, race, or political opinion are incidental. However difficult it is to understand the criteria and to apply them to the particular case before it, what, in the end, the court must decide is whether or not, in the light of the criteria, the reasonably established and so admitted facts show the claimant to be entitled to refugee status.

It is obvious that it will usually be easier to establish some facts than others. To establish that the claimant is outside the country of his nationality is usually not difficult; its function being to disallow applications from one living within his own country. That were he to return to his country he would be in danger of being persecuted is much more difficult to establish. The court must determine what persecution involves and what constitutes a well-founded fear; at once we hit upon the issue of interpretation and application. That the claimant is a member of a particular social group and that he is in danger of persecution *because* he is a member of that group, rather than for some other reason, is still more difficult to establish. That he is unable or unwilling to avail himself of the protection of his country *owing to such fear* is also difficult to establish; for a person might be unwilling to avail himself of protection for some other reason, for instance, because he thought to live under state protection would be unpleasant, or because he preferred to live in the country where he sought refuge.

There has been considerable discussion as to what constitutes 'persecution', 'a particular social group', 'membership of a group', 'well founded fear', and 'protection of his country', and that discussion of criteria may have some bearing on what will count as a relevant fact. Can, for example, the same kind of action count as 'persecution' in one situation or in one jurisdiction but not in another? And what is a 'well founded fear'? A claimant might well honestly consider that his fear of persecution was well founded but the court might equally well conclude that it was not. 'Protection of his country' in the jurisprudence of the English-speaking jurisdictions is taken to mean 'protection by the state'. Or does it mean '*adequate* protection by the state'?

Perhaps the most controversial aspect of the definition of 'refugee' in Article 1(A)2 of the Convention is the meaning of 'a particular social group'.[56]

---

[56] See, for some examples, *Canada (AG) v Ward* 1993 2 SCR 689; *Zefi v Canada (Minister for Citizenship and Immigration)* 2003 FCT 636; *Morato v Minister for Immigration, Local Government and Ethnic Affairs* (1992) 39 FCR 401 (Australia); and *Application S v Minister for Immigration and Multicultural Affairs* (2004) 217 CLR 387 (Australia).

In addressing this issue, the judge's first question is 'What is meant in the Convention by the compound noun "a particular social group"?' But this question is unclear. Does the judge want to know only what it would have meant had he (the judge) used the compound noun or has he some interest in trying to discover what the legislators, however defined, meant? There is a particular and well-known problem here. But all we have is the text; so we ask what it is reasonable to suppose the compound noun means in the text and in the larger context within which it is written. The judge will try to distinguish between 'a group' and 'a particular social group' because he reasonably presumes, until shown otherwise, that the adjectives 'particular' and 'social' have some significance. He makes the mild hypothesis that humans are presumed in the Convention to belong both to groups that are not 'particular social groups' and groups that are 'particular social groups'; were this not the case the adjectives would be redundant. But when he begins to read the text afresh with this clarification, he discovers that it gives rise to some problems. If, for example, left-handed men are persecuted precisely because they are left-handed, does left-handedness convert the group from being not a particular social group to being a particular social group?[57]

Now arises a new issue: is it plausible to read the Convention as meaning that a group that is not a particular social group becomes one when the characteristic that make it a particular social group is concentrated upon by others who now persecute members of the newly noticed group? The group obviously *cannot* be persecuted *as a group* without being first noticed as a group. A particular social group can be instituted not only by members taking themselves to be a group but also by others taking people of a certain type to be a particular social group – foisting, so to speak, 'social-group-ness' upon them. The question at the beginning of this paragraph is still a question about what the text means; but if the answer to the question is that it is not plausible to read the Convention in this way, then the question as to whether or not left-handed men form a particular

---

[57] On the question as to whether or not persecution can transform what is not a particular social group (eg left-handed men) into a particular social group, see *Application A v Minister for Immigration and Ethnic Affairs* (1997) 190 CLR 225 (Australia), where McHugh J: 'Left handed men are not a particular social group in society. But, if they were persecuted *because* they were left handed, they would quickly become recognizable in their society as a particular social group ... But it would be the attribute of being left handed and not the persecutory acts that would identify them as a particular social group.' Many years ago left-handed children were often either required or very strongly encouraged to learn to write with their right hand. Did this educational practice make them a particular social group? Or for people to be a particular social group must they recognize themselves to be members of it? Did being required to write with their right hand give left-handed children a sense of being members of a particular social group? Do left-handed people tend to notice left-handedness in others more than right-handed people do? Robert Hertz's study of the relative social importance of the left and right hands ('La prééminence de la main droite: étude sur la polarité religieuse' (1909) 68 *Revue Philosophique* 553) illustrates how attributes that are from one perspective non-social can become from another perspective social. Some of the markers that serve to identify a social group also define it and some do not. Left-handedness identifies a person as a member of the group and defines the group, whereas a group of English speakers might be identified as New Zealanders from their accents but accent does not define nationality.

social group is not a question about the meaning of the Convention; *it is not, in other words, an interpretive question.* It is a question about how to categorize left-handed men who have been persecuted because they were left-handed men. If the judge decides that, in these circumstances, left-handed men are a particular social group, then, in accord with the Convention, members of that group who are persecuted because they are members of that group are entitled to refugee status if the other conditions are fulfilled.

The judge faced with a claim for refugee status is no longer faced with what 'a particular social group' means; that is, with how this phrase is used in common speech (because unless there is some reason to think that the Convention uses the phrase otherwise than in common speech, there is no reason to understand it otherwise). The judge is faced with the question as to whether the group on which the claimant bases the claim is or is not a particular social group. The judge is not asked to discover if he in some personal and peculiar way thinks of a group as a particular social group but whether it is reasonable within the linguistic and moral context in which he, the legislators and other speakers live to say that the group in question is a particular social group. He should not pretend that the legislators had in mind the question as to whether or not the group now in question is a particular social group. It is patently absurd to think that those who agreed the Convention had every possible social group in mind; it is hardly plausible, for example, to think that they had Pakistani women – *qua* social group – in mind, yet this was validly one of the issues at stake in the well-known UK *Shah and Islam* case.[58]

So the judge is no longer trying to find what the legislators actually thought and thought of; he is trying to determine if a suggested group is a particular social group. It is here that there is going to be, inevitably, what is often referred to as 'pluralism' in interpretation.[59] In *Shah and Islam* Lord Hoffman expressed

---

[58] *R v Immigration Appeal Tribunal and anor, Ex parte Shah and Islam*, 1999 2 All ER 545. *Shah and Islam* concerned two married Pakistani women who were forced by their husbands to leave their homes and who fled to England. Both women claimed refugee status under art 1A(2) of the Refugee Convention, claiming that they had a well-founded fear of being persecuted for reasons of membership of a particular social group. They contended that, if they were forced to return to Pakistan, they would be unprotected by the state and would be subject to various risks, including assault and criminal proceedings for sexual immorality.

[59] Natalie Stoljar suggests that one criterion of adequacy by which a theory of interpretation must be judged is whether the constraints articulated by the theory are capable of generating a plausible answer to the question of authority. This does not mean, she suggests, that it is a criterion of adequacy that a theory of legal interpretation be applicable to all texts or even to all legal texts. Stoljar argues that different theories may be appropriate, for instance, to literary and legal texts, and within law for constitutional and statutory texts. For discussion of these issues in the context of 'law and literature' scholarship, see T Murphy and G Staunton, 'The Envelope and the Letter: Reflections on Law's Ambience' in G Hofmann (ed), *Figures of Law: Studies in the Interference of Law and Literature* (Tübingen: A Francke Verlag, 2007), 21, 31–40. Stoljar argues also that neither do *particular* theories themselves always guarantee single right answers to interpretive questions. Certain 'hard' interpretive questions will be incapable of resolution by any theory of interpretation. Legal interpretation, she concludes, 'is not radically indeterminate, but it is pluralistic', (Stoljar, n 39 above, at 495). Stoljar suggests – correctly, in our view – that this conclusion is consonant with

a view that allows one to think that a particular social group is any group of people that is recognized *by others* as a group even if prior to that recognition the members of that group did not recognize themselves as a group. For example, Africans from Nigeria, Botswana, Zambia, and Namibia and elsewhere do not for the most part think of themselves as a particular social group while they are in their own countries but are often perceived as a particular social group by people in the European countries to which they emigrate and may or may not perceive themselves as one; similarly, Irish, English, Portuguese, and Greeks do not think of themselves as a particular social group but in Australia, although recognized as distinct from one another, are thought of as belonging to the group 'European immigrants', and again they may or may not think of themselves as members of that group. To complicate things further, it can and does happen that outsiders think of a particular set of people as a particular social group because, say, they come from the same country, while the members of the set emphatically do not think of themselves in that way. One judge might think that a particular social group was necessarily a group the members of which thought of themselves as being members irrespective of how others saw them; another judge thinks that others may define a particular social group; yet another judge thinks that a particular social group is self-defining. Is it possible to say which judge is 'right'? This question may have nothing whatsoever to do with the understanding of the original text, because there is no, or insufficient, evidence to know what the original authors thought, or 'what the text means'.

In attempting to understand a legal text the reader may be unable to discern what the original author(s) meant on the grounds that there were so many authors (the group of legislators making up a legislature are commonly thought of as an 'author'). In such instances it is implausible to think that they all had precisely the same intention and so the reader typically invents or constructs an ideal author. But there may be another reason for the inability to discern meaning: there is often a set of associated preliminary texts – such as parliamentary debates or the deliberations of a law reform commission – that may have to be taken into account. If they are to be taken into account, the data for interpretation is not the legislation alone but the legislation and associated texts. If the decision is to confine the data to the legislation, then one has excluded data that in another context would be relevant. If the legislation is to be concentrated upon to the exclusion of texts immediately associated with its framing then the legislation is the data. The legislation is now read within the context of the language in which it is written, within the context of the jurisprudence, and within the intellectual and moral context of the reader.

Neil MacCormick's argument that common law reasoning is pluralistic because different values generate different 'rival' outcomes in cases. See N MacCormick, *Legal Reasoning and Legal Theory* (Oxford: Clarendon Press, 1994), ch 4.

If what constitutes a particular social group is more or less settled, there still remains the question of what constitutes membership of one.[60] To say 'Peter is a member of group A' means something like:

A social group contains more than one member. A group is a collection of persons each one of which has the set of characteristics [the set may contain only one element, ie it is a singleton] that define the group. If Peter has the set of defining characteristics of group A, he is a member of group A. Peter has the set of defining characteristics of group A and, therefore, is a member of, or, in other words, belongs to, group A.

These propositions are an interpretation of the proposition 'Peter is a member of group A'. To claim that the interpretation is adequate is to claim that it adequately states for the audience for which it is intended the interpreter's understanding of the text of which it is an interpretation. To claim that the understanding expressed in the interpretation is correct is to claim 'It is true that "Peter is a member of group A" means "[the above propositions]".' The evidence for the claim is that this is what the text means – that is, this is what the normal speaker would mean were he to assert that 'Peter is a member of group A'. In the absence of any contrary evidence – for a somewhat fanciful example, evidence that the text is in fact a code – it is reasonable to conclude that this is what the original authors meant. Language is essentially public and, used in the normal way, this is what the authors could not but have meant. Someone who wants to controvert the conclusion must produce some evidence to show that the text is to be understood otherwise – such as, evidence that the interpretation suggested fails to take account of some elements in the text or that the text is written in a code based upon English. Were someone to suggest that 'Peter is a member of group A' means that 'Peter has *one* of the elements in the set of elements that define group A' (for example, 'Peter is left-handed and so, although not a woman, belongs to the group of left-handed women'), that person must show some evidence in the text or in the surrounding context to support this view.

What cannot be the case is that the text means that Peter both is and is not a member of the social group, unless it can be shown that it is incoherent and allows both interpretations so that the law as it stands is contradictory and, therefore, impossible to apply.[61] Still, even if we know what to be a member of a group means, we do not yet know what 'a social group' means. By hypothesis, there is insufficient data in the text to determine what is meant. The reader must ask how he uses the term. He invents 'human groups' to help him limit the scope of the term 'social group'; that is, he wants to know to what groups the term

---

[60] See *Morato*; and also *Shah and Islam*, where membership of a group is implicitly defined in the definition of a group.

[61] It is often the case that the data do not allow sufficiently well-grounded understandings; different, plausible but incompatible understandings may be, more or less equally, attested by the available evidence but none prevails because there is insufficient evidence to support any one against another. By itself, the sentence 'I played ball yesterday' grounds equally well two understandings and interpretations, as has been said.

plausibly applies. In most cases it is perfectly plain that the legislators did not have this particular group under scrutiny in mind; they used a very ordinary descriptive complex noun. What did they mean? Unless there is evidence to the contrary what they meant is quite clear: *they meant what any normal speaker would have meant.*

The problem, then, is not how to understand the compound noun, 'social group'. The problem is to determine if a described human arrangement is properly understood as a 'social group'. The compound noun, 'social group', is the type of noun that does not pin down, and is not meant to pin down, precisely and exhaustively, what arrangements are properly called social groups. It is, in fact, a noun that resembles nouns such as 'neighbour', 'land', 'vehicle', and so on, or adjectives such as 'reckless', 'reasonable', 'negligent', and so on. 'Social group' is a term the meaning of which is clear, so that no one hearing or reading that 'someone who is persecuted because he is a member of a particular social group is entitled to refugee status' has any difficulty knowing what the sentence means, but the scope of the term 'particular social group' remains undecided.[62] Lord Hoffman in *Shah and Islam* suggests that the initially non-social group of left-handed men – which is, of course, a group – can move from being non-social to social when left-handed men are subjected to particular treatment, say, persecution, because of left-handedness. Before being persecuted as left-handed, the left-handed men must be recognized as a social group; the characteristic which they in fact share and which makes them a group, albeit a non-social one, is selected and it is this selection that turns them into a social group. But mere selection in the mind of a private person is not enough – someone cannot turn the group of left-handed men who like elephants into a social group merely by thinking. The selection must be accompanied by some social effect. A social group is a group accepted within the community as a group.

So the judge tries to discover, through reflection on a sequence of imaginary cases, the scope of the term; what he is trying to do is to understand and to express his understanding of the data presented to him, in this case about a refugee, namely the appellant's story. The appellant gives a story of his life to support his application; what we try to discover is whether or not his life is to be understood in a certain way; we are not asking 'What do the words "a particular social

---

[62] This characteristic of terms is found as much in everyday as in legal discourse. We know the meaning of 'bright' but are undecided as to what levels of light it refers (that is, we are undecided as to its scope). Different people will apply the term differently and, which is crucial, the person who decides that he will keep a record of when during, say, a month, it got bright in the morning, may not yet know what scope he is going to give the term. For it to become a term in optics requires the invention of a suitable measure of 'brightness'. Everyone understands the word 'dignity', that is everyone has a sense of what it means but to determine whether or not a particular activity has violated human dignity demands more than knowing what the words 'human dignity' means; it demands knowing how they have been used in earlier cases, that is, how its scope has been developed in the jurisprudence and judging whether or not its scope covers, or ought to be enlarged to cover, the instant case. See C Dupré, 'Unlocking Human Dignity: Towards a Theory for the 21st Century' (2009) 2 *European Human Rights Law Review* 190.

group" mean?', we are rather asking 'Is this person's life understood properly by saying that the group he belongs to is a particular social group in the given context?' The judge is not asking for the meaning of the relevant word; he is asking if he is prepared to describe the person as a member of a particular social group. There is not one clearly specifiable ordinary meaning of the word; there is a range, and there are unacceptable meanings. Someone who describes a winter moonless midnight as 'bright' does not know how to use the word. Someone who describes the set of people with A RH+ blood but otherwise unrelated as a social group does not know how to use the word 'social group'.[63] If *all* groupings or classifications of people – that is, all groups – are 'social' then the adjective 'social' is redundant. Outside the ordinary range we are fairly sure about saying that someone is using the word wrongly; inside the range, we often find that someone is prepared to describe something using a word that we would not use for that thing or situation and yet not find the person's usage bizarre or unacceptable; and he might even persuade us to use the word that way in the future.

---

[63] The set of people with A RH+ blood form a biological group; they may *become* a social group if the characteristic becomes socially important as in the example of left-handed men. Women five feet four and half inches tall form a group but not a social group unless the characteristic of being that height becomes socially relevant.

7

Morality, Law, and Legislation

7.1 Introduction

We noted in Chapter 1 that the term 'law' is usually taken to refer to forms of what is typically called 'state law' or 'positive law' and including constitutional law (whether written or unwritten) and enacted legislation (for example, law contained in a common law statute or civil code); law arising from or associated with the courts (common law, case law or, sometimes, 'judge-made law'); and, from many perspectives, elements of international law. This way of understanding the term is common in discussions of the relationship between morality and law, and in these same discussions 'morality' is usually taken to refer to a pre-existing 'moral law' or 'moral code' containing an indefinitely large number of precepts only some of which are explicitly formulated, or, perhaps more often, to a sub-set of the 'moral code' containing only 'private' as distinct from 'public' precepts. We do not use the terms in this way, and we discuss the interrelation between three, rather than between two, elements: namely, morality, law, and legislation. We emphasized in preceding chapters that in our account of law and justice, 'morality' refers to that part of human living governed by deliberation and choice, and 'law' usually refers to the living law or the communal moral tradition, that is, those judgments and choices that in recurrent kinds of circumstances are generally accepted and approved in a particular community. We use 'legislation' in its ordinary sense, that is, to refer to decisions of the legislator, whether the legislator is a single individual or a legislative assembly. Towards the end of this chapter we focus both on how these three forms give rise to *obligation* and on the question of the proper range or scope of legislation, but first we discuss the elements separately.[1]

7.2 Morality

The moral question asks what in given circumstances is to be done. Humans cannot avoid that question; they *must* deliberate and choose. The moral domain

---

[1] The discussion of morality and legislation in this chapter is more detailed than the discussion of the living law or communal moral tradition, which we have discussed already in chs 1 and 3.4.

is the domain of deliberation and choice. The moral domain does not cover the whole of human living: the dilation and contraction of one's pupils, the attempt to recover one's balance, the violent struggle to breathe when being suffocated are examples of spontaneous and unavoidable responses that are at once human and not chosen. The world in which we live is an ever-changing set of events, some but not all of which are subject to our influence. When they had foolishly praised his omnipotence, Canute showed his courtiers that he had no power over the ebb and flow of the tide; but someone knitting a scarf brings about an arrangement of wool that would not otherwise have come about. About what we can, or think we can, influence, we deliberate and choose; about what we cannot, or think we cannot, influence, we do not. Precisely what can and what cannot be influenced is not given once for all. Some diseases formerly beyond human influence no longer are; some building projects become possible only with advances in mathematics, physics, and engineering. What is possible for one person may not be possible for another owing to differences in habitual capacity, lack of equipment, distance from the place where the action is to be undertaken, and so on.

The moral domain exists only if there are things that can be deliberated about and chosen, and if there are those who can deliberate about them, and choose whether or not to act in accord with their judgment about what is to be done. For someone who judges that he should do X, to do X is good, and what will be brought about is a good and to bring it about is a value. Suppose that Peter, in the circumstances in which he finds himself, judges that he should now begin to prepare dinner for his family. (The phrase 'in the circumstances in which he finds himself' is crucial; had they been other than they were, he might well have judged otherwise.) He has judged that to do so is for him a good; the dinner that he hopes to produce is a good, and to produce it is a value. Whether or not to realize that value he has yet to decide, for the judgment 'It would be good that I should now do X' does not determine the decision to do X.

Whether or not Peter should begin to prepare dinner is so commonplace a choice, and so dependent on circumstances that it may not seem at first sight to be a moral issue. Whether or not Peter should return a banknote, which its owner has inadvertently dropped, seems more obviously moral. Peter may accept that in his community it would be thought that in general what is found ought, if possible, to be returned to its owner and that, in the light of that law, he ought in this case to return the money; he may himself accept the communal law or living law. But he might still ask himself whether or not he ought to act, and whether or not he will act, in accord with that law. It is, moreover, possible that Peter might think himself obliged to return the money solely because of the law, and because of his fear of being discovered and punished. The example may incline the reader to suppose that morality is a matter of acting in accord with existing norms. That there are communally accepted norms or laws is both evident and fundamental in our account of law in community but morality is not to be defined as acting or failing to act in accord with them. The moral domain is the domain of personal responsibility, not a sub-domain defined by communally accepted norms or laws that govern both private and public spheres however those spheres are distinguished. Nor is the moral domain confined to what is thought of as 'important'. We chose the example of preparing dinner to emphasize this. The question for personal action, the moral question, is 'What in these circumstances ought I to do?' A community's living law is the set of known and accepted answers to the more abstract set of questions: what ought to be done in this specific type of circumstance? That set of answers forms a large part of the background or context in which the specific moral question arises and is answered.

When a person judges that he ought to do something, he judges that it would be good to do it and that what will be realized through the action is a value to be realized. Clearly, when Peter judges that he ought now to prepare dinner, or that he ought now to return the banknote, he judges that these are values in accord with which he ought to choose. If he actually chooses in accord with them they become actual values for him. When in similar situations – for sometimes situations are relevantly similar – he normally chooses in accord with them, they become his habitual values that may be expressed in more general terms, eg 'A thing that belongs to another is to be returned to its owner if possible', or the like. Had he judged otherwise, eg 'Finders keepers', his values would have been different. Initially, then, values are relative to the judgments and choices of the person judging and choosing.

Values may be disputed. Peter judges that he ought to prepare dinner or return the banknote. Paul thinks that Peter ought to forget about dinner, and would be foolish to return the money. Paul's values are not merely different from Peter's; he thinks that Peter's values are mistaken or wrong. He accepts that for Peter to prepare the dinner or to return the money are values but he takes them for mistaken or wrong values. Conversely, Peter, unless persuaded to change his mind, finds Paul's values mistaken or wrong. Obviously, the question arises as to which of them is right. But before that question can properly arise a more basic issue must be settled: *Can* Peter's values be right or wrong? Paul thinks that Peter is mistaken. Is to be mistaken possible?

The example of the banknote may be slightly adjusted. Peter and Paul together see the owner dropping the banknote. Peter thinks they ought to return the money; Paul thinks they have no obligation to do so but should consult only their own immediate interest in augmenting their resources. Which value is to prevail? If values are simply relative, the only solution is that one person will overcome the other and force the realization of his value. Furthermore, even if values are not simply relative, yet neither can convince the other, once again the only solution is for the more powerful to prevail. There is, however, a crucial difference between the two situations. In the first, by definition, the opposing values are essentially relative to those holding them, neither is better than the other, mistake is impossible, and so force of one kind or another is the only possible solution to disagreement. In the second, by definition, one value is in principle better than the other and so discussion and enquiry, however difficult, however unlikely to succeed, however in the immediate case vain, is not intrinsically pointless.

Our aim in this section is to show that in the moral domain discussion and enquiry are not intrinsically pointless because values are not intrinsically relative. It is important to distinguish between enquiries into what is the case, which conclude with judgments of fact, and enquiries into what ought to be the case, which conclude with judgments of value. Because whether or not to enquire in a particular case is a moral issue – one chooses whether or not to pursue a question – both enquiries – although they differ in other ways – are within the moral domain.[2]

Factual enquiry looks to the discovery of *what is the case*, and judgments of fact state or purport to state the way the world is. To choose to enquire is within the moral domain but the judgment of fact is not itself a moral judgment. Were someone to come across the question as to how to construct, in Euclidean space and without a calibrated measure, a square twice the area of a given square, he might judge that it was not worth his while giving time to the puzzle, and decide not to pursue the matter. That judgment and that decision are within the moral domain but the geometrical question itself is purely factual and intends a purely factual answer. Someone who pursues the matter and concludes that if the length of the sides of the square WXYZ is equal to the diagonal of the given square ABCD, then the area of WXYZ is twice the area of ABCD, propounds his judgment as true. Similarly, one who judges that England is an island propounds his judgment as true. Neither thinks that his judgment is true simply because he judges it to be. Each states what he thinks is the case independently of his judgment. That the geometrical conclusion is true and does state the way the Euclidean world is, while the geographical conclusion is untrue and fails to state the way the geographical world is, does not alter their intentions. Both recognize the possibility of error because both consider that the truth of their respective judgments is not guaranteed by the fact that the judgments have been made. In undertaking their enquiries each intends the answer that, although they can reach it only in their judgment, is true independently of their judgment.[3]

Moral enquiry looks to the discovery of *what ought to be the case*. As with factual enquiry, the judgment that one ought to enquire and the decision to enquire are within the moral domain, but the moral enquiry differs from the factual in what it enquires about. The matter is further complicated by there being two kinds of moral question: first, the question as to what in this concrete existential

---

[2] No one can live without asking some questions and making some decisions but it is, of course, perfectly possible on occasion to fail to pursue a question. But once a question has occurred to a person, he must choose whether or not to pursue it. For that reason, actually to pursue or not to pursue a particular question is a choice; and, being a choice, is within the moral domain.

[3] It is, of course, possible to *redefine* the term 'truth' to mean 'what is asserted in a judgment', in which case what is asserted and what is true are by definition identical. When the term is redefined and used in this way, it cannot be used to say anything interesting about truth defined and used otherwise.

situation the moral actor ought now to do and, secondly, the question as to what in a *type* of situation ought to be done or not done.

In the foregoing example of the dropped banknote both Peter and Paul were faced existentially with the question as to what to do. Their several enquiries led to mutually incompatible judgments: Peter to the judgment that they ought to return the banknote to its owner; Paul to the judgment that they ought to keep it for themselves. A decision consonant with one judgment is incompatible with a decision consonant with the other. Each judgment assigns a value to the action, and each decision realizes that value. If the mutually incompatible judgments are merely 'true for the one judging', then neither is true or false in the way that these words are used of factual judgments. It is, of course, evident that if a person judges that England is an island, he holds that judgment to be true and so must hold that indeed England is an island; in that sense, and in that sense only, the judgment is 'true for him', since it is not possible simultaneously to judge that X is the case and to hold that X is not the case. The possibility of error is based on the possibility of holding that X is the case when it is not, or vice versa. The claim that moral judgments are not intrinsically relative is, in the example of the banknote, the claim that one of the protagonists is right, and the other wrong. And, as with factual judgments, the person whose judgment is mistaken thinks that his judgment is true; if he did not, he would judge otherwise.

The question as to what ought to be done or not done in a *type* of situation differs from the moral question of the existential kind in that it concludes with a judgment of the form: X is to be done or not done in a Y-type situation; for example, 'In case a person loses what belongs to him, that thing is, if possible, to be returned to him by the finder'. Evidently, that judgment does not directly evoke a decision. It does, however, express the background or context within which Peter was acting when faced with the question as to what he ought to do in the situation in which he found himself. That Peter acted within that background or context does not mean that he was following an explicit rule. In contrast, Paul, who judged that there was no demand upon him to return the banknote, was acting within a context that may be expressed thus: 'In case a person drops what belongs to him, the finder may consult exclusively his own interest, and decide to do what at the time in his estimation and judgment suits him best.'

To keep the banknote would augment the resources of both protagonists and we may assume that, abstractly considered, to augment resources is a value for them. A possible, but not the only possible, reason why Peter chooses not to do so in this case is that he takes account of the owner's interest and judges that he is entitled to have the note returned to him. It would seem that the reason why Paul chooses not to return the note is that he prefers to augment his resources, and thinks the owner's interest is at best subordinate, at worst totally irrelevant.

Paul, however, is faced with the further question as to whether or not the person who dropped the note is *entitled* to have it returned to him. If he thinks that the owner is entitled to have the note returned, then his decision not to return it is, whether or not he realizes it, incoherent. If he thinks that the owner is in no sense entitled to have the note returned, his decision is coherent but he is, whether or not he knows it, committed to the position that 'ownership' is no more than another name for 'present possession'; in which case the difference between the protagonists may not be simply that one thinks he ought to do what the other thinks he has no reason to do but maybe that they differ profoundly in their understanding of human society. The one holds that society is a network of entitlements; the other maybe that it is merely conflict of immediate interest and that entitlements are no more than ruses and stratagems by the numerous weak to overcome the few strong.

From a very everyday example we have moved to a possible contrast between two judgments: in the one, human society is a network of entitlements between people of different interests where the interest of others is to be considered in the pursuit of one's own; in the other, human society is the conflict of individual interests where power and opportunity alone are to prevail. The idea that entitlements are ruses of the numerous weak to overcome the few strong is Callicles' position in Plato's *Gorgias*:

CALLICLES: How could anyone be happy when a slave to anybody at all? No, but the naturally noble and just is what I now describe to you with all frankness – namely that anyone who is to live aright should suffer his appetites to grow to the greatest extent and not check them, and through courage and intelligence should be competent to minister to them at their greatest and to satisfy every appetite what it craves. But this, I imagine is impossible for the many; hence they blame such men through a sense of shame to conceal their own impotence, and, as I have remarked before, they claim that intemperance is shameful and they make slaves of those who are naturally better. And because they themselves are unable to procure satisfaction for their pleasures, they are led by cowardice to praise temperance and justice. For to those whose lot it has been from the beginning to be the sons of kings or whose natural gifts enable them to acquire some office or tyranny or supreme power, what in truth could be worse and more shameful than temperance and justice? But the truth, Socrates... is this. Luxury and intemperance and license, when they have sufficient backing, are virtue and happiness, and all the rest is tinsel, the unnatural catchwords of mankind, mere nonsense and of no account.[4]

What Callicles recommends – what in Hobbes is the model of the natural condition, or the war of all against all, over against which stands the order of peace – is an arrangement in which '...nothing can be Unjust. The notions of Right and Wrong, Justice and Injustice have there no place'.[5] Callicles' praise of selfishness has attracted, continues to attract, and, no doubt, will in future attract the powerful tyrant. Against that value stands the value of a self-interest that takes account of others' interests, that is consonant both with a spontaneous

---

    [4] Plato, *Gorgias*, 491e–492c. E Hamilton and H Cairns (eds), *The Collected Dialogues of Plato* (trans WD Woodhead) (Princeton, NJ: Princeton University Press, 1961), 274.
    [5] T Hobbes, *Leviathan*, 188 [63]. What Callicles wants is effectively the natural condition that Hobbes repudiates.

intersubjective sympathy – arising from the social nature of humans – and with an understanding of society as an order which for want of the justice that Callicles derides will be destroyed. The choice is then between two antagonistic and incompatible originating values, between a value that tends to destroy, and if universally or too largely chosen would actually destroy, society, and a value that would sustain it.

It is evident that for the person who judges that to choose the destructive value in the hope that he would gain more from doing so than from choosing the other, that judgment is true for him, and that value is good for him in the sense that we have admitted. And similarly for the person who comes to the opposite conclusion. But what is likewise evident is that neither can find the other's value equally good: '... for whatsoever is the object of any mans Appetite or Desire, that is it, which he for his part calleth *Good*'.[6] Callicles is rationally constrained to hold that his value is, as he says, true, and the other 'tinsel ... mere nonsense and of no account'. And similarly for the person who concludes that to sustain society is the genuine good. Neither can convince the other as long as each judges within the context in which his conclusion seems true.[7] If each is ineradicably confined within his present context, he must come to the realization not that there is no true value, but that it cannot be known. Conversely, one who holds that which of the two values is true can be known must hold that no one is ineradicably confined within his present context. But in fact neither is content to hold that his position is true only within a context; each wants his own to be that from which what is genuinely the case can be reached, for the act of enquiring itself – asking which of the two incompatible values is truly good, the one that tends to destroy society or the one that tends to sustain it – moves the questioner in principle beyond his present confinement. Agreement is in principle possible not because the disputants already share the same context but because in principle *discussion and enquiry* moves them beyond their present context, that is, their present selves.

A value judgment is not extra-contextually true, and so for a proposed value to be genuinely true depends on there being a true context. In the example of the banknote, within Peter's context the genuine value is to restore the banknote to its owner; within Paul's context the genuine value is to augment one's own resources unless there is some reason to believe that to do so would bring a consequence that one would prefer to avoid.

---

[6] Ibid, 120 [24].

[7] The same true proposition may be expressed differently in different contexts or frameworks, as in these sentences, one in English, the other in Icelandic: 'The mountain is snow covered' and 'Fjallið er þakið snjó'. One who knows only one of those languages cannot know that these sentences mean the same thing. There are also contexts within which propositions true in one are untrue in the other; for example, for someone facing north, east is to the right, whereas for one facing south it is to the left, and the sentences 'East is to my right' and 'East is to my left' do not express the same proposition, yet, contextually, each is true. Again, someone unable to make the necessary transformation cannot understand how apparently contradictory propositions can both be true.

A brief examination of promise shows the same crucial difference between a moral agent who takes account of another's interest and one whose sole and over-riding interest is his own convenience. Intrinsic to promise is that it be fulfilled: if Mary promises Anne that she will do something, then she has obliged herself to do it, and Mary's promise entitles Anne to have it done by Mary. That is simply the meaning of promise. When the time comes to fulfil her promise, Mary, find-ing it inconvenient to do so, reneges. As in the foregoing example, Mary allows her present interest to override Anne's entitlement. If Mary's settled habit – in computer jargon her 'default position' – is to fulfil her promises only if it suits her to do so, her context is one in which her own interest is paramount and the inter-est of others is irrelevant.

Were no one to keep promises, no one to return what had been lost, no one to respect ownership – that is, were no one to render what was due unless it was more convenient to do so – the social order would be utterly destroyed. But, of course, the person who decides not to return the banknote or not to keep his word assumes that most others most of the time and on most occasions will do so, and, although he can be shown that his actions undermine the social order, he knows that they are unlikely to destroy it. Hence, he does not want to destroy the order but chooses parasitically to rely on others acting to sustain it. Why should he not do so? There is no axiom or unavoidable rule from which not to do so derives. He is, however, unavoidably faced with the choice between taking his selfish interest as the criterion of action and taking others' interests into account. To persuade Mary that she ought to fulfil her promise it is not enough to remind her of what she already knows – that promises are to be kept. Nor is it enough to persuade Paul that the owner of the banknote is entitled to have it returned; nor enough to show them that their actions undermine the social order; nor to show them that were their attitude to become too prevalent the social order would collapse. Neither can be swayed by these arguments unless they have chosen to be in the context within which they convince, that is, the context in which all can carry on their lives in harmony with one another.

While we very explicitly acknowledge that this context is not an inevitable choice – which, indeed, we must acknowledge as in fact it is not universally cho-sen, and none of us acts within it on all occasions – we nonetheless suggest that it is the more reasonable choice. We suggest, further, that justice, and the entire body of living law and state law that supports it, usually and in principle rests upon the implicit or more or less explicit acknowledgement and acceptance of that choice.[8]

---

[8] Since, as we hold, there are not only particular unjust laws and legislation but also systems unjust at their core, we do not hold that the living or legislated law of any particular jurisdiction at any particular time necessarily rests on mutual respect. What we do hold is that total lack of mutual respect brings about the condition that Hobbes called 'natural' and is a socio-political world in which humans cannot live in mutual harmony.

The example of lying equally reveals the division between, on the one hand, the person who cares exclusively for his own interest and is prepared whenever convenient to override another's interest and, on the other hand, the person who is prepared to take account of another's interest. To lie is to tell to another what one thinks to be untrue. There are occasions when to lie is good, as when the person to whom the lie is told is not entitled to know the truth – for example, when his knowing the truth would lead to his harming one who is entitled not to harmed. To lie wrongly and unjustly is to tell to another, who is entitled to know, and wants to know, the truth, what one knows to be untrue. Why would one decide to lie? The liar wants his interlocutor to believe that the world is otherwise than in fact it is. He knows that his interlocutor is entitled and wants to know the truth. The liar, therefore, harms the person to whom he lies, and does so because he takes his own interest, which is that his interlocutor should believe what is not the case, to override his interlocutor's interest. Evidently, the liar thinks that to lie is in his interest. To lie is for him a value. The context in which it is a value is one in which his own interest is the exclusive criterion, and the liar can be persuaded that to lie is a disvalue only if he can be converted from that context. As long as he remains within that context, he cannot be persuaded because there is no possible argument within that context that would convince him to shift from it to a context in which it is to take another's interest into account is a value, for that another's interest is not to be taken into account is the foundational value of the context in which he is. But again, if that were the prevalent context, it would lead to the breakdown and collapse of the communicative – and thus the social – order. It is for this reason that we consider it – as the living law of any community must do if the community is to survive – a bad or wrong context.

Forms of relativism have emerged as strong themes in postmodernist jurisprudence.[9] Relativism states that a proposition is true for whomsoever holds it to be true, and false for whomsoever holds it to be false. As has been pointed out by many scholars through the ages, this requires the relativist to hold that the proposition expressing the relativist position is true for whomsoever holds it to be true (that is, for the relativist) and false for whomsoever holds it to be false.[10] For the relativist, propositions are in themselves neither true nor false; a proposition is not true because it states what is the case but because it is held to be true. Truth and falsity describe the attitude of the person to the proposition that he asserts or

---

[9] See, for example, M Davies, *Asking the Law Question* (Sydney: Sweet & Maxwell, 1994); cf E Melissaris, 'The Other Jurisprudence: Poststructuralism, Postmodernism and the Law' in T Murphy (ed), *Western Jurisprudence* (Dublin: Thomson Round Hall, 2004), 413.

[10] The basic claim of relativism, as put by Harvey Siegel, is that 'truth and rational justifiability of knowledge-claims are relative to the standards used in evaluating such claims'; in Siegel's account, relativism is demonstrably incoherent, 'because, if it is right, the very notion of rightness is undermined, in which case relativism itself cannot be right'. He argues, however, that the difficulties in formulating a defensible conception of non-relativism have left a vacuum in which there has recently been a resurgence of relativist thought, 'Relativism' in J Dancy and E Sosa (eds), *A Companion to Epistemology* (Oxford: Blackwell, 1992), 429–30.

denies. The terms 'truth' and 'falsity' are thus redefined, and error is impossible. It is in this sense that, as we observed in the Preface, at the heart of relativism is the quest for infallibility. The logic is that if we cannot be sure of reaching the true and the good, we can define the true and the good, right and wrong, as simply what has been decided or held to be the case. But no one consistently holds, or can hold, this position.

Our definition of the term 'truth' differs from that of the relativist. We hold that a proposition is true if and only if (1) it states what is the case; (2) that something is the case; and (3) that what is the case can be discovered. Error is unavoidable but when someone asserts a proposition, at the time of asserting it, unless he is lying and only pretending to assert it, he holds it to be true; for to assert a proposition is to hold it to be true. In that sense, and only in that sense, is a proposition 'true for the person who asserts it'.

There are propositions for which the evidence is overwhelming as it is, for instance, for the proposition that a judge ought not to be biased in favour of one litigant over the other. But even here, the claim that the evidence is overwhelming cannot avoid the fact that it is overwhelming *for someone*. If, in the moral context of a particular judge, the value that his own immediate advantage is always paramount, not alone will he be biased when that is to his advantage, but he will eventually fail to see clearly that to be biased is wrong. The evidence for the proposition is overwhelming within one context but not in another. To persuade the judge who held that it was right for him on occasion to be biased, one would have to persuade him that his advantage was not paramount; one would have to persuade him to move from one context to the other. We acknowledge both that what will seem right in one context will seem wrong in the other, and that to persuade someone to shift from one intellectual and moral context to another, although possible, is not easy.[11] We acknowledge, too, that at any juncture in a society there is likely to be disagreement both within and between contexts.

7.3 Communal Moral Law

We discussed the living law – the communal moral tradition – in Chapter 3.4, when we examined its relationship to the Roman definition of justice. The living law is a communal *moral* law. Morality is about human choice; choices are made in situations; and an explicit moral tradition, the living or communal law, is the set of rules indicating the kind of choices that are, in that tradition, thought good. A living communal law, in other words, indicates the generally approved ways of acting in recurrent types of situations, some of which will be of greater

---

[11] Cf G Barden, *After Principles* (Notre Dame, Ind: University of Notre Dame, 1990), chs 7, 8, 9, 122–31 and *passim*.

and some of lesser importance. Because humans live, and cannot but live, in societies (however different those societies may be), moral traditions will emerge and, generally, members of a community have as children learnt and as adults know the living communal law. Moral traditions will *change* when sufficiently many of those living within them change their minds about how it is good to act. Since it is unlikely that minds will always change in unison, moral traditions at any one time will usually be controversial. We remarked also that the living law can be either general or specific. Living law is general when it applies to all or most members of society; it is specific when it applies to a sub-group (such as the sailing community, which we used as an example).

The communal or living law – like language – is a context within which people communicate with one another more or less well, more or less ambiguously, more or less controversially. It expresses the communal values upon which in practice depends the survival of the order within which people can live together and pursue their several goals in peace. In principle, therefore, it commends actions that realize those values and forbids those that tend to undermine them. The source of many of the particular provisions of the communal law is the evolving practices of those who live together; the practices that become, for a variety of sometimes antagonistic reasons, sufficiently acceptable to survive; and not alone communally acceptable but communally required. Disputes of course occur and so an adjudicative process is established to solve them. As we saw in our discussion of adjudication in Chapter 6, rather than have recourse to violence, disputants who fail to resolve their differences through discussion bring their conflict before an arbitrator or judge, to whose sentence they are required to submit. In other words, in the communal law there commonly emerges a new rule: some disputes are to be settled by an independent and impartial judge.

We argued that the living law or communal moral law tends, generally speaking, to cultivate a moral context within which others' interests are to be considered and this moral context is itself an expression of what is just. When others' interests are considered, and therefore not merely one's own, the tendency is to give to others what is their due. The desire to live peaceably brings with it the requirement of neighbourliness: each person realizes, albeit to a greater or lesser degree, that in order for his interests to be considered by others, in order for him to get what is his due in the community, he must reciprocate and respect and consider others' interests. We argue in favour of the judgment, which we take to be prevalent, that we should take account of others. We think of it as a reasonable conclusion to the question as to how we should live, and suggest that the unreasonableness of the opposite conclusion – that we should take no account of others – is discovered naturally by humans living together. The principle that one should act taking others into account becomes, more or less explicitly, communally accepted as part of the living law.

This general principle is, however, limited in its operation. Moral traditions are necessary if humans are to live together in harmony but it is too easy to take for granted that such traditions – these communal living laws – are in all respects good and just. They are not. The inevitable moral tension between taking only one's own and taking others' interest into account cannot but exist in human societies. No moral tradition will be in all respects good; it will inevitably be corrupted by individual and group bias. Some powerful individuals or groups of individuals will, given time and opportunity, favour traditions that support and enhance their power over others. In every community, as we have said, some persons and some groups are more influential than others, and will inevitably sometimes impose their power to serve their own ends irrespective of the interests of those on whom they impose it.

7.4 Legislation

Legislation introduces sovereign and subject, legislative authority and power, and so there emerges within the social order a new element: the state or state-function. The state legislates and legislation has three components: command, control, and organization. Legislation is a command that is intended to oblige those to whom it applies; it seeks to direct and thus exert control over their activities. In other words, the state acquires entitlements or rights *vis-à-vis* those it commands. Finally, legislation intends to bring about a situation and so organizes the activities of those to whom it applies with a view to bringing the intended situation about. States differ greatly in the scope and limits of these components. In a very small primitive society legislation may be limited to war. The war-leader commands only in that sphere; he controls the time and activities of his temporary subjects only for the duration of the war; and he organizes them during the war so that the goal of defeating the enemy may be achieved. In such a society, the actual presence of the state is, so to speak, intermittent and its scope extremely restricted. It is, however, potentially present and there seems to be no evidence of its total absence from any social order.[12]

When a legislator enacts a law that requires his subjects, those 'formerly obliged to obey him',[13] to do or refrain from doing something, he obviously wants that thing done or avoided. Whatsoever the content of the command may be, the legislator has some reason why he wants the thing done or avoided. The person or persons to whom the law applies – to whom, in Hobbes's words, the command is addressed – need neither know the reason nor approve the command. From his subjects who obey the command simply because it is a command and obliges them, all that is required is that they know that it is a command of the

---

[12] P Clastres, *La societé contre l'État* (Paris: Minuit, 1974), esp ch 11. Anthropologists who write of 'stateless' societies contrast them with societies in which the state is a constant and actual, rather than an intermittent and potential, presence, and in which the scope of its power is relatively much greater.   [13] Hobbes, *Leviathan*, 312 [137].

legislator, understand what it requires of them, and obey.[14] From the perspective of the legislator, however, his command is an answer to his question as to what he wants done or avoided. The legislator deliberates and chooses; the legislative act is, therefore, within the moral domain.

The enacted law or edict embodies the legislator's purpose, which is to bring about his intended goal. When legislation is considered purely structurally, there is no intrinsic limit, beyond impossibility, to its scope. Although the actual scope of legislation in a particular jurisdiction will be limited both by the limits of the legislator's desire and by the limits that subjects successfully impose, recent legislative practice – think of the enormous increase in the amount or degree of legislation and the related enlargement of the domain covered by legislation[15] – shows the scope of legislation to be large and difficult to contain.

To legislate is *necessarily* to act within the moral domain. Every piece of legislation changes, and is intended to change, the institutional context to which it applies. The changed situation is an intended result and so the question as to whether or not it is good to bring about the result cannot be avoided. In some modern legislatures it is sometimes said that a particular piece of legislation involves 'moral issues' which is understood to imply that there are other pieces of legislation that do not involve them. This distinction is incoherent and spurious: every piece of legislation involves a moral issue since the question arises as to whether or not it is good to enact every suggested piece of legislation; and every enacted statute is the result of deliberation and choice.[16] Thus, there remains in legislation an intrinsic openness to criticism. What the legislator commands is by definition what seems to him, for whatever reason, to be good. His command expresses his judgment as to what is valuable, what is right. If these words 'good', 'valuable', and 'right' are misleading synonyms for 'what the legislator commands', there can be no further argument. His subjects may think differently, may have different and opposed values, different and opposed ideas of right, but these, too, are no more than misleading words. Reasonable argument is excluded; right is defined by legislation expressing the legislator's will, and is simply power over others.

---

[14] That subjects must know that what is grammatically a command is legitimately a command addressed to them is Hart's rule of recognition. That a legitimate command, that is, a properly legislated command, obliges those to whom it is legitimately addressed is the nature of a command. That a legitimate but unjust command obliges *in foro externo* but does not obligate – ie does not oblige *in foro interno* – is argued below and in chs 10 and 11.

[15] One UK public lawyer, John Alder, remarks that during the twentieth century, 'it became widely accepted that the state could regulate any aspect of our lives and that whether it should do so was a matter...for the everyday political context', *Constitutional and Administrative Law* (Basingstoke: Palgrave Macmillan, 6th edn, 2007), 77. There may be slight exaggeration in this observation on the range or domain of legislation, and there may be marked differences between states in this regard, but Adler's view of the nature of increasing legislative activity is not too wide of the mark generally speaking. This question is examined further in ch 11 below.

[16] For discussion of this point in the context of drug law reform, see T Murphy, *Rethinking the War on Drugs in Ireland* (Cork: Cork University Press, 1996), ch 4.

7.5 Morality, Communal Moral Law, and Legislation

We now consider in what sense the three potentially obliging forms that we have examined in this chapter give rise to *obligation*. We address that issue in the context of first, morality, secondly, the living or communal moral law, and thirdly, legislation, and we examine also other aspects of their interrelation, including the question of the proper range or scope of legislation.

Morality is the personally unavoidable process of asking oneself what one ought to do in these, or these types of, circumstances; of coming up with a suggested course of action; of reaching a judgment as to whether or not the suggestion is reasonable; and of acting or failing responsibly to act in accord with the judgment. Having raised the question as to what one ought to do, one has embarked on a process of obligation for one already knows that the judgment will oblige. The constant, underlying, and unavoidable demand is to do what one thinks reasonable. One cannot come to a judgment that one ought to do X and not be obliged by the judgment unless on further consideration one judges that one's judgment was mistaken and so comes to a new judgment that one ought not do X or that there is no compelling reason to do X or to do X rather than Y.

If one judges that to do X is a good; then to do X is a value. But whether or not to realize the value has yet to be decided, for the judgment 'It would be good that I should now do X' does not determine the decision to do X. The person's judgment that he ought to do X does not determine the decision; rather it places a demand on him to decide in accord with the judgment. He experiences the judgment as a demand or obligation that he may or may not meet: the core of moral obligation is that *one obliges oneself.*

… normally we have sufficient knowledge and capacity for choice to be able in some fashion to direct our lives. The recognition that we are always influenced by our make up and our environment has not persuaded people to abandon the language of praise or blame, or to cease to try to change our ways or encourage others to change theirs. Which is to say that people generally hold on to the idea of moral *responsibility*, the idea that we are able to make something of ourselves and of our world, and that we are answerable for what we make of ourselves and how.[17]

In relation to morality, we have argued that there are good and bad values and that the adjectives 'good' and 'bad' are not merely relative to those who think them so. None can live without values but it remains the task of each to discover and decide the values by which he chooses to live. That effort of discovery takes place within society with its living laws, customs, and legislation that are handed down and recommended to him as he grows up. Thus, as we have said, he first

---

[17] P Hannon, 'Law and Morality' in T Murphy (ed), *Western Jurisprudence* (Dublin: Thomson Round Hall, 2004), 269, 272 (emphasis in original).

learns his morals as he learns his language. The socially accepted norms define what is generally thought good; they define, so to speak, the social will; but, like the legislator's will, the social will does not define the good any more than the generally accepted 'truths' define what is true. Hence the question arises: How does the living or communal moral law oblige? This law expresses what, in the community, has been thought to be the reasonable course of action in particular types of circumstances. The communal moral law cannot cover the whole moral life because the whole moral life of a particular person is the entire set of choices that confront that person throughout a lifetime. Instead, the communal moral law tells how members of the community are expected to act in reasonably important and recurrent circumstances. To the extent that members of the community share a common outlook the actions that are expected and required by express communally held values. The laws are present in the community as expectations and requirements; failure to act in accord with them attracts punishment of some type. They are present not as recommendations but as obligations.

Consider a community in which there is a communal law forbidding theft and where this law is held to apply to everyone. In what way precisely does this law 'oblige'? Confusion and disagreement reign when no clear distinction is made between two quite distinct ways in which a law obliges. First, a law forbidding theft would not be a law if it did not oblige those to whom it applied. A law obliges those to whom it applies simply because it is a law. It is the character of law to oblige. This type of obligation, however, is 'extrinsic' – in the traditional formula *in foro externo* – and imposes on those who fail to act in accord with the law liability to sanction of some kind. The law, discussed in Chapter 3.4, requiring sailors to go to the rescue of others in peril is present in the community of sailors in such a way that a sailor who failed to act in accord with it would be thought badly of by other sailors. The punishment for breaking the law is distain, ostracism, and the like. The punishment for theft may be, for example, imprisonment. In both cases, there is a communal law, an associated punishment, and a lack of interest in the offender's assessment of the reasonableness of the law. What is important is not what the lawbreaker thinks of the law but what others think of it. Both examples are of laws with which probably most readers agree. But, for this type of obligation, neither the agreement of readers nor the true value of law is of any significance. In other words, for this type of obligation the content of the law does not matter; what a particular person thinks of the law does not matter; all that matters is that it is a law. It obliges *heteronomously*.

There is a second and quite distinct way in which the communal law obliges. A law forbidding theft obliges one who is convinced that theft is wrong but, in this second sense, not simply because it is the law. The sailor who agrees with the communal value expressed in the rule that sailors should attempt to rescue others in peril is obliged to do so not only because it is a rule but because he shares the value that the rule expresses. In each case the law or rule obliges him because in as much as he agrees with the law and accepts the value expressed in it he has already obliged himself. His obligation in this second sense is 'intrinsic' – in the traditional formula *in foro interno*. He is obliged *autonomously*.[18]

The difference between these two senses of obligation appears most clearly in the answers that a person might give to the question as to why he obeyed – that is, acted in accord with – a particular law. One answer is that he obeys the law only because not to obey might lead to inconveniences that he prefers to avoid. For example, a merchant might decide to trade honestly uniquely because the possible consequences of trading dishonestly – litigation, criminal proceedings, loss of reputation with consequent loss of business, etc – seem to him to outweigh the potential benefits. The second answer is that he obeys the law because the law expresses and requires what he requires of himself. So, a merchant might decide to trade honestly because he judges that in exchange he and at least one other are involved, that intrinsic to exchange is a set of mutual entitlements, and that the other's entitlements are to be honoured. For him the law enjoining honest trading requires that each partner transcend his own selfish interest in simply getting, by whatever means, what he wants and what the other has, and expresses what he accepts as the value intrinsic to exchange.[19]

Because there are two distinct senses of obligation, the question: 'Does the law oblige?' is ambiguous; there are, in effect, two distinct questions. We have suggested that to the question 'Does the law oblige in the first sense of oblige?' the answer is that it does because it is the nature or character of law to oblige. To the question as to whether or not it obliges in the second sense, the answer is that it obliges the person who agrees with what is required and obliges himself. We call these two distinct kinds of obligation 'extrinsic' and 'intrinsic'.[20]

In the light of the distinction, the answer to the question as to whether or not an *unjust law* obliges becomes clear. Since a law's extrinsic obligatory character is based not on its content but on its being a law, an unjust law obliges extrinsically. It does not in principle oblige intrinsically because, by definition, it is unjust. However, it is perfectly possible that a person to whom an unjust law applies and extrinsically obliges should agree with the law and so be intrinsically obliged, as a person who is convinced of the truth of what is in fact a mistaken factual proposition must consider the world to be other than it is.

Further and again in the light of the distinction, the answer to the question as to whether or not a *just law* obliges also becomes clear. A person to whom the law applies is extrinsically obliged. In principle, he is intrinsically obliged. But were he to consider the just law to be unjust he would not be intrinsically obliged; as

---

[18] The contrast between heteronomy and autonomy is a dominant motif in Neil MacCormick's *Institutions of Law* (Oxford: Oxford University Press, 2007). We refer to it again in our discussion of the force of law (see ch 10.3 below).

[19] That the form of selfishness for which the other name is 'greed' or 'exploitation' is common cannot be denied and ought not be overlooked in an analysis of an actual market.

[20] Cf HLA Hart, *The Concept of Law* (P Bulloch and J Raz eds) (Oxford: Clarendon Press, 2nd edn with Postscript, 1994), 82–91. When discussing the force of law in chs 10.2 and 10.3 below, we analyse more closely the possible reasons for obeying law.

a person who holds a true proposition to be false cannot, without changing his mind, hold it to be true, and so cannot but hold the world to be other than it is.

Much of what was said of law may be said of legislation. Here, for convenience and clarity, we assume the legitimacy of the legislator and of the laws that he enacts; and we assume legislation to be properly enacted, consonant with all relevant constitutional limitations, and recognized by those to whom they apply.[21] The legislator in enacting a piece of legislation envisages a result that he intends to bring about, and as we have said the legislative act is intrinsically and unavoidably within the moral domain. Within a set of legislative measures there can be unnoticed contradictions, in which cases those to whom the measures apply cannot act in accord with them. They oblige neither extrinsically nor intrinsically. Some actions, although they may be legislatively required without immediately apparent contradiction, nonetheless cannot be effectively required; for instance, no one can be successfully required to believe what he does not believe or to assent to a proposition that he holds to be false, although he can be successfully required to pretend to believe or to assent and to express his pretended belief or assent either in words or actions.

Absent contradiction, a person is *extrinsically* obliged to act in accord with properly enacted legislation. Accordingly, a person can be extrinsically obliged to act *as if* he believed what he does not believe or, more generally, to act in accord with legislation that he considers unjust. A person is *intrinsically* obliged to act in accord with properly enacted legislation only if he considers it to be just or considers that the result of not acting in accord with it would be worse than the result that would follow from acting in accord with it. This distinction justifies civil disobedience in principle *but may not necessarily bring it about in practice.* So, someone required to pay money in taxes to a government that he considered to be deeply corrupt might, and in the circumstances often for good reasons, think it better to pay than to withhold payment. It is, of course, equally possible that he might be intrinsically obliged to withhold payment.

We presume that most readers will accept that Nazi racial legislation was deeply unjust and wrong. The Nuremberg Laws were, quite deliberately, carefully and properly enacted. According to the position worked out here, they extrinsically obliged those to whom they applied. They did not intrinsically oblige those who found them to be deeply unjust and wrong. If they were, as we hold (but do not argue here), in fact deeply unjust and wrong, they in principle intrinsically obliged no one.[22] The question that faced everyone to whom

---

[21] It is crucial to the present discussion to assume legitimacy because if the legislator is not legitimate the status of his legislation is utterly different. An assumption is simply that; it is not a statement of fact. Legitimacy is discussed in ch 11.6 below. We assume also an appropriate degree of enforceability: see ch 10 below.

[22] Those who mistakenly find what is unjust and wrong to be just and right are intrinsically obliged to obey but, being mistaken, they are in the unstable position – although they do not know this – of being intrinsically obliged to obey what they ought not to obey. Their unstable position

they applied, and who considered them to be deeply unjust and wrong, was how to act in the institutional situation that they created. That states enact unjust and wrong laws is not uncommon; the Nuremburg Laws are but one – albeit extreme – example.

The recurrent question asked by the legislator is: what, if anything, ought to be legislated in the present circumstances? Like any moral question, this question is specific and cannot be answered in general. One may, however, ask about the context in which the question is asked. The legislator's question is within the moral domain; he asks what he ought to do, in this case, what he ought to legislate, and, as with every moral question, he may take into account only his own interest or acknowledge the interests of others. Since his enactments change the situation in which others live and impose obligations upon them, the legislator by taking only his own interest into account turns others into his instruments or slaves, and becomes what has traditionally been called a tyrant. To seek to take others' interests into account has traditionally been known as to seek the common good, 'to enlighten the land, to further the well-being of mankind'.[23] To become a tyrant or to take others' interests into account is the fundamental and unavoidable contextual choice between two opposed originating values.

The contextual choice between these opposed values is stark but in human affairs choices are not often utterly clearly made and, indeed, because humans easily deceive themselves, often not clearly seen. Thus the tension between them remains. In a political arrangement in which legislators are periodically elected often by electors who seek their own advantage irrespective of others, the desire to be re-elected will be, more or less dominantly, in tension with, and may well distort, both the desire and the ability to discern the common good and 'to further the well-being of mankind'.[24] The fact that the legislator is faced with the contextual choice between his own restricted selfish good and the common good is the structural tension in the relationship between morality and legislation.[25]

---

resembles that of those who are rationally compelled to hold propositions which they are convinced are true but which are in fact false.

[23] *Code of Hammurabi*, Prologue.

[24] See JM Buchanan and G Tullock, *The Calculus of Consent* (Ann Arbor, Mich: University of Michigan Press, 1965) and the tradition of public choice. This is not to deny that, since election within democracies is a pre-condition of access to the law making power, any person with a desire to exercise that power must be elected, and if his aims for the achievement of the common good involve law-making over more than one term of office, he must also seek re-election. But even if a legislator's desire is wholly and exclusively to promote the common good, in order to do so he must be re-elected and in order to be re-elected he must sufficiently satisfy those who elect him, a group that cannot be presumed to seek only the common good. There is the tension to which we refer – but if a person's only desire is to be re-elected there is no tension.

[25] We noted in ch 2.3 above that the common good is sometimes imagined as an aim or goal common to everyone, and sometimes as the good of the majority, but the common good as we understand it is peaceful and civil society in which humans can, for the most part, live their lives in cooperative harmony.

It is obvious that all legislation must have some content requiring that, in specified circumstances, something specific should be done or not done, or that certain situations should be jurally understood in a specified way. And so there remains the question as to whether or not anything can be said in general about the content and range or scope of legislation: *what ought and ought not to be legislated?* This question properly arises only if there is a distinction between what ought and what ought not to be done and so does not arise in a pure and radical positivist context.[26] In a context in which the question does arise, the obvious answer may seem to be simply that the good is to be required and the bad forbidden. The answer is correct in that an unjust statute, that is, one requiring those to whom it applies to do what ought not be done, to refrain from doing what ought to be done, or to understand a situation in a way in which it ought not be understood, ought not be enacted. That answer is inadequate in that it fails to deal with an aspect of the question: *ought every good act be required and every bad act forbidden?* To understand the question in this way requires a distinction between 'law', as we have defined it, and legislation.

Consider promises. If one person promises another that he will meet him the next day, he intrinsically obliges himself. That is the meaning of promise, and that promises oblige is commonly part of the living law of a community, and those who consistently break their promises lose the trust of those with whom they live and are consequently thought badly of. There could be legislation requiring that all promises whatsoever be kept and that all be justiciable. Most readers would think it bizarre were such legislation to be proposed. Why are some breaches of promise actionable and some not? Why are some vices legislated against and some not? St Thomas suggests that not all vices should be forbidden by legislation primarily because not everyone is perfect and, were all vices forbidden, common practice would so deviate from what was legislated that legislation would be brought into disrepute and would be increasingly ignored. He adds a crucial remark about the proper reach or scope of legislation:

[Legislation] should concentrate on those acts that harm others and which, were they not forbidden, human society could not be sustained; and so human law forbids murder, theft and the like.[27]

Similarly, Thomas Hobbes thinks of legislation as including those fundamental laws 'which being taken away the Common-wealth faileth, and is utterly dissolved; as a building whose foundation is destroyed'.[28]

---

[26] We discuss positivism further when discussing natural law in ch 8.3 below.

[27] *Summa Theologiae*, I–II, q 96, art 3.

[28] T Hobbes, *Leviathan*, 334 [150]. Hobbes's fundamental laws are 'dictates of Reason', human discoveries, theorems or conclusion, before they are 'properly called Lawes' or statutes, which, of course, they become when legislated (216–17 [80]). See G Barden and T Murphy, 'Law's Function in *De Cive* and *Leviathan*: A Re-appraisal of the Jurisprudence of Thomas Hobbes' (2007) 29 *Dublin University Law Journal* 231.

John Stuart Mill, as is well known, considered some vices, judged to be private, to be beyond the proper reach of legislation.[29] He is sometimes mistakenly thought to understand 'private' as not damaging or harmful to another. So understood, his distinction would require every breach of promise to be justiciable since every breach of promise damages another.[30] The private sphere may be understood heuristically to be simply the sphere beyond the proper reach of legislation, for supporting Mill's criterion is the conviction that the citizen is not simply the servant of the state, and that, consequently, there is a sphere beyond the proper reach of legislation. Adam Smith in his *Lectures on Jurisprudence* writes that 'The first contracts that sustained action would be those where the damage done was very great and where there could be no doubt but the person intended to perform.'[31]

None thinks it good to act wrongly; but each thinks it good that in human society some wrong actions be beyond the reach of state legislation. None thinks it bad to act well, but each thinks it good that not every good action be compelled. Their criteria, while not opposed, are different but no suggested criterion automatically yields the correct answer to the question: should X be legislated? Very much more significant than their criteria is their common fundamental position that the fact that an act is acknowledged to be wrong is insufficient reason to forbid it in legislation, and the fact that an act is good is insufficient reason to coerce performance.

No criterion takes away the personal responsibility of the legislator; but the legislator cannot but act within a containing context, and what should or should not be legislated, what the proper reach of legislation should be, cannot be discovered apart from a containing context. If the legislator's purpose is to maintain himself in power and to enrich himself, the containing context will be one in which the reach of legislation will extend to whatever is thought to serve that end. This is the dominant context of many contemporary dictatorships. If the purpose is to impose intellectual and moral conformity, the containing context will be one in which what is to be legislated is whatever is thought to serve that end.

[29] On this question, see W von Humboldt, *The Limits of State Action* [written in 1792 and first published (posthumously) in 1851] (JW Burrows ed) (Cambridge: Cambridge University Press, 1969). In English this book is also called *The Sphere and Duties of Government* and is referred to under that name in the epigraph to Mill's *On Liberty*. See also Isaiah Berlin's essay 'Two Concepts of Liberty' (1958) collected in *Four Essays on Liberty* (Oxford: Oxford University Press, 1969), 118–72; P Braud and F Burdeau, *Histoire des idées politiques depuis la Révolution* (Paris: Montchrestien, 2nd edn, 1992), 74–9 and ch 3; J Freund, *L'Essence du politique* (Paris: Sirey, 1965), esp ch 5; and N MacCormick, *Practical Reason in Law and Morality* (Oxford, Oxford University Press, 2009), esp ch 6.

[30] 'The acts of an individual may be hurtful to others, or wanting in due consideration for their welfare, without going to the length of violating any of their constituted rights. The offender may then be justly punished by opinion, though not by law', JS Mill, *On Liberty* (London: Longmans, Green and Co, 1884), 44.

[31] A Smith, *Lectures on Jurisprudence*, Report dated 1766 (ed RL Meek, DD Raphael, and PG Stein), 472 (Glasgow edn).

This is the dominant context of many ideological tyrannies and theocratic states. If the purpose is to organize the social order so as to achieve greater equality of wealth, the containing context will be one in which what is properly to be legislated is whatever is thought to produce that result. This is, more or less clearly, at least in theory, the dominant context of the centralized organization of communist states. If the legislator's purpose is to maintain an order in which many can pursue their different goals in harmony with one another, the containing context will be one in which what is properly to be legislated is whatever is thought to serve that end. This is, again at least in theory, the dominant context of liberal-democratic states and of those who consider that the social and economic order cannot be organized. These different containing contexts are but models that actual states, more or less closely, tend to exemplify.

In societies in which there is considerable difference of opinion as to what is right, and so no fixed or agreed communal law, the question as to what ought or ought not be legislated becomes more complicated. In the United Kingdom, when the question arose as to whether or not legislation forbidding male homosexual practice should be repealed, the social context was taken to be homogeneous. In a television interview following the publication in 1957 of the *Report on Homosexuality and Prostitution*, Lord Wolfenden, the Chairman of the Committee, said that he and other members of the committee considered homosexual practice to be wrong but to be a private matter beyond the proper reach of legislation. In fact, although the public–private distinction was alluded to, and was important in discussion, more important in raising the issue in the first place was a considerable shift in communal attitudes. Where once homosexual practice had been very widely condemned – at least in public expression – it no longer was, and it was this change of attitude that occasioned legislative reform.[32] In the twentieth chapter of *Leviticus* homosexual practice is one of several forbidden sexual practices: 'If a man lies with a male as with a woman, both of them have committed an abomination; they shall be put to death; their blood is upon them.'[33] Had that, or Justinian's suggestion in the *Novels* that homosexuality was the cause of earthquakes, been the quasi-universal attitude in the United Kingdom in 1957, it is unlikely that homosexual practice would have been considered 'private'.[34]

---

[32] This transformation of communal values regarding homosexuality is often alluded to in arguments for drug law reform. Paul O'Mahony notes that until 1969 in the UK and 1993 in Ireland it was a crime to engage in male homosexual activity, and observes: 'It is clearly possible for society to shift from a position of unambiguous condemnation and harsh repression of an activity to a diametrically opposed position where it is prepared to actively defend the right to engage in that activity and where it regards the right as a fundamental human right. The current widespread, often contemptuous, dismissal of the concept of a human right to use drugs should, therefore, not be taken as evidence that there is any inevitability to the denial of a right to use drugs', *The Irish War on Drugs: The Seductive Folly of Prohibition* (Manchester: Manchester University Press, 2008), 137.

[33] *Leviticus* 20:13.

[34] *Novels*, 77.1.1, quoted in HLA Hart, *Law, Liberty and Morality* (Oxford: Oxford University Press, 1963), 50.

There are four positions. The first is that the legislator is entitled to legislate whatsoever he wills. The second is that he is required to forbid all wrong actions. The third is that he is required to command all good actions. The fourth, the position adopted here, is that he is entitled to legislate within a limited range that must be settled: in legislation neither ought every wrong action be forbidden nor every good action commanded, which necessarily requires the discovery and acceptance of a limiting criterion. No criterion is given; it must be discovered and agreed in argument which ideally will be unbiased, intelligent, reasonable, and responsible. No agreed criterion – such as Mill's that only what is public is within the proper range of legislation – will be an algorithm that automatically generates unquestionable answers to specific questions, for with respect to any action whether or not it is relevantly public remains to be discovered and agreed in argument. The argument ought to be conducted in the light of the criterion, and the conclusion, in this no different from any argument between humans, will be or fail to be the fruit of unbiased attention, intelligence, reason, and responsibility. The expectation that error, brought about through oversight, bias, selfishness, or folly, will be eliminated is itself the fruit of one or more of these perduring human failings.

The arguments about basic position, about criteria or about how to understand a given type of action in the light of the adopted criteria are within the moral domain. Whether or not there ought to be legislation to regulate banks in some particular way is a question within the moral domain just as much as are the questions as to whether or not there ought to be legislation permitting procured abortion under certain conditions, or as to whether or not the conditions defining citizenship ought to be relaxed or made more stringent, or as to whether or not third level education ought or ought not to be provided and paid for by government. Questions concerning what is to be done in these types of situation are moral questions; all legislation concerns what is to be done in these types of situation; accordingly, all legislative questions are within the moral domain.

8

Natural Law

8.1 Introduction

We come now to the natural law tradition, an ancient and enduring tradition in Western jurisprudence. Thus far in this book we have advanced an account of law that draws a great deal on the idea of *natural justice*. From the Roman definition of justice as the giving to each what is due, we developed the idea of natural justice in our explications of jural community, the living law, the various forms of justice, and adjudication and interpretation. In each of these contexts, we argued, to discover what is naturally just requires an examination of the intrinsic nature of a given situation or circumstance. We offered the example, given the nature of ownership, of a person finding a wallet and the naturally just situation being restored when it is returned to whoever owns it. Similarly, that a borrowed book is to be returned is naturally just, that is, it is intrinsic to the practice of lending and borrowing. Again, since it is in the nature of a promise that it produces an obligation, it is naturally just that a promise produces an obligation. But our discussion up until this point has not included any detailed reference to *natural law*, which is a far more common topic in jurisprudential literature than natural justice. This chapter sets out our understanding of natural law and its place in the broader account of law and justice in community presented in this book.

When in Chapter 4.2 we discussed some of the multifarious meanings of the word 'natural', we emphasized that the terms 'natural law' or 'natural justice' are never used in this book to mean the divine law believed by religious Jews, Christians, and Muslims to have been revealed. We emphasized also that these terms are never used in this book to mean a set of inbuilt infallible moral axioms from which appropriate moral or legal rules may be deduced. One of these two meanings – a revealed divine law or a set of infallible axioms – is usually what is meant when 'natural law' is referred to in jurisprudence. Our view is that the natural law is *not* a superior set of axioms or provisions that, for whatever reason, are not, or may not be, actually part of the law of the particular jurisdiction, but against which, nonetheless, a subordinate law may be tested and perhaps found wanting. As we explained in Chapter 4.2, we use the word 'natural' to refer to what is *intrinsic* to a given situation or circumstance or to a practice or set of practices, that is, to the nature of the case. When discussing natural law, 'the case' is the human condition. Natural law, as we argue in this chapter, refers primarily to the moral experience of being human, or, to put it another way, to the responsibility intrinsic to being human.

Natural *law* is primarily *ethical*, but is related intimately to the primarily *political* concept of natural *justice*. Historically, many have understood it in a way incompatible with our account. That understanding, which has been, as we think wrongly, associated with St Thomas Aquinas, is of natural law as revealed divine law or, in its secular versions, as a set of infallible axioms. While we hold that St Thomas's view is consonant with ours, this remains disputable, but does not affect our position.

8.2 Natural Law as Moral Experience

We understand natural law to refer primarily to the moral experience of being human. By 'moral experience of being human' we mean that, as humans, we must, constantly and always, ask the moral or ethical question: What am I to do? As we have said, this is the moral or ethical question because it is the question of deliberation and choice, the question that defines the moral or ethical domain. How we, as individuals, are to act in any given situation or circumstance is what ethics is fundamentally about. As we have also said, it is irrelevant what type of situation is involved, whether it is a trivial or a serious matter: if it requires deliberation and choice then it is in the ethical – ie the moral – domain. The first principle or precept of morality is the basic feature of natural law in humans: namely, *that we, who are naturally social animals, are responsible for how we live and what we do.* This first principle is the natural law in that it is natural to us. It indicates, in other words, the kind of beings that we are. It is not in any sense a command; nor can it be formulated as a command. It is a principle intrinsic to enquiry as to how to act, as to how to answer the moral question of what one is to do.[1] It is a principle that we cannot avoid because we cannot avoid the question.

Natural law in humans arises from the human need and ability to discern what is good and bad. The first principle – that we, who are naturally social animals, are responsible for how we live and what we do – means that we are required to decide responsibly. In order to decide responsibly we have to judge reasonably. In order to judge reasonably we must try to understand, in the world in which we find ourselves, what is a good course of action. To act reasonably and responsibly is the demand *intrinsic* to our moral experience as humans, and once we have discovered what to do then there is an *intrinsic* demand to do it. 'Act reasonably and

---

[1] It is possible to conceive of this theory of natural law in theological terms: one can consider the intrinsic demand to act reasonably and responsibly as our participation in the eternal law, which is traditionally understood as God's mind related to creation. Obviously, only someone who believes in God can possibly agree with this theological perspective. Our account of natural law is not based on such belief; neither is it incompatible with it.

responsibly' is not added on to us; we are demands to and on ourselves because we cannot avoid asking what we are to do and, at this level of ourselves, we choose to act to bring about a result; *omne ens agit proter finem, qui habet rationem boni* ('every being acts because of a goal which seems good') and humans are responsible for their actions including the choice of the results that they wish to bring about; what seems good is what one wants to bring about.[2]

This conception of natural law focuses on individual morality and requires an analysis of human decision that finds that it is possible to discover, albeit fallibly, what is right.[3] An analysis that does not find this to be the case may discover a demand to act reasonably and responsibly but hold that the demand cannot be met. But reasonableness and responsibility *can* be discovered; it *is* possible to discover – again, albeit fallibly – whether or not a proposed course of action is good or reasonable without referring either to an established positive law, convention, or agreement.

This version of natural law does not purport to constitute a substantive conception of political justice. It does not set up a given, objective morality as a standard against which actions can be judged to be right or wrong, good or bad. But in another sense our ethical theory of natural law and our political theory of natural justice are closely interdependent. We have argued that humans have always lived together: civil society is a social *order* and not a contract-based organization. The function of law, of the jural order, is to promote the common good, that is, to contribute to the maintenance of a social order within which people can pursue their lives in peace. The intrinsic demand to act reasonably and responsibly gives rise to what we term the 'natural law', and that which is intrinsic to the social order is what we term the 'naturally just'. This is the best way of understanding these terms in relation to one another: reasonable and unbiased enquiry reveals the natural law that we ought not to steal; and it is the social rule forbidding theft that expresses the naturally just.

When considering natural law or natural justice the term 'higher law' is misleading because it gives the impression that the natural law and the naturally just are already fully formed and imposed from above. They are not. The naturally just is discovered to be common to different societies but, before it is *discovered* to be common, it is *in fact* common, and represents similar responses to similar exigencies. Similarly, the natural law is not a superior set of axioms or provisions that, for some reason, are not actually in the law of the particular jurisdiction, but against which a subordinate law may be tested and perhaps found wanting. Rather, the natural law comes about because of the requirement that we, as humans, are required to decide responsibly. And, as we have said, in order

---

[2] To repeat a key quotation from the Western philosophical tradition: 'Every act and every investigation', wrote Aristotle at the outset of the *Nicomachean Ethics*, 'and similarly every action and pursuit, is considered to aim at some good. Hence the Good has been rightly defined as "that at which all things aim"', Aristotle, *Ethics* I.1094a.1–2 (trans and ed JAK Thomson) (Harmondsworth: Penguin, 1976), 63.   [3] See ch 7.2 above.

to decide responsibly we have to judge reasonably about what to do; this in turn requires the effort to understand what, in the world in which we find ourselves, is a good course of action. In other words, awareness and knowledge of natural laws is the fruit of careful analysis of our social lives by means of intelligent enquiry and reasonable judgment. What as explicit and accepted laws they enjoin or prohibit is often very obvious, spontaneous, and fundamental to the survival of society. In practical matters, the goal is to discover not what is the case but what ought to be done and so the enquiry has from the outset engaged our decision orientated responsibility.

There is no derivation from 'is' to 'ought' in our account of natural law because the ought is contained in the first principle of morality: that we, who are naturally social animals, are responsible for how we live and what we do.[4] It is a part of human nature that we ought to be responsible in this way. The present or given situation of any human involves the moral or ethical question as to what one is to do. So the principle of responsibility is intrinsic to the enquiry as to how to act.

From the first principle of morality and the fact that we are social beings is derived the judgment that we should take account of others. We think of it as a reasonable conclusion to the question as to how we should live. We have suggested that the opposite conclusion – 'We should take no account of others' – is not equally reasonable. The principle that one should act taking others into account becomes communally accepted more or less explicitly; it may or may not be posited in a statute. A particular person may rarely take others into account and it may hardly ever occur to him to do so, but it is invariably the case that he lives in a jurisdiction where to take others into account is expected and the idea that one should do so is used by the courts in assessing action.

Derivation is best understood by means of a particular example. In a community where people drive cars, from the fundamental precept that we should judge reasonably and decide responsibly and the derived principle that we should take account of others may be derived the rule that we should drive carefully and with due care for *oneself* and for others.[5] We then have to discover what driving carefully and with due care involves. Some of the actions that are involved in driving carefully are intrinsic to the activity, and some activities are excluded. We make such discoveries by investigating further the nature of driving. Critically, this process of 'natural law discovery', which we undertake as individuals, has implications, when social activity is involved, for what is the naturally just. This reflects the fundamental relation between ethics and politics: issues pertaining to

---

[4] There is much reference to the empiricism of David Hume (1711–76) in the jurisprudential literature on natural law. In his *Treatise of Human Nature* (1739/1740), Hume claimed that any 'system of morality', including natural law, was flawed in that it could not support its derivation of values from facts, or of an 'ought' from an 'is'. *A Treatise of Human Nature* [III.I.I] (ed EC Mossner) (Harmondsworth: Penguin, 1969), 521. Our position, as explained in the text, is that the 'ought' is in the 'is' and so no derivation of values of this type takes place.

[5] Obviously, to drive with due care for oneself is not a rule against deliberate recklessness with the intention of committing suicide.

how one ought to live *cannot* be considered in isolation from issues pertaining to how we, as a communal group or society, ought to live.

Obviously, to have successfully learned how to drive a car is required for one's being able to drive carefully and with due care. To allow a space between your car and the one ahead of you such that you will be able to stop in an emergency without running into it is required. And you must know how much space is required and how this is related to speed. Equally obviously, to drive utterly drunk through a crowded street at 120 kph at night and without lights is excluded. The principle expresses the reason why one should not do so; if one is asked why one should not drive in this manner, the answer is: 'Because that is not driving carefully, and with due care'. From the principle that one should drive carefully may be derived also that one should not drive while extremely tired and precisely the same answer satisfies the question as to why one should not.[6] These are discoveries that we make as individuals that have consequences for the social regulation of driving; both the natural law and the naturally just come into play.

The basic principle that one should drive carefully and with due care may be expressed in legislation: 'Drive carefully, and with due care for others'. If it is so expressed, it is not the fact that it is legislated and promulgated legitimately that makes it right to act in this way; to act in the way described in the legislation is right whether or not it is commanded. Yet in order that people may drive safely it is not enough that each drives carefully; there must arise customs or enacted laws that establish arrangements to allow safe driving to be effectively possible. Some of these arrangements will be good because they are posited. It is essential that drivers know and accept which side of the road to drive on; it does not matter which side is chosen but one must be. Why is it good to drive on the left side of the road in Ireland? Because if safe driving is to be possible, then one side of the road must be chosen, known and agreed; and, in Ireland the left side has been chosen. Although there are of course historical reasons why this particular side was chosen in Ireland, these are irrelevant to the fact that the custom or legislation is conventional: it is conventional in Ireland to drive on the left side of the road; but it is natural, not conventional, that one side *must* be chosen, known, and agreed if there is to be an environment in which it is possible to drive carefully and with due care for others.[7] Some principles *require* customary or legislative institution. A conventional side of the road is necessary. The blood alcohol level established in a particular jurisdiction is not randomly selected; it has to do with drunkenness

---

[6] It is noteworthy that it is usually the case that in a particular jurisdiction there is legislation forbidding drunken driving but none forbidding driving while extremely tired. Most would agree that the latter is extremely dangerous but it is something that cannot yet be measured easily or conveniently.

[7] And sometimes a side of the road is chosen that will later be changed by a new conventional decision, as happened, for example, when, in September 2009, Samoa changed the side of the road on which automobiles are driven from the right to the left.

and capacity to drive carefully; but the precise level selected may reasonably be somewhat different in different jurisdictions.

8.3 St Thomas Aquinas and Natural Law

Because the belief that the laws set down in the *Torah* were revealed by God to Moses has been of great importance in the Western Tradition, in a discussion of St Thomas and natural law it is as well to begin by considering that idea. Ten of those laws, commonly known as the Ten Commandments or Decalogue, are singled out both in *Exodus* and *Deuteronomy*. Four have to do with the proper way for the Israelites to worship their God; the remaining six are very ordinary injunctions having to do with the proper way to treat others.[8] About these commandments there are theological and jurisprudential questions. On the assumption that they were revealed there arises the theological question as to the meaning of such revelation. A key jurisprudential question is the question for a legislator within a tradition in which these commandments are known: *should any or all of the six commandments that deal with social life be part of the positive law?* In the Western tradition some have never been, namely, the ninth and tenth that forbid one to covet one's neighbour's wife or goods; some have been but, in many jurisdictions no longer are, namely, the seventh that forbids adultery; some remain in the enacted law in many jurisdictions, namely, the fifth that forbids murder, the sixth that forbids theft, and the eighth that forbids perjury.[9]

There is also another, deeper, and for us more important, jurisprudential question regarding the Decalogue. This deeper question derives from what is known as 'the *Euthyphro* dilemma'.[10] The most common theological version of this question

---

[8] That these six injunctions are not peculiar to the Ten Commandments is obvious, and it seems unlikely that they entered the Roman or Western legal traditions *exclusively* from the *Torah*.

[9] Quite often these are implicit and referred to by their associated punishment or other consequence. The rhetoric of the *Torah* is dominantly one of direct command – 'Thou shalt/Thou shalt not' – whereas the rhetoric of both the *Twelve Tables* and the *Code of Hammurabi* is dominantly 'If X is done, Y is to be the consequence', eg 'If any one is committing a robbery and is caught, then he shall be put to death' (*Code of Hammurabi* 22) and 'When a person makes bond and conveyance, according as he specified with his tongue so shall be the law' (*Twelve Tables* VI.1).

[10] The dilemma appears in Plato's *Euthyphro*: 'Is what is holy holy because the gods approve it, or do they approve it because it is holy?', *Euthyphro*, 10a, in E Hamilton and H Cairns (eds), *The Collected Dialogues of Plato* (trans L Cooper) (Princeton, NJ: Princeton University Press, 1961), 274. The *Euthyphro* dilemma involves a conflict between two types of ethical theory: voluntarist theories and rationalist theories. If one takes the view that what is holy is holy 'because it is loved by the gods' then one is responding to the dilemma in voluntarist terms. If, on the other hand, one considers that what is the holy is 'loved by the gods because it is holy' then the source of moral authority – here, the source of the judgment that something is holy – is something other than command. This implies that in order to judge that something is holy, and that the holy is good, one must in some way discover this. Reason and intellect, therefore, rather than simply will, are central to this ethical theory: the theory is rationalist, T. Murphy, 'St Thomas Aquinas and the Natural Law Tradition' in T Murphy (ed), *Western Jurisprudence* (Dublin: Thomson Round Hall, 2004), 94, 105–18.

is to ask if the commandments of the Decalogue are good because commanded, or commanded because good.[11] In as much as the Ten Commandments have been considered within Western jurisprudence the *Euthyphro* dilemma has been expressed in the question: is what is commanded in the Ten Commandments right because it is commanded or commanded because it is right?[12]

The tradition that came to prominence with the fourteenth-century English theologian, William of Occam (1290–1345), is that the commands in the Decalogue are right because commanded and not otherwise discoverable. For Occam, everything other than God exists contingently and the only restriction on God's power is the principle of non-contradiction: 'Anything is to be attributed to the divine power when it does not contain a contradiction.'[13] The actions commanded or forbidden by the commandments are right or wrong, according to Occam, *because* commanded by God. Consider again the example of theft, specifically, the sixth commandment forbidding theft. The rule against stealing is thought of by Occam as a command that could well have been other. John Selden, in the Occamian tradition, writes in the chapter on the 'Law of Nature' in his *Table-Talk*:

I cannot fancy to myself what the Law of Nature means but the Law of God. How should I know I ought not to steal…unless some body had told me so? Surely, 'tis because I have been told so! 'Tis not because I think I ought not to do them, nor because you think I ought not; if so, our minds might change: whence then comes the restraint? From a higher Power; nothing else can bind. I cannot bind myself, for I may untie myself again; nor an equal cannot bind me, for we may untie one another: it must be a superior, even God Almighty. If two of us make a Bargain, why should either of us stand to it? What need you care what you say, or what need I care what I say? Certainly because there is

---

[11] Theologically, the dilemma raises the question of the extent of God's power. If the commandments of the Decalogue are commanded because they are good, then the source of their moral authority would seem to be other than God's will, in which case God's power would be limited. To avoid this position William of Occam concluded that the good was what God commanded, and that God could command everything but the contradictory or the impossible, William of Occam, XI.4, *Quodlibeta*, III.13 in P Boehner (ed), S Brown (revised edn), *Ockham: Philosophical Writings* (Indianapolis, Ind: Hackett, 1990), 144–7. (Occam's name is spelt differently by different writers.) On Occam's voluntarist account of law, see M Bastit, *Naissance de la loi moderne* (Paris: Presses Universitaires de France, 1990), esp chs 7–10.

[12] John Kelly expresses the *Euthyphro* dilemma as follows: 'Had God so commanded Moses because the order of nature had, all along, already contained the precepts which the Decalogue expressed? Did the Decalogue contain natural, already-established precepts, or was it an expression of God's will? If so, had the Decalogue been necessary? Conversely, if what was perceived as the law of nature was in fact itself only the outcome of God's will, it was open to God to change the rules: in which case nature could not be looked to as an infallible, invariable rule of conduct', *A Short History of Western Legal Theory* (Oxford: Clarendon Press, 1992), 103. Kelly does not here make clear what is meant by 'an already-established precept', thus possibly giving the impression that a natural law is a command to be obeyed.

[13] William of Occam, *Ordinatio*, qu. i, n *sqq.*, in P Boehner (ed), *Ockham: Philosophical Writings*, 25, quoted in MJ Osler, *Divine Will and the Mechanical Philosophy* (Cambridge: Cambridge University Press, 1994), 29–30.

something about me that tells me *Fides est servanda* ['A promise is to be kept']; and if we after alter our Minds, and make a new Bargain, there's *Fides servanda* there too.[14]

Although it is not utterly clear in Selden, the obvious sense here is that not alone can one not know the unjust character of stealing unless one is told, but that its unjust character is established for the first time by the injunction against it. Before the command, stealing was a matter of indifference; in other words, to steal is unjust only because it is forbidden by convention.

For Occam the actions commanded or forbidden by the commandments were right or wrong because commanded by God. If the words 'by God' are omitted, the road to a pure positivism is opened. For the *pure* positivist, in the absence of a sovereign's command, it is impossible to discover what is right, for the simple and powerful reason that, absent the command, there is no right.[15] 'Law of the State' may replace 'Law of God' without changing the basic structure of the Occamian argument. The root of legal positivism is here; for, in all its versions, its foundational principle is that law is authoritative command. Whether the authoritative source is the secular ruler or God is a dispute *within* legal positivism. Some natural law theories turn out to be positivist in that their claim to be natural is based on the theory that the source of law is God's command, and the Decalogue is understood as the imposition of divine authoritative command on what was originally indifferent.

Indeed, in later thought the ethical tradition established by Occam divides into three streams. The first two are versions of voluntarist or command theory: the religious stream, where *God's command* remains the criterion, and the secular, positivist stream, where *the command of the Sovereign* replaces the command of God.[16] Critically, the modern natural law tradition is the third stream arising out of Occam's thought, in which God's command becomes the innate moral law, conceived as a set of propositions, and the stream where ethics conceived as geometry with unassailable axioms is most at home.

---

[14] J Selden, *Table Talk: Being the Discourses of John Selden* [1689] (London: Dent, 1956), 73–4.

[15] Not all writers who think of themselves as 'positivists' are radical in this way. Oran Doyle holds that Hart, when he writes of there being no necessary connection between law and morality, claims that a 'law' – Hart has legislation in mind – is valid law if properly enacted. Hart does not claim that every purported distinction between just and unjust laws is spurious; what he rejects is the extreme interpretation of St Augustine's idea that an unjust law is not a law. See O Doyle, 'True Morality and the Necessary Connection Thesis', Paper at the Irish Jurisprudence Society Symposium, University College Cork, 17 April 2010. If this is a correct interpretation of Hart, we agree with Hart on this point. Here, however, we refer to a positivism defined as a theory within which a law cannot be just or unjust except in so far as it is properly enacted or not.

[16] The first stream is substantially that of Protestant religions, associated with thinkers such as Martin Luther (1483–1546), Karl Barth (1886–1968), and Jacques Ellul (1912–94). The second stream is usually said to include Thomas Hobbes (1588–1679), Jeremy Bentham (1748–1832), John Austin (1790–1859), Hans Kelsen (1881–1973), and HLA Hart (1907–92). For the argument that Hobbes's positivism is impure and that his thought is much closer to St Thomas's than is commonly assumed, see G Barden and T Murphy, 'Law's Function in *De Cive* and *Leviathan*' (2007) 29 *Dublin University Law Journal* 231.

Many modern jurists endorse this view of natural law in that they understand natural law theory as involving some definitive idea of justice that invariably comprises an independent and unassailable moral order capable of expression in the form of axioms or principles. It is not surprising that this view is perpetuated especially by jurists since this understanding of natural law is tantamount to conceiving of natural law as a system of principles or axioms similar in form – but superior in status – to that of modern legal systems. Proponents of this version of natural law usually insist that positive law, in order to qualify as valid law, must not contradict the supervening natural law principles.[17] JW Harris, for example, refers to three characteristics of the classical doctrine of natural law: (i) that it is universal and immutable; (ii) that it is a 'higher' law; and (iii) that it is discoverable by reason.[18] As to the substance of these characteristics, Harris suggests that the first two emphasize the 'legal' quality of natural law. The universality and immutability of natural law imply that 'it is one conception of "justice", in the sense in which justice stands for the righting of wrongs and the proper distribution of benefits and burdens within a political community'; that it is a 'higher' law means 'it has a relationship of superiority towards laws promulgated by political authorities'.[19]

This is modern natural law theory and it is often presented as an account of what St Thomas Aquinas meant by 'natural law'. In our view, St Thomas's idea of natural law was quite different. According to St Thomas, the precepts commanding how humans ought to treat one another in the Decalogue may be understood as *the clarification of what could be discovered*. The precepts, revealed in the divine law, were commanded *because they were right, and could be discovered by natural reason to be right*. So, to the question in the *Euthyphro* dilemma as to whether an act was good because the gods commanded it – the act being, therefore, intrinsically or naturally neutral – or whether the gods commanded an act because it was good, St Thomas's answer is unequivocal: God commanded acts that are naturally or intrinsically good and forbade those that are naturally or intrinsically wrong and evil. He did not think of God's commands in the Decalogue having to do with ordering our relations with one another in society as mere conventions that might just as well have been different, but as manifestations of what was truly and intrinsically right and good.[20]

---

[17] As John Kelly remarked: 'A central problem of jurisprudence is whether a law, in order to be recognized as such, need conform only to formal criteria, or whether its validity depends also on its not infringing some permanent, higher, "natural" standard', *A Short History of Western Legal Theory* (Oxford: Clarendon Press, 1992), 19.

[18] JW Harris, *Legal Philosophies* (London: Butterworths, 2nd edn, 1997), 7.

[19] Ibid. By way of emphasizsing this 'legality', Harris writes: 'If it were merely a system of private ethics, it would not *eo ipse* [in and by itself] be mete for enactment by legislatures and judges and would not set criteria for obedience.'

[20] St Thomas did think that the commandments that have to do with our relations, not to one another, but to Yahweh, enjoin actions that are good because commanded. So, for example, to keep the Sabbath (Saturday) holy is good because commanded. This commandment remains within Judaism, but not within the New Law as Christians think of their religion, where Sunday replaces

St Thomas thought that basic acts like not stealing, for example, were good and in accord with the created nature of humans as social beings.[21] According to St Thomas one can discover, yet neither easily nor inevitably, the unjust character of stealing from an examination of ownership. To steal deprives another of what is due, and so undermines human society, whereas not to steal respects what is due to another, and so contributes to sustaining it. For St Thomas this is a discovery that we, as humans, can make both for ourselves *and* for the social context in which we find ourselves.[22] We discover as *individuals* that stealing is naturally or intrinsically unjust and wrong and we understand that therefore we should not steal. The *social* and explicit rule against stealing is a formulation of an understanding that stealing is naturally or intrinsically unjust. For that reason no decision can make it just. Similarly, that contracts ought to be kept is existentially discovered in the making of contracts, and theoretically discovered in the effort to understand the nature of contract – what a contract is – and does not depend upon the command to keep contracts; that something is due to one who has suffered from another's breach of contract is discovered in the effort to understand what is intrinsic to breach of contract.

In his discussion of the essence of law, St Thomas arrives at a definition of law as 'a reasonable command of the person who has care of the community, ordered to the common good, and promulgated'.[23] He identifies four varieties of law: the eternal law, the divine law, the natural law, and positive law.[24] The 'eternal law', which is not in any sense posited, is God's mind with respect to the created world and includes, for instance, the laws of mathematics, physics, biology, zoology, and so on.[25] The divine law refers to that part of the eternal law that God chooses

---

the Sabbath as the day to be kept holy – even if some Christians mistakenly refer to Sunday as the Sabbath.

[21] It is worth remarking that Hobbes thought of the laws of nature as immutable and eternal, and held that they 'can never be made lawfull'. Hence, for Hobbes, the source of fundamental laws, 'which being taken away, the Common-wealth faileth', is not the sovereign's will, *Leviathan*, 215 [79] and 334 [150].

[22] As we mentioned in ch 1 above, most jurisprudential scholarship, when discussing St Thomas's natural law theory, refers exclusively to his discussion of law in Questions 90 to 97 in the *first* part of the second part of his *Summa Theologiae* [I–II], the so-called 'Treatise on Law'. There is little or no reference to his discussion of justice and what is just, found in Questions 56 to 71, 120, and 122 of the *second* part of the second part [II–II]. To this practice the late Michel Villey is the great and influential exception. [23] *Summa Theologiae*, I–II, q 90, art 4.

[24] Another variety of law, the law of concupiscence, is rarely mentioned in contemporary accounts of St Thomas's natural law thought. Although, following this practice, it will not be referred to again in this chapter, it may be noted that the law of concupiscence is the inclination of sensuality that is a deviation from reason. In the Christian theological tradition, this inclination, which is manifestly present in humans, is usually discussed as an effect of original sin.

[25] St Thomas's account of divine Providence provides that the whole community of the universe is governed by divine reason; this rational guidance of created things on the part of God has the nature of a law and, since it is not subject to time, it can be called the eternal law, *Summa Theologiae*, I–II, q 91, art 1. The eternal law, in other words, is the divine intelligence; MDA Freeman has described it as 'God's plan for the universe', *Lloyd's Introduction to Jurisprudence* (London: Sweet & Maxwell, 8th edn, 2008), 100.

to reveal, either through Scripture or supernaturally. In as much as the divine law refers to the Ten Commandments and other ordinances in the *Torah*, it is clearly a law in the ordinary sense of St Thomas's definition: the acts commanded are reasonable; God, as well as the secular ruler, has care of the community; the commands in the Decalogue are ordered to the common good; and they are promulgated in the *Torah*. The divine law, we suggest, is a positive law because what makes a law *positive* has not to do with *what* is posited but with *the fact that it is posited*. Of what is posited, St Thomas writes in the *Summa Contra Gentiles*:

From what has been said earlier it is clear that according to the divine law a person is led to follow a reasonable ordering of those things for which he can be responsible. Among those things for which one can be responsible are especially other people. Man is naturally a social animal who needs from others what alone he cannot provide. It is, accordingly, suitable that humans should be required by the divine law to be reasonably ordered towards one another.[26]

It is perfectly clear that St Thomas's conception of human action is far from a concept of morality as obedience to given norms and precepts. As we have argued, the basic feature of natural law in humans is that we, who are naturally social animals, are responsible for how we live and what we do.[27] It is natural to humans to be responsible for themselves, to discover intelligently, to judge reasonably, and to decide responsibly how they are to be. Part of this discovery is the appropriateness of being reasonably ordered towards one another.

Of 'natural law', St Thomas asks the question whether this law is 'within us'. In replying in the affirmative, he establishes the link between the eternal law and the natural law:

Since all things are regulated and measured by Eternal Law ... it is evident that all somehow share in it, in that their tendencies to their own proper acts and ends are from its impression.

Among them intelligent creatures are ranked under divine Providence the more nobly because they take part in Providence by their own providing for themselves and others. Thus they join in and make their own the Eternal Reason through which they have their natural aptitudes for their due activity and purpose. Now this sharing in the Eternal Law by intelligent creatures is what we call 'natural law'.

That is why the Psalmist after bidding us, *Offer the sacrifice of justice*, adds, as though anticipating those who ask what are the works of justice, *There be many who say, Who will show us the good?* and replies, *The light of thy countenance, O Lord, is signed upon us*, implying that the light of natural reason by which we discern what is good and what evil, is nothing but the impression of divine light on us.

---

[26] *Summa Contra Gentiles*, III.128. G Barden, 'Of Natural Law or Reasonable Action' (2005) 56 *Milltown Studies* 71.

[27] For St Thomas, natural law as it exists in animals or plants is different to the extent that they are not responsible for themselves. See the second and third objections and their answers in *Summa Theologiae* I–II, q 91, art 2.

Accordingly it is clear that natural law is nothing other than the sharing in the Eternal Law by intelligent creatures.[28]

The natural law operates to its proper effect in human beings when they act in accord with the divine intelligence, that is, reasonably and responsibly. Humans participate in the eternal law, the divine mind, simply in that they are human. They participate in the eternal law in a more excellent way than do the other creatures in as much as they are rational. Dogs do not participate in the eternal law by obeying rules that they know about; rather to be a dog and, accordingly, to act as dogs act is to be that kind of creature, and the entire existence and nature of creatures is the expression of God's eternal understanding and decision. When Galileo discovered how balls run down an inclined plane, he discovered one of the ways in which they participate in the divine mind. The divine mind is promulgated to balls and dogs simply in that they are balls or dogs.

The human, moral task is to discover 'the way' through virtuous reflection and action.[29] A question arises: in the light of St Thomas's definition of law, in what sense is natural law a law? If the natural law is not a superior law, as we say, because natural law is not posited, not a command and not promulgated, then it would seem that it is not a law in the ordinary sense of St Thomas's definition. Since we can discover how to act well, we can express the discoveries in law and the person who has care of the community can command them (promulgate and command). But natural laws are discovered, not given; and *reason* is the possibility of discovery.[30] For St Thomas the proximate origin of intelligent and reasonable practical conclusions of things to be done or omitted is human reason. Human reason is the way in which humans participate in the eternal law, which, being identical with God, is the origin of reason. As to *how* such discoveries are made, St Thomas thought that human beings, made in the image of God,[31] possess natural reason, which incorporates certain natural dispositions.

---

[28] *Summa Theologiae*, I–II, q 91, art 2.

[29] The notion of 'the way' as representing a 'path', 'road', or 'route' to truth or enlightenment is common and found in very many of the world's religions or moral teachings. We do not use the term in a technical way here but rather suppose that the reader will understand what is meant in the present context.

[30] While our claims as to the meaning of 'natural law' in St Thomas's writings may appear novel in the jurisprudential context, it is worth remarking that the status of 'law' in his work is hugely controversial in several other disciplines. Cristina Traina has noted that contemporary scholars of St Thomas 'disagree vehemently over the proper status of law in his theology generally and over the proper role of law in his ethics in particular. In the language of theological anthropology, this is the question, whether human conformity to divinely established ends involves adherence to principle or development of habits or character. Virtue theorists insist that reducing Thomas's ethics to law ignores his emphasis upon growth in the virtues and upon the flexibility of practical reason in pursuit of the good; others counter that it is impossible to ignore the treatise on law or the important role law plays in the extensive ethical discussions in part II–II of the *Summa Theologiae*', CLH Traina, *Feminist Ethics and Natural Law* (Washington, DC: Georgetown University Press, 1999), 58.

[31] The doctrine of *imago Dei* is that each person, as evidenced by the twin endowments of rationality and freedom, is made in the image of God. God's reason may therefore be disclosed to human

Synderesis is one such disposition and it is fundamental, along with prudence, to practical reasoning and practical knowledge.

In the *Summa Theologiae* St Thomas writes of *synderesis* which he thinks of as a 'natural habit of intellect' that is said 'to incite us to good and deter us from evil, in that through first principles we begin the investigation and judge what we find'.[32] Later, he writes that '*synderesis* is the law of our intellect, in so far as it is the habit containing the precepts of natural law, *which are the first principles of human action*'.[33] The first principles of action are not moral propositions, injunctions, or commands, they are the spontaneous operations involved in moving from question to decision; from the question that begins the investigation, through careful and intelligent enquiry to the judgment that concludes it, and evokes but does not determine decision, for the moral judgment neither compels nor guarantees decision in accord with it. For St Thomas, our practical conclusions as to what is to be done or omitted are laws that each of us gives him or herself.[34]

It is not that command is absent from St Thomas's account of law: for him a suggestion that something should be done becomes positive law when it emanates either from the entire population or from the public person on whom falls the care of the whole population.[35] Thus, proposals that are not simply expressions of 'laws of nature', however reasonable they may be – for example, that motor vehicles must not travel at over 100 kph – become laws only when properly legislated, that is, when the command is posited. Proposals in the form of suggested ways of communal living – rules of etiquette are a good example – can also be properly legislated or posited, by the entire population or by part of the entire population: such 'positing' is in the form of acceptance and approval and gives rise to the living law. A suggested provision becomes state law only when properly legislated but it remains the case that reason is properly the source of law and the criterion of its adequacy. Nor is it the case that for St Thomas an unreasonable law is not a law. It is a law, but an inadequate one.[36] A law intrinsically is a reasonable

---

reason. The broader context here is that St Thomas's effort is to understand reasonable action in relation to God; theology is for him the study of God and of other things in as much as they are ordered to God as to principle and end, *Summa Theologiae*, I, q 1, art 7.

[32] *Summa Theologiae*, I, q 79, art 12. For St Thomas, a habit is the characteristic practical disposition or inclination to act in a certain way. A habit could be of the intellect or of the will, innate or acquired, natural or supernatural, good or bad. On *synderesis*, see T Murphy, 'St Thomas Aquinas and the Natural Law Tradition' in T Murphy (ed), *Western Jurisprudence* (Dublin: Thomson Round Hall, 2004), 94, 114–15.

[33] *Summa Theologiae*, I–II, q 94, art 1 (emphasis added). See also I–II, q 91, art 2.

[34] *Summa Theologiae*, I–II, q 90, art 3.

[35] *Summa Theologiae*, I–II, q 90, art 3: 'And therefore to make law pertains either to the entire multitude or to the public person to whom falls the care of the entire multitude.' What St Thomas here calls the 'public person', Hobbes, in *Leviathan*, 312 [137], refers to as the '*Persona Civitatis*, the Person of the Commonwealth', which in principle, may be the entire population.

[36] *Summa Theologiae*, I–II, q 95, art 2. In this article St Thomas quotes St Augustine (*On Free Will*), for whom an unjust law was not a law. At the end of the same paragraph St Thomas subtly dissents from this view with the suggestion that 'a law discordant with natural law [that is, with reason] will not be not a law but a corruption of law' (*iam non erit lex sed legis corruptio*).

solution to a practical problem; when it is not in fact a reasonable solution, it is an inadequate or, in the limit, a corrupt law.[37]

If we take the moral discovery that we should take account of others as basic, we have discovered it as a good way to act; but, obviously, another might think of it as a bad or indifferent way to act. Someone might suggest, for instance, that we should take account of others only to the extent that not to do so would at least in some, and perhaps most, circumstances make it more difficult for us to achieve what we want.[38] An example of such a suggestion would be that the only good reason to be polite is that our own desires will be more easily and more often fulfilled; if we thought that by taking no account of another our desires will be achieved – think of successfully jumping a queue – then it would be more reasonable to take no account of others. Here are two rival accounts of the good but both assume that it is possible to arrive at a definition of the good. One position is Occam's: that we cannot make moral discoveries because courses of action are always indifferent in themselves, so there is nothing to discover. On this view, courses of action get their good or bad character from the will of the person commanding them. Our position – and we suggest that this is also that of St Thomas – is that we are able to discover the genuine moral character of courses of action, and that some courses of action are intrinsically, naturally, right; some are bad; and some are indifferent. Reasonableness and responsibility, it need hardly be added, are constant demands rather than constant achievements.

Hans Kelsen opens his *Pure Theory of Law* with an argument against St Augustine's idea that an unjust law is not a law. He comes in the end to the conclusion that what is properly legislated or adjudicated is law and, therefore, *within the perspective of the pure theory of law*, is just or right. In other words, the 'just' or 'right' is defined to be what is properly legislated or adjudicated.[39] Our suggestion,

---

Somewhat similarly, a mistaken proposition is a proposition, but an inadequate one: a proposition is the answer to a question; a question looks not merely for an answer, but for the correct answer; hence, a mistaken or incorrect answer is an answer, but an inadequate answer. As an example in elementary logic, the proposition 'Iceland is not an island' is as good as 'Iceland is an island'; as proposed answers to the question as to whether or not Iceland is in reality an island, they are not equally good.

[37] At *Summa Theologiae*, II–II, q 60, art 2, it is said that a judgment *contra rectitudinem iustitiae* is called 'perverse or unjust'. A judgment is *contra rectitudinem iustitiae* when it is unreasonable. Of course, there is no automatic, unintelligent, irresponsible, or infallible way of knowing that a judgment in the jural domain is unreasonable, any more than there is an automatic, unintelligent, irresponsible, or infallible way of knowing whether a particular scientific or commonsense judgment is reasonable or unreasonable.

[38] As we said, one whose effective and affective orientation is always to ignore others' interests in favour of his advantage will find valuable what one whose effective and affective orientation is to take account of others' interests will find valueless. The choice is between taking account of others' interests and allowing one's own absolute primacy; between supporting society and subverting it. Thus, the choice between these orientations is the fundamental moral choice.

[39] The phrase 'within the perspective of the pure theory of law' is italicized to emphasize that we do not claim that Kelsen personally held that laws were right merely because properly legislated; only, he found no way of distinguishing between right and wrong within the pure theory, that is, for Kelsen properly legislated laws are necessarily right or just . See T Murphy, 'Hans Kelsen's Pure

by contrast, is that the living law of a community – the communal moral law – expresses more or less explicitly both communally approved and required ways of acting and communally accepted entitlements; that what is legislated is state or positive law; and that what the court determines is established. What is by law, legislation and court decisions handed down – the jural tradition – is neither infallible nor perennial, but is subject to changes that, themselves being neither infallible nor perennial, are subject to further changes. To this extent, we agree with the positivist. More or less clearly, positivists may go further and suggest either that legislation or judicial decisions are necessarily correct or that they are correct by definition. If the decision is necessarily correct, there may be a correct and an incorrect answer to a problem, but the legislator or judge in coming to an answer is infallible. If the decision is correct by definition, the term 'correct' has become a synonym for 'the legislator's or judge's decision'. In other words, positivism holds that the lawmaker's decision is correct either because the lawmaker cannot err (that is, his decision is necessarily correct), or because the claim that the lawmaker's decision is correct adds nothing to the claim that the lawmaker's decision is the lawmaker's decision. We differ from this position in that we hold that, however difficult they may be to reach, there are right and wrong answers, but that legislative and judicial enquiries, like scientific enquiry, indeed like any human endeavour, are fallible, and their conclusions subject to discussion. To the adage *Res judicata pro vere tenetur* we add *pro tempore*: the judgment is taken to be true – for the time being.

In summary, then, the natural law of human moral action is, at its most basic level, simply the fundamental originating principles of action: that one raises the question as to what one ought to do in the circumstances in which one finds oneself; that one investigates the situation carefully; that one makes a sustained effort to understand it; that one attempts genuinely to judge reasonably; and that

---

Theory of Law' in T Murphy (ed), *Western Jurisprudence* (Dublin: Thomson Round Hall, 2004), 251. This is not our view but we stress again that we do not hold that there are given true and unquestionable propositions from which right solutions may be simply deduced. See N MacCormick, *Rhetoric and the Rule of Law* (Oxford: Oxford University Press, 2005), 272: 'Especially by the end of his life, Kelsen's "pure theory of law" embraced the view that decisions by authorized persons are necessarily right, there being no possibility of logical and demonstrative arguments using the raw materials of the law, which are decisions, not assertions, acts of will not acts of thought.' Footnote 25 to this passage may also be consulted, and see also MacCormick's *Institutions of Law* (Oxford: Oxford University Press, 2007), 214: 'Hans Kelsen . . . said that from the standpoint of his non-moralistic Pure Theory of law, all wrongs in law are prohibited wrongs and are thus wrong in the same way and for the same reason – because prohibited.' Kelsen's position comes down to this: within the horizon of his pure theory of law, the right or just is what is commanded or allowed in a particular jurisdiction; the wrong or unjust is what is forbidden in that jurisdiction. We agree with this position in that we agree that what is commanded or allowed or forbidden within a particular jurisdiction is precisely what in that jurisdiction is commanded, allowed, or forbidden. The crucial question is whether or not a further question as to the rightness or justice of what is commanded, allowed, or forbidden properly arises. Only if it does, as we have tried to show that it does, is there the possibility of there being just and unjust laws. If it does not, Kelsen's horizon marks a limit beyond which one cannot go.

one decides responsibly in the light of one's judgment. Naturally and inescapably, when one asks what one ought to do one enters a context or universe of value. And so naturally and inescapably, there arises the question of what good one will choose to bring about both in general and in the particular case. We argue that the cardinal point on which one's basic moral context turns is the choice between taking one's own interest as paramount and over-riding, and taking account of others' interests as well as of one's own. That choice emerges upon, yet is not determined by, the judgment as to which of these ought to prevail. The choice is not determined, but choice is unavoidable. That one must choose is the moral aspect of the human.

Although our focus is not the interpretation of St Thomas, we have neverthe-less suggested that, consonant with our own, his account of knowing and doing what is naturally right is discovered in a reasonable judgment that evokes but does not determine responsible decision. Cardinal to his, and our, account of natural law is that sometimes it is possible to know what is right and just by examining the situation in which we – as social, interpersonal, intelligent, reasonable, and responsible beings – find ourselves; and that sometimes it may not be. We cannot avoid deliberate action; we cannot avoid choosing what seems good to us, what seems valuable; we cannot avoid trying to discover what is good. But it is *we* who enquire as to what is to be done, *we* who discover what seems good to us, *we* who decide. And what will seem good to us depends on what we have become, on how we see things, on how we feel about others and ourselves.

9

Rights

9.1 Introduction

Our account of rights is grounded in the Roman definition of justice. Rights, whether they are classed as 'natural', 'individual', 'subjective', 'fundamental', or 'human', are a function of justice understood as the giving to each what is due. In other words, we consider rights to be entitlements that are discoverable objects of justice; what is discovered to be 'due' to a party in instances of disagreement is established as a right. In this chapter we give an account of rights followed by some observations on the historical development of rights discourse.

9.2 Rights as Jural Relations

The distinction between classical and modern theories of rights is that classical theory emphasizes the jural relation between people within society while modern theory emphasizes subjective rights. We reject the modern theory of rights in which there is a faith in the *reality* of rights as a form of 'higher law'; this is a version of command theory because it considers abstract statements of rights to be definitively normative in cases of disagreement regarding justice.[1] By contrast, we advance a version of classical theory that focuses on the jural relation between people within society. Because rights and claims are three place relations, they are necessarily social. A right is a juridical construct with three elements: an entitlement associated with a type of person and, therefore, with an individual of that type; the recognition of that entitlement by others, and without which recognition the entitlement would not effectively exist; and the enforcement of that

---

[1] The first distinction in Gratian's *Decretum* – ie his *Concordia Discordantium Canonum* ('A Concordance of Discordant Canons') of about 1140 – illustrates a rhetorical shift from the description of the naturally just as discovered in the relations between people to a rhetoric that stresses command and higher authority: 'The human race is ruled by two [means] namely by natural law and by usages. Natural law [*ius naturae*] is what is contained in the Law and the Gospel by which each is commanded to do to another what he wants done to himself and forbidden to do to another what he does not want done to himself. So Christ in the Gospel: "Therefore all things whatsoever ye would that men should do to you, do ye even so to them: for this is the law and the prophets"' (*Matthew* 7:12).

entitlement, without which it would be vacuous. In the jural community, rights are entitlements; they are what is discovered to be due. Rights – entitlements – come into being only when they have been recognized, established, and honoured in particular situations.[2]

Rights and claims are three place relations: A is entitled to X from B, or A claims X from B. From the fact that A is entitled to X from B, it follows that B is indeed *obliged* to give X to A. X may refer to what B is obliged to do or to what B is obliged not to do. For example, if A is entitled to have a loan repaid by B, then B is obliged to repay the loan to A; and if A is entitled to walk across a bridge, then B is obliged to refrain from hindering A from so doing. In this latter case, B refers to everyone, but the obligation comes into play only when B is in a position to hinder A.[3] Although *claims* are also three place relations – A claims X from B – a claim is not a right. If A claims X from B, B is obliged to give X to A only when the claim is established as a right. Many claims are controversial, and a claim that is not recognized as a right is effectively not a right.[4]

To say that a right is natural is to say that the alleged right is natural to the situation when the situation is correctly understood. Hence, for example, to say that a lender is naturally entitled to – or has a natural right to – have a loan repaid is to say that this is how a loan is correctly understood. Rights are established; sometimes they are established in general as when there is a general law to the effect that a loan is to be repaid. But in particular situations something that is established in general as a right may not be a right. So a drunk person who intends to drive his car may not be entitled to have his car keys returned to him. In such a case, his claim that he is entitled to be given the keys that belong to him by whomsoever holds the keys is not – and does not become – a right, natural or otherwise.

To say that rights and claims are three place relations and therefore social is to say that since rights and claims require A, B, and X, rights and claims emerge only in society. And because both A and B, as well as X, are required for there to be a right, for a right effectively to exist both A and B must recognize the right. From this it follows that, were there only one person, that person would have no rights and no claims. The phrase 'were there only one person' is to be taken literally, in

---

[2] Because rights are established entitlements, rights may be legislated either by or within particular jurisdictions or by international bodies such as the United Nations, the decisions of which are accepted by particular jurisdictions. Thus, the rights enshrined in the 1948 Universal Declaration of Human Rights, in as much as they are established and accepted in particular jurisdictions, are rights.

[3] It seems at first sight exceedingly odd to suggest that if A has a right to cross a particular bridge in Tallow, a small country town in Ireland, then everyone in Japan has the duty – which, presumably, few if any know is their duty – not to hinder A. To deal with the oddity we have said that the duty comes into play only when the possibility of such hindering actually arises.

[4] Our theory is quasi-Hohfeldian: WN Hohfeld's *Fundamental Legal Conceptions As Applied in Judicial Reasoning* [1913/1917] (ed W Wheeler Cook) (New Haven: Yale University Press, 1964) identified eight types of jural relations, namely, claims, duties, liberties, no-claims, powers, liabilities, immunities, and disabilities.

the sense of 'no other person existing'. Were one to be the only human left in the world, one would have no rights and no claims. The phrase 'were there only one person' does not apply to the solitary castaway on an island. The castaway has latent claims because were anyone to land on the island he would be confronted with his way of life, and the castaway confronted with the new demands that the newcomer would make. The castaway and the newcomer would, in both words and actions, make explicit their perfectly ordinary claims to a way of living that would allow them to live together in mutual harmony. Such claims, were they to be mutually accepted, either through words or actions, would become rights. The shift from being claims to being rights would depend on both in fact agreeing – almost certainly more in their practice than in a formal and explicit contract – to live together in a peaceful social order. Were they to fail to make that shift; were, for instance, either one intent on expelling the other (in the limit by killing him), the mutual rights upon which a peaceful social order depends would not exist. The peaceful social order would not exist and their lives together would be what Hobbes described as the 'natural condition'. It is not the emergence, but rather the survival, of a peaceful social order – the common good – that depends on agreement.

It is important to emphasize that a right is an entitlement that can be either a benefit or burden. In modern English, in which rights are understood to attach to individuals as positive entitlements only, it is distinctly odd to speak of a require-ment or an obligation as an 'entitlement'. But in classical rights theory – given that rights are jural, social, three place relations – 'entitlement' works, so to speak, both ways.[5] The oddity in English points yet again to the fact that the Latin *ius* is virtually untranslatable; there is no word in English that is used in quite the same was as *ius* is used in Roman law.[6]

The Roman law definition of justice has been criticized for its emptiness in that it offers no help in the effort to discover which rights do exist or to distin-guish between just and unjust arrangements or distributions. The criticism is true enough but also irrelevant. What is just in a particular situation – what is to be recognized as a right – is to be discovered in and through discussion and inves-tigation of that situation. In practice, certain rights are in fact recognized and thereby established; others are not. There are two main varieties of rights that may be recognized, depending on the nature of the particular jural community in which claims are made. Some rights are those established by institutions such as states, corporations, federations, and clubs; other rights – which may be called 'living law rights' – include customary and moral rights, created by moral rules and principles that evolve over time in line with practice. Whatever the context,

---

[5] Gaius thinks of a *ius* (a right, what is due, an entitlement) in this way when he writes that it may be a person's *ius*, traditionally called a servitude, to allow his neighbour's drain to pass through his land. Gaius, *Institutes*, ii.14; Justinian, *Institutes*, II.II.3 and 4; *Digest*, viii.3.1.Preamble.

[6] Interestingly, in Gerhart Hauptmann's Middle High German play *Der Arme Heinrich* (c 1190) the word *recht* (right) is sometimes used to refer to what in modern English is called a 'duty'.

a right is discovered when a claim is acknowledged as creating an obligation. Rights, in other words, are ways of talking about, or ways of understanding, jural relations.

This account of rights is consonant with that of St Thomas who offers the following version of the Roman definition of justice: 'the habit whereby a person with a lasting and constant will renders to each his due'.[7] He claims that the object or objective of justice, that is, the situation that a just act is intended to bring about, 'is called the just, which is the same as "right"'. Hence, it is obvious that right is the object of justice'.[8] Thus, a 'right' comes into existence only when it is established, that is, when something is recognized as being due to someone. St Thomas argues that 'right' is fittingly divided into natural right and positive right:

Right or what is just is a fair arrangement of mutual entitlements. This can be measured in two ways. One, from the very nature of the case, as when somebody gives so much in order to receive as much in return: this is called natural right. The other is when the balance is settled by agreement or mutual consent, as when a person counts himself content to receive such or such in return. And this may come about in two ways. First, by private agreement, as when the parties bind themselves to a contract; and secondly, by public agreement, as when the whole civil community agrees that one thing be taken to be equated or commensurate with another or when this is so ordained by the sovereign authority who is responsible for and represents the people: this is called positive right.[9]

Here 'natural right' refers to the recognition of entitlement in a situation where no prior convention or law establishes its rightness; a right is natural if the claim to entitlement is natural to the situation when the situation is correctly understood. 'Positive right' refers to the recognition of entitlement in a situation where the entitlement depends wholly on having been agreed either privately or publicly. Every contract, as St Thomas observes, is an example of the private creation of positive rights. Modern constitutional bills of rights and international human rights charters are examples of publicly agreed positive rights, and so too are legislative measures setting out social welfare entitlements, the general manner in which shareholders in a company must be treated, the range of punishments for various crimes, and so on.

Ronald Dworkin is both an anti-positivist thinker and one of the leading rights theorists in contemporary jurisprudence. Dworkin's theory of law is 'interpretive' in that the law is whatever follows from a constructive interpretation of the insti-

---

[7] *Summa Theologiae*, II–II, q 58, art 1.   [8] *Summa Theologiae*, II–II, q 57, art 1.
[9] *Summa Theologiae*, II–II, q 57, art 2. The example given here of natural right is hardly illuminating; perhaps what St Thomas had in mind is a loan for consumption as when it is naturally right to return a bottle of milk to the person from whom one has borrowed a bottle of milk for consumption. A positive or agreed right is established when, for example, two people agree to buy and sell an object for a mutually agreeable price. It sometimes happens that a fixed ratio between goods and money is authoritatively set, and it is to this that St Thomas refers in the final part of the quotation.

tutional history of the legal system.[10] His theory of 'law-as-integrity' requires that interpretations 'fit' with community or political morality and it emphasizes the role of *principles* in the legal order: arguments of principle carry more weight than either rules of law or social policy considerations; principles are, for Dworkin, propositions of political morality that demonstrate the existence of rights, and rights, once discovered, must be protected.[11] For Dworkin, rights are best understood as 'trumps' over some background justification for political decisions that state a goal for the community as a whole. Dworkin believes courts are the most appropriate forum in contemporary democracies for engaging with and authoritatively resolving debates about moral and political principles. The superhuman judge, Hercules, emerges in Dworkin's work in order to provide an ideal example of how 'law-as-integrity' might function in practice, that is, Hercules is the judge who correctly uses the applicable body of rules, principles, and policies to reach the 'right answer': a decision that fits with the political morality of the community.[12]

Dworkin does not believe that rights exist only in positive or state law, but rather, as one commentator has put it, 'that our intuitions about justice are based on the assumption that people do have rights and that one right is fundamental'.[13] For Dworkin, the fundamental right is a version of the right to equality that he terms the right to 'equality of concern and respect':

We may therefore say that justice as fairness rests on the assumption of a natural right of all men and women to equality of concern and respect, a right they possess not by virtue of birth or characteristic or merit or excellence but simply as human beings with the capacity to make plans and give justice.[14]

This basis for justice – which has led to Dworkin's jurisprudence being referred to as a form of natural law theory[15] – is very different from the Roman definition that underpins the account of law and justice put forward in this book. We referred in Chapter 6 to Michel Villey's observation that adjudication is always an effort to discern what is the just in each case, and that the judgment, to succeed, must rest upon the virtue of justice, including, in the first place, the cognitive part of the virtue. It is sometimes possible, by an examination of the circumstances, to discover what is intrinsically and in that sense naturally just, and sometimes impossible to do so. When it is possible to do so, this is not done by appeal to a set of principles thought of as propositions or axioms or to any higher law but through

[10] C Harvey, 'Talking about Human Rights' in T Murphy (ed), *Western Jurisprudence* (Dublin: Thomson Round Hall, 2004), 291, 299–303.
[11] 'If the Government does not take rights seriously, then it does not take law seriously either', R Dworkin, *Taking Rights Seriously* (Cambridge, Mass: Harvard University Press, 1977), 205.
[12] R Dworkin, *Law's Empire* (Cambridge, Mass: Harvard University Press, 1986). The political morality of a community resembles in some senses the living law of the community.
[13] C Harvey, 'Talking about Human Rights', 300–1.
[14] R Dworkin, *Taking Rights Seriously*, 182.
[15] See, for example, C Covell, *The Defense of Natural Law* (New York: St Martin's Press, 1992).

an examination and discussion of the case in the light of the jural background or context. When it is impossible to discover a just intrinsic to a situation, when several solutions seem good, what is just must be established by convention.

The first principles of moral – including jural – enquiry are not propositions but rather natural, spontaneous, and unavoidable orientations of intellect: to ask what is to be done, to try to understand, critically to examine one's hypothesis, to judge it to be correct, probable, or incorrect in the light of the available evidence, and to decide and act in accord with one's judgment. Dworkin, in the quotation given above, writes of 'the assumption of the natural right of all men and women to an equality of concern and respect'. We agree with him that equality of concern and respect ought to exist, although when that principle is so expressed, how it applies to particular cases is yet to be discerned. It is not an algorithm, any more than is 'render to each what is due'. There is, moreover, a certain paradoxical ambiguity about the principle, for to treat everyone with equal concern and respect does not demand that one respect the fraudster who has damaged many and ruined some as one would respect the honest investor. What the principle demands is that one not discriminate *unjustly* between people. What is important about the principle, however it is formulated, is that it is not simply an assumption but is the expression of a sensitive, intelligent, reasonable, and responsible, even if rather general, conclusion to the enquiry as to how people ought to treat one another. A right to be treated with equal concern and respect is not attached to isolated individuals but is a reciprocal right between people who live together in community. To be in any jurisdiction an existing right and not simply either a claim or an aspiration, it must, obviously, be accepted as a right and then what counts as equal concern and respect remains open to more precise specification.

From what we have said here and throughout about rights, it is evident that if A has a right to do Y, it would be nonsense to claim that B has a right to prevent A from doing Y; if B has a right to prevent A from doing Y, this means that A has no right to do Y. If it is established that 'A has a right' the argument is concluded. So we agree, as given our account of rights we must, that rights are to an extent 'trumps' because that is simply what is meant by the assertion that A is entitled (or has a right) to X from B. But that Dworkin considers rights to be 'trumps' over utilitarian considerations tends to conceal his underlying presupposition that some abstract rights are absolute such that no situation can overcome them. So, in his account, neither the legislative nor the adjudicative question is squarely faced. The first, the legislative question, asks what rights there ought to be in the general case; the second, the adjudicative question, asks what in these circumstances is this person's right, and, in attempting to answer that question, the court considers the person not only as an individual but as a *type* of person; a ship's pilot arraigned for incompetence is both an individual – this particular person – and a type of person – a ship's pilot.

For Dworkin each party to a dispute under adjudication has the right to be treated with equal concern and respect; the right resides, as such, in each of the parties. Dworkin here expresses the element of subjectivity that pervades modern rights theory. In our account the right or entitlement derives from – or resides in – the situation at hand, that is, in how the adjudicative question is to be answered. It is intrinsic to adjudication that parties be treated with equal concern and respect. For that reason, we have argued that the rights to present one's case (*audi alteram partem*) and to be judged impartially (*nemo iudex in causa sua*) are intrinsic to adjudication, which is to say that each litigant is to be treated equally. To that extent at least, our position resembles Dworkin's.

The effort to discover what entitlements are present in any dispute – and not what 'fits' with any fundamental right – is the essence of the adjudicative and interpretive processes. Our understanding of a 'right' as 'that to which someone is entitled' allows that the 'right answer' is an as yet unknown goal to be kept in mind by the judge and tended towards – but there will often be a *range* of possibly correct answers or solutions. In Dworkin's account, the decision to apply the judgment in *Donoghue v Stevenson* in *Grant v Australian Knitting Mills Ltd* – the ousting of the privity rule by the 'neighbour' principle – was the right answer; in our account, it would not have been manifestly unjust to have decided *Donoghue* otherwise, nor, given that it had been decided in favour of Donoghue, to have distinguished *Grant* from it, as, indeed, was done in a lower court.[16]

This is one of the fundamental differences between Dworkin's theory of adjudication and ours. A related difference concerns his antipathy towards the idea that judges make law. Judges do not make law precisely as legislators do but they do – in some cases – inevitably make law. The judges in *Donoghue v Stevenson* made law – extremely important law at that – that, for the time being, stood. It could have been overturned in later legislation – as can any court decision or legislated enactment be overturned in later legislation – but, in fact, it was not. When a judge goes beyond the written enactment because, in his estimation, it fails to deal with the instant case he cannot but make law. In such cases the type of 'law-making' at work differs from the typical legislative process, which involves considerable debate on policy, including discussion in the public realm. Adjudication – including its interpretive aspects – is a different enterprise. The court in handing down its judgment in the instant case does not make general law but because similars are similarly understood, and no particular case can be so peculiar that in principle it can in no way resemble any other case, the scope of the judgment cannot but go beyond the instant case to influence the course of future efforts to discern what is just. Courts address the questions: *in the case now being considered*, what is due to whom? In answering these questions a court gives a judgment in the instant case that ought to be impartial, intelligent, reasoned, and fair but that on any specific occasion may be biased, unintelligent, unreasonable, and unfair. That there may be an undemocratic element involved

---

[16] We referred to these two cases in ch 3.3 above. Cf JM Kelly, *A Short History of Western Legal Theory* (Oxford: Clarendon Press, 1992), 407–9.

in adjudication is undeniable as when, for example, judges are not elected.[17] But, however judges are appointed, judicial law-making, as we have described it, is intrinsic to adjudication and so unavoidable.

9.3 Some Remarks on the Historiography of Rights

There is much confusion concerning the historiography of natural rights discourse, the tradition that preceded the modern human rights tradition. The main schools of thought concerning this question locate the origins of natural rights discourse in either the thought of William of Occam during the fourteenth century or in the emergence of individualistic liberal philosophy during the seventeenth and eighteenth centuries. The second view represents the predominant view and from this perspective contemporary human rights law has its direct source in the natural rights philosophy of the eighteenth century, and human rights are said to have 'an indirect source to natural law dating back to the philosophy of the Greeks'.[18] This supposed lineage provides the basis for modern human rights theory, which maintains that all persons are entitled to certain forms of treatment independent of their communal bonds, social roles, historical period, and cultural traditions. Frederic Kellogg remarks that the concept of *a priori* subjective natural rights involves the notion that certain definable fundamental goods or opportunities are 'morally wed to individuals or groups'.[19] 'Individuals have rights,' observes Robert Nozick, 'and there are things no person or group may do to them (without violating their rights)'.[20]

This historiography of rights considers the individualism often associated with the Protestant Reformation as the foundation upon which the multifarious versions of modern natural rights theories developed.[21] During the Reformation period the appeal to reason against authority led to a new conception of the legal order as a device to secure a maximum degree of individual self-assertion. It is typically asserted that the theoretical underpinning of modern rights theories took place somewhat later – during the seventeenth and eighteenth centuries, and particularly in the thought of Thomas Hobbes, John Locke, and

---

[17] J Waldron, *Law and Disagreement* (Oxford: Oxford University Press, 1999); J Waldron, 'The Core of the Case against Judicial Review' (2006) 115 *Yale Law Journal* 1346.

[18] MCR Craven, *The International Covenant on Economic, Social and Cultural Rights* (Oxford: Clarendon Press, 1995), 10.

[19] F Kellog, 'Natural Rights' in CB Gray (ed), *The Philosophy of Law: An Encyclopedia (Vol II)* (New York: Garland, 1999), 581–2.

[20] R Nozick, *Anarchy, State and Utopia* (Oxford: Blackwell, 1974), ix. Joel Feinberg's definition of rights suggests a similar understanding: 'generically moral rights of a fundamentally important kind held equally by all human beings, unconditionally and unalterably', *Social Philosophy* (Englewood Cliffs, NJ: Prentice-Hall, 1973), 85.

[21] For an overview of the rise of modern individualism, see Erich Fromm, *The Fear of Freedom* [1941] (London: Ark, 1984), chs 2 and 3. Cf J Witte Jr, *The Reformation of Rights: Law, Religion, and Human Rights in Early Modern Calvinism* (Cambridge: Cambridge University Press, 2007).

Jean-Jacques Rousseau. Locke and Rousseau were major influences on the American states' joint *Declaration of Independence* of 1776 and the French *Declaration of the Rights of Man and of the Citizen* of 1789 respectively. The truth-claims of these documents assert themselves to be self-evident: they refer to the existence of simple and indisputable principles – expressed in the form of natural rights – as the ultimate standard and the basis of political obligation.[22]

The most important of these natural rights theorists was John Locke (1632–1704).[23] In his *Two Treatises on Civil Government* (1690), Locke sought to underpin intellectually the ending of the Stuart dynasty and its claims to divine right in kingship. He did so in his account of the basis of government in terms of a social contract that was different from that in Hobbes's *Leviathan*. Locke's legitimation of the 'Glorious Revolution' of 1688 was based on an idea of a state of nature in which man lived according to the law of nature, accessible to him through his reason. In such a situation, argued Locke, men would not injure the 'property' of others, where others' property is understood in the broad sense of their 'lives, liberties and estates', nor would they expect encroachments on their property, but in order to make such original property rights secure, civil society was instituted:

But because no political society can be, nor subsist, without having in itself the power to preserve the property, and in order thereunto punish the offences of all those of that society, there, and there only, is political society where every one of the members hath quitted this natural power, resigned it up into the hands of the community in all cases that exclude him not from appealing for protection of the law established by it.... Those who are united into one body, and have a common established law and judicature to appeal to, with authority to decide controversies between them, and punish offenders, are in civil society one with another.[24]

'Political society', in other words, emerged when individuals ceded their natural rights to a community designed to safeguard property rights.[25] The main

[22] In addition to the influence of modern individualism in both of the revolutionary rights declarations, their rationalist style is also easily identifiable. AP d'Entrèves remarked that reason for the Roman lawyer was really another name for experience: *Natural Law* (London: Hutchinson, 2nd edn, 1970), 52; he also commented that for the medieval philosopher reason was the gift of God, ibid, 49. In both cases, he notes, 'the evidence of reason had to be implemented, and indeed confirmed, by some other evidence – of fact or of faith. But [in the Declarations of 1776 and 1789] the evidence of reason is in itself sufficient', ibid, 52.

[23] Locke has been described accurately by István Mészáros as 'the idol of modern Liberalism', I Mészáros, 'Marxism and Human Rights' in AD Falconer (ed), *Understanding Human Rights: An Interdisciplinary and Interfaith Study* (Dublin: Irish School of Ecumenics, 1980), 49.

[24] *Two Treatises on Civil Government* (ed WS Carpenter) (London: Dent, 1924) [II.VII.87], 159. When the members of this civil society choose a government for themselves, they do so by means of the will of the majority; Locke believed that this was the appropriate method for decision-making in a political community, ibid, [II.VIII.95–6] 164–5.

[25] In his discussion of the ends of political society and governments, Locke asks why free, 'natural' man surrenders his freedom and responds that the answer is obvious: '[T]hat though in a state of Nature he hath such a right, yet the enjoyment of it is very uncertain and constantly exposed to

American revolutionary document – the states' joint *Declaration of Independence* in 1776 – distils Locke's concept of natural rights and his interpretation of the social contract. Moreover, as John Kelly remarks, the original Bill of Rights, consisting of the first 10 Amendments annexed in 1791 to the United States Constitution of 1787, 'although using as its practical model the English Bill of Rights of 1689, clearly belongs in the doctrinal tradition shaped by Locke'.[26] The French *Declaration of the Rights of Man and of the Citizen* was in the same tradition as the American Declaration, but it was 'neither a pure expression of natural rights ideology nor a mere imitation of admired English or American precedents': according to d'Entrèves, the proclamation in the preamble of the French *Declaration* of the 'natural, inalienable and sacred rights of man' marks 'the end of an era and the beginning of contemporary Europe'.[27] On this account, the individualistic perspective underlying modern rights theories was a major new departure for the natural law tradition. It reflected the growing influence of individualism and economic principles associated with the expansion of the market order.[28]

As mentioned above, an alternative view of the historiography of rights discourse is that the fourteenth-century theologian, William of Occam, was the originator of subjective rights theories.[29] We discussed in the previous chapter how Occam was the key figure in opposing St Thomas's ideas concerning natural law and in contributing to the emergence of the several modern theories of natural law. Through his analysis of the terms *ius* and *ius naturale*, Michel Villey identifies William of Occam as the one who gave the first clear analyses of subjective right [*droit subjectif*] and as the originator of the subjective natural rights tradition.[30]

---

the invasion of others; for all being kings as much as he, every man his equal, and the greater part no strict observers of equity and justice, the enjoyment of the property he has in this state is very unsafe, very insecure. This makes him willing to quit this condition which, however free, is full of fears and continual dangers; and it is not without reason than he seeks out and is willing to join in society with others who are already united, or have a mind to unite for the mutual preservation of their lives, liberties and estates, which I call by the general name – property', ibid, [II.IX.123], 179–80.

[26] JM Kelly, *A Short History of Western Legal Theory* (Oxford: Clarendon Press, 1992), 270.

[27] AP d'Entrèves, *Natural Law* (London: Hutchinson, 2nd edn, 1970), 48.

[28] Louis Dupré remarks: 'The equation of a doctrine of natural law with one of natural rights developed out of a more radically individualistic questioning of the social pretenses of the contractual theory. Though the theory of rights may be *reinterpreted* within the general context of natural law…its original individualism was far removed from the natural law's fundamental assumption of the essentially social nature of the person', 'The Common Good and the Open Society' in R Bruce Douglass and D Hollenbach (eds), *Catholicism and Liberalism* (Cambridge: Cambridge University Press, 1994), 172, 180 (emphasis in original).

[29] See M Bastit, *Naissance de la loi moderne* (Paris: Presses Universitaires de France, 1990), 171–304.

[30] M Villey, 'Les origines de la notion du droit subjectif' in *Leçons d'histoire de la philosophie du droit* (Paris: Dalloz, 1962), 240. See also his 'L'idée du droit subjectif et les systèmes juridiques' (1946) 24 *Revue historique de droit français et étranger* 201; and *Seize essais de philosophie du droit* (Paris: Dalloz, 1969) Essays X, XI, and XII, 140–220, and esp Essay X, 140–78 on Occam and the genesis of subjective right.

Villey suggests that Occam persistently twisted the sense of *ius* (right or entitlement, whether positive or negative) to give it a meaning of *potestas* (power). This combination of two ideas that had formerly been quite distinct is said by Villey to have been destructive of the whole preceding natural law tradition.[31]

We have been greatly influenced by Villey's account of the nature of justice and law but we acknowledge that his account of the historical origins of subjective right has been questioned. Brian Tierney and others claim that the canon law of the twelfth and thirteenth centuries possessed both a fully developed concept of subjective rights and nascent theories of natural rights.[32] Tierney acknowledges that the phrase *ius naturale* is 'a semantic minefield',[33] but is convinced that it was in the two centuries after Gratian's *Decretum* of about 1140 – and not any later – that the phrase *ius naturale* began to acquire the sense of a subjective natural right. The *Decretum* begins with reference to the distinction between the *ius naturale* and human usages, and therefore the commentators on the *Decretum* could not avoid detailed scrutiny of the term *ius naturale*.[34] Although the scrutiny revealed that Gratian used the term inconsistently, and only sometimes meant subjective right, the subjective definitions given to *ius naturale* in some twelfth-century canonistic glosses were transmitted to seventeenth-century rights theorists in part through the encyclopedic works of late medieval lawyers and the works of sixteenth-century Spanish 'late scholastic' jurist-theologians such as Francisco de Vitoria (c 1485–1546) and Francisco de Suárez (1548–1617).[35] The other main channel of transmission was Occam, who relied more on earlier canonistic teachings than on his own innovative nominalist philosophy in formulating his theory on natural rights.

These are the diverse historical strands that led to modern subjective rights theory and in particular to the phenomenon of human rights in contemporary law. Since the end of World War II, the world has witnessed a dramatic rise in the territorial and substantive scope of human rights law. United Nations' and regional charters of rights have emerged and provided the backdrop for increasing numbers of national constitutional bills of rights. Although human rights

[31] After Occam, on this view, *ius naturale* was identified as a natural power or 'right' of an individual. Occam is thus nominated as 'the destroyer of the prior Thomistic harmony', and a line is drawn 'from Occam's rights-based polemics to the excesses of the French Revolution and eventually to modern "excesses"', CJ Reid, 'The Canonistic Contribution to the Western Rights Tradition: An Historical Inquiry' (1991) 33 *Boston College Law Review* 37, 37–8. Cf M Bastit, *Naissance de la loi moderne* (Paris: Presses Universitaires de France, 1990), 171–304.

[32] See B Tierney, *The Idea of Natural Rights* (Atlanta, GA: Scholars Press, 1997). See also B Tierney, 'Origins of Natural Rights Language: Texts and Contexts, 1150–1250', *History of Political Thought*, Vol X, No 4, winter 1989, 615.

[33] B Tierney, 'Origins of Natural Rights Language', 619.

[34] We quoted these lines in fn 1 of this chapter, and the reader may have noted that in the *Decretum* the term used is *ius naturae*.

[35] The late scholastics were the most important theologians during the period of transition from medieval to modern thought. Natural rights language was employed in their objections to the conquest and maltreatment by their compatriots of the peoples of the New World.

law is 'now a near-omnipresent phenomenon',[36] it remains incontrovertible that no *agreed* normative justification for human rights has ever been proffered by anyone, irrespective of the extent to which they have been adopted in positive law.[37] In contemporary debates, the underlying question as to whether rights can be proved actually to exist is usually developed as a series of questions concerning the *foundation* of human rights. Most common is an attempt to ground human rights in some form of political, moral, or legal theory based on the rational nature of the human being, but even among these approaches there remains persistent disagreement.[38]

The classic contemporary example of natural rights theory is John Finnis's *Natural Law and Natural Rights*. Finnis attempted a modern, secular reconstruction of St Thomas's theory and claimed that the 'basic forms of human flourishing'[39] are discernible by means of 'a simple act of non-inferential understanding [that allows one to grasp] that the object of [an] inclination which one experiences is an instance of a general form of good, for oneself (and others like one)'.[40] According to Finnis, these basic forms of human flourishing, or 'basic goods', are: life; knowledge; play; aesthetic experience; sociability or friendship; practical reasonableness; and religion. Finnis also argued that there are certain 'basic methodological requirements' of practical reasonableness. These include, for example, 'a coherent plan of life', 'no arbitrary preferences amongst values' or amongst 'persons', 'detachment and commitment', 'the [limited] relevance of consequences', 'the requirements of the common good', and 'following one's conscience'.[41] For Finnis, as MDA Freeman puts it, '[t]he "basic goods" and the "basic methodological requirements" together constitute the universal and unchanging principles of natural law'.[42] Finnis proposes that the maintenance of human rights is a 'fundamental component of the common good'.[43] He argues in favour of a range of

exceptionless or absolute human claim-rights – most obviously, the right not to have one's life taken directly as a means to any further end; but also the right not to be positively lied

---

[36] M Cohen-Eliya, 'Foreword' (2007) 1 *Journal of Law and Ethics of Human Rights* 3, 3.

[37] Obviously, if a right established in the positive law of a particular jurisdiction is labelled a 'human right' then, as we have said, in that jurisdiction in which it now exists, there is a human right.

[38] For examples, see D Richards, *A Theory of Reasons for Actions* (Oxford: Clarendon, 1971); R Dworkin, *A Matter of Principle* (Cambridge, Mass: Harvard University Press, 1985); and A Gewirth, *The Community of Rights* (Chicago: Chicago University Press, 1996). For discussion of the problematic foundations of modern human rights law, see R O'Connell, 'Do We Need Unicorns When We Have Law?' (2005) 18 *Ratio Juris* 484, 484–92. Attracta Ingram – in *A Political Theory of Rights* (Oxford: Clarendon Press, 1994) – grounds the notion of rights of the person against the state thus: 'On my account a proposition of rights is a political claim which gets its sense from the status of persons as self-governing members of a liberal democratic polity' (215). Her account seems to move from 'subjective rights' attached to lone individuals towards an understanding of rights as relations of entitlement between, in this case, the person and the state.

[39] JM Finnis, *Natural Law and Natural Rights* (Oxford: Clarendon Press, 1980), 23.

[40] Ibid, 34.   [41] Ibid, 100–33.

[42] MDA Freeman, *Lloyd's Introduction to Jurisprudence* (London: Sweet & Maxwell, 8th edn, 2008), 89.   [43] JM Finnis, *Natural Law and Natural Rights*, 218.

to in any situation (e.g. teaching, preaching, research publication, news broadcasting) in which factual communication (as distinct from fiction, jest, or poetry) is reasonably expected; and the related right not to be condemned on knowingly false charges; and the right not to be deprived, or required to deprive oneself, of one's procreative capacity; and the right to be taken into respectful consideration in any assessment of what the common good requires.[44]

Finnis's references to these rights as 'absolute' and 'exceptionless' may seem to indicate the idea of unassailability that is often associated with modern natural law thought but Finnis agrees with St Thomas in that he does not commit himself to the position that, in order to be a valid law, a law must not contradict supervening moral principles.[45] Moreover, it is difficult to consider his seven 'basic goods' as other than a reasonable account of basic values that arise in communal life; Finnis's account of basic goods is the expression of a sensitive, intelligent, reasonable, and responsible conclusion to the enquiry as to what people value. The list of basic goods is not a given, nor does Finnis think that it is. Few would disagree entirely with him but some would incline to subtract some good or add others, or to alter the meaning of one or more goods. We do not disagree with his list but think of rights differently. For us rights are jural relations arising from the fact of humans living in community; they are a function of communal life, not derivatives of any set of 'basic goods' combined with methodological principles.

   We contend that the legal system and rights discourse perform the same essential function: they provide practical and intellectual fora in which discovery of *entitlement* takes place. Again, as St Thomas wrote, the object or objective of justice 'is called the just, which is the same as "right". Hence, it is obvious that right is the object of justice'; in other words, a 'right' actually exists only when something is recognized as being due to someone or some type of person.[46] Thus, there are no *given* rights – just as there is no given natural law and no given natural justice. The first principles of moral, including jural, enquiry are not propositions but rather natural, spontaneous, and unavoidable orientations of intellect: to ask what is to be done, to try to understand, critically to examine one's hypothesis,

---

[44] Ibid, 225.

[45] 'Aquinas carefully avoids saying flatly that "an unjust law is not a law: *lex injusta non est lex*". But in the end it would have mattered little had he said just that. For the statement either is pure nonsense, flatly self contradictory, or else is a dramatization of the point more literally made by Aquinas when he says that an unjust law is not law in the focal sense of the term "law" [ie *simpliciter*] notwithstanding that it is law in the secondary sense of the term', Finnis, *Natural Law and Natural Rights*, 364. Finnis is even more explicit later on: 'Far from denying legal validity to iniquitous rules, the tradition explicitly (by speaking of unjust laws) accords to iniquitous rules legal validity, whether on the ground and in the sense that these rules are accepted in the courts as guides to judicial decision, or on the ground and in the sense that, in the judgement of the speaker, they satisfy the criteria of validity laid down by constitutional or other legal rules, or on both these grounds and in both these senses. The tradition goes so far as to say that there may be an obligation to conform to some such unjust laws in order to uphold respect for the legal system as a whole...', ibid, 365.   [46] *Summa Theologiae*, II–II, q 57, art 1.

to judge it to be correct or incorrect in the light of the available evidence, and to decide and act in accord with one's judgment. The Thomist tradition of natural law theorizing is primarily about careful, intelligent, and reasonable deliberation and responsible choice.[47] Finnis acknowledges this when he writes of the purpose of natural law theory:

> The dominant concern is with *judging for oneself* what reasons are good reasons for adopting or rejecting specific kinds of option. Societies and their laws and institutions are therefore to be understood as they would be understood by a participant in deliberations about whether or not to make the choices (of actions, dispositions, institutions, practices, etc) which shape and largely constitute that society's reality and determine its worth or worthlessness.[48]

The type of theoretical foundation for rights that is commonly searched for is a chimera. Rights-claims of any kind – including of course claims that an individual or human right exists in a given situation – represent claims to entitlement. *All* law – and *all* justice – is in this sense about 'rights': to ask what type of person in the general case and what individual in a particular case is entitled to is to ask what right exists and who has what right in that particular case. Rights, therefore, like law and 'the just', are *discovered and decided*. All law, moreover, is about potential or actual conflicts of claims, for the function of a dispute over conflicting claims is to discover and determine rights. There can be conflicting claims; only incoherently and temporarily can there be conflicting rights. The question of the substantive justice raised in particular situations by claims and arguments for rights is a matter for juridical discussion, discovery, and decision. What is *always* discovered in court is a right that resolves a conflict of claims.

[47] B Lonergan, *Method in Theology* (London: Darton Longman and Todd, 1972), chs 10 and 11.
[48] JM Finnis, 'Natural Law: The Classical Tradition' in J Coleman and S Shapiro (eds), *The Oxford Handbook of Jurisprudence and Philosophy of Law* (Oxford: Oxford University Press, 2002), 3–4 (emphasis in original).

10

The Force of Law

10.1 Introduction

The theme of law and force or coercion is an old one in the philosophy of law. The first rule or law in the oldest code we know, the *Code of Hammurabi* reads, 'If any one ensnare another, putting a ban on him, but he cannot prove it, then he that ensnared him shall be put to death',[1] and is manifestly vain if the threat cannot be enforced. As in many laws, in this the direct element of command is absent. Those to whom Hammurabi's laws are addressed are often not directly commanded, but are rather told what will result if they disobey what is implicitly commanded. Some laws, on the other hand, explicitly command or forbid but leave the threat of force implicit, as does the the first law on the tenth table in the early Roman *Twelve Tables*: 'None is to bury or burn a corpse in the city'.

In this chapter we set out a theory of law and force. A person is *directly* forced to act (or to refrain from acting) when to refrain from acting (or to act) is made physically impossible for him. Direct force may be exerted by a natural event or by another's action: by a natural event as when a storm leaves fallen trees on a road and forces one to refrain from successfully driving one's car any further; by another's action as when a thief physically constrains one to yield one's purse. A person is *indirectly* forced to act (or to refrain from acting) when the unavoidable or anticipated consequences of refraining from acting (or acting) are judged by him to outweigh the anticipated benefits of acting (or refraining from acting). Indirect force may also be exerted by a natural event or by another's action: by a natural event as when, for example, heavy rain leads one to decide not to go for a walk; by another's action as when, for example, one decides to hand over one's purse in the face of a threat of injury if one does not. As both examples of indirect force indicate, in that type of situation there remains an element of choice.

We are concerned in this discussion only with force, direct or indirect, exerted by another's action. We first examine the force of law in the specialized sense of legislation, ie enacted state or positive law; then the force of the living or communal moral law, ie custom; and, following that, the force of threat. We then discuss different possible reasons for obedience and distinguish between autonomy

---

[1] *Code of Hammurabi*, 1.

and heteronomy. We continue by clarifying further the distinction between indirect and direct force and we consider the criterion of effectiveness as a measure of the severity of a threat. The function of the threat of undesired consequence following non-compliance is to make compliance more likely. Whether or not it is effective depends entirely on the person against whom it is directed. Finally, we consider another criterion as a measure of the severity of a threat – that of taking into account the interest of the person subjected to a threat.

Throughout the chapter, we prescind from authority and legitimacy, and so distinguish force from authority and legitimacy. To prescind from something involves the idea of taking one thing at a time – what is likely to happen if a person drops a china cup on hard ground is a question that prescinds from the question as to whether or not the person has any authority or reason to do so. Similarly, what will happen if a person commands someone to do something and threatens him with dire consequences if he does not obey prescinds entirely from the question as to whether or not the person is in any way authorized or legitimately entitled to command him. Although it is not uncommon for writers to conflate the issue of the force of state law with that of its authority or legitimacy, we do not do so because we are concentrating on the fact that force can and does exist without authority or legitimacy. Because we prescind from any questions of authority or legitimacy, we effectively subsume legislation, custom and threat under command that is effective precisely because the person or persons commanding can exert force. When one prescinds from questions of authority and legitimacy to concentrate on force alone, it is clear that the command of the bank robber to the teller is then structurally identical with the command of 'sovereign' to 'subject'.[2]

10.2 The Force of Legislation, of Custom, and of Threat

Suppose that there exists in a particular jurisdiction legislation forbidding the driver of an automobile to use a mobile phone while driving. What kind of force, if any, does this exert? The question can be answered only when it is known what consequences, if any, follow, or may follow, upon using or attempting to use a mobile phone in the relevant circumstances. If there are none, then the legislation exerts no force whatsoever. The legislation is in such case no more than advice or counsel because, in St Thomas's words, '[It] has not the coercive force that law should have'.[3] Obviously, a command can exert force only if there are in the community those who can and will effectively impose the consequence of their

---

[2] These are within quotation marks to remind the reader that the terms 'sovereign' and 'subject' slip in notions of authority and legitimacy so that the sovereign's entitlement to command and the subject's duty to obey are present, as it were, by definition.
[3] *Summa Theologiae*, I–II, q 90, art 3.

disobedience on those who disobey; in other words the legislation can exert force only when an effective enforcement apparatus is in place.

Suppose that the consequence is the possibility of the driver having his licence endorsed with four penalty points. The possibility is an immediate consequence; the realization of the possibility is not. A driver who acts in accord with the traffic rules *solely* because he judges that the possible consequences outweigh the benefits is indirectly forced to refrain from using his phone. He is not actually prevented from using the phone; no direct force is exerted upon him. It is, of course, possible to imagine a situation in which a rule forbidding the use of mobile phones in a particular place directly forces compliance, as when a signal blocking reception is in place.

In the following examples we assume that, were it not for the rule, the person would act differently from the way in which the law requires him to act. Therefore, in the absence of the rule and its possible consequences, the driver would use his mobile phone; that is to say that, were the rule and its possible consequences not in place, he would understand his self-interest to be served by using the phone. Suppose that he considers that the imposition of the sanction would outweigh the benefits. If he is sure that the sanction will be imposed, he will not use the phone. But the imposition of the sanction may be merely a possibility, even a remote possibility. He will assess the risk of detection, consequent conviction, and sanction. If his assessment is that there is almost no risk of detection he may use the phone, although whether or not he does so will depend also on how unwelcome he considers the sanction to be. If his assessment is that the risk is very great he is likely not to use the phone. If he considers that detection and consequent inconvenience is certain, since by hypothesis, he considers that the imposition of the sanction outweighs the benefit of using the phone, he will not use it. Thus, his decision to use or not to use the phone depends on whether or not the perceived risk of detection and consequent inconvenience is greater than the perceived benefit of using it.

Generalizing from the example, we may say that if someone acts in accord with a rule *solely* because of the possibility of sanction, then he will disobey it whenever the perceived benefit of doing so outweighs the perceived risk of detection and consequent inconvenience. It follows that a sanction forces compliance only to the extent that a particular person considers that the probability of its imposition outweighs the perceived benefit of non-compliance. In other words, legislation forces compliance only to the extent that a person accepts the probability of the imposition of a sanction as a *reason* for acting in accord with the rule. It may be, and commonly is, the case that what will count as a reason for one person will not count as a reason for another. For someone who otherwise would not obey, legislation has coercive force only in so far as the desire to avoid the anticipated consequence of disobedience counts as a reason to obey. In this context, then, the force of law is *always* indirect, never direct.

When the force of legislation is understood in that way, it becomes clear on reflection that, structurally, it is no different from the force of the communal moral law expressed in custom: as is said in Justinian's *Institutes*, '... long last-ing customs confirmed by usage resemble law'.[4] Because the living or communal moral is older than law understood as legislation, we might better say, 'Legislation resembles custom'. Customs are socially approved ways of behaving in the appro-priate circumstances – the living law comprises those judgments and choices that in recurrent kinds of circumstances are generally accepted and approved in a particular community. Acting in accord with these customs brings approbation, approval, praise, and esteem; flouting them brings disapprobation, disapproval, blame, scorn, and derision. Humans, for the most part, look for and enjoy the esteem of those whom they admire. They try to avoid their scorn and derision. We do not first decide to prefer the esteem of such people to their scorn, and only then prefer the one to the other; we find that we do so; this is the kind of beings that we are. Why we are beings of this kind is no doubt a further question, but it is easy to forget that the question arises upon the prior discovery of the fact.

A coherent relativism would hold that the moral character of a custom – whether it is good or bad – is dependent on its being, for that community, approved or disapproved of. We made clear in Chapter 7 that we are not relativ-ists. However, it will more clearly illustrate our argument if we consider a custom that most readers will find wrong but that we suppose to be approved within a particular community.[5] We are concerned with the person who acts in accord with a custom *solely* because he thinks that the risk of discovery and subsequent scorn on the part of those whose esteem he wants outweighs the good of flouting it. A teenager, who in principle would prefer to pay his bus fare, might well decide to avoid paying it when the chance of getting away without paying presented itself thus avoiding his companions' 'scorn and derision'. The custom that he fol-lows is the approved way of acting among those whose esteem he values.

The force of the communal moral tradition – of custom – is, then, like the force of legislation, always indirect. Our hypothetical person, who would act differ-ently from the way in which the law requires him to act, chooses to act in accord with the custom only when he finds that the advantages of doing so outweigh the anticipated cost of not doing so. The anticipated cost does not directly force com-pliance. He *chooses* to comply with the customary rule rather than incur the cost of non-compliance. Indirect force offers *an anticipated fact* – scorn and derision – which the person *chooses to take as a reason* for acting. As we have acknowledged, different people perceive advantages and disadvantages differently, and accord-ingly act differently. As with legislation, custom has this indirect coercive force only if there are those in the community who can and will effectively impose the consequence of non-compliance on those who fail to act in accord with it.

---

    [4] Justinian, *Institutes*, I.III.9.
    [5] That there are differences between people as to what is considered good or bad is patent; to that extent what is good or bad is relative. Whether or not what is considered good or bad is, or could possibly be, really good or bad and to whom the real good or bad becomes clear are entirely differ-ent questions. See ch 7.2 above.

What is true of legislation and the communal moral tradition expressed in custom, is true also of threat. The gang running a protection racket threatens a shopkeeper with a consequence following the non-payment of protection money. The shopkeeper would prefer not to be threatened and will yield to the threat only if both of two conditions are fulfilled. First, he must perceive the disadvantage of the threatened consequence to be greater than the advantage of keeping his money. Secondly, he must expect that those who threaten him will carry out their threat. It may take some time and thought for him to conclude that the conditions are fulfilled but, if he concludes that they are, he will yield. As with legislation and custom, a threat constitutes indirect force. The person who makes a threat gives to the person he threatens what he hopes will be a convincing reason to yield to the threat. The person threatened and who yields is not, for instance, physically compelled to yield his money as he might be in a violent mugging or were his bag snatched from him. As with legislation and custom, he takes the threat as a reason, and chooses to act for that reason. In fact, under different guises and different names, legal sanction, communal disapproval, and threat are species of the same thing.

10.3 Other Possible Reasons for Obedience

In each case above we have assumed that the person would act otherwise were it not for the indirect force exerted by legislation, custom, or threat. There are, of course, other types of situation in which people obey the legislated rule. A second possibility arises in the case of someone utterly indifferent, in the absence of a rule, as to which way to act, but who nonetheless wishes to avoid the consequence of disobeying. To such a person, legislation enjoining a certain way of acting gives him a reason for acting in that way. For a driver indifferent as to whether or not to use dimmed headlights during daylight hours, a rule requiring their use and imposing an undesirable consequence on not using them gives him a reason to use them. To use dimmed headlights is, by hypothesis, not for him an inconvenience. Nonetheless, he uses them because of the anticipated inconvenience of not using them. The anticipated inconvenience is his reason and is, therefore, the indirect force of the legislation that produced the rule.

There is a third possibility: a person may act precisely as the rule commands but not because of the command. He may simply completely agree that the way in which the rule requires him to act is the way in which he thinks reasonable, and how he would act in its absence. Legislation or custom may require one to honour a contract that one has freely entered into. But the person who has entered into a contract may be – quite independently – of the view that he ought to honour his contract and be completely willing to do so. By entering into a contract he accepts that he puts this obligation on himself. Legislation and custom simply express what he already knows and accepts to be the case. They add only the undesirable consequence of non-compliance but this is not for him a reason. It would become a possible reason only were he tempted to break his word. St Thomas Aquinas describes those who act in this way as 'observing the law internally' rather than observing it through fear of punishment:

[T]hey are law unto themselves, having charity, that in place of law so inclines them that they act freely. Therefore, it was not necessary to impose the external law for them; but only for those who of themselves are not inclined to the good. Hence it is said in I Timothy 1:9: 'the law is not made for the just but for the unjust'. This is not to be understood, as some have done, as if the just are not held to fulfil the law; rather they are inclined of themselves to do what is just, even without the law.[6]

There is also a fourth possibility: a person may disagree with a particular rule yet consider that more harm than good would be done in the circumstances by disobeying; and so freely and autonomously, even if reluctantly, act in accord with it. But the important point is that the force of legislation, like the force of custom or threat, comes into play when fear of an anticipated, undesirable, consequential penalty becomes the reason for the person's fulfilling the law; this may arise in cases where a person would act differently if the penalty did not exist or in cases where the person is indifferent as to how to act. But force does not come into play if a person simply agrees with the way in which he is required to act and how he would act in the absence of legislation. To obey because of the threat of sanction, however wise it may be on occasion to do so, is to obey 'under coercion, not willingly'.[7] The shopkeeper who reluctantly pays for 'protection' may be wise to do so; nonetheless he does so under coercion, not willingly; he acts coerced by another's will, heteronomously, rather than autonomously.[8]

10.4 The Distinction between Direct and Indirect Force

In the light of what has been said thus far, we may clarify further the distinction between indirect and direct force. It is evident that indirect force does not

---

[6] *Summa Contra Gentiles*, III.128. St Thomas here assumes the goodness and legitimacy of law. Our present argument does not require us to make this assumption. St Thomas uses the word '*lex*' (law) in several related ways but in the question 'On the Essence of Law' where he defines law (*Summa Theologiae*, I–II, q 90, art 1) he tends to think of a law as a deliberate enactment either by the community as a whole or by the public person who has charge or care of the community and that has coercive power. In I–II, q 97, art 3, he distinguishes law (*lex*) from custom (*consuetudo*).

[7] *Summa Contra Gentiles*, III.128. What we have translated by 'under coercion, not willingly' is more literally 'in a servile manner, not freely' (*serviliter non liberaliter*), but the words are used here much as we would use them in 'When threatened, the cashier handed over the money under coercion and not willingly'.

[8] See Neil MacCormick's discussion of autonomy and heteronomy in his *Institutions of Law* (Oxford: Oxford University Press, 2007), esp 249–51. In this discussion MacCormick writes: 'If I give up smoking, not because I reflectively decide that it is right or good to do so, but because of pressure exercised by family and peer-group, or become of some enforced unavailability of tobacco, or under pressure of a legal ban on smoking in enclosed public spaces, the resultant state (my not smoking) may be on some view better than the former, but no moral credit belongs to me for this.' This is an example of acting heteronomously as opposed to autonomously.

compel performance. It is effective only when the threat of the direct force consequent on non-compliance is perceived to outweigh the advantages. In the limit, it is ineffective since a person may choose, and in fact many have chosen, death rather than compliance, showing that the direct force consequent on non-compliance has not forced compliance.

A jail sentence consequent on fraudulent dealing follows fraudulent dealing because the indirect force, the threat of punishment, has failed. The sentence is direct force in that it limits the fraudster's freedom by means of imprisonment. In as much as it may become a reason for future compliance, it can exert only indirect force. It is important to note also that direct force is not to be identified with physical force. Torture is an example of physical force, but is indirect. The torturer's expectation is that the anticipation of further, and perhaps more extreme, torture will become for his victim a reason for agreeing to the torturer's demands.

Legislation is supported by direct force in cases where the action forbidden is rendered impossible or the action commanded is rendered inevitable as when a state legislates against some usages of the internet and, more or less successfully, blocks the signal; or forbids a radio station to broadcast and physically closes it down; or requires residents to pay a tax and deducts the money at source; or forbids people to enter a particular area and uses law enforcement officers physically to prevent them. The list is indefinitely long but the examples show that when a person is directly forced to act or to refrain from acting, choice is absent. It is, therefore, better to say that, rather than acting, he is acted upon.

10.5 The Criterion of Effectiveness

The measure of the success of a threat is its effectiveness, for the function of the threat of an undesired consequence following non-compliance is to make compliance more likely. Whether or not it is effective depends entirely on the person against whom it is directed. It is obvious that the same threat directed to many different people in general may be, and in fact usually is, effective in the case of some, and ineffective in the case of others. So, a parent dealing with several children may on occasion threaten different children with different consequences on the grounds that what is likely to be an effective deterrent for one is unlikely to be for another. However, when dealing with many unknown people, it is often impracticable to make different threats. If one's *sole* purpose is to bring about compliance, and one's power to do so is indefinitely great, one will make a threat that one expects to be effective in most or even in all cases. The bank robber, whose only criterion is the success of his threat, will not hesitate to threaten death in the expectation that this threat will be effective in almost all cases. Similarly, the well-established, well-protected, megalomaniac dictator is likely to threaten whatever consequence he thinks will be effective.

The person who is convinced that to inflict torture on his captive will produce the desired result, whose sole interest is in getting the result he desires, and who has no concern whatsoever for the moral character of the means – in this case, torture – will inflict ever more extreme and inhumane torture. Such a torturer might be convinced by an argument that attempted to show that torture was an ineffective means; that is, by an argument that attempted to show that his chosen means would not achieve the intended result. But he would not be convinced by an argument that attempted to show that his chosen means was wrong in any other respect; for, by hypothesis, he has no interest in the means beyond their presumed effectiveness. Provided, therefore, that the *sole* purpose is to achieve a result and the moral character of the means is taken to be irrelevant, the choice of what is taken to be an effective means is comprehensible and, in one use of the word, even rational.

When anticipated effectiveness is the sole criterion, there is no reason to balance the severity of the threat against the seriousness of the action. In this context, the only question that arises following the suggestion to threaten execution if a driver is discovered to have used his mobile phone while driving is whether or not the threat would be effective. Although there is a distinction between effectiveness which pays no attention to cost, and efficiency which does, when anticipated effectiveness is the sole criterion, neither the question of cost nor even the question as to whether one should threaten no more than what is thought to be necessary to ensure compliance arises. If effectiveness is the sole criterion, the only argument against a threat is that it is likely to be ineffective. Conversely, someone who has chosen not to make a threat that he thought would have been effective *vis-à-vis* a desired result cannot but have been influenced in his choice by some other criterion.

When a threat is directed against a large number of people who differ from one another, the question as to its effectiveness becomes more difficult. Suppose there are 100 people and the purpose of the threat is to deter everyone from disobeying a rule that prohibits the use of a mobile phone while driving. Suppose that three threats are suggested as consequences of disobedience: (1) four penalty points in a system where the consequence of 12 accumulated points is loss of licence for one year; (2) immediate loss of licence for three years; (3) immediate loss of licence for 10 years. Since by definition a threat is supposed to be effective, a threat that is expected to deter no one is pointless. On the supposition that each of the three proposals is expected to be in some measure effective, which one is it rational to choose *when effectiveness is the only criterion*? If the first penalty were expected to deter only 20 people, the second a further 40, and the third a further 20, then, on the criterion of effectiveness, the third would be the only rational choice. One would be left with the remaining 20. If one supposed that a more severe penalty would be effective – for instance, the death penalty – it would be rational not to impose it only in case one was in fact using another criterion.

In this chapter we have concentrated on force, and have deliberately prescinded from questions relating to the authority and legitimacy of the legal system and its legislation. We have prescinded also both from the *content* of the command and from any function that it might properly have beyond the benefit to the person commanding. No question of benefit to the person or persons commanded has yet been raised. But that question is in the wings and makes its first appearance in the next and final section of this chapter.

10.6 The Criterion of the Interest of Those Commanded

No question beyond its effectiveness can arise when a threat is considered in the context within which effectiveness is the sole criterion. A question as to its severity, considered apart from effectiveness, can arise only within another context. In this new context, precisely what is excluded in the more restricted context is included: namely, *the interest of the person or persons commanded*. In our absurd example of a death penalty for using a mobile phone while driving, the proposed penalty overrides any benefit to the person commanded; whoever finds the penalty too severe does so, not because he thinks that it will be ineffective, but precisely because he thinks the benefit, namely the benefit to the person commanded of remaining alive, is to be taken into account.

The example is absurd; therefore, let us place our discussion in a more realistic context. What is neither absurd nor imagined is the gradual abandonment of capital punishment in Europe. That gradual dialectical movement is associated with a conviction that in principle it is wrong to injure another, and therefore that for the most part to kill another is wrong, which latter conviction is associated with the conviction that, again for the most part, humans desire to remain alive. The modern expression of these convictions can obscure the idea that the right is linked to the spontaneous desire, an idea central to both St Thomas and Hobbes.[9]

Why is capital punishment thought to be wrong?[10] There are three very different types of reason. First, it may be thought ineffective, or not as effective as some other possible threat. Secondly, it may be thought to be dangerous

---

[9] *Summa Theologiae*, I–II, q 94, art 2. In this question St Thomas quite explicitly links a prohibition against murder with the spontaneous desire or inclination to remain alive: 'And from this inclination [the desire to continue in being] it follows that it belongs to natural law to maintain human life and to oppose what impedes it.' In *Leviathan* Hobbes writes: 'For he that should . . . performe all he promises . . . where no man els should do, should make himselfe a prey to others, and procure his own certain ruine, contrary to the ground of all Lawes of Nature, which tend to Natures preservation', 215 [80].

[10] The question may be glossed by an addition: Why is capital punishment thought to be wrong *by those who think it wrong*? Those convinced that capital punishment is wrong easily overlook the fact that this conviction is not universally shared. Many people in states where capital punishment no longer exists remain in favour of it; in many states throughout the world it survives.

in that it is likely to lead to civil unrest and the consequent danger of the overthrow of those in power from whom the threat emanates. The exercise of power that utterly ignores the interests of those over whom the power is wielded undermines their acquiescence and can, and in the end often does, lead to revolt against it, and so runs against the interest of the person commanding who wishes to remain in power.[11] Thirdly, capital punishment may be thought wrong because the interest of the condemned person is wrongly overridden.

The first and second of these reasons may be wholly within the context or perspective of the ruler's exclusive interest. The third reason is simply not a reason within that context. If one's actions are guided by one's exclusive interest, the interest of others, unless it affects that exclusive interest, is an irrelevant fact that is not, for the actor, a reason for action. The third reason takes account of the interests of others; it is a reason only for someone whose moral context or perspective includes the value that account is to be taken of others' interests. The fact that a person desires to remain alive and not to be executed has, when this value is included, become at least a possible reason for not executing him. Abstracted from that context, the person's desire not to be executed is simply a fact. Nothing at all in any way follows from that fact until it is placed in the context of valuing others' interests.[12]

As we have argued throughout this book, the precept that one should take account of others' interests pervades the Western and other jurisprudential traditions. The argument here is that to the discussion of threat and the force of law it brings in principle, and in fact has brought, a criterion other than effectiveness. Because humans are social beings and cannot but live in association with one another, it is impossible to ignore the fact that others may have interests other than one's own; a command is supported by sanction precisely because the person commanding anticipates that the interest of at least some of those to whom the command is given may be to disobey. Yet the fact that another's interest may run counter to one's own prompts the question as to how to deal with others' interests. It does not determine the answer. The criterion, expressed in the three

[11] This issue arose starkly in 1968 during a famous televised discussion between William F Buckley Jr and Norman Mailer. Mailer had been sentenced to five days in prison as a result of his involvement in an anti-Vietnam war demonstration (which involvement had inspired his Pulitzer-Prize winning 1968 book, *The Armies of the Night* (New York: New American Library)). Mailer stated that he had been fully prepared deliberately to break the law and to serve such a sentence because he wished to protest strongly against the war. When pressed by Buckley as to what severity of punishment might have made him decide not to disobey the law, Mailer responded that if the punishment for his protest were to be life imprisonment he would 'go underground', 'leave the country' or turn into 'an enemy of the country'.

[12] With Hume, we hold that no value follows from a sheer fact; hence, we insist that only within a context of value – here the valuing of another's interest – does anything follow from the person's desire not to be executed.

precepts of justice in Justinian's *Digest*, however traditional it may be, is but one of the possible answers.[13]

It is bootless to make a threat that is universally ineffective or that the person threatened knows will not be carried out. Clearly, however, the known threat has been ineffective in the case of a person who, despite it, has disobeyed. What the new criterion brings is the idea that it is not unquestionably right to make a threat indefinitely more severe. The new criterion – the valuing of others' interests – gives, to the person who disobeys a law, a new right that limits the right of the person imposing the law. What the limits should be in a particular case remains to be determined; the new criterion raises a new question, the answer to which in different situations is yet to be determined. So we do not deduce from the idea that another's interest is to be taken into account, the idea that in all cases to kill another is wrong.[14]

The criterion that the other person's interest is to be taken into account allows an important and clear distinction between one who accepts that criterion and one who ignores it. The robber who requires the bank teller to hand over money or be shot issues a threat that stems purely from the criterion of effectiveness. The ruler who commands his subjects to act in a certain way on pain of a fine, although he expects that this threat will not be in all cases effective, acts, whether or not he recognizes this explicitly, from the criterion of others' rights. These examples may, however, seriously mislead. It is perfectly possible to imagine a robber who accepts a limit based on his acceptance of the others' interest; there are robbers who are prepared to wound but not to kill. Equally, it is perfectly possible to imagine a ruler whose interest is exclusively his own and whose threats are based solely on their anticipated effectiveness in ensuring that what he commands is done. For this reason, Cicero does not contrast robber and sovereign but rather uses the more traditional contrast between tyrant and good ruler.[15]

We have not here dealt with the issue of the legitimacy and authority of command: in what circumstances, if any, is X entitled to command Y? We raise that question in the next chapter when we discuss the authority and legitimacy of law. Here, we have been concerned only with the force that one who issues a command to another is *able* to use. But even if someone is *entitled* to command, even if what he commands is good, the assertion that he is entitled to use indefinite force is sustainable only if it is assumed that he acts – and is entitled to act – within a context wholly defined by his exclusive interest. Only within that context is he

---

[13] The association between doing harm to another and justice is taken up in the second of the three precepts of justice in Justinian's *Digest*: 'The basic principles of right are to live honourably, not to harm any other person, to render to each his own', *Digest*, I.I.10; *Institutes*, I.I.3.

[14] Cicero writes of killing another as the greatest crime yet discusses, in Book III of *On Duties*, why it is moral to kill a tyrant. See our discussion of this in ch 11.6 below.

[15] Cicero, *On Duties*, Book III.

'entitled' to command whatever he wills whilst others are 'entitled' to nothing. The argument that he is not so entitled rests on the idea that others' interests are to be taken into account. Only in a context in part defined by that idea does the idea of the subject's yet to be determined entitlement make sense. Perhaps few rulers have reached the limit where the independent interest of their subjects – those in their power – is utterly irrelevant but that there have been, are, and no doubt will be, those whose rule approaches that limit cannot be doubted.

11

The Authority and Legitimacy of Law

11.1 Introduction

In our discussion of the force of law we prescinded completely from questions of authority and legitimacy. Now, turning to discuss the authority and legitimacy of law, we prescind from force. Both the living law and legislation are supported by force; the threat of punishment associated with command is neither vain nor merely extrinsic, for when force is entirely absent a command becomes merely counsel or advice. Similarly, it is normally the case that adjudication is combined with the power or force to ensure that decisions are implemented. However, the source of the authority of custom, legislation, or judicial decision is not merely the force that happens to be available to community, ruler, or judge, unless 'authority' is no more than a deliberately misleading name for a force the real character of which it is intended to conceal.

What, then, is the source of authority? This is an ancient, recurrent, and contentious question. We first deal with the word 'authority' and distinguish between two senses or meanings that attach to it for there are two distinct aspects to authority. The first is when it is used to refer to the relation of ruler to subject: authority in this modality means that the ruler is entitled to command, and the subject is obliged to obey. Entitlement and obligation are reciprocal so that it makes no sense to say that a ruler is entitled to command if his subject is in no sense obliged to obey; nor does it make sense to suggest that a subject is obliged to obey a ruler who is not entitled to command him.

Secondly, 'authority' is also used to refer to the relation between teacher and student, between expert and learner. So, to take a very ordinary example of this second sense of the term, if Peter is lost in a city unfamiliar to him, he may approach someone whom he takes to be knowledgeable and ask the way to where he wants to go. His hope is that the person is an authority in the relevant domain, here the geography of the city, and will agree to tell Peter what he wants to know. Suppose that Peter has chosen rightly. The person knows how, and is willing, to guide Peter. In this brief encounter the person asked is the teacher or expert, the questioner is the student or learner. The person asked is an authority because he knows. When he is asked the way, he is faced with two basic choices. He must decide whether or not to answer; and, if he has decided to answer, he must decide whether or not to tell the truth.

When the questioner asks the way, he asks in effect two questions. He wants to know the way; but also he wants to know if he has hit upon an expert. The honest and helpful person unfamiliar with the city is likely to say that he is sorry that he cannot help because he is not an expert, not an authority. The honest and helpful person who is an authority is likely to give a set of directions. His answer tells the questioner, implicitly, that he is an authority and, explicitly, that if the directions are followed the destination will be reached.

What is the position of the questioner relative to the answer he has been given? In this second sense of 'authority', he is, in this example, not obliged to follow the directions that the authority has given him. Nonetheless, there is something quite odd about someone who, having asked how to get to to where he wants to go, and having been given, and having believed, an answer giving him directions, simply ignores the directions, and continues his journey as if he had not been given them.[1] His action is unreasonable. Believing what he has been told, he now accepts, for example, that if he wants to get to where he wants to go, he should take the next right turn and yet when he comes to the turn he deliberately continues straight along. The meaning of 'should' here is not that he is obliged to follow the instructions given because they were given by the authority; if it makes any sense to say that he should follow the instructions, it is that he should do what he considers to be reasonable. He understands that, in order to reach his desired destination, he should turn right; but his thinking this is founded on his belief in the truthfulness and expertise of the person who gave the directions. In this second sense of 'authority', an authority is one who is both truthful and expert, that is, reliable. Still, unless one supposes an authority to be infallible in the relevant domain, the question arises as to the correctness of the authority's opinion. What is crucial is not that the authority be infallible, for this is impossible, but that he be sufficiently expert for it to be reasonable to believe him. Crucial also is that there *are* correct answers, and that it is possible intelligently and reasonably to reach them. In the absence of the possibility of correct answers, authority in this second sense is fraudulent.[2]

There are, then, two senses of 'authority'. First, a ruler is said to be in 'authority' over his subject in that the ruler is entitled to command his subject who, reciprocally, is obliged to obey. We have as yet said little about the source of authority of

---

[1] 'To believe' is commonly used as, or nearly as, synonymous with 'to know'. It is not so used here. Here 'to believe' is 'to hold something to be the case on the authority of another whom one presumes to know it to be the case'. 'A belief' is the content of an act of believing. Someone who personally works out that a belief is true, moves from believing to knowing.

[2] If, because error is always possible, an authority should never be believed, there would be no reason ever to ask even so commonplace a question as how to get to somewhere. If one is utterly lost but in the company of one familiar with the locality, one need not think one's companion infallible to think it wise to follow his lead. If no proposed answer is better than any other, the very idea of authority in this second sense is meaningless; the suspicion that this is the case is at the root of radical positivism (and, indeed, relativism) in which the law can be nothing more than what the authority in the first sense, or sheer force, establishes.

this type. Secondly, a person is said to be an 'authority' in as much as he is expert in a domain and worthy of belief, although not infallible. The source of authority of this type is expertise, truthfulness or, in moral affairs, wisdom.

We must eventually discuss the relationship between these different types of authority in the legal domain, but first we consider a story from the life of Cormac Mac Airt, a High King of Ireland in the third century AD. The story contrasts the two distinct senses of authority. It is significant that Cormac Mac Airt was a 'king-judge', both the legislator and the adjudicator, because the two senses or modalities of authority are relevant to both roles. Our focus initially in this chapter is on adjudication. After considering the story, we address the questions of why adjudicative authority emerged in human society, and why its authoritative position is based on its supposed ability to discern what is just. Adjudication is a method of resolving disputes peacefully. Two further questions arise. First, what evidence is there that adjudication is a method of resolving disputes peacefully? Secondly, why would contending parties accept the method? We emphasize the reasonableness of the adjudicative procedure as a method of maintaining and achieving peace. The source of authority in the second modality is wisdom: the judge's authority rests on his ability and willingness to discover what is just in a given set of circumstances. Such knowledge, ability, and willingness, in the context of a given set of material and jural facts, are required and expected in adjudication. They are, in other words, fundamental prerequisites of authoritative adjudication in addition to those relating to a judge's formal entitlement to adjudicate. Finally, we discuss the essentially contestable and ambiguous nature of the 'legitimacy' of the sovereign or other holder of authority. Although the discussion of authority concentrates on adjudication and the discussion of legitimacy on legislation, an understanding of both modalities of authority is necessary in both the adjudicative and the legislative domain and the reader may extrapolate our arguments and conclusions from one domain to the other.

11.2 A Tale of Two Modalities of Authority

The tale of Cormac Mac Airt's judgment on trespassing sheep as recounted in Fergus Kelly's *A Guide to Early Irish Law* contrasts the two modalities of authority:

As a young man he [Cormac] was approaching the gates of Tara [the seat of the High King] for the first time, when he saw the steward of king Mac Con telling a woman something which caused her to weep. He enquired what was wrong, and was told that the woman's sheep had broken into the queen's woad-garden and had eaten the leaves off the plants. Mac Con had passed judgement that the woman's sheep be forfeit for their offence, and this was the cause of her distress. Cormac immediately pointed out to the steward that the judgement should have been 'one shearing for another' i.e. the woman should have had to forfeit only the shearings of her sheep in recompense for the shearing of the woad-plants. When Mac Con was told of this judgement he immediately realized that he had been guilty of injustice, and handed over the kingship of Tara to Cormac.

Kelly remarks that 'Though this tale is obviously apocryphal, it serves to illustrate the enormous importance which the early Irish attached to the concept of *fír flathemon*, "king's justice".'[3]

For a discussion of authority, this story is extremely illuminating. King Mac Con, the Irish High King and therefore supreme ruler *and* judge, had handed down a judgment in a commonplace, but socially important (since the queen was involved) civil dispute. The woman's sheep had broken into and damaged the queen's woad-garden. No contributory negligence on the queen's part is suggested and it is assumed that the owner of the woad-garden has some claim against the owner of the sheep. This particular dispute is a particular instance of the court's question as to what in these circumstances belongs to whom and is in the realm of rectificatory justice.[4] It is a particular instance of the court's question as to what in these circumstances belongs to whom. As we have reiterated throughout this book, the function of the judge is to declare what in the instant case the entitlements are.

In this case, sheep entered a place where woad was growing and ate the leaves of the plants. These are the essential non-jural, sometimes called material, facts. Again, by 'non-jural' or 'material' we mean facts that simply describe what took place and that do not refer to the bundle of entitlements that make up the jural community. All the other facts are jural; among the more significant of these are that the garden and the woad leaves were owned by the queen; that the woman owned the sheep; that her sheep ought not have broken into the queen's garden; that the woman was responsible for what her sheep had done; and that, consequently, the queen was entitled to bring an action for damages against her. Whatever questions may have arisen at an earlier stage in the society concerning the movement and behaviour of domestic animals, and the responsibility of their owners for damage caused by them, by the time of the story they had been answered. Cormac Mac Airt, when he argues against King Mac Con's judgment, takes it as given that the woman was responsible for her sheep, and that they ought not to have broken into the garden. That King Mac Con is the proper

[3] F Kelly, *A Guide to Early Irish Law* (Dublin: Dublin Institute for Advanced Studies, 1988), 240. The word *fír* translated here by Kelly as 'justice' has also the meaning 'truth'; and from it come into modern Irish and Scots Gaelic *fíor* and *fír* both of which mean 'truth'. It is worth noting that in the story Cormac is not just any passerby but one already known for his wisdom and already a possible successor. T Ó Cathasaigh, *The Heroic Biography of Cormac Mac Airt* (Dublin: Dublin Institute for Advanced Studies, 1977). It is also worth remarking that Ireland in the third century AD was not a unified state and that the High King-judge did not closely resemble a modern legislator. He was more like a Supreme Court (as he is in the tale).

[4] It is possible to argue that the justice involved is distributive since the task of the court is in the circumstances to distribute the remaining relevant goods among the relevant owners. The distinction between rectificatory and distributive justice, as we remarked in ch 4 above, is very much a rule of thumb rather than a strict or rigid analytical distinction.

person before whom the dispute between the litigants should have been brought is also taken for granted. The question as to who should adjudicate in such cases had been settled.[5]

Cormac argues against Mac Con's judgment that the sheep should be forfeit, and suggests that only the shearings are due. Mac Con's reason for his judgment is not given. Cormac's judgment is reasoned: one shearing for one crop. It is plain, however, that both judgments are of the same form: a statement of what is due to each person involved. The queen is due – that is, entitled to – the ownership of the sheep in Mac Con's judgment but, in Cormac's judgment, is entitled only to the shearings. The woman's due or entitlement is to hand over her sheep according to Mac Con, or only the shearings according to Cormac.[6]

'When Mac Con was told of this (Cormac's) judgment he immediately realized that he had been guilty of injustice, and handed over the kingship of Tara to Cormac.' The injustice of which he had been guilty was what he only now sees as a mistaken assessment of what was due to each litigant. The clear suggestion in the story is that Mac Con discovered his mistake only on learning of what seemed to him to be the manifest correctness and justice of Cormac's determination of entitlements. The story presents Mac Con's judgment as mistaken, and Cormac's judgment as correct, and tells that Mac Con, convinced of this and for that reason, resigned his position to Cormac. There is no suggestion that Mac Con acted otherwise improperly.

Both modalities of authority are at work in the story. In the first modality, the High King is entitled to hear and settle disputes. Others are required to bring their disputes to him if they cannot settle them peaceably and without resort to violence. The king's judgment is to be implemented. Those to whom the judgment is handed down are required to implement it. Force is present in the background, but in the foreground is the idea that the king's judgments ought to be followed. The judgment establishes what the entitlements are, and commands that they be implemented.

The second modality of authority is at work also. Cormac, when he hears of the King's judgment, at once points out that it is mistaken. Mac Con, when he learns of Cormac's judgment, agrees with it, and hands over the kingship. Thus Kelly writes that the tale highlights the enormous importance which the early Irish attached to the concept of *fír flathemon*, the ruler's judgement, or truth. It illustrates not only the enormous importance of the *fír flathemon* but also, implicitly yet clearly, an important jurisprudential notion of the relationship between the just judgment and the authority of the judge.

---

[5] Less obvious, perhaps, but equally important, is the assumption in the story that the disputants should bring their dispute before the king-judge rather than resort to violence. That question, too, had been settled.

[6] In modern English it is distinctly odd to speak of the requirement laid on the woman to hand over her sheep or their shearings as an 'entitlement', but see our discussion of rights as entitlements in ch 9.2 above.

Regarding the first modality of authority, the existence of the judicial position is accepted. The king is the person entitled to hear and pronounce judgment on the cases brought before him. The 'rule of law' is so developed that disputants are required to bring their disputes forward if they are unable to settle them peaceably themselves, and required to accept the king's judgment.[7] There are two aspects to the requirement. On the one hand, it is an element in the rule of law that disputants accept the judgment; they are, in principle, morally obliged or obligated to do so. Their obligation is intrinsic. On the other hand, they are obliged – ie compelled or coerced – in that the king's judgment will be enforced on those who refuse to act in accord with it. Their obligation is extrinsic.[8]

Why are disputants morally obliged or obligated to act in accord with the king's judgment? Not simply because the king is entitled to hear the case and they are required and compelled to bring it before him rather than to have recourse to violence in case they fail to resolve it peacefully between themselves. They are morally obliged because the king-judge is supposed to be authoritative in the second sense of the term; his judgment will tell what is just, what in these circumstances is due to whom. The judge's authority, in the second modality, rests on his ability and willingness to discover what is just on this occasion. In the tale, Mac Con is very obviously not corrupt; his honourable character is shown in his willingness to resign when he discovers his error. He was simply mistaken. He knew that his task was to balance the damage done by a suitable recompense. The damage done cannot be undone; it is accepted that the owner is responsible for the damage caused by the sheep; it is accepted that the specific question is this: what is due from the woman who owned the sheep to the woman who owned the woad-garden? Mac Con, it may be surmised, considered that the garden had been destroyed and that, consequently, the flock should be given in compensation. The woman who owned the sheep was, for obvious reasons, upset by the judgment but may also have been unconvinced by it. Still, as must be the case in any adjudication system, *res judicata pro vero tenetur*; the judgment, although not infallible and so possibly mistaken, must be acted upon, for in practical jurisprudential matters time presses otherwise than in pure enquiry, and undue delay compounds injustice.

The tale implicitly rejects a completely positivist account of adjudication in which the 'just' or 'correct' solution is stipulated to be what the judge decides. 'Cormac immediately pointed out to the steward that the judgment should have been "one shearing for another"'. Cormac's judgment is based on a different jural interpretation of the material facts from that of Mac Con: the sheep did not destroy the garden; they destroyed only this year's crop. The sheep are said to

---

[7] Cf *The Twelve Tables*, Table 1.1: 'If anyone summons a man before the magistrate, he must go. If the man summoned does not go, let the one summoning him call the bystanders to witness and then take him by force.'

[8] See HLA Hart, *The Concept of Law* (Oxford: Clarendon Press, 2nd edn, 1994), ch. V, §2 'The Idea of Obligation', 82–91.

'have eaten the leaves off the plants'; had they been goats, that might well have eaten the bushes also, the situation would have been relevantly different. Having destroyed only this year's crop, the just balance was not the transfer in perpetuity of the flock from the woman to the queen, but the transfer of the corresponding crop yielded by the flock, namely, this year's shearing. Mac Con, being both honourable as well as juridically intelligent, at once realized and acknowledged his error, and, having done so, recognized that Cormac, not he, was the authority, that is, the one more adept at discovering the just solution. Once he recognized Cormac's authority in the second modality, Mac Con 'handed over the kingship', that is, the authority in the first sense of the word, to him.

From a strictly positivist perspective, the tale is jurisprudential nonsense. Mac Con is judge, the 'just solution' is stipulated to be what the judge decides, and so, on the assumption that his is the court of final appeal, Mac Con's judgment is the correct solution. From such a perspective there is no more to be said. Since Cormac is not a superior judge and so does not have judicial authority his judgment is irrelevant to the dispute. But neither he nor Mac Con thinks so. Both are convinced that there is a just solution to be found; that one proposed solution may be discovered, and agreed, to be better than another. The importance of agreement is emphasized in the tale by Mac Con's acceptance of Cormac's judgment and his realization 'that he had been guilty of injustice', and that consequently he had done the woman an injury.[9]

Authority in both modalities is central to the tale; if either one is overlooked the tale deviates into incoherence. Overlook the first modality of authority and the relative positions of Mac Con and Cormac disappear; neither one is entitled to judge and Mac Con, who in the tale hands over the kingship, that is, among other things, the entitlement to judge, has nothing to hand over. Overlook the second modality of authority and there is no reason at all for Mac Con to hand over the kingship. To understand the tale properly, both modalities of authority must be kept in mind.

There is one more crucially significant notion underlying the story. Mac Con hands over the kingship – authority in its first modality – because it is Cormac, not he, who gave the better judgment, is the better judge, and so has authority in its second modality. Thus, in the story, it is authority in its second modality that underlies and can undermine authority in its first modality; the entitlement to judge is thought to be based on an ability to discern what is just; but a supposed ability to discern what is just is fraudulent if what is just in no sense whatsoever exists to be discerned.[10] It is equally important to make clear that a person's ability to discern what is just does not *ipso facto* confer on him the entitlement

---

[9] 'For a person against whom the praetor or judge pronounces an unjust sentence is said to have received an injury', Justinian, *Institutes,* IV.IV.Preamble.

[10] If what is just *in no sense whatsoever exists* it cannot be found; if it exists precisely how it exists is another, difficult, and disputed question. Certainly, the as-yet-undiscovered-just does not exist in the same way that the as-yet-undiscovered-fact exists.

to judge. The two authorities are related but they remain distinct, and even if one depends fundamentally on the other, it does not derive from it alone.

The relationship between the two senses of 'authority' may be illustrated in another domain. Consider an historian perfectly well able to teach history in a university – he is an authority in the second modality – but until he is appointed he is not yet entitled to teach – he has not authority in the first modality. If the historian presents himself as a candidate for a teaching position – that is, seeks authority in the first modality – those considering his candidacy will normally investigate his eligibility – that is, they will attempt to discover whether or not he is an authority in the second modality. However, it sometimes happens that those who make such appointments err, and choose a candidate who is not in fact an authority in the second sense of the term. He is given the position, that is, authority in the first modality is conferred on him; but the competence that should ground his entitlement to teach is missing. His authority in the first modality remains but is vitiated; he cannot do properly what he has the authority to do. His entitlement to teach derives directly from his appointment, but is related to a mistakenly supposed capacity on the basis of which the appointment was made.[11]

In the tale, Mac Con hands over the kingship because he recognizes that he is no longer an authority in the second sense of the term, and that Cormac is the one with this authority.[12] In the tale, had the kingship not been handed over, Cormac, despite being presented as giving the correct judgment, and thus having authority in its second modality, lacked authority in the first modality, and so was not entitled to administer justice. The story of Mac Con and Cormac subtly plays with the two modalities of authority and thus implicitly depends upon a theory of jurisprudence that was almost certainly not explicit in the writer's mind. The idea that the judge's entitlement to render judgment rests on his ability to judge correctly is not peculiar to this tale; it is very ancient and appears already as the fifth law in the *Code of Hammurabi*:

If the judge try a case, reach a decision, and present his judgement in writing; if later error shall appear in his decision, and it is through his own fault, then he shall pay twelve times the fine set by him in the case, and he shall be publicly removed from the judge's bench, and never again shall he sit there to render judgment.[13]

The reader may remark that the sanction for one misjudgment on the part of the judge in both the tale and in Hammurabi's *Code* is severe: the judge loses the entitlement to adjudicate, that is, he loses authority in its first modality. There

---

[11] It is worth noting, in passing, that those that made the appointment had the first-modality authority to do so, and that that authority was associated with a presumed second-modality authority to judge prudently as to the eligibility of candidates.

[12] The Irish story does not say that in every case of misjudgment the judge is required to resign; being a story it simply recounts one occasion on which resignation followed mistake. It may also have been that resignation was the only way for Mac Con to vacate his judgment.

[13] *Code of Hammurabi*, 5.

are some differences between them: the nature and extent of adjudicative error warranting loss of adjudicative entitlement is formally set out in the *Code*, and the judge must be at fault, a feature that is absent from the Irish tale, in which the misjudgment is presented as simply an error although the ideal that the judge ought to be able to judge justly remains and is known to, and understood by, the various parties involved. It is a feature of the living law that forms the background to judgment. There is nothing remarkable about the fact that in the tale Mac Con hands over the kingship to Cormac although it is nowhere written down that he should do so; it is not remarkable, precisely because, as Fergus Kelly says, it reflects the enormous importance that the early Irish attached to the concept of 'king's justice' or truth.

Contemporary legal systems do not generally enforce a severe sanction for the misuse of adjudicative authority. Partly owing to what is seen as the need for strict judicial independence, which is expressed strongly in separation of powers theory, the impeachment sanction is not frequently invoked in any jurisdiction. Moreover, judges tend not to resign voluntarily for erroneous judgments that they may accept that they have made. Judges do, however, sometimes in subsequent judgments and sometimes when writing extra-judicially or from the vantage point of retirement, acknowledge mistakes on their part. One can say that in doing so they acknowledge the importance of adjudicative authority in its second modality even if they work within a system that does not require, as was required in ancient Babylon and in the ancient Irish story, that a single misjudgment should entail the loss of the entitlement to judge.

That the tale contrasts two distinct senses or modalities of authority is no guarantee that they exist. The jurisprudential theory that is the presupposition of the tale may well be mistaken, and reliance on it for guidance in an adjudicative system may well be misplaced. Still, two senses or modalities of authority are clearly distinguished. They exist, if not in reality, at least as ideas. It is worth examining each one separately. Because they are distinct, it is not unreasonable to work on the hypothesis that the reasons for their emergence will be different. We must ask, then, in relation to the first modality of authority, why adjudicative authority emerged; and in relation to the second modality, why that authority is based on its supposed ability to discern what is just.

11.3 Authority as Legal Entitlement

Considering authority in the first modality (and prescinding as far as possible from discussion of authority in the second modality), we may ask: why did judges and the function of adjudication emerge in human society? We have discussed, in Chapter 6, how impartiality is intrinsic to adjudication; here our focus is on impartiality as intrinsic to *authoritative* adjudication. Thomas Hobbes gives his answer in his discussion on what he calls 'the other Lawes of Nature' in the third chapter of *De Cive* and in the fifteenth chapter of *Leviathan*. Hobbes's two answers to the question are not identical but the core meaning is the same. We quote here from *De Cive*, and give the version from *Leviathan* in a footnote:

> Furthermore because, although men should agree to make all these and whatsoever other laws of nature, and should endeavour to keep them, yet doubts and controversies would daily arise concerning the application of them unto their actions, to wit, whether what were done were against the law or not, which we call the question of right; whence will follow a fight between the parties, either side supposing themselves wronged: it is therefore necessary to the preservation of peace, because in this case no other fit remedy can possibly be thought on, that both the disagreeing parties refer the matter unto some third, and oblige themselves by mutual compacts to stand to his judgment in deciding the controversy. And he to whom they thus refer themselves is called an arbiter. It is therefore the fifteenth precept of the natural law, *that both parties disputing concerning the matter of right, submit themselves unto the opinion and judgment of some third*.[14]

This conclusion, theorem, dictate of reason, or 'natural law' is clearly Hobbes's answer to the question: why are adjudicators – Hobbes uses indifferently 'arbiters', 'arbitrators', 'judges', 'umpires' – necessary? Hobbes's overarching question to which others are subordinate is this: what is needed if 'men in multitudes' are to live together without a state of constant war 'where every man is an Enemy to every man'?[15] To which question the answer is 'Peace'. Consequently, '... the first, and Fundamentall Law of Nature ... is, *to seek Peace, and follow it*'.[16] The possibility that society will degenerate into a state of war is a constant; that it does so degenerate, either into outright civil war or to some lesser violence is all too common. It does happen, and will continue to happen, that controversies will arise between people. How are these to be resolved when each one thinks himself right, and his opponent wrong? Violence can and does break out and the winner's 'right' prevails. In this situation, as Hobbes rightly says, 'The notions of Right and Wrong, Justice and Injustice have there no place'.[17] How can violence be avoided and peace preserved? Only if, as Hobbes writes in the passage quoted above, 'the

---

[14] *De Cive*, 145–6 (emphasis in original). The corresponding passage from *Leviathan*, 213 [78] reads: 'And because, though men be never so willing to observe these Lawes, there may neverthelesse arise questions concerning a mans action; First, whether it were done, or not done; Secondly, (if done) whether against the Law, or not against the Law: the former whereof, is called a question *Of Fact*; the later a question *Of Right*; therefore unlesse the parties to the question, Covenant mutually to stand to the sentence of another, they are as farre from Peace as ever. This other, to whose sentence they submit, is called an ARBITRATOR. And therefore it is of the Law of Nature, *That they that are at controversie, submit their Right to the judgement of an Arbitrator*' (emphases in original). An earlier version of the same natural law occurs in his *The Elements of Law*: Hobbes, *Human Nature and De Corpore Politico* (ed JCA Gaskin) (Oxford: Oxford University Press, 1994), 95.

[15] *Leviathan*, 186 [62].

[16] Ibid, 190 [64]. Hobbes, as we saw in ch 2.4 above, does not mistakenly derive what men ought to do from a fact; the structure of his argument is this: if peace is to be maintained, this is what must be done. Having contrasted imaginatively the two states, he thinks that his readers will share his conviction that a state of peace is preferable to a state of perpetual war. Someone who does not share this conviction will not be convinced.   [17] Ibid, 188 [63].

disagreeing parties refer the matter unto some third, and oblige themselves by mutual compacts to stand to his judgment in deciding the controversy'.

Adjudication, where '*... they that are at controversie, submit their Right to the judgment of an Arbitrator*',[18] is the solution to what is found to be a problem. It is considered in light of a desire for peace and, if a peaceful society is to be brought about, 'unlesse the parties to the question, Covenant mutually to stand to the sentence of another, they are as farre from Peace as ever'.[19] The answer to the question as to why judges emerge in society is therefore this: Peace is the desired condition. Conflicts between members of the society will arise. The peaceful condition will be undermined and the conflicts will be resolved by violence between the contending parties unless a peaceful way of resolving them is discovered and implemented. Adjudication, when the contending parties submit their dispute to a judge and agree to abide by the judge's verdict, is the only way to resolve them peacefully, 'and where there is no judge, there is no end of controversy, and therefore the right of hostility remaineth'.[20]

Adjudication, then, is a method of resolving disputes peacefully. It is one thing to think of a method, but quite another to implement it. In the context of the broader issue of why adjudicative authority emerged, we must therefore ask two sub-questions. First, what evidence is there that adjudication is a method of resolving disputes peacefully? Secondly, why would contending parties accept the method?

As to the first of these questions, we have already suggested that a judgment is the proposed solution to a practical problem. The proposed solution to a practical problem does not correspond to an already existing situation. The judgment proposes a possible course of action 'which, as yet, is not a fact but just a possibility'.[21] What kind of evidence supports the judgment that a possible course of action would be a solution to the practical problem that the questioner desires to solve? The problem is that the contending parties cannot agree on a solution to their dispute. Suppose that in the division of property following a divorce, both husband and wife may each want two-thirds of the value of the house that they jointly own. Each may feel entitled to it and be unwilling to agree to a mutually acceptable outcome. Clearly, the required result is a mutually accepted outcome. The crucial shift is, obviously, from 'mutually acceptable' – that is, a solution with which each will be content – to 'mutually accepted' – that is, a result which each will, however reluctantly, *accept*. The search for a way to resolve the dispute has now reached a heuristic solution: the contenders cannot agree between

[18] *Leviathan*, 213 [78].   [19] Ibid, 213 [78].
[20] Hobbes, *The Elements of Law*: Hobbes, *Human Nature and De Corpore Politico* (ed JCA Gaskin) (Oxford: Oxford University Press, 1994), 95.
[21] B Lonergan, *Insight* (London: Longmans, 1957), 610; but see the whole of ch XVIII and the same author's treatment of moral judgment in his later *Method in Theology* (London: Darton Longman and Todd, 1972), ch 2; see also W Matthews, *Lonergan's Quest* (Toronto: University of Toronto Press, 2005), ch 25.

themselves (had they been able to do so the problem would not have persisted); and so the next step is to discover how to reach a result that they will both accept. This basic insight yields the proposal that a result to be worked out by an impartial third person, which the contending parties agree in advance to accept, would solve the original problem. Is there sufficient evidence that the proposed method would work? What is sought is a result that the contending parties will accept. Their agreement in advance to accept the ruling of the adjudicator provides such a result. Thus, there is sufficient evidence for the judgment that if the proposed method is implemented, the desired solution is obtained.

An obstacle remains. As our second sub-question states: *why* would contending parties accept the method? They have been unable or unwilling to find a mutually acceptable result. Why would they be willing to accept the judgment of a third person, however impartial? One obvious reason – still supposing they prefer not to, or cannot, resort to violence – is that time passes. They want a result but have reached an impasse; further dispute is a waste of their time. This is a good reason but insufficient. Were they interested solely in breaking out of the impasse, they might as well toss a coin or draw straws. Either of these methods would yield a result, and only if they are interested in a result that relies on more than mere chance will it be reasonable for them to refuse an aleatoric method. What, then, are they looking for? Obviously, each would prefer a result in his or her favour, but tossing a coin is as good as any way of reaching that if, in fact, there is neither the possibility of violently overcoming the opponent nor a right result. (When in cricket a coin is tossed to determine which captain may choose whether to bat or field first, there is no right result, 'right' and 'wrong' being here irrelevant.) The only good reason to choose an impartial third person over tossing a coin is the conviction that there is a right or just result to be determined; the precise character of just results and how they are to be found are further issues. As we have discussed, the result is called 'right' or 'just' because what is sought is a result that yields to each what each is due which is how, in this context, the terms 'right' and 'just' are properly used.

That a judge in a dispute between contending parties should be impartial is an ancient and universal discovery contested by none. In an unresolved dispute between two people, neither one would accept that the other should be appointed judge for

seeing every man is presumed to do all things in order to his own benefit, no man is a fit Arbitrator in his own cause: and if he were never so fit; yet Equity allowing to each party equall benefit, if one be admitted to be Judge, the other is to be admitted also; & so the controversie, that is, the cause of War, remains, against the Law of Nature.[22]

---

[22] *Leviathan*, 213–14 [78]. This is the seventeenth law. The corresponding law, the sixteenth, in *De Cive* reads: 'But from this ground, that an arbiter or judge is chosen by the differing parties to determine the controversy, we gather that the arbiter must not be one of the parties. For every man is presumed to seek what is good for himself naturally, and what is just only for peace's sake and accidentally; and therefore cannot observe that same equality commanded by the law of nature, so

That the chosen arbitrator should not, for whatever reason, antecedently prefer the victory of one contender over the other, or one solution to the dispute over the other, is also an ancient and universal discovery contested by none; for if he prefers one outcome, he has taken the side of the contender who desires that outcome, and may be expected to determine the controversy in his favour.[23]

For the same reason interference with the adjudicative process in the form of bribery is universally forbidden. As it is written in *Exodus*, 'You must not accept a bribe, for a bribe blinds clear-sighted men and is the ruin of the just man's cause'.[24] Notice at once that the ancient command includes a reason: a judge should not accept a bribe *because* a bribe blinds and leads to unjust decisions.[25] Therefore, in Hobbes's words,

no man in any Cause ought to be received for Arbitrator, to whom greater profit, or honour, or pleasure apparently ariseth out of the victory of one party, than of the other: for hee hath taken (though an unavoydable bribe, yet) a bribe; and no man can be obliged to trust him. And thus also the controversie, and the condition of War remaineth, contrary to the Law of Nature.[26]

In these 'laws of nature', more properly called dictates or theorems of reason, is discovered a source of authority that is not based on force. The judge is authorized to declare the solution to the unresolved dispute between contending parties who cannot themselves settle their dispute without recourse to violence. A state of peace is to be maintained and impartial arbitration is the *only* method by which unresolved disputes can be settled peacefully.

Impartiality is intrinsic to any adjudication whatsoever whether or not disputants choose to accept it; it is intrinsic to authoritative adjudication in that there would otherwise be no reason to accept it. The arbitrator or judge must be impartial and accepted by contenders to be impartial, for a partial or prejudiced judge is biased and 'no man can be obliged to trust him'. The sense of 'can be obliged' in Hobbes's sentence is that it is unreasonable to require someone to trust the decision of one whom he knows to be prejudiced against him. He does not mean that no man can be forced to accept such a judge, for in that sense of 'obliged'

---

exactly as a third man would do. It is therefore in the sixteenth place contained in the law of nature, *that no man be arbiter in his own cause.'*

[23] See our discussion of impartiality in the context of adjudication in ch 6.4 above.

[24] *Exodus* 23:8. The translation is from *The Jerusalem Bible*. In the fourth chapter of *De Cive*, 'That the Law of Nature is a Divine Law', Hobbes cites this verse in the translation from the Authorized King James Version: 'And thou shalt take no gift: for the gift blindeth the wise, and perverteth the words of the righteous.' We discussed in ch 6.4 above how the explicit discovery of the need for impartiality in adjudication is both ancient and widespread. Once it has been discovered and formulated it is passed down from generation to generation and no one knows or can now know its original discoverer. Its formulation in *Exodus* is its earliest appearance in the *Torah*; whether or not *Exodus* is the main channel through which it flowed to the West from its ancient source is an historical question.

[25] The prohibition against taking a bribe is one of the few laws in the *Torah* for which an explicit reason other than God's will is given.   [26] *Leviathan*, 214 [78].

undeniably one can be obliged to do so. One cannot be forced to trust, but force can be used, and often with success, to bring about acceptance.

What we have emphasized so far is the reasonableness of the adjudicative procedure as a method of maintaining peace. One is obliged to accept the procedure simply because it is the reasonable solution to a problem that one wants solved. No man can be obliged to trust a dishonest and biased judge because it is not reasonable to do so. As we have suggested, to be 'obliged' in this context is not to be compelled by another; it is to be reasonably obliged, or not obliged, by oneself. This is what we have called *intrinsic* obligation – the obligation to become, as it were, the lawgiver for oneself.[27] When one realizes that adjudication by a third person is the only way to resolve a dispute without recourse to violence, and so to sustain the peaceful order that one wants to maintain, then one finds oneself obliged to accept adjudication. This, and this only, is the *structure* of moral obligation. One is not free to be, or not to be, obliged; but it is the nature of moral freedom that one may or may not decide to fulfil an obligation. The dictates of reason, in other words, oblige but do not compel.

The adjudicative procedure will not emerge in a society until the idea of such a procedure occurs; until it is fairly sufficiently commonly understood that the procedure is a method that will solve what is acknowledged to be a problem; and until it is sufficiently commonly agreed to implement the suggested procedure. In a society in which the idea has occurred to no one, clearly no adjudicative procedure will exist and disputes, when they arise, will be solved violently or by means of other forms of pressure. In a society in which the idea is known but in which violence is an acceptable way to solve disputes, the adjudicative procedure will not prevail over violence, or will prevail only intermittently. Only in a society in which the idea is known, and in which violence is an unacceptable method, will adjudication emerge and survive. Hence, adjudicative procedures are the product of intelligent discovery, reasonable judgment, responsible decision, and agreement.

It would be ridiculous to suggest that in a society in which adjudication has become the acceptable way to resolve disputes, everyone will on every occasion agree to be bound by the adjudicative process. One whose sole interest is an outcome that favours himself, and who considers himself to be able to bring about that outcome violently and without recourse to an adjudicative process that puts him on an equal footing with his opponent, may well not agree willingly to submit the dispute to adjudication. He will submit to adjudication only when forced to do so. Since he will not oblige himself, he must be compelled. Accordingly, unless one imagines a society composed only of reasonable and responsible members who will oblige themselves and so agree to the adjudication

---

[27] See St Paul's *Epistle to the Romans* 2:14 and St Thomas's comment on this passage in the *Summa Theologiae*, I–II, q 90, art 4. See the discussions of the distinction between intrinsic and extrinsic obligation in chs 4.3 and 7.5 above.

process, some will submit, not because they agree, but only because they are forced
to submit. Here, as we mentioned above, authority and force come together, but
it should also be remarked that this does not *necessarily* negate the fact that an
issue may arise as to the reasonableness of compelling them to undergo them.

It would also be ridiculous to suggest that in a society in which adjudication
has become the acceptable way to resolve disputes it will on each occasion be
good adjudication. Throughout this book we have stressed human error and fallibility and how these may impinge upon various aspects of the workings of legal
systems. Clearly, this is particularly significant when considering the authority
of law, whether adjudicative or, as we discuss later in this chapter, legislative.
Consider again the example of an historian seeking to teach in a university. As
we said, if he presents himself as a candidate for a teaching position it can happen that that those who make such appointments err, and choose a candidate
who is not in fact an authority in the second modality and the competence that
should ground his entitlement to teach is therefore missing. Obviously, the same
can happen in the appointment of a judge and many instances of poor judgment may ensue. Partly because of the strength of separation of powers doctrine,
impeachment laws are rarely invoked and therefore bad judges may, and do, continue in office. Such judges may fail to be authoritative adjudicators in the second modality, just as a legislator may fail to be an authoritative legislator in that
modality, to which we now turn.

11.4 Authority as Ability and Willingness

Because partiality and bias undermine authority in the first modality, the idea
that the judge be impartial has brought to the discussion a requirement that
properly belongs to authority in its second modality. And so to this authority
we now turn. The source of this authority is wisdom, that is, the judge's ability
and willingness to discover what is just. As we shall now see, this ability and
willingness – in the context of a given set of material and jural facts – are required
and expected in adjudication. They are, in other words, fundamental prerequisites of authoritative adjudication. Here we concentrate on what is required for
wise, even if not infallible, judgment; for no one would willingly submit to an
adjudicator who, however impartial, was also both uninterested in justice and
unwise. In two places in his *Summa Theologiae*, St Thomas Aquinas asks if it is
legitimate to judge, that is, to determine what is just. In both cases he has in mind
the practical judgment that intends to determine or discover what is just, rather
than speculative or theoretical judgment that intends to state what is the case. In
the first passage he writes:

Judgment is licit to the extent that it is an act of justice ... [I]t is plain that for a judgment
to be an act of justice three things are required: first, that it proceeds from a just inclina-

tion; secondly, that it stems from the authority of the person presiding; thirdly, that it is given according to prudential right reason.[28]

A second passage is similar but not identical and the order in which the three requirements are set out is different. It may be read as a comment on the first discussion:

Three things are required for judgment. First, the power to compel those judged: hence it is written in *Ecclesiasticus* 7,6: *Do not seek to be made judge unless you are strong enough to stamp out injustice.* Secondly, zeal for right, so that the judge does not give judgment out of hatred, envy or spite, but from a love of justice: according to *Proverbs*, 3,12: *For God chastises whom he loves, as a father the son in whom he delights.* Thirdly, wisdom, according to which the judgment is formed; so it is said in *Ecclesiasticus*, 10,1: *The wise judge will judge his people.* Of these three, the first two are prerequisites of judgment: but proper to the third is the form of judgment, for the reason of a judgment is the law of wisdom or truth, according to which judgment is made.[29]

The requirements are similar yet not identical. In the first passage the second requirement is that the person who is to judge be entitled to judge: the judgment must come from the authority of the person presiding. This entitlement or authority is close to our authority in its first modality. In the second passage this is the first requirement. It is formulated differently and concentrates on the judge's power to impose his decision, and hence is directly related to force. But force, as we have said, although present and possible, and in practice often required, is required only in cases where at least one of those involved does not agree to submit to adjudication. The first requirement as set out in the first passage is that the judgment proceeds from 'a just inclination' (*ex inclinatio iustitiae*); in the second passage this is the second requirement: a 'zeal for right', so that the judgment is not based on hatred, envy, or spite but on a love of justice. The third requirement is wisdom in the second passage, and in the first is prudence, which is wisdom in the practical domain.

One of the three requirements refers to authority in its first modality, that is, the entitlement to judge. The other two refer to authority in its second modality, that is, to the judge's intellectual and moral competence. Unless each requirement is met, the judgment comes from a tainted source and is 'vicious and illicit'. If the first requirement is lacking, the judgment is illicit in as much as the person who has set himself up as judge had usurped the authority. If either of the remaining two are lacking, the judgment is 'perverse or unjust'.

---

[28] *Summa Theologiae*, II–II, q 60, art 2.
[29] *Summa Theologiae*, III, q 59, art 1. In the passages quoted here from the Old Testament, the judge is obviously also the ruler as he was in the old Irish story and as, until early modern times in Europe generally, the judge was thought or imagined to be the representative of the king's justice. The image remains in England in the names 'King's or Queen's Counsel' and 'King's or Queen's Bench', and many modern monarchs or presidents retain some powers to commute sentences.

The decision of a judge who, for whatever reason and irrespective of the relevant evidence and precedent, favours one outcome over another will not be just except by accident; unless – in accord with the positivist account of adjudication – what is just is *stipulated* by the judgment, in which case, precisely the contrary judgment, handed down by a judge with a contrary bias, would also, and equally, be just. If what is just is stipulated to be whatever the judge decides, then his judgment is necessarily infallible, not because he infallibly discovers what is just but because what is just is whatever he decides and his competence an irrelevance; only his entitlement to judge is important. This is, in the end, no better than a decision based on the toss of a coin; only considerably more expensive, complicated and time consuming.

Even if one does not accept that what is just is in principle what the judge defines, that is, when the just is not stipulated by the judge, the judgment handed down is to be accepted and, at least for the time being, and for immediate practical purposes, does 'define' what is just. Thus, a judgment stating that Mary is entitled to some land, the ownership of which is disputed between her and Anne, gives the ownership of the land to Mary, and, for practical purposes, 'defines' what is just. Unless one supposes a court's decision to be an infallible discovery of what is just, it seems that what is decided to be just, is simply the best available opinion and determines, in practice and for the time being, what is just.

We have argued that what is just in the circumstances under consideration is to be discovered. 'The just' is the name for 'what is to be discovered by the court' and 'what is to be discovered by the court' is 'what in these circumstances belongs to whom; who is entitled to what?' Adjudication, as we have seen in detail in Chapter 6, is a process of enquiry. When enquiry begins, the answer is as yet unknown; were it known, the enquiry would already be concluded. Hence, a judge who thinks that he already knows the answer cannot genuinely enquire.[30] The specific answer is unknown but, for the enquiry to go forward, the heuristic form of the answer must be known; in the jurisprudential domain, the heuristic form of the answer is: X is entitled to Y from Z.

11.5 Authoritative Adjudication in a Claim for Residence

The question before the Court as to what belongs to whom – as to who is entitled to what – always arises in specific circumstances. The circumstances are both the material and the jural facts. Suppose that Amélie, who is not a citizen of

---

[30] The presumption of innocence in a criminal trial is obviously based on this idea even if in such cases the focus of enquiry is on whether or not the evidence presented is sufficient to support the judgment that the hypothesis presented by the prosecution is correct. Those who are to judge are not asked 'Who committed this crime?' but 'Is there sufficient evidence to convince us that the accused person committed it?'

Ecalpemos, claims before a court that she is entitled to residence in that state.[31] Already that basic description of her action contains almost nothing but jural facts. The terms in the description – 'citizenship', 'Ecalpemos', 'claims', 'court', 'entitlement', 'residence', 'state' – are jural.

The specific circumstances of the case, what the situation is, are in part jural or institutional, and contribute to making up the jural context in which the case is to be considered. Suppose, further, that Amélie, who has been refused residence and issued with a deportation order by the immigration authorities on the grounds that she is legally separated from her husband, appeals against the order on the grounds that she is entitled to residence because her husband, from whom she is legally separated but not divorced, is an Ecalpemosian citizen. All the facts adduced are jural or institutional except some features of the fact that she has been refused residence and issued with a deportation order, and that she has appealed against it. The form of the question before the Court ('who is entitled to what?') is specified to become: 'is Amélie entitled to residence in Ecalpemos?' As is usually the case, many of the alleged facts are agreed between the disputants. In the example, the disputants agree that Amélie is not an Ecalpemosian citizen; that she has been refused residence and issued with a deportation order; that the reason for the refusal and consequent issue of the order is that she is legally separated but not divorced from – and, therefore, still married to – her husband; and that were she not legally separated from her husband, who is a citizen, she would be entitled to residence. The question before the Court becomes: 'is Amélie's entitlement to residence, which is based on the fact that she is married to an Ecalpemosian citizen, nullified because she is legally separated from her husband although not divorced from him?' In other words, 'is her entitlement to residence based upon marriage alone or upon marriage without legal separation?'

Amélie's claim against the immigration authorities is based on what she believes the jural context to be. Let us assume that the right to residence is lost if the marriage upon which it is based is dissolved. It is clear that a marriage which has been dissolved is different from one in which the partners are legally separated. When a marriage is dissolved, it is reasonable to conclude that entitlements that depend *wholly* on being married are extinguished. There is a difference between an entitlement that depends on X having been married to Y, and one that depends on X being now married to Y. Which entitlements depend on being married and which on having been married must be determined. It is plausible – but not necessarily very important – to imagine that the legislators who established the entitlement to residence based on marriage to a citizen had marriage without legal separation at least vaguely in mind. In our example, what the legislators may have had in mind is not stated, and, although a marriage in which the partners are legally separated is – or, let us suppose, was when the legislation was enacted – rarer than

---

[31] This story is based on a real situation in which the deportation order was carried out; the case did not come before a court.

one in which they are not, such marriages do, for a number of reasons, exist, and the wording of the entitlement to residence does not explicitly exclude them.

Thus, in its effort to determine that to which Amélie is entitled, the court must determine if, for the purposes of determining an entitlement to residence, a marriage where the partners are legally separated is equivalent to a dissolved marriage. More succinctly, are divorce and legal separation in this context equivalent? The deportation order is based on the claim that they are equivalent; Amélie's counter claim is that they are not.

No one will dispute that whether or not Amélie is entitled to residence depends on the answer to the question as to whether or not divorce and legal separation are in this context equivalent. Their equivalence is a sufficient reason or ground for the conclusion that Amélie is not entitled to residence, and so sufficient reason to allow the conclusion that the deportation order is just. Contrariwise, their non-equivalence is sufficient reason to support Amélie's claim that she is entitled to residence, and, therefore, sufficient reason to allow the conclusion that the deportation order is unjust. Thus the antecedent question before the court is whether or not legal separation and divorce are *in the circumstances* equivalent. This is not our question; our question is to discover how that question can be answered.

Legislation can be amended or rescinded, and new legislation can be enacted. So, it would be perfectly possible for a modern state to establish a rule stating that '(i) a non-national married to, and neither legally separated nor divorced from, a national has a right to residence; (ii) if a non-national, whose right to residence depends upon him or her being married to, and not legally separated from, a national, becomes legally separated from his or her spouse, then the non-national's right to residence is lost'. If such a rule contributed to the definition of the situation, the question of equivalence would already have been answered. Such, by hypothesis, is not the case in our example. The question of entitlement arises in a jural or institutional context, and the entire point of the old distinction between the *ius gentium* and the *ius civile* is to show that jural contexts differ from jurisdiction to jurisdiction according to the particular arrangements even if, for some problems, jurisdictions discover broadly similar solutions.

Questions of entitlement arise within jurally defined contexts and so, it follows, that entitlements may, and sometimes will, differ from jurisdiction to jurisdiction. In our example, what Amélie is entitled to within the Ecalpemosian jurisdiction may be different from what she would be entitled to in another jurisdiction. Thus, inevitably, justice, inasmuch as the situation is in part defined by the rules of justice proper to a jurisdiction, is relative to jurisdictions. Rules defining entitlement to residence differ from state to state, and, within the same state, from time to time; a right of residence is a conventional entitlement (as is entitlement to citizenship or refugee status); and the convention institutes the context within which disputes are examined and resolved.

In the case of Amélie, the court is asked to determine whether or not she is entitled to residence. The jural context within which the court asks its question is one in which she is entitled to residence if married to an Ecalpemosian citizen. The immigration authorities claim that she loses that entitlement if she has legally separated from her husband. It is not disputed that there is a jural distinction between marriage, legal separation, and divorce. We have assumed that in Ecalpemos were she divorced from her husband Amélie would not be entitled to residence. We have assumed also that there is no applicable precedent; which is to say that the general case, of which Amélie's is a particular instance, has not been settled. It is already known that the solution must be either that Amélie is entitled to residence or that she is not, and that this must be determined within the Ecalpemosian jurisdictional context. However, the Ecalpemosian context, as it has been until now understood, does not clearly decide the issue. In coming to its decision, the court has no option but to develop the context. If it decides to refuse the right of residence it develops the context to equate, in these circumstances, divorce and legal separation. If, on the other hand, it grants the right, it develops the context by distinguishing, in these circumstances, between them. Again, in this and other situations of the same type, the court cannot but 'fill the gap in the law' and, to that extent, 'make law'.[32]

Here the two modalities of authority are clearly shown. If there is no accepted authority, the issue cannot be decided. In our discussion we have taken the court to be the accepted authority. In the story of King Mac Con and Cormac Mac Airt, the king was the accepted authority; but notice that when dispensing justice the king fulfilled the essential function of adjudication. Not only was he the accepted authority, his *duty* was to fulfil that function. It is told of the Roman Emperor Hadrian that he met an old woman on the road who asked him to adjudicate in a dispute. Hadrian responded that he was busy and she should not bother him, whereupon the old woman retorted: 'And don't you be king, then'.[33] Ashamed, Hadrian bothered. The story is told of other rulers, of whom Philip of Macedon is said to be the first. What is universal is not who should fulfil the adjudicative function but the function itself.

The court or whatever institution fulfils the adjudicative function is entitled to judge but its authority to judge continues to be quietly accepted because those who willingly submit to it suppose that it will, not infallibly but for the most part, judge wisely and well.[34] In Amélie's case, the court must decide whether or not she

---

[32] We discussed this in chs 6.5 and 9.2 above.

[33] This story is told by Robin Lane Fox in his *The Classical World* (Harmondsworth: Penguin, 2005), 200.

[34] The two fundamental presuppositions underpinning adjudicative authority as wisdom have long been known, and are explicit in Justinian's *Digest* (I.1.Preamble and 1): 'Ulpian *Institutes, Book 1*: A law student from the outset of his studies ought first to know the derivation of the word *ius*. For in terms of Celsus's elegant definition, the law is the art of goodness and fairness. 1. Of that art we [jurists] are deservedly called the priests. For we cultivate the virtue of justice and claim awareness of what is good and fair, discriminating between fair and unfair, distinguishing lawful from unlawful, aiming to make men good not only through fear of penalties but also indeed under allurement of rewards, and affecting a philosophy which, if I am not deceived, is genuine, not a sham.'

is entitled to residence. If, quite literally, one decision is as good, as wise, as just, as another, then discussion and argument are an irrelevant and costly waste of time; as we have said, there is no reason why the matter cannot be settled by tossing a coin. Furthermore, if there is in principle a just outcome but it is impossible even to go towards discovering what it is, discussion and argument are once more a waste of time. No one intelligently and reasonably tries to find what he knows to be a non-existent solution, or one that, although it in some sense exists, he is convinced cannot be found. The operative presuppositions underlying a decision to bring a dispute to the judge are that there is a just outcome to be found, and that the judge – given that it is a judge's primary professional function and duty to adjudicate fairly and justly – is better equipped than others to find it.

11.6 The Question of Legitimacy

We have now said a great deal about authority, but what of legitimacy? As mentioned in the introduction to this chapter, in considering the issue of legitimacy we switch focus from the adjudicative to the legislative domain. But first let us consider the legitimacy of human society itself. Although it is difficult entirely to eradicate the image of society as the product of contract, in a discussion of legitimacy it is imperative to do so. If several people together decide to establish a society – say, for example, a society for the protection of birds – it is possible and relevant to ask whether or not they are entitled to establish it. If they are so entitled, their decision and, consequently, the society, are legitimate. If they are not so entitled, their decision and, consequently, the society are illegitimate. What is true of a society for the protection of birds is true of human societies or communities if, and only if, they are the product of contract. If, however, as we argue, they are not the product of contract no question of their legitimacy or illegitimacy properly arises.[35]

In our view, society – human societies considered more generally – is not 'legitimate' or 'illegitimate'; it is simply the given network of relationships and entitlements. No society is, or can be, without a living or communal moral law – that is, customs – just as no society is, or can be, without language. These customs form the living law of a society that we have discussed in earlier chapters. Language exists habitually in that the members of that linguistic order know how to speak to one another; it exists actually whenever anyone speaks to another. Similarly, customs are habitually known, and actually exist whenever anyone acts in accord with them. There exists in every society acceptable ways

---

[35] Societies are not the product of contract. States and quasi-states, however, to a greater or lesser extent, often are. The European Union is an obvious recent example of a contracted entity, and, however much their detailed histories differ, many modern states are the products of, not necessarily recent, contracts, agreements, or pacts, often following wars.

of speaking, eating, and so on. These customs are learnt as ways in which one ought to behave. So children learn the acceptable way of eating, and usually put that into practice when they eat. There can be good and bad customs but both are equally customs: customs that are thought to be good are taught and learned as what, normally, one ought to do; those that are thought to be bad are taught and learned as what, normally, one ought not to do. Customs, good and bad, survive only if people act in accord with them. Customs change not because change is legislated but because some people begin to act in a different way and others follow.

As we use the term, it is not illuminating to think of the living law, that is, of customs, as legitimate or illegitimate, and this for several reasons. First, to ask if a custom is legitimate seems to be no more than to ask if it is effectively a custom. Secondly, and because we use the adjective 'legitimate' only if 'illegitimate' is also possible, it seems that a custom could possibly be illegitimate only if it is a practice that has grown up despite legislation forbidding it. Thirdly, we do not use 'legitimate' and 'illegitimate' as synonymous with 'good' and 'bad'.

Consider the game of chess. In chess, a set of rules governs the moves that the different pieces are permitted to make. The castle may move only backwards or forwards across or along the length of the board in a straight line; the bishop may move only diagonally. Only these moves are legitimate. A player who moves a castle diagonally makes an illegitimate move. The legitimacy or illegitimacy of the move is defined relative to the rule. In a chess match between two players, both are entitled to make alternate legitimate moves. A third person who is not a player is not entitled to make a move. Legitimate moves made by the players are legitimate; moves made by the non-player, however legitimate as moves in themselves, are illegitimate. Again the legitimacy or illegitimacy of the moves is defined relative to the rule.

Is the set of rules itself legitimate or illegitimate? In itself a set of rules is simply that. Intending players, faced with a written set of rules, may ask two questions. First, is the set coherent? Secondly, is the set of rules correct, that is, is this set that purports to be the rules of chess in fact the rules of chess? If the set is coherent it will be possible for the intending players to play a game the legitimate moves of which are set down. Whether or not the defined game is chess is a distinct question that arises upon the presupposition that there is a game that is properly called 'chess' and is distinguishable from even very similar games. The questioner presupposes that there is a legitimate set of rules, that is, a set of rules that legitimately define the game of chess.

Can some of the rules within the set of rules be changed? Over time practices evolve without the intervention of any authority; such evolutionary changes in human living are simply changes that have come about because someone has introduced them and others, thinking the changes to be improvements, have taken them up, or, as often happens in linguistic shifts, speakers discover that they have begun to talk in the new way. Games, like other human practices, may evolve in this manner. It happens, however, that some games become more formalized. Governing bodies are established that consider and approve or disapprove rules and rule changes. The character of the set of rules is transformed; the governing body is entitled to approve and disapprove rules and only those rules approved by it are legitimate.

The question of legitimacy turns on the issue of entitlement. At once the foundational question arises: whence is the governing body's *entitlement*? The success of the governing body's attempt to impose a new rule depends on *acceptance* of the rule by those to whom it is addressed. Acceptance may be achieved for several reasons: by agreement as when those on whom the rule is imposed agree with the rule and follow it for that reason only; by force as when they accept it only because they prefer to act in accord with it than to incur the consequences of contravening it; or by prior agreement as when they have already agreed to accept the governing body's decisions regarding the rules of chess. The reasons for acceptance of the rule are clearly different. Success may be achieved if any one of the reasons prevails. Which, if any, confers entitlement?

If Paul acts in accord with Peter's command *only* because he agrees with the suggestion, he has accepted the suggestion as counsel not command. If Paul acts in accord with Peter's command *only* because he fears to act otherwise, he in effect treats the suggestion as if it was a command but may not accept that Peter is entitled to command him. Only if he acts in accord with Peter's command because he accepts Peter's entitlement to command him does he accept the command as legitimate. The ruler's entitlement rests on the subject's acceptance and whether or not he ought to accept is a serious moral question.[36] In practice, of course, a person may respond to a particular command for more than one of these reasons.[37]

While a person may join a chess club or federation and, in doing so, formally agree to be bound by the ordinances of the governing body regarding the rules of chess, this is not how a person joins a human social order or ordinarily becomes a citizen of a state organization. In a modern state persons in dispute over a contract are required to submit to the decision of a court if either one insists upon it. The disputants, having learnt of it as they grew up in the society, know of this requirement. It is unreal to suppose that either one at any stage made a deliberate prior agreement to act in accord with it. Each accepts the institution but may do so for different reasons. One may think that the resolution of disputes in court by an impartial judge is good and be willing to submit to the court's decision that, necessarily, is not known in advance and with which he may, in the event, disagree. The other may submit only because he prefers to do so rather than suffer the consequences of his refusal to do so.

---

[36] Julian, in the *Digest* at 1.3.32.1, is quoted as saying that the '... statutes themselves are binding upon us for no other reason than that they have been accepted by the judgment of the populace'.

[37] We discussed various possible reasons for obeying a command, in the context of force, in ch 10.

Imagine a state in which one group accepts the court and another does not. The group that accepts the court imposes it on the group that does not. Is the court legitimate? For the members of the group that accepts it, the court is legitimate. But is that group entitled to impose it on the other? Is the court legitimate for the members of the group that does not accept it? It is easy to find a realistic example. During a war an army invades and occupies the territory of one of its enemies. The occupying power more or less pacifies the population, and establishes civilian courts with its own judges that follow its civil laws. Are these courts legitimate? If they are not immediately legitimate when, if ever, do they become so? If the occupying power, having won the war, establishes itself as sovereign – the Roman Empire in Europe, the Mughal empire in India, the Manchu or Qing dynasty in China, are examples of some of the many empires that endured sometimes for several centuries – is it plausible to say that its rule *never* becomes legitimate?

To establish and maintain the idea of legitimacy and, more important, to support a claim to legitimacy, there was invented in Europe at least, the notion of 'right of conquest': to the victor, legitimately, the spoils. The historian Tacitus quotes a speech by Petilius Cerialis to the Gauls arguing for the legitimacy of Roman rule that nicely illustrates the rhetorical use of this right and introduces another aspect of legitimacy, the goodness of the ruler's laws:

73. What they [the Germans] have really wanted is to abandon their marshes and deserts, and gain control of this rich soil and of yourselves. But 'liberty' and other fine phrases serve as their pretexts. Indeed, no one has ever aimed at enslaving others and making himself their master without using this very same language.
74. Throughout the whole of Gaul there were always despots and wars until you passed under our [Roman] control. We ourselves, despite many provocations, imposed upon you by right of conquest, only such additional burdens as were necessary for preserving peace. Stability between nations cannot be maintained without armies, nor armies without pay, nor pay without taxation. Everything else is shared equally between us... if the Romans are expelled – which Heaven forbid! – what else will result but world-wide war in which each nation's hand will be turned against its neighbour?... At present, victors and vanquished enjoy peace and imperial citizenship upon an equal footing, and it is upon these blessings that you must lavish your affection and respect. Learn from your experience of the two alternatives not to choose insubordination and ruin in preference to obedience and security.[38]

Petilius Cerialis obviously expects his audience to accept the 'right of conquest' behind which lies the assumption that the legitimate ruler is the one who succeeds in ruling. Once established, of course, the ruler would rely on the acceptance by his subjects of another right, 'that the legitimate ruler not be overthrown'. This latter right, too, has been accepted, despite its tension with the former, in order

---

[38] Tacitus, *The Histories*, 4:73 and 74 (trans K Wellesley) (Harmondsworth: Penguin, 1964), 258–9.

to ensure, as best could be, a peaceful order within which people could carry on their lives. It is to this right that Petilius refers, for it is only under relatively stable rule that peace is more or less well assured. This, we will recall from our discussion in Chapter 2, is the very function of law, of the jural order.

That the right of conquest and the right not to be overthrown are in tension shows an unavoidable ambiguity at the heart of legitimacy. The entitlement to rule depends on the ruler's ability to rule; but his ability depends on his ability to fend off rivals and maintain sufficient acquiescence of his subjects. The right not to be overthrown, however, in the end depends on his ability 'to keep the peace'. These two come together in that failure to keep the peace, failure to allow his subjects to live their several lives in mutual cooperation, is a failure, owing to incompetence or tyranny, to maintain sufficient acquiescence. Hence, a third right, and Cicero's recurrent example of unusual duty in particular circumstances: the right to overthrow tyrants:

For there can be no fellowship between us and tyrants – on the contrary there is complete estrangement – and it is not contrary to nature to rob, if one can, a man whom it is honourable to kill. Indeed, the whole pestilential and irreverent class ought to be expelled from the community of mankind....[39]

The question concerning the legitimacy of a command properly arises only if illegitimate commands are possible. If Peter commands Paul to do something, Paul will ask if Peter is entitled to command him to do it only if he knows that there is at least the logical possibility of Peter not being so entitled. Faced with a notice forbidding walking on the grass, Paul will ask, first, if the injunction is directed to him; secondly, if the injunction requires him to do something that he finds, absent the injunction, not morally wrong to do; and, thirdly, if the person issuing the injunction is entitled to do so. If he answers all three questions affirmatively he will, all other things being equal, consider himself obliged to comply. It must be constantly kept in mind that a person who considers himself obliged to obey an injunction may nonetheless decide not to obey it. But, clearly, he asks these questions only because each one could be answered negatively. The injunction might not apply to him; might require him to do something morally wrong; or might have been issued by someone not entitled to command him.

These questions are not equally easy to answer. Often a person will have little difficulty in determining whether or not an injunction applies to him. 'Do not walk on the grass' will normally be taken to apply to everyone who reads it; but may in the actual social context be known by residents to apply only to visitors. Occasionally, too, a command or sign is ambiguous. Is a sign indicating that a lavatory is suitable for disabled people simply that, or does it include

---

[39] Cicero, *On Duties*, III.32 (ed M Griffin and M Atkins; trans M Atkins) (Cambridge: Cambridge University Press, 1991), 111.

the injunction that it is not to be used by those who are not disabled? It is not uncommon for it to be difficult to determine how precisely complicated legislation, for example revenue or social welfare measures, apply to a particular individual.

The person to whom the command is addressed judges whether or not what is commanded is morally wrong. He may accept that in the normal case the person issuing the command is entitled to command him but judge that on this occasion what is commanded is morally wrong. He may, as we have constantly stressed, be mistaken, but moral obligation arises from personal moral judgment and no one can be morally obliged to do what he judges to be morally wrong. On this position – traditionally known as the primacy of conscience – what a person is morally obliged to do is not what is right, but what he judges to be right. It may happen that a legislator judges that what he requires of citizens is right, whereas a citizen judges that it is not. An important and recurring example of this is the conflict arising out of the requirement on conscientious objectors to fight in a war. In this type of situation the question arises as to whether or not a sovereign is morally entitled to force someone to do, or to punish for failing to do, what the sovereign judges to be morally right but what the person to whom the injunction applies judges to be morally wrong.

Behind the foregoing questions – whether or not the command applies, whether or not the person commanded thinks it to be morally wrong – is the question of authority in the first modality: is A *entitled* to command B? The bank robber commands the teller to hand over money but is not entitled to do so, and what he commands is wrong. To be legitimate the person commanding must be entitled – have authority in the first modality – to command the person to whom the command is addressed. That authority is not enough but it is one of the two sources from which legitimacy flows. If Peter is entitled to command Paul, he acts legitimately and his injunctions are legitimate in the first modality. Why, then, is Peter entitled to command Paul? The perennial appeal and the kernel of truth in contract theory become at once apparent: Peter is entitled to command Paul because Paul has agreed to be – or at the very least has acquiesced in being – commanded by Peter. Most people in any community in practice agree to live peacefully within it; the developing living law within which they carry on their lives together expresses the moral – or less comprehensively the jural – character of the community which positive law adds to and adjusts. That agreement in practice is in no sense an original founding contract. Even had there been such a contract it would not bind later generations.[40] The fundamental laws without which a society would collapse are not agreed once for all; they are agreed in the decisions that we make in our everyday lives. A child learns that to steal is wrong and whenever in adulthood he chooses, for that reason, not to steal, he agrees with that fundamental law, and, as we have said, contributes to the maintenance

---

[40] See GN Casey, 'Constitutions of No Authority' (2010) 14 *The Independent Review* 325.

of the peaceful order.[41] The entitlement of legislators to legislate and the entitlement of judges to adjudicate are *for the most part* accepted, and in that acceptance they are established. That is 'the social contract'. Legitimacy in the end rests on its being accepted. Acceptance is, however, provisional. Not every power will be accepted as legitimate, nor every command, even of one entitled to command, approved. To determine and agree what is just or unjust is both difficult and controversial, but it remains that the legitimate power is not entitled to command what is unjust.

It seems, therefore, that the sovereign or legislator *is legitimate if the subjects accept his legitimacy*. The Manchus invaded China in the mid-seventeenth century and following some resistance founded the Ching (Pin-Yin: Qing) dynasty which lasted for 296 years. When did the Manchus become legitimate? The best answer seems to be: when their rule was accepted. This answer is close to Kaarlo Tuori's who has written that, 'The law enjoys empirical legitimacy, if among the relevant group there exists a sense of obligation to obey it', except that we find some difficulty with his distinction between empirical and normative legitimacy, in which '[n]ormative legitimacy, in turn, can be equated with ethically and morally justified obligation to obedience'.[42] How is the 'sense of obligation to obey' in the definition of empirical legitimacy to be understood and distinguished from the 'ethically and morally justified obligation to obedience'? In the bank clerk faced with the robber's command to hand over money there exists or could exist a sense of some kind of obligation to obey; but this 'obligation' is based entirely on force, a fact that is recognized in everyday English in that a clerk who had handed over money could say either that he was 'forced' or 'obliged' to do so.[43] This perfectly good ordinary usage of 'obliged' in English prompted Hart's well-known distinction for clarity in analysis between 'being obliged' and 'being obligated'. If force is sufficient basis for empirical legitimacy, we would say that a merely empirically legitimate command is not a law; to extend Hart's usage, it may *oblige* but does not *obligate*. On the other hand, if the sense of obligation in empirical legitimacy includes the idea that the person commanded thinks that he ought to obey, then in our analysis, he is morally obliged. But from this follows that 'accepted' in our claim that Manchu rule became legitimate when it was accepted is to be understood as 'accepted as

---

[41] In a modern state, most citizens or residents, often unquestioningly, acquiesce in a socio-political arrangement, and only rarely does a citizen or resident formally agree to become a subject; an exception is when an adult non-national becomes a citizen by mutual contract.

[42] K Tuori, 'Legitimacy' in CB Gray (ed), *The Philosophy of Law: An Encyclopedia (Vol II)* (New York: Garland, 1999), 493. See also his 'Discourse Ethics and the Legitimacy of Law' (1989) 2 *Ratio Juris* 125.

[43] See ch 10 above. A bank clerk illegitimately commanded under threat of serious injury or death to hand over money is not morally obliged, that is, not obligated, by the illegitimate command but he may well be morally obligated to hand over the money because he judges that the value of his staying alive or unharmed outweighs the value of not giving the money. The crucial point is that he is not *obligated by the command*. Similarly, one living under a regime *de facto* in power but illegitimate may for his own reasons consider himself to be obligated to act in accord with, but not obligated by, its illegitimate commands.

morally binding' or, in Kuori's usage, as 'normatively legitimate'. We take his 'empirical legitimacy' to be '*de facto* in power'. The rule of an occupying power in war – for example, Nazi rule in at least some of the occupied countries during World War II, Soviet rule in occupied Finland – is *de facto* rule but it is not legitimate because it is not accepted.

If the analysis is correct, it follows that legitimacy as entitlement to rule is essentially contestable which is by no means to suggest that whether or not to accept the legitimacy of state or court is nothing more than a matter of arbitrary whim. Nonetheless, legitimacy is in principle contestable, and is in reality often contested. Seeing clearly that this is so, Hans Kelsen puts an axiom of legitimacy – the *Grundnorm* – at the head of a pure theory of law. Revolutionaries, of whatever stamp, who would overthrow the *de facto* power, commonly base their entitlement to do so on their conviction that the *de facto* power is not legitimate. It is the essential contestability of legitimacy that gives rise to the saw that 'one man's terrorist is another man's freedom fighter'.[44] When within a state there are those who accept its legitimacy and those that do not, the essential contestability of legitimacy is *actually* contested.[45] Those who reject the legitimacy of the legislation and of the ruler of the state in which they live are constrained to ask how they ought to behave. Those who accept them are equally constrained to ask how they ought to behave. The contexts within which the members of these diverse groups enquire as to what they ought to do differ radically. The legislators who *de facto* legislate commonly think of their state as legitimate, of themselves as legitimate legislators, and of their legislation as legitimate. When legislators do not in fact consider themselves to be legitimate, they tend nonetheless to act *as if* they do, and to develop a political rhetoric to persuade the population of their legitimacy.[46] In either case they are constrained to ask how to deal both with those who reject the state's

[44] For example, the IRA in the United Kingdom contested the UK parliament's jurisdiction in Northern Ireland, and in Ireland (the state, not the island) contested the legitimacy of the Irish state, T Murphy, 'The Evolving Constitution of Northern Ireland' (2006) 1 *Lögfræðingur* [*Lawyer*] 14. Other examples abound: ETA in Spain contests the national government's jurisdiction in the Basque Country; FARC in Colombia . . . the list is long. We could as well choose examples of revolutionaries with whom we would expect all readers to agree: for example, the various resistance movements in the European states occupied by the Nazis.

[45] The majority of Spaniards accepts the legitimacy of the national parliament; in the Basque country the majority accepts its legitimacy although some in that majority support negotiated and agreed secession; ETA rejects the legitimacy of the national parliament and considers itself entitled to work violently towards secession. Roughly the same can be said of the situation in Northern Ireland before the Belfast Agreement with the considerable difference that before the change in its Constitution associated with the Agreement, the Irish state rejected the legitimacy of United Kingdom of Great Britain and Northern Ireland in as much as it rejected the legitimacy of Northern Ireland's membership of the United Kingdom. In Scotland some look for Scotland's secession from the United Kingdom and some do not, but the vast majority, both of those who look for, and of those who oppose, secession, accept the Union's present legitimacy. The same is true of Wales.

[46] See G Barden, 'Rhetorics of Legitimacy' (1998) 2 *European Journal of Law, Philosophy and Computer Science* 47.

legitimacy and engage in a form of civil war, and with those who simply disobey its laws.[47]

In sum, then, the authority of the court, that is, of whatever institution fulfils the adjudicative function, rests on two bases. Its entitlement to adjudicate,
authority in its first modality, rests on the perceived need to mediate authoritatively between disputants if peace is to be maintained and disputes are to be
resolved without resort to violence. This entitlement to adjudicate is generally and
implicitly agreed, and where agreement is absent is supported by force. The base
of adjudicative authority in the second modality is the possibility of reaching a
just conclusion. The court must attempt to discern in the details of the case before
it, and in the light of the jural context, what is just, what is due. If there is literally
no sense in which there is a *ius* – a right, 'what is due' – or literally no possibility of
discovering what is due, then in any dispute whatsoever any conclusion is as good
as any other. The story of Mac Con and Cormac contrasts two judgments and
few readers will genuinely hold that they are equally good, however difficult they
may find it to say precisely and utterly convincingly why they are not. The story of
Amélie ends with two possible but mutually incompatible judgments; both cannot be right; they can be equally good only if right does not exist. Both cannot be
implemented. If they are equally good it must be a matter of indifference which is
chosen, and a matter of indifference how the choice is made.

We have suggested that there is a *ius* – a 'what is due' – to be discovered, and
that it is the task of the court to discover it. Were this not so, there would be
nothing but the random and the arbitrary. We have been at pains to make clear
that neither the court nor the jural context within which it deliberates is infallible
or perfect; were this not so there would be no possibility of development. As in
science, so in adjudication, what we must be content with is not the unquestionable opinion but rather the best available opinion. Humans approach truth and
justice asymptotically; yet we do approach them.

We claim that a legislature and its laws are legitimate and oblige those to
whom they apply if they are recognized or ought to be recognized by them and
if legislation is confined within the proper range. This excludes a legislature's
entitlement to command not alone what is evil but also to command or forbid
those other actions, not in themselves evil but beyond the legitimate range, that
must be identified and about which there will sometimes be dispute and serious disagreement.[48] The idea that a legitimate legislature's entitlement is limited

---

[47] The legitimacy of states with respect to other states is of course also contested and contestable. Kosovo seceded from Serbia and declared itself to be legitimately a sovereign state in
March 2008. Some countries accepted this; others did not. The political reasons behind these
acceptances and non-acceptances showed how in such instances states often do 'what they can get
away with'.

[48] That the range of the legislation ought to be limited has been discussed in ch 7.4 above. The
issue became central in European theoretical political discussion in von Humboldt's *The Limits of
State Action* and Mill's *On Liberty* (1869) and has remained so. Isaiah Berlin's essay 'Two Concepts
of Liberty' (in *Four Essays on Liberty*, Oxford University Press, 1969) remains an illuminating

is the ground upon which St Augustine bases his theory that a law that goes beyond the legitimate range – his example is a law that commands what is evil but the notion of legitimate range is more complex and comprehensive – is not a law. We think – and here, again, we are more in line with St Thomas than with St Augustine – that it is clearer to say that a law that goes beyond the legitimate range remains a law and so 'legally' binds but is defective and does not 'morally' bind; *it obliges but does not obligate.*

We conclude briefly. Legitimate authority rests on two bases. The first, on which the pure positivist – to an extent a straw man – exclusively depends, is the entitlement to legislate: what is properly legislated is law. The second, upon which the pure Augustinian – likewise a straw man – tends exclusively to concentrate, is the just character of what is legislated: an unjust law is not a law. The positivist overlooks the authority of wisdom; the Augustinian the authority of entitlement. Rejecting the exclusivity of both, we have argued that legitimacy rests on both modalities of authority. Unlike the pure positivist, we hold that an unjust law is defective. Unlike the pure Augustinian, we hold that an unjust law remains a law.

discussion as do the works by Braud and Burdeau, and MacCormick that we referred to in ch 7.5. See also J Green, *L'Essence du politique* (Paris: Sirey, 1965), ch 5. Where precisely at any time the limit is to be drawn is, as Berlin wrote, 'a matter of argument, indeed of haggling' (124).

12

Conclusion

The account of law and justice developed in this book is built on six pillars. First, we are social animals: we make, and cannot but make, our individual lives in association with one another – this is 'human community' or 'human society'. As time passes and situations change, as, following new discoveries and new practices, different ways of living together emerge, human societies adjust and develop, but they are not initially invented. Secondly, society is an order that is simply the vast and enduring human context brought about by continually changing interactions between humans. Thirdly, the many laws and customs common to every human society and those peculiar to different societies are prior to legislation and are the accepted, or acquiesced in, living law – or communal moral law – of the society. This communal law is not necessarily in all respects good, for in every society there are the relatively more or less powerful, and the more powerful can, and do, to a greater or lesser extent impose their biased and selfish interests upon the less powerful. Societies are at all times and inevitably dialectical. Fourthly, particular societies are different versions of the human context and share some fundamental features; but societies differ and each society, in addition to those common features without which it could not survive, has and must have other customs and laws unique to itself and others that are shared by some, but not all, societies. Fifthly, justice is the virtue that inclines each to render to others what is due; the virtue that requires that each take account of both their own and others' interests; and if justice is to be done, if what is due is to be rendered, then what is due, both in the general and in the particular case, must be discovered and established. The sixth and final pillar is that the survival of a society depends on its members acting to a sufficient degree in a way that allows each to live in accord with others, and so demands that each has what is due or, which is almost equally important, the possibility of discovering and establishing what is due at any time. Because of the intrinsic and inevitable dialectic of biased interests, unjust institutions will arise and, although they carry within them the seeds of their own destruction, will for a shorter or longer time survive. And when one unjust institution – for example, slavery – is eliminated, others emerge. Nonetheless, the demand for justice remains, and if the demand is insufficiently answered the society will be destroyed.

In the effort to discover what is due and because we are responsible for how we live our lives, we must pursue our own interests, that is, we are 'self-interested'. But it is of cardinal importance to distinguish self-interest from selfishness; confusion here ineradicably distorts analysis. Self-interest drives a person's choices. Someone does something because he wants to bring about a new situation that is the object of his desire. In choosing we become responsible both for the object of our choice and for the means that we choose to bring it about. One who wants bread may go to the baker either to buy or to steal it. Were he to choose to steal rather than to buy the bread from its owner, the means to achieve the object would be unjust; for 'to steal' is 'to take something to which one is not entitled'. Anyone who argues that theft is not unjust will be found to hold that the 'owner' does not really 'own' the thing 'stolen'; indeed, if a thing is not owned, it *cannot* be stolen. The injunction against theft is inextricably linked to ownership in the absence of which it is meaningless. The decision not to steal is to take account of another's interests, to accept what is due, to be just.

The traveller who wants to go from one place to another may go on foot, by bicycle, car, bus, train, boat, plane, etc, but his choice may be limited by the physical environment. Whatever the limitation imposed by the environment, the choice to make the journey, and to make it by this means rather than that, is taken in the human context that always and inescapably includes others; and, even if it be supposed that there is nothing reprehensible, nothing unjust, about the traveller's decision, his choice remains self-interested. Suppose that for good reasons a person decides to go from one city to another. Suppose that he decides to go by car rather than by train. That decision is taken within a context that includes other people and their interests, and questions arise in the present world about the moral appropriateness of choosing to go by car rather than by train. (When a question is genuine this indicates that the answer is unknown not that it is obvious.) If he decides to go by car, the carrying out of the decision is within a context that includes many others – drivers and pedestrians – all of whom are going about their self-interested business in the context of the self-interested business of others. Driving from one city to another cannot be done at all unless there are some commonly recognized traffic rules and customs, whether or not they are legislated; it cannot be done safely unless the rules are both prudent – that is, likely, if followed, to bring about a safe driving environment – and, for the most part, obeyed. The driver who wants to arrive safely at his destination knows that he depends on the rules being prudent and on their being generally observed. Thus, there emerges in the traffic rules – whether the traffic be by land, by sea, or by air – the fundamental rule or originating principle from which all the detailed rules intelligently, reasonably and responsibly derive, namely, 'travel safely', 'drive carefully', or some equivalent expression.

That fundamental rule is not given as a logical axiom; it is, as the Romans had it, the fruit of natural reason; in other words, it is the natural law of traffic. To any normally intelligent person it is obvious. Were one to ask a sailor why there were collision rules or customs, he would find the question odd, but might still answer that they were to help avoid collisions between ships. If the questioner pursued the matter and asked why it was desirable to avoid collisions, the sailor would think the questioner to be extremely unintelligent for it is obvious that sailors want their vessel to reach port safely, and that to do so demands that collisions be avoided. *Obviously* the driver who wants to reach his destination safely wants to avoid a crash. The many drivers pursue their own different interests but they share, each self-interestedly, the desire for the reasonably safe environment that following the traffic rules will go towards producing. The rules themselves do not produce the environment; those that drive in accord with them contribute to bringing it about. Thus, each driver is responsible for his contribution to the production of the safe environment. The safe environment is the product of many moral choices and is, therefore, a moral as well as a material thing; and, in contributing to its production, each driver, whether or not he adverts to it, takes the interests of other drivers into account.

Selfishness is utterly different from such irreproachable self-interest. The selfish driver allows his self-interest to override the interests' of others. He will flout the rules whenever, and for whatever reason, they impede his own interest, and thus he contributes to the breakdown of the safe environment in which, ideally, he and others drive. The selfish driver does not always flout the rules; he keeps them when, but only when, it is more in his interest to keep them than to flout them. The selfish driver does not want to crash and so impede himself, but he is indifferent as to whether his driving brings about damage to others to whose interests he is at best indifferent, and at worst, hostile. Selfishness, then, is a distorted self-interest that is always indifferent, and sometimes antagonistic, to the self-interest of others.

What is true of driving is true of human living in general. The basic traffic rule – 'drive safely' or 'drive with due care' – is a specification of a yet more basic rule or principle: 'take account of others' interests'. That more basic rule is simply another formulation of the traditional rule of justice: 'render to each what is due'. Different reasons incline one to be just, to render what is due. One who does the just thing only because he fears the consequences of not doing so does not care for others' interests, has no interest in bringing about the just for its own sake, and obeys the rule in a slavish manner. The just person, whose habitual desire is to render to each what is due, does the just thing *because* he respects the interests of everyone involved, including himself. *He remains self-interested but chooses to act justly.* For him the law, supposing it to be just, is not so much a constraint as a clarification of what is due. Few of us are completely just; for if justice is the constant and enduring determination to render to each what is due, selfishness is the constant and enduring temptation – in some, the settled determination – to do otherwise whenever it is more convenient to do so.

The rules of justice in a society state what is thought to be just in those types of circumstances that commonly arise. They command *and* clarify. Because contracts are made – and because that contracts are to be kept is a rule of justice natural or intrinsic to contract, absent which the pretended making of a contract would be empty words or play-acting – it is necessary that what constitutes a contract be clear, communally known, and accepted. When what constitutes a contract is not known, the contracting parties cannot know whether or not they have contracted: one party may think that a contract had been made while the other may be convinced that it had not. Contract is intrinsic to the order; what constitutes a valid contract, what counts as adequate fulfilment, what renders a contract void and so on must be discovered and decided both in a general rule or custom, and, when disputes arise, in the instant case. For even when the rules of contract are set down clearly, there arise situations in which the parties involved disagree, and in such cases adjudication is needed to settle whether or not there had been a valid contract, whether or not the contract had been properly fulfilled, and so on.

Ownership, the right to alienate one's resources, and contract, the order according to which promises are binding, are essential to a trading order in which people agree to exchange one thing for another. Without these a reciprocal entitlement between those who would engage in mutual trade is impossible. When trading partners freely and mutually agree upon a price, and make what in their society is accepted to be a valid contract, that price establishes the reciprocally just transaction-values of what is to be exchanged between them. At the moment of exchange each partner is, for whatever reason and however enthusiastically or unenthusiastically, satisfied with the price; but there neither is, nor can there be, any guarantee that each will in retrospect *remain* satisfied with the price or the contract made.

The trading order, the market, is simply the continuing set of transactions between trading partners. To deal fraudulently is a temptation. The order can survive some fraud but not an indefinitely large amount, for fraud erodes the mutual confidence upon which the order depends. The engine of exchange is mutual self-interest. Honest trading sustains the order; fraud is selfishness, the refusal to take due account of others' interests, and it undermines the order by undermining the confidence, the credit upon which its survival depends. As a trading order develops and most make their living by trading both the temptation and the opportunity for greed increases, and, as will always be the case, the more powerful will attempt to subvert law to their own advantage and to the disadvantage of the less powerful. Still, the order cannot in the longer period survive too much injustice and the justice proper to it is the reciprocal justice inherent in free exchange.

The reciprocal justice inherent in the trading order has nothing to do with the outcome that at any moment is the unforeseen and unintended result of the entire set of exchanges. We have insisted that the trading order, concerned as it is only with reciprocal justice, neither does, nor can, solve all the questions of justice that may arise in the society as a whole. Those who cannot survive by trading – children, the severely disabled, those whose skills are not demanded – survive otherwise than by trading or not at all. It is not a rule intrinsic to the trading order that all must survive by participating within it. Perhaps it is more important to make utterly clear that it is not intrinsic to the encompassing social order that no question arises concerning those who cannot survive by trading.

In every society a question arises concerning the survival of those who cannot fend for themselves in the prevailing economic order. Children too young to sustain themselves provide the obvious, universal, and incontrovertible example. Designated adults, usually parents or close kin, are responsible for their survival. In the societies in which most readers live, in which wealth is generated within a trading order in which government substantially intervenes, and in which government, through its power to raise revenue through taxation, provides a vast number of services, many must make their living by hiring their time and skill. Some, through no fault of their own, fail to do so, and cannot effectively survive unless provided for by others. From the limited perspective of the trading order, their failure is simply a fact. From the perspective of the encompassing social order, their failure places a demand on those who do make their their living by hiring their time and skill. A demand is actually placed only on one who recognizes and accepts it, precisely as a teacher actually teaches only when the student is learning. The demand to care for those who have been unable to fend for themselves can be recognized and accepted only by one within whose intellectual and moral context it seems to be a demand – that is only by one who accepts that to each is due the possibility of survival within the social order and that, accordingly, to render what is due may require what has more traditionally been called benevolence, and that *in extremis* may mean that what one in normal circumstances owned and might justly dispose of as one wished, one can no longer justly so dispose of it. How that demand is to be met is a further question but, for one whose intellectual and moral context is one in which the other is a 'second self', that it is to be met is clear. Outside that context this will not, and cannot, seem to be so. If contexts are ineradicably unarguable, moral judgments are ineradicably relative. We have argued that they are not but unequivocally acknowledge both that different contexts exist and that to persuade someone to move from one context to another is difficult and often unsuccessful.

Controversies arise, rival claims are made. The desire to dominate, the biased conviction of one's own right, selfishness, greed, even genuine uncertainty as to what is just, give rise to the need for, and the emergence of, adjudication, which to be just must be unbiased, for it is useless and intrinsically fraudulent if the interests of one are to be – in principle and apart from the facts and jural context – preferred to the interests of the other. To be unbiased is a natural law of adjudication, and is discovered by reflection on the practice and on what it is intended to achieve: the discovery and implementation of what is due. Adjudication must be intelligent and contextual; neither an unintelligent adjudicator, nor one ignorant of the jural context, will do. Adjudication requires interpretation and application. The first question before the adjudicator may be, for example, in the context of the established rules as they are properly understood in the jurisdiction, whether there was a contract in a paricular circumstance. That question seeks an answer clarifying the jural or institutional fact (interpretation) and its relevance to the instant case (application); and it is evident that no adjudicator can in all circumstances guarantee an infallibly true answer. Hence, our insistence throughout on the court's fallibility, and on the adage that the *res iudicata pro vero tenetur* to which we have added *pro tem*: 'what has been adjudicated is to be taken as true *for the time being*'. Because judgment is fallible, it is subject to revision. Hence there emerge lower and higher courts but eventually, because time presses in practical affairs differently than in purely theoretical matters (although even in the natural sciences the best available opinion stands for the moment and is subject to revision), there is a highest court whose judgment for the moment stands, and is implemented. When the questions as to whether or not there had been a contract, whether or not fraud had so vitiated the supposed contract as to render it void, whether or not the contract had been adequately fulfilled, whether or not there had been undue delay in fulfilling the contract – when these questions have been answered, the question arises as to what is now due to the litigants. The answer to that question concludes the first part of the adjudicator's task; what is just has been discovered. The decisive task remains, for what is due is to be rendered to those to whom it is due; what is just must be done.

Although disputants can agree between themselves upon an adjudicator, and agree to be bound by his decision, it is a very ancient practice in human societies for adjudicators to be imposed, and for litigants in certain circumstances to be required to submit their quarrels to them. So emerged the ruler-judge and eventually a distinction between legislator and judge. When adjudicators emerge, with their emergence the question arises as to their authority: who is entitled to adjudicate, and on what grounds does his entitlement stand? Our proposed answer involves a distinction between two modalities of authority: the modality of entitlement and the modality of competence. Not everyone is entitled to adjudicate, and not everyone entitled to adjudicate turns out to be competent to do so. Those not entitled to adjudicate but who nonetheless impose themselves have usurped the position; the incompetent undermine it, and bring the courts into disrepute; and the adjudicator uninterested in discovering what in the instant case is just has no concern for the interests of others. He breaks the fundamental rule: 'take others' interests into account' or, equivalently, '(discover and) render to each what is due'.

In cases of doubt and dispute what is due must be discovered; and it is the task of courts and legislators to discover it. What is due to a person is that person's entitlement or right. No human society exists, has existed, or can survive, in which no one is entitled to anything, where no one is due anything in any circumstance, where there are no rights. Because human societies develop, new situations raise new and different problems; new understandings and new sentiments evoke questions about the wisdom, relevance, or justice of former solutions. Human societies are open to development and also to decline, although what constitutes either one is endemically open to discussion and dispute. A claim that something ought to be a right is an implicit acknowledgement that it is not yet recognized to be, and not yet established as, a right. Again, human societies are dialectical. Claims supported by some are opposed by others. There will be incompatible claims but only temporarily and inconsistently can there be incompatible rights. Because change is often disputed, claims will often be opposed, sometimes, indeed, on selfish grounds, and no one is surprised when those who expect a new proposed right to be disadvantageous to themselves oppose its establishment. Nor is anyone surprised when those who champion the cause of a new claim are indifferent to the disadvantages its success may bring upon others. For bias is neither unknown nor unexpected, and, being the product of selfishness, it cannot be expunged from human community.

The function of the court is to discover and render what is due to the contending parties in the light of the actual situation and the prevailing jural context. Sometimes, the appropriate form of justice will be distributive as when, in case of dissolution, partners in a firm or a marriage, dispute the division of the joint property. Sometimes, rectificatory justice is involved as when one party has been shown to have damaged another, or – which is a species of damage – one party has taken more than his due. In criminal cases what is thought to be due to the convicted criminal, namely, punishment, has overshadowed the question as to what is due to the victim.

The two modalities of entitlement in adjudication – the entitlement to hold the position or role of adjudicator and the entitlement rooted in the moral and intellectual competence of the adjudicator – are likewise present in legislation. The same questions arise: Who is entitled to legislate? What is the legislator entitled to legislate? The law, properly legislated by one entitled to legislate, imposes a legal, but not necessarily a moral, obligation on those to whom it properly applies. It obliges, but does not necessarily obligate. We have argued that the entitlement to legislate is essentially contestable, and that the ground of the entitlement must include acceptance or acquiescence by those to whom it applies.

A law properly legislated by one entitled to legislate may nonetheless be unjust, for law has a function, namely to command and clarify the context in which people, without impeding one another, can live their lives together in peace, and a law that fails to fulfil its function, when, for example, it supports only the selfish purpose of a tyrannical legislator and his supporters, or oversteps the limits of what a legislator is entitled to require or forbid, is unjust. There is no formula from which can be deduced which laws are just and which unjust, which laws, although commanding what is reasonable, nonetheless overstep the limits of what the legislator is entitled to legislate. Still, precisely because the law's function is to sustain the common good, a law that fails to do so is unjust. It obliges legally – otherwise it would not be a law – but not necessarily morally. It obliges, but does not intrinsically obligate. A law that properly fulfils its function, however, obliges both legally and morally. It obliges *and* obligates.

What in detail a good social context will be cannot in detail be known in advance, for new attitudes, new understandings, new situations, new problems, and new solutions to old problems constantly arise. Despite such changes, and following one of the great traditions in Western jurisprudence, we hold that the basic context in which people can live together in peace is common to human societies, and requires some discoverable features that form the set of fundamental principles. These principles are discoverable, but not all are inevitably discovered or, if discovered, implemented in laws whether customary or statutory. Societies are in great part moral constructions. They can collapse, and selfishness carries the seeds of their decay. We have argued that these fundamental principles are discovered in the practice of living together, and in reflection on that practice; they are not a given set of propositions. Running through our account in various registers is the constant theme that the survival of human societies depends on taking others' interests into account, rendering to each what is due. Justice is the foundation of society; the prevalence of injustice must in the end utterly destroy it. This is how we understand Njál's words in the Saga: *By law is the land built; by lawlessness destroyed.*

Index